海军工程大学涉外丛书

外训系列教材

Fundamentals of Warship Electric Circuits

舰艇电路原理

主 编 单潮龙 钟 斌
副主编 稽 斗 汪小娜 邓 波

武汉大学出版社

图书在版编目(CIP)数据

舰艇电路原理/单潮龙,钟斌主编. —武汉:武汉大学出版社,2018.1
海军工程大学涉外丛书
ISBN 978-7-307-18912-6

Ⅰ.舰… Ⅱ.①单… ②钟… Ⅲ.军用船—电路—高等学校—教材 Ⅳ.U674.7

中国版本图书馆 CIP 数据核字(2016)第 289074 号

责任编辑:王智梅　胡国民　　责任校对:汪欣怡　　版式设计:马　佳

出版发行:**武汉大学出版社**　(430072　武昌　珞珈山)
　　　　　(电子邮件:cbs22@whu.edu.cn　网址:www.wdp.com.cn)
印刷:虎彩印艺股份有限公司
开本:720×1000　1/16　　印张:26　　字数:467 千字　　插页:1
版次:2018 年 1 月第 1 版　　2018 年 1 月第 1 次印刷
ISBN 978-7-307-18912-6　　定价:55.00 元

版权所有,不得翻印;凡购我社的图书,如有质量问题,请与当地图书销售部门联系调换。

Introduction

This book is written based on the requirement of teaching standards for foreign trainee of NUE. Taking into account the application characteristics of the military institutions and the practical engineering, the main contents are: circuit model and Kirchhoff's laws, circuit system analysis method, resistive circuit equivalent and circuit theorem, sinusoidal AC circuit analysis, coupled inductor circuit analysis, resonant circuit, three-phase circuit, the first-order dynamic circuit, application of Matlab and EWB to analyze the circuit, circuit experiments.

This book can be used as training or undergraduate textbook of military academy in following professions: electrical engineering, electronic engineering, weapons engineering, navigation, communications engineering and computer applications and other profession, it can also be used as undergraduate textbook of other institutions in electronics, computer science, etc. or used by the relevant professional and technical personnel as a reference material.

Preface

This book is written in accord to the requirement of foreign training teaching and curriculum system reform. It is stroked to inherit the tradition, enhance the application and reflect the advancement in the textbook. The book content is characterized by: laying the groundwork on the basic concepts and theoretical system, focusing on the combination of theory and practical application, strengthening application of modern computer-aided analysis software to analyze the circuit. Each chapter contains examples of EWB and Matlab circuit analysis applications that are compatible with the content, it lays the basis for theoretical and methodological learning for practical circuit analysis. This is not only conducive to improving students' interest in learning, to expand their horizons, but also to improve students' ability to analyze problems and solve problems. By solving the problem in the example to show solving ideas, too much text description is removed. In the use of EWB and Matlab for the circuit analysis, in addition to direct analysis of the circuit with EWB, Matlab programming circuit analysis is also introduced through examples, so that students can have a detailed understanding of how the computer circuit analysis, rather than simply use software to solve problems, which is conducive to the cultivation of students' innovative ability.

The structure of the book and the characteristics of the system design are: Chapter 1 discusses the circuit model and Kirchhoff's laws, it lay the foundation for the book. Discussion of resistive circuit is divided into three chapters, Chapter 2 discusses the resistive circuit equivalent simplification, Chapter 3 discusses circuit systematic analysis method, Chapter 4 discusses some important circuit theorems. The analysis and reduction methods discussed in these three chapter are very useful and can be used for next chapters. Discussion of AC circuit is divided into four chapters, that is, Chapter 5 discusses the basic knowledge of sinusoidal AC circuit analysis, Chapter 6 discusses the coupled inductor AC circuit, Chapter 7 discusses the resonant circuit, and Chapter 8 discusses the three-phase circuit. The transition analysis of first-order dynamic circuit will be discussed in chapter 9. The content about experiments are given in appendix.

To help the reader to learn, the beginning of each chapter outlines the contents of the chapter and the main points, each chapter are accompanied by exercise problems, answers of exercise problems are given in appendix of the book.

The book writing is divided into: Shan Chao Long prepared the chapter 1, 2, 3, 4, 9, Wang Xiao Na prepared Chapter 5, Ji Dou prepared the chapter 6, 7, 8, Zhong Bing is responsible for the overall planning, Deng bo prepared appendix and all the exercises. The book Manuscripts is reviewed by Shan Chao Long. Thanks to Professor Wang Jian of Huazhong University of Science and Technology who reviewed the first draft of the book and made a lot of valuable amendments.

In the course of the preparation of this book, we have learned a lot from the experts and scholars of the literature. Professor Wu Zhengguo of the Naval Engineering University had provided many valuable opinions on the preparation of this book.

Due to the limitation of the authors level, there may be some omissions and mistakes in the structure of the book, the arrangement of the system, the choice and narrative of content and other aspects of book. We urge the readers' correction.

Content

Chapter 1 Circuit Model and Kirchhoff's laws 1
   1.1   Circuit and Circuit Model 1
   1.2   Voltage and Current and Their Reference Direction 5
   1.3   Kirchhoff's Laws 8
   1.4   Passive Circuit Elements 13
   1.5   Active Circuit Elements 23
   1.6   Example of Computer-Aided Analysis of Circuits 31
   Exercise 33

Chapter 2 Equivalent Resistive Circuits 41
   2.1   The Equivalent Circuit of One-Port Network 41
   2.2   Equivalent Resistance of Passive One-Port Networks 48
   2.3   Delta-to-Wye Equivalent Circuits 58
   2.4   Equivalent Simplification of Active One-Port Networks 69
   2.5   Equivalent Simplification of Controlled Source Circuit 79
   2.6   Example of Computer-Aided Analys of Circuits 83
   Problems 85

Chapter 3 Systematic Analysis of Circuits 89
   3.1   The Basic Concept of Graph Theory 90
   3.2   2b Method and Branch Analysis Method 101
   3.3   Loop Analysis and Mesh Analysis 114
   3.4   Node Analysis and Modified Node Analysis 126
   3.5   Example of Computer-Aided Analysis of Circuits 140
   Problems 146

Chapter 4 Circuit Theorems 153
- 4.1 Superposition Theorem 153
- 4.2 Substitution Theorem 163
- 4.3 Thevenin's Theorem and Norton's Theorem 168
- 4.4 Tellegen's Theorem and Reciprocity Theorem 186
- 4.5 Computer-Aided Analysis of Circuits 199
- Exercise 200

Chapter 5 Sinusoidal Steady-State Analysis 207
- 5.1 The Basic Concept of Sinusoidal Quantity 207
- 5.2 Phasor Representation of Sinusoidal Quantity 213
- 5.3 Kirchhoff's Laws and VCR in Phasor Form 219
- 5.4 Impedance and Admittance 225
- 5.5 Analysis of Sinusoidal AC Circuit 234
- 5.6 Power in Sinusoidal AC Circuit 242
- 5.7 Examples of Computer-Aided Analysis of Circuits 252
- Problems 255

Chapter 6 Magnetically Coupled Circuits 264
- 6.1 Mutual Inductance and VCR of the Coupled Inductor 264
- 6.2 Analysis of Coupled Inductor Circuit 273
- 6.3 Air-Core Transformer and Ideal Transformer 283
- 6.4 Examples of Computer-Aided Circuit Analysis with Matlab 297
- Exercises 298

Chapter 7 Resonant Circuit Analysis 305
- 7.1 Series Resonant Circuit 305
- 7.2 Parallel Resonant Circuit 312
- 7.3 Examples of Computer Aided Circuit Analysis 323
- Exercises 326

Chapter 8 Three-Phase Circuits 330
- 8.1 Balanced Three-Phase Circuits 330

8.2　Unbalanced Three-Phase Circuits ······· 339
8.3　Power of Three-Phase Circuits ········ 344
Exercises ········ 349

Chapter 9　First-Order Circuits ········ 352
9.1　The Basic Concept and Circuit Switching Rule ······· 352
9.2　Zero-Input Response of First-Order Circuit ······· 357
9.3　Zero-State Response of First-Order Circuit ······· 365
9.4　Short-Cut Method for Complete Response of First-Order Circuit ········ 369
9.5　Step Response and Impulse Response of First Order Circuit ······ 373
Exercise ········ 381

Appendix A　Experiment ········ 388

Appendix B　Reference Answers for Partial Exercises ······· 399

References ········ 407

Chapter 1

Circuit Model and Kirchhoff's laws

This chapter mainly introduces the concept of circuit model, the reference direction of voltage and current, Kirchhoff's laws (including Kirchhoff's current law and Kirchhoff's voltage law) and basic circuit elements (including resistors, inductors, capacitors, voltage sources, current sources, and controlled sources). Circuit model is the object for circuit research. It is required to understand the internal relationship and difference between the actual circuit and circuit model. Voltage and current reference direction is an important concept in circuit analysis. Kirchhoff's laws and elements characteristics of the circuit are the basis of the circuit analysis and should be mastered proficiently.

1.1 Circuit and Circuit Model

1.1.1 Function and Structure of Circuit

An electric circuit consists of several electrical components which are connected with each other, it is the path of the current and is also known as the electric network.

Each circuit has its specific function. Although the shape of the circuit structure and the tasks that can be accomplished are diversified, the functions of circuits can be classified into two categories. One is transmission and conversion of electric power, a typical example is power system. The other is processing and transmission of signal, for examples, temperature measurement, radio, television, etc. Regardless how complicate of the structure, a circuit is divided into three parts: a power source or a signal source, an intermediate link and a load. For the circuit with first kind of function, the power source may be a generator in which other forms of energy is transformed into electrical energy; the load may be a electric motor, lamp or oven in which electrical energy is converted into other forms of energy. The intermediate links is a transmission line or transformer which is used to connect the power source and load, it plays a role of transmission and distribution of electric energy. For the circuit with second kind of function, the signal source may be a galvanic, a receiving antenna in which the information of the temperature or electromagnetic wave are converted to voltage signal, then these signals are transmitted or processed by intermediate link (magnification, the setting, the detection, etc.) to a load (for example, millivoltmeter, speaker, kinescope, etc.) to restore the original messages.

For two kinds of circuit, voltage or current of power supply or signal source are usually called excitements which drives the current to flow in the circuit. The voltage or current in other part of the circuit driven by the excitement are called the responses. Sometimes the excitement is also called the input and the response called the output.

1.1.2 Circuit Model

The circuit consists of practical elements or devices which have different roles, such as resistor, capacitor, coil, switch, generator, transformer, motor, transistor, and so on. Their electromagnetic properties are complicate. To facilitate the circuit analysis and mathematical description, the practical elements are idealized, i.e. under certain conditions, to highlight its main electromagnetic nature, to ignore the secondary factors, they are considered to be the ideal circuit elements (also called components). For example, if the main effect of a device is shown as the electric energy loss, it can be modelled as a resistor. If main effect of a devices is shown as energy storage in magnetic field, it can be modelled as an inductor. If main effect of a device is shown as energy storage in electric field, it can be modelled as a capacitor. So, resistor, capacitor and inductor are ideal elements.

A circuit consisting of ideal circuit elements is called the circuit model of an actual circuit. For example, for the actual circuit of a electric torch, as indicated in Fig.1.1.1a, the battery inside the torch can be modeled as a voltage source in series with a internal resistor, the lamp modeled as a resistor. So, the torch can be modeled as an ideal circuit shown in Fig.1.1.1b.

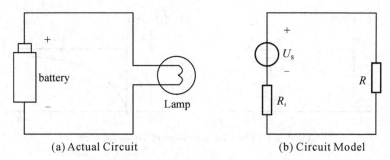

(a) Actual Circuit   (b) Circuit Model

Fig.1.1.1 Actual Circuit and Its Model

1.1.3 The Linear Time-Invariant and Lumping

1.1.3.1 The Linear Circuit

The circuit made up only of linear elements is called linear circuit. Basic characteristic of a linear circuit is additivity and homogeneity, as shown in Fig.1.1.2.

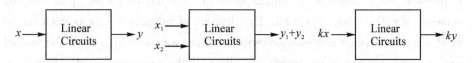

Fig.1.1.2 Description of Additivity and Homogeity

Strictly speaking, the actual linear circuit does not exist in practice. However, a lot of actual circuits can be regarded as linear circuits if certain conditions are satisfied. In circuit theory, the linear circuits have been studied for a long time, there are fine theories and methods that can be used. As an elementary course, we mainly focus on discussing linear circuit.

1.1.3.2 The Time-Invariant Circuit

The component parameters of a circuit does not change with time, is called time-invariant circuit. For this kind of circuit, the characteristic curve of element in y-x plane does not change with time, as illustrated in Fig.1.1.3.

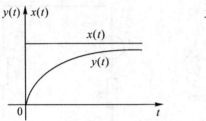 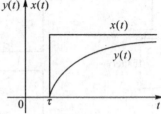

Fig.1.1.3　The Characteristics of Time-Invariant

1.1.3.3　Lumping Circuit

In circuit theory, we mainly study the electromagnetic phenomenon occurred in the circuit. Current, voltage (sometimes using charge, flux) is used to describe the process inside the circuit. Usually, we are only interested in the current through and voltage across the devices. We don't deal with the physical process involving inside the internal devices. This is reasonable only if the circuit is supposed to be a lumping circuit.

If the size of an circuit element is small enough comparing with its operational wavelength, it is called as a lumping element. The circuit consisting of lumping elements is called lumping circuit. The diagram of lumping circuit is made up of ideal wires and circuit elements according to a certain connection rule. The symbol size of circuit elements, the length and shape of the connection in the diagram is not important.

The geometry dimension of real circuits varies considerably. For transmission lines, whose operating frequency is 50 Hz, it's wavelength is 6000km. So a transmission line of a 30km long is only 1/200 of wavelength. It can be considered as a lumping circuit. While a transmission line of hundreds and thousands of kilometers cannot be considered as a lumping circuit.

To sum up, a circuit consisting of time-invariant lumping linear elements and connected by ideal wires is said to be linear time-invariant lumping circuit. This textbook discusses lumping circuits only. Because analysis of non-lumping circuits is complicate and requires to apply the distributing-parameter circuit theory, it will not be discussed in the textbook.

1.2 Voltage and Current and Their Reference Direction

The electrical properties of circuit may be generally described by a group of variables which are a function of time, and the common variables used are current, voltage and power. In this section the reference directions of current and voltage are important concepts.

1.2.1 Current

The amount of charge passing through cross section area of a conductor in the unit of times is defined as current intensity, simply said the current, represented by the symbol i,

$$i = \frac{dq}{dt} \qquad (1.2.1)$$

where q is the amount of charge passing through cross section area of the conductor. When the magnitude and the direction of the current does not vary with time, it is called direct current (DC), usually denoted in capital letter I.

In the international system of units (SI), charge is coulomb (C), time is second (s), and current is measured in amperes (A).

Due to the historical reason, the direction of the movement of the positive charge is considered as the actual direction of current. But in specific circuits, the actual direction of current often varies with time. Even if the current does not vary with time, the direction of current in some places of circuit is also difficult to determine. Therefore, it is often difficult to set the actual current direction in the circuit. So, it is necessary to introduce the concept of reference direction of current, as shown in Fig.1.2.1.

The reference direction of current can be selected arbitrarily. It is also known as positive direction and can be indicated with an arrow in the circuit, as shown in Fig.1.2.1. After the reference direction of current is selected, the current becomes an algebraic quantity. If the reference direction of current is same as the real direction, the value of current is positive ($i>0$), as shown in Fig.1.2.1a. If the reference direction of current is opposite to the real direction, the value of current is negative ($i<0$), as shown in Fig.1.2.1b. Then, with the reference direction and

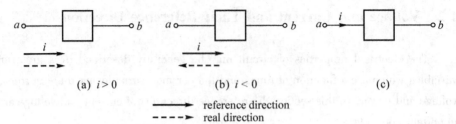

Fig.1.2.1 Reference Direction of the Current

the value of current, the real direction can be determined easily. Obviously, if the reference direction of current is not given, there are not meaning for that current is positive or negative. The reference direction of current is often denoted with an arrow in the wires, as shown in Fig.1.2.1c.

Reference direction of current can also be represented by double subscripts, for example, i_{ab} indicates that reference direction is from a to b. In this textbook, we only mark the reference directions in circuit diagrams, and don't mark the real directions.

1.2.2 Voltage

In electric circuit, the work that the electric field does in driving unit positive charge from one point to another point is defined as the voltage between the two points, also known as the potential difference:

$$u = \frac{dw}{dq} \tag{1.2.2}$$

As the same concept of current, when analyzing a circuit, we should define the reference direction or polarity of voltage. The reference polarity of voltage can be defined by using the symbols " + " and " - " in the diagram. We can also be used an arrows to indicate the reference direction of voltage, as shown in Fig.1.2.2.

In the international system of units (SI), the voltage is measured in volt (V).

Reference direction of current or voltage plays a very important role in circuit analysis. The current or voltage are algebraic quantity. Both value and sign have their physical significances. The current or voltage that have only value without the reference direction makes no sense.

1.2 Voltage and Current and Their Reference Direction

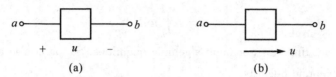

Fig.1.2.2 Reference Direction of Voltage

The reference direction of voltage or current of an element or a segment of circuit can be independently specified arbitrarily. If the reference directions of voltage and current are same, it is known as standard reference direction, as shown in Fig.1.2.3a. On the contrary, the reference directions of voltage and current are not standard, as illustrated in Fig.1.2.3b.

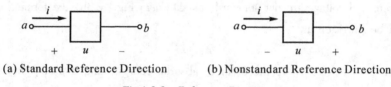

(a) Standard Reference Direction   (b) Nonstandard Reference Direction

Fig.1.2.3 Reference Direction

1.2.3 Power and Energy

The power are closely related with voltage and current. The movement of positive charge from the positive polarity to the negative polarity of voltage across a circuit element is caused by work done by strength of electric field, and in this case, the element absorbs energy. Conversely, when positive charge moves from the negative polarity to the positive polarity of voltage across circuit element, it is required to do work to the charge with outside force (chemical, electromagnetic force, etc.). In this case, the circuit element supplies energy.

According to the formula (1.2.2), from t_0 to t time, the energy w absorbed by elements is

$$w = \int_{q(t_0)}^{q(t)} u\,dq$$

Under the condition of the standard reference direction, the energy w

absorbed by elements can be expressed from expression (1.2.1) as

$$w = \int_{t_0}^{t} ui \, dt \quad (1.2.3)$$

where u, i are time functions and algebraic quantities. So, w is also a function of time and algebraic quantity.

The changing rate of energy with respect to the time is called electric power, simply power. Thus, power absorbed by circuit element is

$$p = \frac{dw}{dt} = ui \quad (1.2.4)$$

It needs to mention that expression (1.2.4) is obtained in case the directions of current and voltage are standard (as shown in Fig.1.2.3a). So, if $p>0$, the element absorbs supply energy, if $p<0$; the power absorbed by the element is a negative value, in fact, it will supply or produce energy. If the reference directions of current and voltage are not standard, as shown in Fig.1.2.3b, the formula (1.2.4) should be rewritten as

$$p = -ui \quad (1.2.5)$$

In this case, if $p>0$, the element absorbs energy, and if $p<0$, the element delivers energy.

In the international system of units (SI), energy is measured in joule (J), power is measured in watt (W).

1.3 Kirchhoff's Laws

The circuit is a whole connected each other by some elements. The currents and the voltages of each element in the circuit are constrained by two types of governing equations. One is the constraints among the currents and among the voltages and they are called topological constraints. Another is the constraints of elements characteristic, i.e., the relationship existing between the currents and the voltages of element itself and it is called element constraint. The former will be discussed in this section and the element restraint will be discussed in next section.

Kirchhoff's laws are important in lumping circuits, they are the cornerstones of the circuit theory. To facilitate the illustration of Kirchhoff's laws, let's introduce some terms of circuits.

(1) The Branch. The branch is known as any current path in the circuit. A branch can be an element, can also be several components connected in series. The currents flowing through each element of a branch are the same. As shown in the Fig.1.3.1, there are 5 branches in the circuit.

(2) The Node. The connecting point of three or more branches in the circuit is a node. For example, in the circuit shown in Fig.1.3.1, points labeled 1, 2, 3 are nodes, there are three nodes.

(3) The Loop. The closed path consisting of several branches in the circuit is known as the loop. For example, for the circuit of Fig.1.3.1, closed path of branches (4,3,2,1,4) and (1,3,2,1) are loop. Totally, there are 7 loops in the circuit.

(4) The Mesh. For a planar circuit, the loop without any branches inside it is called mesh. For example, for the circuit of Fig.1.3.1, loop (1,3,2,1) is a mesh, loop (4,3,2,1,4) is not a mesh, for there is a branch inside the loop.

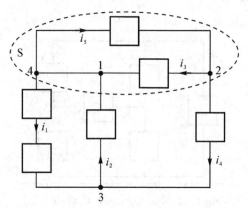

Fig.1.3.1 The Circuit for Interpretation of Terms

1.3.1 Kirchhoff's Current Law

Kirchhoff's current law (KCL) can be stated as follows: for each node in the lumping circuit, at any time, the sum of the currents leaving the node is equal to the sum of the currents entering the node.

For example, the circuit shown in Fig.1.3.1, the KCL at node 1 can be

written as
$$i_2+i_3=i_1+i_5$$

If it is stipulated that "+" sign is used for the current entering the node, is, "−" sign is used for the current leaving node. Then, above equation can be rewritten as follows
$$i_2+i_3-i_1-i_5=0$$

So, KCL can also be stated as: for any node in the lumping circuit, at any time, the algebraic sum of the currents at the node is equal to zero.
$$\sum i = 0$$

Normally, KCL is applied to the node. However, it can also be generalized to apply to a closed surface (generalized node) including several nodes. For example, choose a closed surface S as shown in Fig.1.3.1, KCL can be written as
$$-i_1+i_2-i_4=0$$

Example 1.3.1 For the circuit shown in Fig.1.3.2, given: $i_1 = 5A$, $i_2 = -1A$, $i_6 = -2A$. Find i_4.

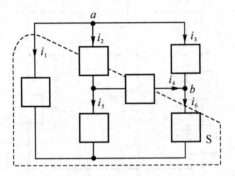

Fig.1.3.2 The Circuit for Example 1.3.1

Solution To find i_4, applying KCL to node b, there is
$$i_3+i_4=i_6$$
So,
$$i_4=i_6-i_3$$
Next, to find i_3, applying KCL to node a, we have
$$i_1+i_2+i_3=0$$
or

So, it is derived that
$$i_3 = -i_1 - i_2 = -5 - (-1) = -4A$$
$$i_4 = i_6 - i_3 = -2 - (-4) = 2A$$
Or choose a closing surface S, as shown in Fig.1.3.2, according to KCL, we have
$$i_1 + i_2 - i_4 + i_6 = 0$$
Then, there is
$$i_4 = i_1 + i_2 + i_6 = 5 - 1 - 2 = 2A$$

1.3.2 Kirchhoff's Voltage Law

Kirchhoff's voltage law (KVL) can be stated as follows: For any loop of lumping circuit, at any time, the algebraic sum of the voltages around the loop is zero,
$$\sum u = 0$$
For example, for the loop in the clockwise direction as shown in Fig.1.3.3, KVL can be written as
$$u_1 - u_2 + u_3 - u_4 = 0$$

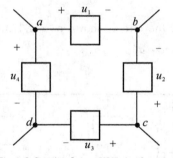

Fig.1.3.3 Applying KVL in the Loop

where, the reference direction of u_1 and u_3 is the same as loop direction, so, "+" is chosen in the expression, instead, the reference direction of u_2 and u_4 is opposite to the loop direction, so, "−" is choose in the expression.

KVL can be extended to apply to find the voltage between any two points. For example, to find voltage between a and c in Fig.1.3.3. The KVL equation for this

loop is
$$u_1 - u_2 + u_3 - u_4 = 0$$
It is known that
$$u_{ab} = u_1, u_{bc} = -u_2, u_{cd} = u_3, u_{da} = -u_4$$
Then
$$u_{ab} + u_{bc} + u_{cd} + u_{da} = 0$$
Due to $u_{cd} = -u_{dc}$, $u_{da} = -u_{ad}$, so there is
$$u_{ab} + u_{bc} = u_{ad} + u_{dc}$$
On the left-hand side of expression, it is the voltage along the path a, b, c, that is
$$u_{ac} = u_{ab} + u_{bc} = u_1 - u_2$$
On the left-hand side of expression, it is the voltage along the path a, d, c, that is
$$u_{ac} = u_{ad} + u_{dc} = u_4 - u_3$$
Both are equal.

In the lumping parameter circuit, any two points (such as p and q) is equal to the algebra sum of all the branch voltages along any path from p to q, that is,
$$u_{pq} = \sum_{\substack{along\ a\ path \\ form\ p\ to\ q}} u \qquad (1.3.1)$$

Example 1.3.2 For the circuit shown as Fig.1.3.4, given: $u_1 = 10V$, $u_2 = -2V$, $u_3 = 3V$, $u_7 = 2V$. Find: u_5, u_6, u_{cd}.

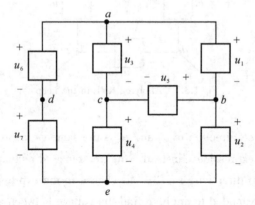

Fig.1.3.4 The Circuit for Example 1.3.2

Solution By inspection the circuit in the figure, it is seen that
$$u_5 = u_{bc}$$
Applying KVL along the path b, a, c, we get
$$u_5 = u_{ba} + u_{ac} = -u_1 + u_3 = -10 + 3 = -7V$$
For
$$u_6 = u_{ad}$$
And as well, applying KVL along the path a, b, e, d, we get
$$u_6 = u_{ad} = u_{ab} + u_{be} + u_{ed} = u_1 + u_2 - u_7 = 10 - 2 - 2 = 6V$$
$$u_{cd} = u_{ca} + u\ ad = -u_3 + u_6 = 3V$$
applying KVL along the path a, b, e, d, we get
$$u_{cd} = u_{ca} + u_{ab} + u_{be} + u_{ed} = -u_3 + u_1 + u_2 - u_7 = -3 + 10 - 2 - 2 = 3V$$

Kirchhoff's voltage law and Kirchhoff's current are basic laws of the lumping circuit. KCL describes the constraint relationship of each branch current at each node of the circuit. KVL describes the constraint relationship of each branch voltage around each loop of the circuit. KCL and KVL is the topological restraint relationship of the interconnection elements. KCL and KVL apply not only to linear circuits, also apply to nonlinear circuit, time-invariant circuits and time-varying circuits. The only limitation for KCL and KVL is that the circuits must be a lumping circuit, so it is widely used and very important.

1.4 Passive Circuit Elements

In the lumping circuit, the circuit element is the basic block to form a circuit. It is an ideal model of a actual device, there should be the strict definition for them. In this section and the next section, several types of circuit elements will be discussed.

1.4.1 Resistor

1.4.1.1 The Definition of Resistor

Resistance is the parameter which is used to express the ability of resist current in the circuit, or the amount of the energy loss. Resistor is used to simulate the loss of electric energy. It is an ideal element in which electrical energy can be converted into other forms of energy, such as heat energy. From characteristics of element, it can be divided into linear or non-linear, time-invariant and time-varying resistor. From the angle of power, it can be divided into active resistor and passive resistor. From the number of terminals, it can be divided in the two-terminals resistor and multi-terminals resistor. In the following, the two-terminal resistor is defined and its concept can be extended to multi-terminal resistor.

1.4.1.2 The Linear Resistor

The volt-ampere characteristic of a linear resistor element is a straight line passing through the origin on a u-i plane, as shown in Fig.1.4.1a. Its symbol is shown in Fig.1.4.1b. The value of linear resistor is equal to the slope of the line. If the slope of the line varies with time, it is called time-varying linear resistor, otherwise, it is called linear time-invariant resistor.

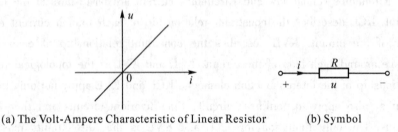

(a) The Volt-Ampere Characteristic of Linear Resistor (b) Symbol

Fig.1.4.1 Volt-Ampere Characteristic Curve and Symbol of Linear Resistor

It is known from the volt-ampere characteristic curve that linear resistor is a bidirectional element. i.e. if the polarity of the voltage is changed, direction of current will also changes. At any time, the relationship between the current and the voltage of a linear resistor must obey Ohm's law. When the reference directions of voltage and current are standard, the relationship between the voltage and current can be written as

$$u = Ri$$

or

$$i = Gu$$

where the resistance R is a constant, independent of the current and voltage of resistor. The conductance G is the reciprocal of resistance, namely, $G = 1/R$. In the international system of units, resistance is measured in Ohm (Ω) and conductance is measured in Siemens (S).

In particular, when the current and voltage of resistor are nonstandard direction, Ohm's law must be rewritten as

$$u = -Ri$$

or

$$i = -Gu$$

1.4.1.3 The Open Circuit and Short Circuit

There are two types of specific resistance to be noted: open circuit and short circuit. For any two-terminal element (or circuit), if the current flowing through this element is always zero whatever its voltage is, it is considered as an open circuit. Open circuit can be treated as an resistor with infinite resistance. Instead, for any two-terminal element (or circuit), if the voltage across this element is always zero whatever its current is, it is considered as an short circuit. Short circuit can be treated as an resistor with zero resistance or a ideal wire.

1.4.1.4 The Power of Resistor

If the voltage and current are in standard reference direction, the power of resistor is

$$p = ui = Ri^2 = Gu^2$$

For most cases, the resistance and conductance are positive constant, so, the power of resistor is always a positive value or zero. It shows that resistor always absorbs energy. In case that the of voltage and current are not in standard reference direction, the power of resistor will be

$$p = -ui$$

Due to

$$u = -Ri \quad \text{or} \quad i = -Gu$$

so, the power of resistor

$$p = -ui = -(Ri)i = Ri^2$$

is still a positive value. It indicates that resistor always dissipates the power, i.e. at any moment, it is impossible for a resistor to supply power or energy. Usually, electric energy is absorbed by a resistor and is converted into thermal energy. So a linear resistor is an passive element of energy dissipation.

1.4.2 Capacitor

The capacitor is an ideal element to simulate a device capable of storing energy in electric field. This capability of storing energy in electric field is represented by capacitor. A real capacitor can be considered as consisting of two parallel plates of conductive plate. Insulating material is filled between two parallel plates. The symbol of capacitor is shown in Fig.1.4.2a.

If Coulomb-Volt characteristic curve of element does not vary with time, the element is time-invariant capacitor.

The symbol of a linear capacitor is shown in Fig.1.4.2b. Its Coulomb-Volt characteristic curve is a straight line passing through the origin of q-u plane, as shown in Fig.1.4.2c. Under the condition that voltage polarity is the same as the charge polarity, at any time, the relationship between the voltage and charge of capacitor can be written as

$$q = Cu$$

where C is capacitance, its unit in SI is Farad(F). Sometimes F is too big unit, so, μF and pF are also be used, $1\mu F = 10^{-6}$ F, $1pF = 10^{-12}$ F, u is the voltage across the capacitor, in Volts.

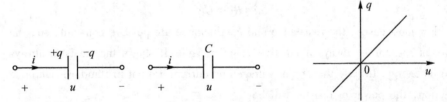

(a) Capacitor Symbol (b) Linear Capacitor Symbol (c) Coulomb-Volt Characteristic Curve

Fig.1.4.2 Symbol and Coulomb-Volt Characteristic of Capacitor

Now, considering the voltage-current relationship of capacitor element, if the reference direction of the voltage and current are i.e. assumed the same, as shown in Fig.1.4.2a, with $i = \dfrac{dq}{dt}$, we can get the following expression

$$i = \frac{dq}{dt} = C\frac{du}{dt} \tag{1.4.1}$$

This expression is called the voltage-current relationship of capacitor element. It is a differential equation. It shows that, at any instant, the current of capacitor is proportional to the ratio of change of voltage. So, if the voltage changes fast, the current is large. Instead, if voltage changes slowly, the current will be very small. If voltage does not change with time, then $\frac{du}{dt}=0$, the current $i=0$, the capacitor can be considered as an open circuit. So, a capacitor is considered to be open-circuited for direct current.

From expression (1.4.1), we get

$$du = \frac{1}{C}idt$$

By taking integral for above expression from t_0 to t (to avoid making mixture up limit t of integral with variable t of integral, select ξ as integral variable), we get

$$\int_{u(t_0)}^{u(t)} du = \frac{1}{C}\int_{t_0}^{t} i(\xi)d\xi$$

$$u(t) - u(t_0) = \frac{1}{C}\int_{t_0}^{t} i(\xi)d\xi$$

$$u(t) = u(t_0) + \frac{1}{C}\int_{t_0}^{t} i(\xi)d\xi \qquad (1.4.2)$$

where t_0 is a fixed instant, or a starting instant. If $t_0=0$, then

$$u(t) = u(0) + \frac{1}{C}\int_{0}^{t} i(\xi)d\xi \qquad (1.4.3)$$

where $u(t_0)=\frac{1}{C}q(t_0)$ is the voltage at the starting instant t_0. The expression (1.4.3) can also be called as the voltage-current relationship of capacitor. It is an integral equation. It shows that, at any instant, the voltage u of capacitor is contributed by initial voltage $u(t_0)$ and all the currents from time t_0 to time t. So, we can say that capacitor element is a kind of "memory" element.

When voltage and current are in the standard reference direction, the power of capacitor is

$$p = ui = Cu\frac{du}{dt} \qquad (1.4.4)$$

So, in the interval from t_0 to t, the energy absorbed by capacitor is

$$w(t) = \int_{t_0}^{t} p(\xi)d\xi = C\int_{t_0}^{t} u(\xi)\frac{du(\xi)}{d\xi}d\xi = C\int_{u(t_0)}^{u(t)} udu = \frac{1}{2}Cu^2(t) - \frac{1}{2}Cu^2(t_0)$$

Assuming $u(t_0)=0$, then

$$W(t) = \frac{1}{2}Cu^2(t) \tag{1.4.5}$$

This is the energy storage formula of capacitor, it can also be used to represent the state of energy storage in capacitor at instant t.

From t_1 to t_2, the energy absorbed by a capacitor can be written as

$$w(t) = C\int_{u(t_1)}^{u(t_2)} u\,du = \frac{1}{2}Cu^2(t_2) - \frac{1}{2}Cu^2(t_1) = W(t_2) - W(t_1) \tag{1.4.6}$$

i.e., it is equal to the difference of energy storage in the electric field between the instant t_2 and instant t_1.

When capacitor is charged, its voltage will rise, $|u(t_2)| > |u(t_1)|$, and $W(t_2) > W(t_1)$, $w(t) > 0$. So, capacitor absorbs electric energy and stores all energy in the electric field. When capacitor is discharged, its voltage will drop, $|u(t_2)| < |u(t_1)|$, $W(t_2) < W(t_1)$, $w(t) < 0$. It releases the electric energy from the electric field energy. An ideal capacitor is a kind of energy storage element. It does not dissipate the energy. The released energy will not exceed the absorbed energy, so, a capacitor is also a passive element.

Example 1.4.1 For a capacitor $C = 0.5F$ in Fig.1.4.3a is given, its current is given

$$i(t) = \begin{cases} 0 & -\infty < t < 0 \\ 2A & 0 \leq t < 1s \\ -2A & 1 \leq t < 2s \\ 0 & t \geq 2s \end{cases}$$

Its waveform is shown in Fig.1.4.3b, Find the voltage $u(t)$, the power $p(t)$ and the energy $w(t)$, and draw their waveforms.

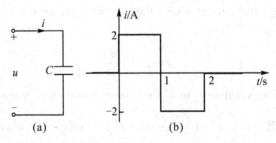

Fig.1.4.3 The Figure for Example 1.4.1

Solution As shown in Fig.1.4.3a, the voltage and current are assigned in associated direction. Since current i is always zero when $t < 0$, according to expression (1.4.3), when $-\infty < t < 0$, $u(t) = 0$, so, $u(0) = 0$.

When $0 \leq t < 1s$,

$$u(t) = u(0) + \frac{1}{C}\int_0^t 2d\xi = 4t$$

$$u(1) = 4V$$

When $1 \leq t < 2s$,

$$u(t) = u(1) + \frac{1}{C}\int_1^t (-2)d\xi = 4 - 4(t-1) = 4(2-t)$$

$$u(2) = 0V$$

When $t \geq 2s$

$$u(t) = u(2) + \frac{1}{C}\int_2^t 0 d\xi = 0$$

That is

$$u(t) = \begin{cases} 0 & -\infty < t < 0 \\ 4t & (V) & 0 \leq t < 1s \\ 4(2-t) & (V) & 1 \leq t < 2s \\ 0 & t \geq 2s \end{cases}$$

Its waveform is shown in Fig.1.4.4a.

From expression (1.4.4), the power of capacitor is

$$p(t) = \begin{cases} 0 & -\infty < t < 0 \\ 8t & (W) & 0 \leq t < 1s \\ -8(2-t) & (W) & 1 \leq t < 2s \\ 0 & t \geq 2s \end{cases}$$

Its waveform is shown as imagine line in Fig.1.4.4b.

According to expression (1.4.5), the energy of capacitor is

$$u(t) = \begin{cases} 0 & -\infty < t < 0 \\ 4t^2 & (J) & 0 \leq t < 1s \\ 4(2-t)^2 & (J) & 1 \leq t < 2s \\ 0 & t \geq 2s \end{cases}$$

Its waveform is shown in Fig.1.4.4b.

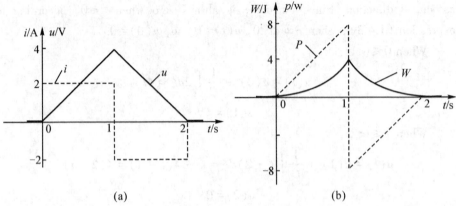

Fig.1.4.4 The Diagram for Example 1.4.1

The capacitor used in the actual circuit has a large variation in the capacitance range, and the leakage current of most capacitors is very small. When the operating voltage is low, an ideal capacitive element can be used as its circuit model. When the leakage current cannot be ignored (such as electrolyte capacitors), you can use an ideal capacitor and the ideal resistor components in parallel as its circuit model. In the case of high operating frequencies, it is also necessary to connect an ideal inductive element in series to form the circuit model of the capacitor. In addition, in practical circuit, to change the size of the capacitance, capacitor is often made up of copper plate whose area is adjustable, known as adjustable capacitors, such as channel-selecting capacitors used in FM.

1.4.3 Inductor

It is known from physics that when there is a current flowing through the conductor, a magnetic field is generated around the conductor. The changing magnetic field allows the conductor to be placed in the magnetic field to generate a voltage that is proportional to the rate of change of the current that produces the magnetic field over time. The inductor discussed here is the ideal element for simulating the actual inductor device. The definition of the two-terminal inductor is given below.

A two-terminal element, if at any time, the relationship between its flux and

ψ its current i can be determined by a fixed ψ-i curve on the plane, it is called the inductor. This curve is called Weber-Ampere characteristic curve of the inductor. If the characteristic curve is a straight line passing through the origin and does not change with time, it is called a linear time-invariant.

Fig.1.4.5 shows the characteristic curves and component symbols for linear time-invariant inductor. When the reference flux direction and the reference direction of the flux and the reference direction of the current match the right hand spiral relationship, at any time, the relationship between the flux and the current is

$$\psi(t) = Li(t)$$

where L is called inductance. In the international unit system, the magnetic flux and flux units are Weber (Wb), the unit if inductance is Henry (H). For linear time-invariant inductive elements, L is a real constant.

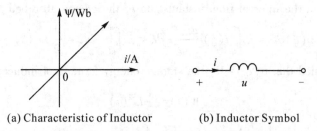

(a) Characteristic of Inductor   (b) Inductor Symbol

Fig.1.4.5 Characteristic of Inductor and Symbol

As mentioned above, the time-varying magnetic field will produce a voltage, assuming that the inductor-side voltage is in the associated reference direction with respect to its current reference direction, as shown in Fig.1.4.4b. According to Lenz's law and (1.4.6), the voltage of inductor can be written as follows

$$u = \frac{d\psi}{dt} = L\frac{di}{dt} \qquad (1.4.7)$$

The above equation is called the volt-ampere relationship of the inductance element. This equation shows that at any time, the voltage on the inductive element is proportional to the rate of change of current at that time. If the current does not change with time, then $u = 0$, the inductance element is equivalent to short circuit.

The relationship between the inductor current and its terminal voltage is derived from equation (1.4.7)

$$i(t) = i(t_0) + \frac{1}{L}\int_{t_0}^{t} u(\xi)d\xi \tag{1.4.8}$$

where $i(t_0)$ is the inductor current at starting instant t_0. Expression (1.4.8) shows that the current i of inductor is contributed by initial current $i(t_0)$ and all voltages from t_0 to t. So, inductor is also a kind of "memory" element.

If starting instant is selected as $t_0 = 0$, then

$$i(t) = i(0) + \frac{1}{L}\int_{t_0}^{t} u(\xi)d\xi$$

Assuming that the voltage is in the associated reference direction with respect to its current reference direction, the power absorbed by inductor is

$$p = ui = Li\frac{di}{dt} \tag{1.4.9}$$

Then, in the interval from instant t_0 to t, the energy absorbed by inductor is

$$w(t) = \int_{t_0}^{t} p(\xi)d\xi = L\int_{t_0}^{t} i(\xi)\frac{di(\xi)}{d\xi}d\xi = L\int_{u(t_0)}^{u(t)} idi = \frac{1}{2}Li^2(t) - \frac{1}{2}Li^2(t_0)$$

If it is assumed that $u(t_0) = 0$, the storage energy formula of inductor is

$$W(t) = \frac{1}{2}Li^2(t) \tag{1.4.10}$$

In the interval from instant t_1 to t_2, the energy absorbed by inductor is

$$w(t) = L\int_{u(t_1)}^{u(t_2)} idi = \frac{1}{2}Li^2(t_2) - \frac{1}{2}Li^2(t_1) = W(t_2) - W(t_1) \tag{1.4.11}$$

i.e., it is equal to the deference between the inductor energy at instant t_2 and the inductor energy at instant t_1.

If $|i|$ increases, then $W(t_2) > W(t_1)$, $w(t) > 0$, inductor absorbs electric energy and transforms it to electromagnetic storage energy in inductor. Instead, If $|i|$ decreases, then $W(t_2) < W(t_1)$, $w(t) < 0$, inductor releases electromagnetic storage energy in inductor and transforms it to electric energy. It can be seen that the ideal inductor is a kind of energy-storing element and it does not dissipate energy. Furthermore, for the released energy will not exceed the absorbed energy, so, it is also a passive element.

There are many types of inductor coils used in the actual circuit, the inductance range varies greatly, and the coil wires are always resistive, especially when the wires are long and thin, the resistance of the wires cannot be ignored. In this case, a series connection of a linear resistor element and a linear inductance element can be used as its circuit model. In the case of higher frequency, the impact of the coil turn-to-turn capacitance must be considered, so, a capacitor more should be connected in parallel with it.

1.5 Active Circuit Elements

1.5.1 Independent Power Source

A power supply or source is a device that provides energy and is an active circuit element that is an idealized model for a variety of energy-producing devices. There are two categories of power supply, i.e. independent power supply and power controlled source. The so-called independent power source, is an active circuit components which is able to independently provide voltage and current to the circuit. Independent power source can be divided into independent voltage source and independent current source.

1.5.1.1 The Voltage Source

If considering a two-terminal element, regardless of the value of the current through it or whatever the external circuit connected, its voltage is always maintained for a certain fixed time function $u_S(t)$, it is called an independent voltage source, referred to as the voltage source, the circuit symbols is shown in Fig.1.5.1a. The voltage source, in which the voltage is kept constant, is called a DC voltage source or a constant voltage source, represent by U_S. Its volt-ampere characteristic is shown in Fig.1.5.1c. It is a straight line parallel to the current axis. If $u_S(t)$ changes over time, the line parallel to the current axis also changes its position, as shown in Fig.1.5.1d. When the DC voltage source is a battery, symbol as shown in Fig.1.5.1b is commonly used.

When the voltage source $u_S(t)$ is not connected to the external circuit, as shown in Fig.1.5.2a, the current is always zero, but the voltage at both ends is still $u_S(t)$, known as the voltage source open circuit, $u_S(t)$ is known as open circuit voltage. When the voltage source is connected to the external circuit, as shown in

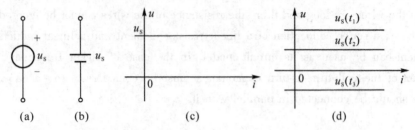

Fig.1.5.1 Characteristic and Symbol of the Source Voltage

Fig.1.5.2b, the current of the voltage source is determined by the voltage source and the external circuit connected to it. It varies with the external circuit, but its terminal voltage is always $u_S(t)$, it has nothing to do with the external circuit. If the voltage of the voltage source is equal to zero, its volt-ampere characteristics coincide with the current axis, which corresponds to a short circuit.

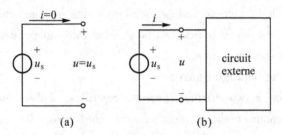

Fig.1.5.2 Characteristics of Voltage Source

Incidentally, the voltage and current of the voltage source are often used in nonstandard reference directions, as shown in Fig.1.5.2b. At this point, the power of the voltage source $p=-ui$. If $p<0$, then the voltage source generates power, it acts as a power supply; if $p>0$, then the voltage source absorbs power, and acts as a load.

1.5.1.2 Current Sources

For a two-terminal element, regardless of the value of its terminal voltage or the external circuit, its output current always maintain a certain time function $i_S(t)$, it is called the independent current source, or simply the current source. Its circuit symbol is shown in Fig.1.5.3a. If the current of source is always a constant, it is known as the DC current source or constant current source, indicated as I_S. Its volt-ampere characteristics is shown in Fig.1.5.3b, it is a straight line parallel to the voltage axis at any time. If it changes over time, the line parallel to the voltage axis also changes its position, as shown in Fig.1.5.3c.

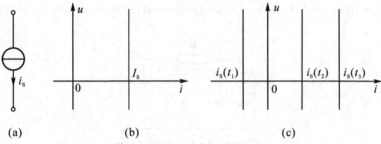

(a) (b) (c)

Fig.1.5.3 Characteristics and Symbols of Power Source

When the external circuit of the current source is a short circuit, its terminal voltage $u=0$. However, its output current is still $i_S(t)$, that is, the current source current is a short-circuit current, as shown in Fig.1.5.4a. When the external circuit of the current source is not short-circuited, as shown in Fig.1.5.4b, the terminal voltage of the current source is determined by the current source and the external circuit connected to it, which varies with the external circuit while the current is always $i_S(t)$, independent of the external circuit. If the current source $i_S(t)$ is equal to zero, its volt-ampere characteristic coincides with the voltage axis, which is equivalent to an open circuit.

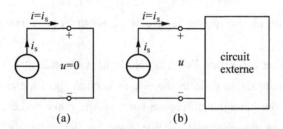

(a) (b)

Fig.1.5.4 Characteristics of Current Source

Incidentally, the voltage and current of the current source are often used in a nonstandard reference directions, as shown in Fig.1.5.4b. At this point, the power of the voltage source $p = -ui$. if $p<0$, then the current source generates power, it acts as a power supply; if $p>0$, then the current source absorbs power, and it acts as a load.

Example 1.5.1 For the circuit shown in Fig.1.5.5, given: $I_S = 0.5\text{A}, R = 10\Omega, U_S = 10\text{V}$. Find the power generated by voltage source and current source.

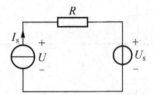

Fig.1.5.5 The Circuit for Example

Solution Knowing from the figure, the voltage and current of the voltage source are in the standard reference direction, then the power of voltage is
$$P_{U_S} = U_S I_S = 10 \times 0.5 = 5\text{W}$$

As the value of power is positive, so the power consumption of the voltage source 5W, i.e. the power generated by voltage source is −5W.

According to KVL, the voltage if current source is
$$U = RI_S + U_S = 10 \times 0.5 + 10 = 15\text{V}$$

For the voltage and current of the current source are not in the standard reference direction, so the power of current source is
$$P_{IS} = -UI_S = -15 \times 0.5 = -7.5\text{W}$$

As the value of this power is negative, so the power generated by current source is 7.5W.

1.5.1.3 The reference Point or Node in a Circuit

In circuit analysis, a node in the circuit is often specified as a reference point or node. Then, the potential difference between the other nodes and the reference node is known as the potential of that node or the voltage of that node. The potential of reference point is zero, commonly indicating with a ground symbol "⊥", as shown in Fig.1.5.6.

In the circuit shown in Fig.1.5.6a, if the node d is assigned as the reference node, the potentials or voltages of the nodes a, b, and c relative to the reference point are denoted as V_a, V_b, V_c respectively.

$$V_a = u_{ad} = u_{S1}, \quad V_b = u_{bd} = R_3 i_3, \quad V_c = u_{cd} = -u_{S2}$$

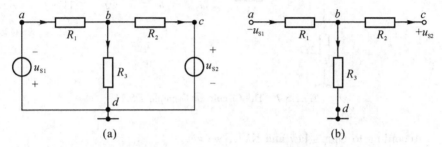

Fig.1.5.6 Illustration for Reference Node

In order to simplify the circuit diagram, the voltage source with one terminal connecting to the ground (reference node) is usually not drawn with the voltage source symbol, instead, the value and the polarity of the voltage are indicated at the ungrounded end of the voltage source. According to this rule, the circuit of Fig. 1.5.6a can be drawn as Fig.1.5.6b.

It is important to note that the potential of a node in the circuit varies with the position of the reference node, and it is meaningless to refer to the potential of a node without specifying the reference node; and the voltage is the potential difference between the two nodes and has nothing to do with the selection of the reference node.

Example 1.5.2 For the circuit shown in Fig.1.5.7, the potential of node b is given as −8V. Find:

(1) resistance R;

(2) the power of voltage source.

Solution First, the reference direction of resistor voltage U and some currents I_1, I_2, I_3 are assigned, as shown in Fig.1.5.7.

(1) To find R, find U and I_2 first.

By using generalizing KCL, find the current

$$I_1 = 2\text{A}$$

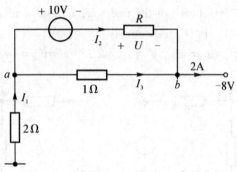

Fig.1.5.7 The Circuit for Example 1.5.1

According to Ohm's law and KVL, we get
$$U_{ab}=V_a-V_b=-2\times2-(-8)=4\text{V}$$
$$U_{ab}=10+U$$

So,
$$U=-6\text{V}$$
$$I_3=\frac{U_{ab}}{1}=\frac{4}{1}=4\text{A}$$

For node a, write down KCL equation as
$$I_2=I_1-I_3=2-4=-2\text{A}$$

Finally, according to Ohm's law, the resistance is
$$R=\frac{U}{I_2}=\frac{-6}{-2}=3\Omega$$

(2) Since the 10V voltage and current I_2 of voltage source are in the associated reference direction, so its power is
$$P=UI=10\times(-2)=-20\text{W}$$

Due to $P<0$, so the voltage source will generate 20W power.

1.5.2 Controlled Source

The controlled source is a special power source whose output voltage or current is not a given time function but is controlled by a branch voltage or current in the circuit.

The controlled source is an active two-port element, among whose two ports, one is the power port, acts as a voltage source or current source, can provide power; and the other is the control port, acts as a control voltage or control current. The power on the control port is always zero, i.e. when the voltage u_C is controlled, the control port current i_C is zero; when the current i_C is controlled, the control port voltage u_C is zero. Since the control of the controlled source is achieved by a voltage or current of some other element in the circuit, and the source can be voltage or current, it follows that there are four possible types of controlled sources, namely, a current-controlled voltage source (CCVS), a voltage-controlled voltage source (VCVS), a current-controlled current source (CCCS) and a voltage-controlled current source (VCCS). The circuit symbols of the four controlled sources are shown in Fig.1.5.8, and their port characteristics are

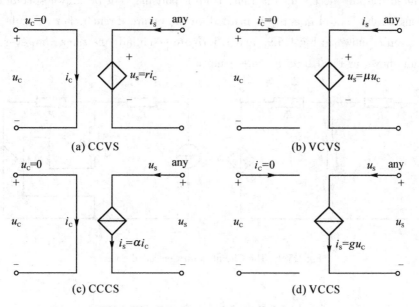

Fig.1.5.8 Four Forms of Controlled Sources

$$\text{CCVS} \quad \begin{cases} u_S(t) = r i_C(t) \\ u_C(t) = 0 \end{cases} \qquad (1.5.1)$$

$$\text{VCVS} \quad \begin{cases} u_S(t) = \mu u_C(t) \\ i_C(t) = 0 \end{cases} \qquad (1.5.2)$$

$$\text{CCCS} \quad \begin{cases} i_S(t) = \alpha i_C(t) \\ u_C(t) = 0 \end{cases} \quad (1.5.3)$$

$$\text{VCCS} \quad \begin{cases} i_S(t) = g u_C(t) \\ i_C(t) = 0 \end{cases} \quad (1.5.4)$$

Where r, μ, g, α are the control coefficient. Among them, r and α are dimensionless, and μ and g has the dimensions of resistance and conductance, respectively. When these coefficients are constants, the controlled quantity is proportional to the control quantity, and these kinds of controlled sources are called linear time-invariant controlled sources. This book deals only with such controlled sources.

Because the power of control port is zero, it is either open-circuited or short-circuited. So, in the circuit diagram, control port may not be drawn specifically, as long as the control quantity is marked on the control branch. For example, the two circuits shown in Fig.1.5.9a and 1.5.9b are essentially the same, however, the circuit shown in Fig.1.5.9a is more concise.

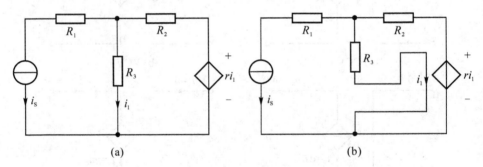

Fig.1.5.9 The Circuits with Controlled Sources

It must be pointed out that independent and controlled sources are two different concepts. The independent source, which is an model of the electric power or electrical signals in the actual circuit; and the controlled source is an model that describes the control of a branch in the electronic device over another branch, and does not supply power in the circuit.

Example 1.5.3 For the circuit shown in Fig.1.5.10, find voltage u.

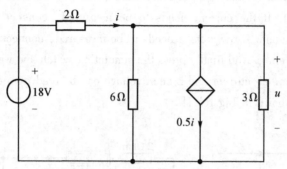

Fig.1.5.10   The Circuit for Example 1.5.2

Solution   The circuit in Fig. 1.5.10 is a circuit with controlled current source. According to KCL, the current i is

$$i = \frac{u}{6} + 0.5i + \frac{u}{3}$$

or

$$i = u$$

Again, according to KVL, we can write

$$2i + u - 18 = 0$$

By solving this equation, we can find the voltage

$$u = 6V$$

1.6   Example of Computer-Aided Analysis of Circuits

EWB is known as Electronics Workbench. It is a electronic circuit computer simulation design software developed by Canada's Interactive Image Technologies Ltd in 1988. The software is perfect in design features, friendly in user interface and very easy to master.

Using EWB to analyze simple DC circuits will be discussed in this section.

Example 1.6.1   Fig.1.6.1a shows a simlpe DC circuit. If the current and voltage of each branch are required to find by using EWB, the required components can be selected from the component library according to the schematic diagram, and moved to the workspace. In parameter settings dialog box of the component model, set the value of components, and then connect them to form the required circuit. If the current needs to be measured, connect the ammeter in series to the branch. If the voltage needs to be measured, connect the voltmeter in parallel with branch. And finally press the simulation switch and wait a second, the values of the branch current and branch voltage can be read from the ammeter and voltmeter, as shown in Fig.1.6.1b.

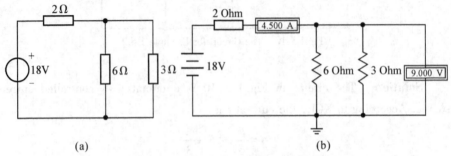

Fig.1.6.1 The Circuit for Example 1.6.1

Example 1.6.2 Fig.1.6.2a shows a schematic diagram of a DC circuit that requires to find the current and voltage of each branch. According to the circuit diagram, follow the simulation steps, select the required components from the component library and drag it to the workspace, through the component model parameter settings dialog box, set the component values, labels and numbers, and then wire them into the desired circuit. Finally press the simulation switch and wait a second, the values of the branch current and branch voltage can be read from the ammeter and voltmeter, as shown in Fig.1.6.2b.

After establishing the schematic diagram in the workspace, you can also select the Schematic Options command from the Circuit menu in the command menu. In the dialog box that is activated, select Show Nodes, the node number will be displayed on the schematic, as shown in Fig. 1.6.2c. Then, select the DC Operating Point command in the Analysis menu of the command menu. The EWB will analyze the DC operating point of the circuit. The result of the analysis is shown in the DC Bias column of the Analysis Graphs window, where each node voltages and branch currents of voltage sources is shown, as shown in Fig.1.6.2d.

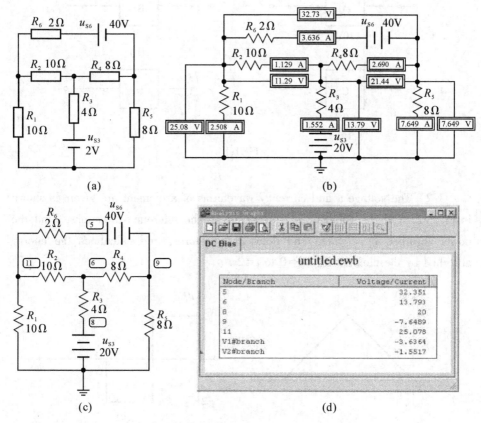

Fig.1.6.2 Figure for Example 1.6.2

Exercise

1-1 Four elements are given as shown in Fig.1-1.

(1) Find the power absorbed by element A;

(2) Find the power generated by element B;

(3) If the power generated by element C is 10W, find current i;

(4) If the power generated by element D is -10W, find voltage u.

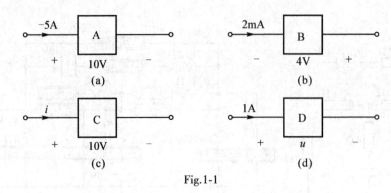

Fig.1-1

1-2 The voltage u and current i waveforms of a element are given as shown in Fig.1-2. And the voltage and current are in the reference directions. Find the power absorbed by element and draw its waveform, and calculates the energy absorbed by the element from $t=0$ to $t=2s$.

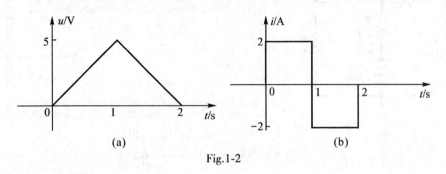

Fig.1-2

1-3 For the circuit shown in Fig.1-3, given: $I_1 = 0.01\mu A$, $I_2 = 0.3\mu A$, $I_5 = 9.61\mu A$. Find currents I_3, I_4 and I_6.

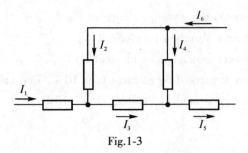

Fig.1-3

1-4 For the circuit shown in Fig.1-4, find voltage u_1 and u_{ab}.

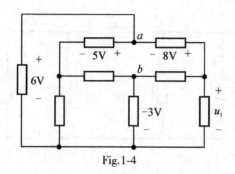

Fig.1-4

1-5 For the circuit shown in Fig.1-5, given: $I_1 = 2A$, $I_3 = -3A$, $U_1 = 10V$, $U_4 = -5V$. Find the power absorbed by each element.

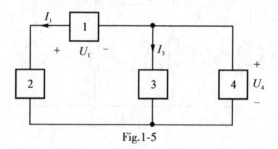

Fig.1-5

1-6 For the circuit shown in Fig.1-6, find current i.

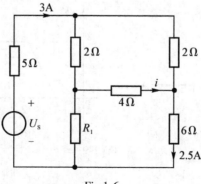

Fig.1-6

1-7   For the circuit shown in Fig.1-7, find resistance R.

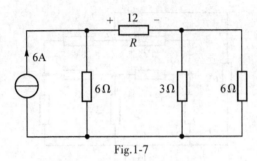

Fig.1-7

1-8   For the circuit shown in Fig.1-8, find u and i_S.

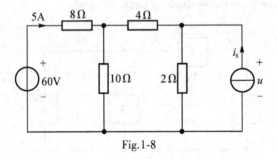

Fig.1-8

1-9   For a capacitor element shown in Fig.1-9a, its voltage waveform is given as shown in Fig.1-9b, and $C = 100\text{pF}$, find current i.

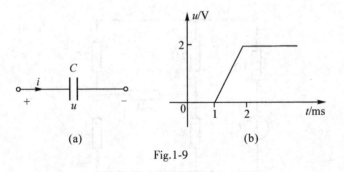

Fig.1-9

1-10   The current waveform of a 0.2H inductor element is given as shown in

Fig.1-10. And the reference directions of voltage and current are in the associated direction. Find the voltage waveform of inductor.

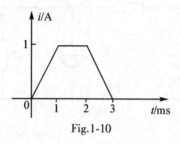
Fig.1-10

1-11 For a $C = 0.2F$ capacitor, its current waveform is given as shown in Fig.1-11, if at $t=0$, its voltage is given $u(0) = 0$, find its voltage u.

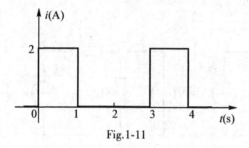
Fig.1-11

1-12 For the circuit shown in Fig.1-12, $R = 2\Omega$, $L = 1H$, $C = 0.1F$, $u_C(0) = 0$. If $i(t) = e^{-t} A$. Find: u_R, u_L and u_C when $t > 0$.

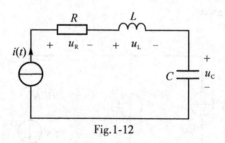
Fig.1-12

1-13 Find the voltage u in the circuit shown in Fig. 1-13. If the 20Ω

resistance is changed to 40Ω, what is the impact on the results, why?

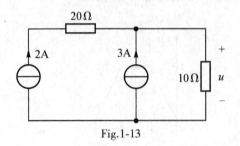

Fig.1-13

1-14 The circuit is shown in Fig.1-14. find:
(A) the current i in Fig.1-14a;
(B) the terminal voltage u of the current source in Fig.1-14b;
(C) the current i in Fig.1-14c.

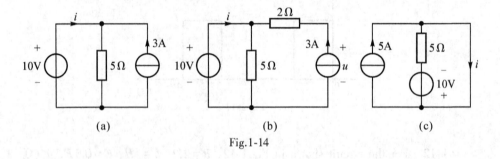

Fig.1-14

1-15 For the circuit shown in Fig.1-15, find the voltage u_1 and the power absorbed by each element.

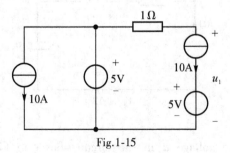

Fig.1-15

1-16 For the circuit shown in Fig.1-16, find potentials V_a, V_b and V_c.

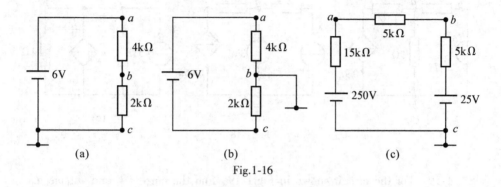

Fig.1-16

1-17 For the circuit shown in Fig.1-17, find:
(1) The potential at node A in Fig.1-17a;
(2) The voltage u in Fig.1-17b.

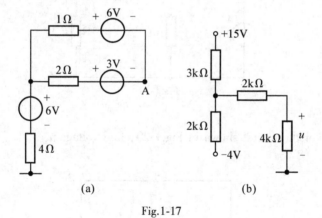

Fig.1-17

1-18 For the circuit with controlled source shown in Fig.1-18, find:
(1) The current i_1 and voltage u_{ab} in Fig.1-18a;
(2) The voltage u_{ab} and u_{cb} in Fig.1-18b;
(3) The voltage u and current i_1, i_2 in Fig.1-18c.

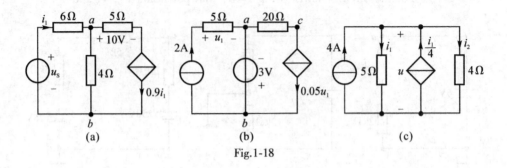

Fig.1-18

1-19 For the circuit shown in Fig.1-19, find the current i_1 and voltage u.

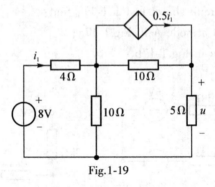

Fig.1-19

1-20 For the circuit shown in Fig.1-20, find voltage u_{ab}.

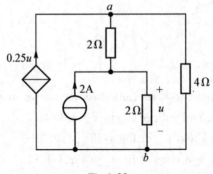

Fig.1-20

Chapter 2
Equivalent Resistive Circuits

In the analysis of the network, sometimes it is not required to find all the voltages and currents, and only some of the voltages and currents is required to be found. In this case, we can usually reduce the part of the network which do not contain the required voltages and currents and make the circuit easy to solve. This chapter will discuss the method for getting equivalent circuits of resistive circuits.

First, the concept of equivalent transformation of one-port network is introduced, then the methods for obtaining equivalent resistive circuits are introduced. It includes the equivalence of passive one-port network, the series/parallel and the hybrid connection, balanced bridge circuit, equivalent transformation of Y to $\triangle$ connection, equivalent simplification of active one-port network, equivalent circuits with the controlled sources.

The methods for equivalent circuits described in this chapter are very useful in circuit analysis and engineering practice and should be mastered.

2.1 The Equivalent Circuit of One-Port Network

The concept and method of equivalent simplification of one-port network are very important in circuit analysis, and are often used in electrical engineering. In this section, some concepts of equivalent circuit for one-port network will be introduced.

2.1.1 Ports

For a network with two terminals, if the current flowing into one terminal is equal to the current flowing out of the other terminal, the two terminals are defined as a port. As shown in Fig.2.1.1a, if $i=i'$, then the terminals 1 and 2 constitute a port. The condition that the current flowing into one terminal is equal to the current flowing out of the other terminal is called the port condition. From the definition of the port, it can be seen that not all two terminals selected from the network can be a port. For example, there is no port in the network as shown in Fig.2.1.1b.

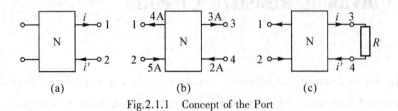

Fig.2.1.1 Concept of the Port

To ensure that the two terminals selected can form a port, it should be noted that if the current flowing into one terminal is equal to the current flowing out of the other terminal. If only one element is connected between the two terminals, as shown in Fig.2.1.1c, according to KCL, there is $i = i'$, the port conditions are met, so the terminals 3 and 4 constitute a port.

2.1.2 One-Port Network

The network which is connected to other circuits only with two terminals is known as a two-terminal network, also known as one-port network. Why can we call a two-terminal network as a one-port network? For the two-terminal network shown in Fig.2.1.2a, according to KCL, it is easy to prove that there is always $i = i'$, so the terminals 1 and 2 constitute a port. Any two-terminal network is a one-port network. Similarly, a network with two ports is called a two-port network. According to whether they contains independent sources or not, one-port networks are divided into active one-port network and passive one-port network. An active one-port network refers to a one-port network with independent sources, as shown in Fig.2.1.2b, and a passive one-port network does not contain any independent source, however it may contain controlled sources, as shown in Fig.2.1.2c.

In the circuit analysis, a part of the circuit in the network is often called a block. If the block is connected to the external circuit only with two terminals, and the current flowing through the two terminals will be the same, this block can be considered to be a one-port network. By using this concept of a one-port network, a larger network, such as the network as shown in Fig.2.1.3a, can be divided into

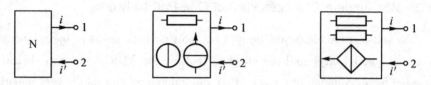

(a) Single-Port Network   (b) Active Single-Port Network   (c) Passive Single-Port Network

Fig.2.1.2   Single-port Network

two smaller networks N_1 and N_2, as shown in Fig. 2.1.3b, then it is easier to analyze the network N_1 and N_2 by applying equivalent circuits or other analysis methods. This is the main idea of circuit analysis discussed in this chapter.

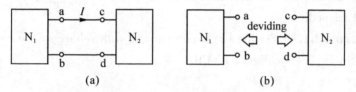

Fig.2.1.3   Dividing the Network

When the concept of one-port network is applied, it should be noted that the one-port network must be "clear" one-port network. What is a clear one-port network? If the one-port network does not contain any element which is coupled electrically or non-electrically (such as magnetic coupling, optical-coupling, etc.) with some variables outside of the network, then the one-port network is said to be clear. In the later discussion, only the clear one-port network will be discussed.

In general, there are three ways to describe one-port network:

(1) specific circuit model.

(2) The relationship between the voltage and current of the port, that is, the volt-ampere relationship(VCR) of a one-port network (expressed by an equation or a curve). It is the most common method, which is equivalent to the constraint condition of the component.

(3) Equivalent circuit.

2.1.3 Volt-Ampere Characteristics of One-Port Networks

The volt-ampere characteristic of a one-port network refers to the relationship between the port voltage and the current, that is, the VCR of the port. It can be expressed by an equation or a curve. Port volt-ampere relationship is very important in the circuit analysis, it is the basis to determine if the two one-port networks are equivalent or not. This principle can also be extended to the three-terminal network and two-port network.

Generally, by externally connecting a voltage source or a current source to the port, the port volt-ampere relationship of network can be derived by experiment measurement or calculation. For series or parallel connection of one-port networks, their port volt-ampere characteristics can be synthesized by a graphical method or analytical method.

Example 2.1.1 For the single-port network with voltage source and resistor, as shown in Fig.2.1.4a. Find its VCR.

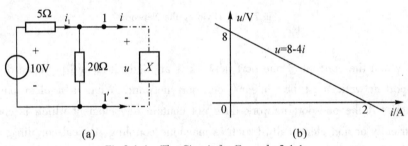

(a)   (b)

Fig.2.1.4 The Circuit for Example 2.1.1

Solution The VCR of a one-port network is determined by its components and structures, and it is independent of the external circuit. So its VCR can be derived by connecting to any external circuit X, as shown in Fig.2.1.4a. To find its VCR, first, let's list the equations for the entire circuit with KCL, KVL and Ohm's law, and it is not required to write the VCR of component X:

$$10 = 5i_1 + u$$
$$u = 20(i_1 - i)$$

Then by cancelling all variables except u and i, the following equation can be

derived. So, there is:
$$u = 8 - 4i$$

This expression is the VCR of the single-port network in case of standard reference direction of the u, i. Fig.2.1.4b shows its VCR curve in u-i plane.

The VCR of a single-port network is independent of the external circuit, so it is possible to derive its VCR in case of connecting an simplest external circuit. Finding voltage by applying external current source and finding current by applying external voltage source are two common methods, they are also the basis to derive VCR with the experimental method.

Example 2.1.2 For a one-port network with independent source, resistance and controlled source, as shown in Fig.2.1.5, find its port VCR.

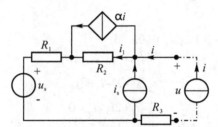

Fig.2.1.5 The Circuit for Example 2.1.2

Solution By connecting a current source i on the port of the one-port circuit, following KVL equation can be derived by inspection.
$$\begin{aligned}u &= (i+i_s-\alpha i)R_2 + (i+i_s)R_1 + u_s + iR_3\\ &= [u_s + (R_1+R_2)i_s] + [R_1+R_3+(1-\alpha)R_2]i\end{aligned}$$

It is the port VCR we need.

From these examples, it is seen that the VCR of an active one-port network can be written in the form of $u = U_0 + Ri$.

Example 2.1.3 For the one-port network which is consist of resistor only, as shown in Fig.2.1.6a, find its VCR.

Solution Applying a voltage source u to the port of the network, as shown in Fig.2.1.6b. If the directions of branches and 3 loops are assigned as shown in Fig., the KCL equations are

$$\begin{cases} i-i_1-i_2=0 \\ i_1-i_3-i_4=0 \\ i_2+i_3-i_5=0 \end{cases}$$

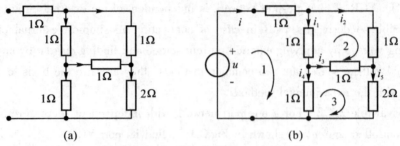

(a)   (b)

Fig.2.1.6   the Circuit for Example 2.1.3

Applying KVL to 3 loops, there are
$$\begin{cases} i+i_1+i_4=u \\ i_2-i_3-i_1=0 \\ i_3+2i_5-i_4=0 \end{cases}$$
By solving equations, it is derived
$$u=\frac{24}{11}i$$
This is the port VCR of the network.

In general, the VCR of a purely resistive single-port network can always be expressed in the form of $u=Ri$, where R is the equivalent resistance of a one-port network.

2.1.4   Equivalent Circuit of One-Port Network

If the volt-ampere relationship of a one-port network N_1 is exactly the same as volt-ampere relationship (external characteristic) that of another single-port network N_2, then two single-port networks N_1 and N_2 are said to be equivalent. As shown in Fig.2.1.7. The two networks are equivalent, it means that they have exactly the same VCR at the equivalent port, although two networks may have totally different structures.

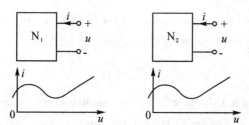
Fig.2.1.7 Equivalent Circuit of Single-Port Network

According to the equivalent concept, in the study of one-port network N_1, it can be replaced with N_2 to achieve the goal of simplifiing circuit structure and analyzing easily.

It is important to note that, when the equivalent circuit method is applied to analyze the circuit, the part where the voltage and current remain unchanged is only limited to the part outside of the equivalent circuit, that is, equivalent is valid only to the external circuit. For the inside of the equivalent circuit, it is not equivalent. For example, as shown in Fig.2.1.8, the part of the circuit in dashed box (Fig.2.1.8a), has a totally different structure from the part of the circuit in dashed box (Fig.2.1.8b). However, for external circuit M in both Fig., since they are equivalent to each other, their electrical behavior are identical.

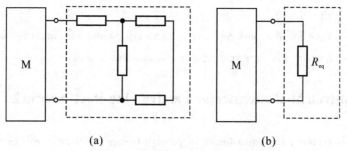

(a)　　　　　　　　(b)
Fig 2.1.8 Equivalent to the External Circuit

The equivalent circuit is also a description of the one-port network, the simplest and most basic situation is the equivalent resistance of series resistaors and the parallel resistors. respectively, They are all equivalent to a single resistor with the same VCR relationship.

Fig.2.1.9 shows a one-port passive resistive network, the equivalent resistance is defined as the ratio of the port voltage and current, that is,

$$R_{eq} = \frac{u}{i} \qquad (2.1.1)$$

It should be noted that, only for the passive one-port network, there is an equivalent resistance. For active single-port network port, the ratio of voltage and current is generally not a constant, so it is meaningless.

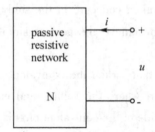

Fig.2.1.9 A Single-Port Network

The method of equivalent circuit can be summarized as follows:

(1) If the external characteristics of the two circuits are the same, then the two circuits are called equivalent circuit.

(2) If two two-terminal networks are equivalent, one can be replaced with the other in the circuit.

(3) Except for the part replaced by the equivalent circuit, the voltages and currents of the part which is not replaced keep unchanged.

2.2 Equivalent Resistance of Passive One-Port Networks

In this section, the equivalence of passive one-port networks will be discussed, including the resistors in series, in parallel and neither in sevies nor in parallel.

2.2.1 Equivalent Resistance of Resistors in Series

The basic connections form of the linear time-invariant resistor in the network are series connection and parallel connection. The series connection is characterized

2.2 Equivalent Resistance of Passive One-Port Networks

by the fact that the same current flows through all the resistors. The parallel connection is characterized in that the voltages across and the resistors are the same. Both connections can be equivalently simplified.

First, the series connection of two linear time-invariant resistors are discussed. The series connection of two linear time-invariant resistors can be regarded as a two-terminal network N whose internal structure is known, as shown in Fig.2.2.1a.

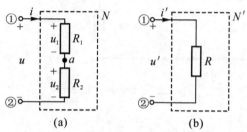

Fig.2.2.1 The Series of Two Resistors and Its Eequivalent Resistance

KVL equation of this two-terminal network can be written as follows
$$u = u_1 + u_2 \tag{2.2.1}$$
According to KCL, the current flowing through the two resistors is the same, i. In addition, we also know that the characteristics equation of the two linear resistor are
$$u_1 = R_1 i$$
$$u_2 = R_2 i$$
Substituting the above two expressions into the expression (2.2.1) gives
$$u = R_1 i + R_2 i = (R_1 + R_2) i \tag{2.2.2}$$
This equation is the external characteristic equation of the two-terminal network N.

And let's consider a two-terminal network N' with only one resistor R, as shown in Fig.2.2.1b, the external characteristic equation of this two-terminal network is
$$u' = Ri' \tag{2.2.3}$$
In comparison with (2.2.2) and (2.2.3), it is seen that, if $R = R_1 + R_2$, then $i' = i$; and, $u' = u$ so if $R = R_1 + R_2$, N and N' are equivalent.

Similarly, for the series circuit of n resistors shown in Fig.2.2.2a, set u to represent the total voltage, i to represent the total current, R_1, R_2, $\cdots$, R_n are the resistance of each resistor, u_1, u_2, $\cdots$, u_n are the voltage across each resistor respectively. Applying KVL, yields

$$u = u_1 + u_2 + \cdots + u_n$$

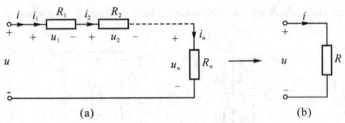

Fig.2.2.2   Resistors in Series

and applying Ohm's law gives

$$u_1 = R_1 i, \ u_2 = R_2 i, \cdots, \ u_n = R_n i$$

$$\therefore \quad u = R_1 i + R_2 i + \cdots + R_n i = (R_1 + R_2 + \cdots + R_n) i = Ri$$

where $R = R_1 + R_2 + \cdots + R_n = \sum_{k=1}^{n} R_k$, is known as the total resistance or equivalent resistance of n resistors in serie. Its equivalent circuit is shown in Fig.2.2.2b.

It follows that the two-terminal network in series with n linear time-invariant resistors R_1, R_2, $\cdots$, R_n is equivalent to a two-terminal network with only one linear time-invariant resistor R and $R = R_1 + R_2 + \cdots + R_n$. That is, the total resistance or the equivalent resistance of the series resistance is equal to the sum of the each resistors in series.

The above conclusions can also be extended to the linear time-variant resistors in series, that is, the equivalent resistance of the n linear time-variant resistors in series is

$$R(t) = \sum_{k=1}^{n} R_k(t)$$

For a two-terminal network N made up of n linear time-invariant resistors in series, its power is:

$$P = ui = (R_1 + R_2 + \cdots + R_n) i^2 = R_1 i^2 + R_2 i^2 + \cdots + R_n i^2 = Ri^2$$

The above equation shows that the total power absorbed by multiple series resistors is equal to the sum of the power absorbed by each resistor and is equal to the power absorbed by the equivalent resistor.

A common application of series resistance is voltage division.

For a two-terminal network N connected in series by n linear time-invariant resistors $R_1, R_2, \cdots, R_n$, the voltage on each resistor can be derived as

$$u_k = R_k i = \frac{R_k}{R} u$$

It can be seen that the voltage of each resistor in series is proportional to the resistance of that resistor, or the total voltage is distributed according to the resistance of each series resistance. The larger the resistance is, the bigger the resistor voltage is. The smaller the resistance is, the smaller the resistor voltage is. The above expression is called voltage division.

In the most case, only two resistors are connected in series, then the voltage division is

$$u_1 = \frac{R_1}{R_1 + R_2} u$$

$$u_2 = \frac{R_2}{R_1 + R_2} u$$

2.2.2 Equivalent Resistance of Resistors in Parallel

Two linear time-invariant resistors in parallel can also be regarded as a two-terminal network N whose internal structure is known, as shown in Fig.2.2.3a. all the resistors in parallel bear the same voltage.

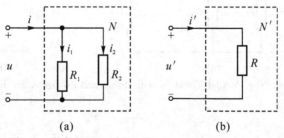

Fig.2.2.3 The Parallel Circuit of Two Resistor and Its Equivalent Resistance

Writing the KCL equation for the network shown in Fig.2.2.3a, gives
$$i = i_1 + i_2 \tag{2.2.4}$$
Applying Ohm's Law, yields
$$i_1 = \frac{u}{R_1} = G_1 u$$
$$i_2 = \frac{u}{R_2} = G_2 u$$
Substituting the egu.(2.2.4), into egu.(2.2.4) gives
$$i = G_1 u + G_2 u = (G_1 + G_2) u \tag{2.2.5}$$
Let's consider a two-terminal network N' with only one resistor R, as shown in Fig.2.2.3b. The external characteristic equation of N' is
$$i' = \frac{u}{R} = G u' \tag{2.2.6}$$
In comparison with (2.2.5) and (2.2.6), it can be seen that, if the condition $G = G_1 + G_2$ or $\frac{1}{R} = \frac{1}{R_1} + \frac{1}{R_2}$ is satisfied, then $u' = u$ only if $i' = i$; or $i' = i$ only if $u' = u$. Thus, if $G = G_1 + G_2$, N and N' are equivalent.

Similarly, for the parallel circuit of n resistors, as shown in Fig.2.2.4a, if i is the total current, u is the total voltage, G_1, G_2, $\cdots$, G_n are the conductances of each resistor and i_1, i_2, $\cdots$, i_n are the currents in each resistor. By applying KCL, there are
$$i = i_1 + i_2 + \cdots + i_n = G_1 u + G_2 u + \cdots + G_n u = (G_1 + G_2 + \cdots + G_n) u = G u$$

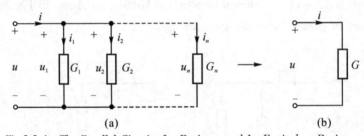

Fig.2.2.4 The Parallel Circuit of n Resistors and Its Equivalent Resistance

where
$$G = \frac{i}{u} = G_1 + G_2 + \cdots + G_n$$

is called the total conductance or equivalent conductance of the resistors connected in parallel, which is equal to the sum of their individual conductance.

$$\because G=\frac{1}{R}, G_1=\frac{1}{R_1}, G_2=\frac{1}{R_2}, \cdots, G_n=\frac{1}{R_n}$$

$$\therefore G=\frac{1}{R}=\frac{1}{R_1}+\frac{1}{R_2}+\cdots+\frac{1}{R_n}$$

So, there are

$$R=\frac{1}{\frac{1}{R_1}+\frac{1}{R_2}+\cdots+\frac{1}{R_n}}$$

Normally, it is more convenient to handle the resistance in parallel with the conductance than with the resistance

From the above discussion, it can be seen that, for the two-terminal network N which is connected by n linear time-invariant resistors R_1, R_2, $\cdots$, R_n in parallel, it is equivalent to a two-terminal network N' with only one linear time-invariant resistor R, and total conductance is $G=G_1+G_2+\cdots+G_n$. Resistance R is called the equivalent resistance of the n resistance in parallel, its conductance is

$$G = \sum_{k=1}^{n} G_k \tag{2.2.7}$$

The total power of n resistor R_1, R_2, $\cdots$, R_n in parallel is derived as follows

$$P=ui=(G_1+G_2+\cdots+G_n)u^2=G_1u^2+G_2u^2+\cdots+G_nu^2=Gu^2$$

That is, the total power of the parallel resistors is equal to the sum of the powers of each conductance or equal to the power of equivalent conductance.

A common application of parallel resistors is current division. If the resistors are connected in parallel, the current in each resistor can be derived as

$$i_k=G_k u=\frac{G_k}{G}i$$

It can be seen that the current in the shunt resistor is proportional to the conductance of each resistor, or the total current is distributed according to the conductance of each shunt resistor.

For the case that there are only two resistors, as shown in Fig.2.2.12, the currents in each resistor are

$$i_1=\frac{G_1}{G}i=\frac{1/R_1}{1/R_1+1/R_2}i=\frac{R_2}{R_1+R_2}i$$

$$i_2 = \frac{G_2}{G}i = \frac{1/R_2}{1/R_1 + 1/R_2}i = \frac{R_1}{R_1 + R_2}i$$

From the above equation, it can be seen that, the greater R_1 is, the smaller i_1 is, the larger R_2 is, the smaller i_2 is. It should be noted that, this feature is different from the resistance in series, for which the greater resistance, the greater the voltage. Since these two formulas are often used, it should be remembered.

From the formula of the parallel resistance, a feature can be found, that is

$$R = \frac{1}{\sum_{k=1}^{n}\frac{1}{R_k}} = \frac{1}{\frac{1}{R_1} + \frac{1}{R_2} + \cdots + \frac{1}{R_n}} < R_k, k = 1, 2, \cdots, n$$

Therefore, the total resistance of the parallel resistor is less than any individual resistance in parallel.

For two resistors in parallel, the equivalent resistance is

$$R = \frac{1}{1/R_1 + 1/R_2} = \frac{R_1 R_2}{R_1 + R_2} \triangleq R_1 \parallel R_2$$

This formula is often used and should also be remembered.

2.2.3 Equivalent Resistance of Resistors-Parallel

The resistor connection with both series and parallel is called the resistor in mixed connection. For a mixed connection circuit, as shown in Fig.2.2.5, R_3 and R_4 are connected in series and then connected in parallel with R_2, and finally connected in series with R_1. For a mixed connection circuit, the series resistance formula and the parallel resistance formula can be applied repeatedly to derive the equivalent resistance or the total resistance of the entire circuit.

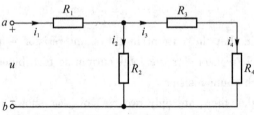

Fig.2.2.5 The Resistance in Mixed Connection

For example, for the mixed connection circuit shown in Fig.2.2.5, the circuit

2.2 Equivalent Resistance of Passive One-Port Networks

equivalent resistance can be derived as follows

$$R = R_1 + R_2 \parallel (R_3 + R_4) = R_1 + \frac{R_2(R_3+R_4)}{R_2+R_3+R_4}$$

The general analysis steps of the mixed connection circuit are as follows:

(1) find the equivalent resistance R or equivalent conductance G of the whole circuit;

(2) apply Ohm's law to find the total voltage or total current circuit;

(3) apply the voltage division formula and current division formula to find the voltage and current on each resistor.

Example 2.2.1 As shown in Fig.2.2.5, it is given $u = U_S$. Find the voltage and current on each resistor.

Solution Apply the above results of equivalent resistance, the total current is derived as

$$i_1 = i = \frac{U_s}{R_1 + \frac{R_2(R_3+R_4)}{R_2+R_3+R_4}}$$

Then, the voltages accross resistor R_1, R_2 are

$$u_1 = R_1 i_1$$

$$u_2 = u_{34} = (R_2 \parallel R_{34}) i = \frac{(R_3+R_4)R_2}{R_2+R_3+R_4} \cdot i_1$$

The currents flowing through R_2, R_3 are

$$i_2 = \frac{u_2}{R_2} = \frac{(R_3+R_4)R_2}{(R_2+R_3+R_4)} \cdot \frac{i_1}{R_2}$$

$$i_3 = i_4 = \frac{u_2}{R_3+R_4}$$

Finally, the voltages of resistor R_3, R_4 are

$$u_3 = R_3 i_3$$
$$u_4 = R_4 i_4$$

Example 2.2.2 Fig.2.2.6a shown a DC divider circuit with dual power supplies. Find the changing range of the potential at terminal a if the sliding terminal of the potentiometer is moved.

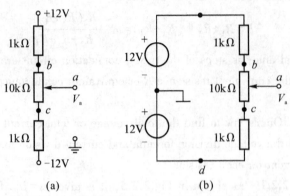

Fig.2.2.6 A DC Divider Circuit with Dual Power Supplies

Solution By replacing the two potential values with two voltage sources, a circuit shown in Fig.2.2.6b is obtained.

If the sliding terminal of potentiometer is moved to the bottom, the potential of terminal a is

$$V_a = U_{cd} - 12\text{V} = \frac{1\text{k}\Omega}{1\text{k}\Omega + 10\text{k}\Omega + 1\text{k}\Omega} \times 24\text{V} - 12\text{V} = -10\text{V}$$

If the sliding terminal of potentiometer is moved to the top, the potential of terminal a is

$$V_a = U_{bd} - 12\text{V} = \frac{10\text{k}\Omega + 1\text{k}\Omega}{1\text{k}\Omega + 10\text{k}\Omega + 1\text{k}\Omega} \times 24\text{V} - 12\text{V} = 10\text{V}$$

Therefore, if the potentiometer sliding terminal is moved up from the bottom gradually, the potential at terminal a will continuously change from -10V to $+10\text{V}$.

Example 2.2.3 For the circuit shown in Fig.2.2.7, find each branch current.

Solution First, find the equivalent resistance R_{ab} between the terminal a, b.

$$R_{de} = 30\Omega \parallel 60\Omega = \frac{30 \times 60}{30 + 60} = 20\Omega$$

$$R_{db} = 20\Omega + 10\Omega = 30\Omega$$

$$R_{eb} = 30\Omega \parallel 30\Omega = \frac{30 \times 30}{30 + 30} = 15\Omega$$

$$R_{ab} = 15\Omega + 25\Omega = 40\Omega$$

2.2 Equivalent Resistance of Passive One-Port Networks

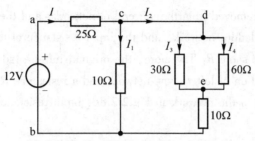

Fig.2.2.7 The Circuit for Example 2.2.3

According to Ohm's law, the total current is,

$$I = \frac{12}{R_{ab}} = \frac{12}{40} = 0.3\text{A}$$

Then according to current division formula, other branch currents are derived..

$$I_2 = \frac{30}{30+R_{db}}I = \frac{30}{30+30} \times 0.3 = 0.15\text{A}$$

$$I_1 = I - I_2 = 0.3 - 0.15 = 0.15\text{A}$$

$$I_3 = \frac{60}{30+60}I_2 = 0.10\text{A}$$

$$I_4 = I_2 - I_3 = 0.15 - 0.1 = 0.05\text{A}$$

Example 2.2.4 The network shown in Fig.2.2.8a is known as an infinite ladder network. All resistors in the network are linearly resistors. Where R_S is called the series-arm resistance, R_p is called the parallel-arm resistance. If $R_s = 2\Omega$, $R_p = 1\Omega$, try to find input resistance R_i of the entire network.

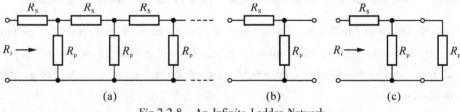

Fig.2.2.8 An Infinite Ladder Network

Solution Obviously, this network is made up of an infinite number of so-called left Γ networks as shown in Fig.2.2.8b. Since the network is infinite, if one left Γ network is removed from the left end of network, and the remaining network is still an infinite ladder network, and the input resistance of the network can still be regarded as the same R_i. Therefore, the original infinite ladder network can be seen as a combination of left Γ-type network and a resistance Ri, as shown in Fig. 2.2.8c. According to the network in Fig.2.2.8c, input resistance Ri can be written immediately as

$$R_i = R_s + R_p \parallel R_i = R_s + \frac{R_p R_i}{R_p + R_i}$$

By solving this equation, it is derived that

$$R_i = \frac{R_s + \sqrt{R_s^2 + 4R_p R_s}}{2}$$

Substitute the given number $R_s = 2\Omega, R_p = 1\Omega$ into above expression, there is

$$R_i = 2.73\Omega$$

There is still another solution $R_i = -0.73\Omega$, but it is disagree with the meaning of problem.

2.3 Delta-to-Wye Equivalent Circuits

Sometimes, the resistors in the circuit are neither in series nor in parallel, such as the wheats tone bridge. In this case, if it is required to find the equivalent of the circuit, the equivalent transformation of resistances in Y and delta connection can be applied.

2.3.1 Resistances in Delta-Connected and Wye-Connected Resistors

As shown in Fig.2.3.1a, by connecting one terminal of each resistor together to form a common point, the other terminal of each resistor is connected to the external circuit, this kind of connection is called Y connection, also known as star connection.

For the circuit shown in Fig.2.3.1b, by connecting three resistors with head to tail to form a triangular and leading to external circuit from the connection, this kind of connection is called a Δ(or delta) or triangular connection.

2.3 Delta-to-Wye Equivalent Circuits

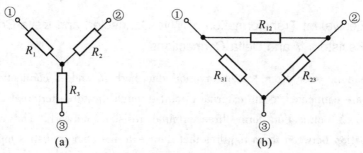

Fig 2.3.1 Resistances in Y and Δ

For a bridge circuit as shown in Fig.2.3.2a, if Δ connection composed of R_1, R_2, R_3 is equivalent to a Y connection composed of R_a, R_b, R_c, as shown in Fig.2.3.2b, then the equivalent resistance between a, b (total resistance) can be derived by applying the series and parallel resistance formula as.

$$R_{ab} = R_a + \frac{(R_4+R_b)(R_5+R_c)}{R_b+R_5+R_c+R_4}$$

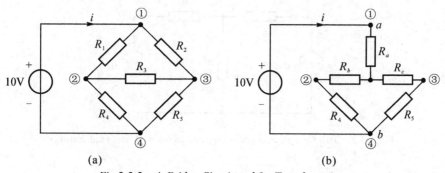

Fig.2.3.2 A Bridge Circuit and Its Transformation

Similarly, if the resistances in Y composed of R_1, R_3 and R_4 is transformed into the resistances in Δ, the total resistance between a and b can also be derived by applying series and parallel method as.

$$R_{ab} = \frac{R'_a \left(\dfrac{R_2 R'_b}{R_2+R'_b} + \dfrac{R_5 R'_c}{R_5+R'_c} \right)}{R'_a + \dfrac{R'_2 R'_b}{R_2+R'_b} + \dfrac{R_5 R'_c}{R_5+R'_c}}$$

2.3.2 Equivalent Transformation of Wye-Connected and Delta-Connected Resistors Y and Delta Connections

It can be seen from the observation that both Y and Δ connection of the resistors are connected to the external circuit through the three terminals, resistors in Y and Δ connection form three-terminal resistive network. The equivalent transformation between them requires that their external characteristics must be the same. The so-called external characteristics are the same, refers to that if the same voltages are applied to the corresponding terminals, then the currents of the corresponding terminal must also be the same.

In general, the port characteristics of the resistive three-terminal network can be characterized by two algebraic equations that relate to these voltage and current relationships.

For Y-connected three-terminal resistance network, two current sources i_1 and i_2 are applied, as shown in Fig.2.3.3.

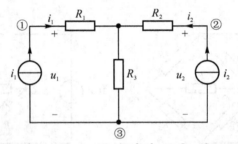

Fig.2.3.3 Two Current Sources is Applied to a Star-Connected Network

Appling KVL, the expressions of port voltage u_1 and u_2 are derived as

$$\begin{cases} u_1 = R_1 i_1 + R_3 (i_1 + i_2) \\ u_2 = R_2 i_2 + R_3 (i_1 + i_2) \end{cases}$$

Finishing up, there are

$$\left. \begin{aligned} u_1 &= (R_1 + R_3) i_1 + R_3 i_2 \\ u_2 &= R_3 i_1 + (R_2 + R_3) i_2 \end{aligned} \right\} \quad (2.3.1)$$

For the three-terminal Δ-connectell resistive network shown in Fig.2.3.4a, by adding two current sources i_1 and i_2 and converting the current source in parallel with the resistor into a voltage source in series with resistor, the circuit shown in

Fig.2.3.4b is obtained.

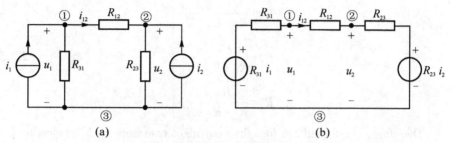

Fig.2.3.4 The Resistive Network of Δ Connection

By applying Ohm's law, there is

$$i_{12} = \frac{R_{31}i_1 - R_{23}i_2}{R_{12}+R_{23}+R_{31}} \quad (2.3.2)$$

By applying KVL, there are

$$\begin{cases} u_1 = R_{31}i_1 - R_{31}i_{12} = R_{31}(i_1 - i_{12}) \\ u_2 = R_{23}i_{12} + R_{23}i_2 = R_{23}(i_2 + i_{12}) \end{cases}$$

Substituting i_{12} expression into the above two expressions, it is derived that

$$\left.\begin{aligned} u_1 &= \frac{R_{31}(R_{12}+R_{23})}{R_{12}+R_{23}+R_{31}}i_1 + \frac{R_{23}R_{31}}{R_{12}+R_{23}+R_{31}}i_2 \\ u_2 &= \frac{R_{23}R_{31}}{R_{12}+R_{23}+R_{31}}i_1 + \frac{R_{23}(R_{12}+R_{31})}{R_{12}+R_{23}+R_{31}}i_2 \end{aligned}\right\} \quad (2.3.3)$$

The expressions (2.3.1) and (2.3.3) are the VCR equations for resistive networks in Y connection and Δ connection, respectively.

If the resistive networks in Y connection and Δ connection are equivalent, the corresponding coefficients of the above two VCR equations are required to be equal, i.e.

$$\left.\begin{aligned} R_1 + R_3 &= \frac{R_{31}(R_{12}+R_{23})}{R_{12}+R_{23}+R_{31}} \\ R_3 &= \frac{R_{23}R_{31}}{R_{12}+R_{23}+R_{31}} \\ R_2 + R_3 &= \frac{R_{23}(R_{12}+R_{31})}{R_{12}+R_{23}+R_{31}} \end{aligned}\right\} \quad (2.3.4)$$

Thus, it is derived that

$$\left. \begin{array}{l} R_1 = \dfrac{R_{31}R_{12}}{R_{12}+R_{23}+R_{31}} \\[6pt] R_2 = \dfrac{R_{12}R_{23}}{R_{12}+R_{23}+R_{31}} \\[6pt] R_3 = \dfrac{R_{23}R_{31}}{R_{12}+R_{23}+R_{31}} \end{array} \right\} \quad (2.3.5)$$

Therefore, the formula to find the equivalent resistance in Y connection from Δ connection is

$$R_i = \frac{Product\ of\ two\ resistances\ connected\ to\ node\ i}{Sum\ of\ three\ resistances\ in\ \Delta}$$

Where R_i is the resistance connected to node i in Y connection, $i=1, 2, 3$.

If $R_{12} = R_{23} = R_{31} = R_\Delta$, there is

$$R_1 = R_2 = R_3 = R_Y = \frac{1}{3}R_\Delta$$

From expression (2.3.5), it is derived that

$$\left. \begin{array}{l} R_{12} = \dfrac{R_1R_2+R_2R_3+R_3R_1}{R_3} \\[6pt] R_{23} = \dfrac{R_1R_2+R_2R_3+R_3R_1}{R_1} \\[6pt] R_{31} = \dfrac{R_1R_2+R_2R_3+R_3R_1}{R_2} \end{array} \right\} \quad (2.3.6)$$

So, the formula to find the resistance in Δ connection from the Y connection is

$$R_{mn} = \frac{Sum\ of\ products\ of\ each\ two\ resistances\ in\ Y}{The\ resistance\ which\ is\ not\ connected\ to\ terminal\ m,n} \quad (2.3.7)$$

where R_{mn} is the resistance in Δ connection and it is connected between node m and n, $m, n = 1, 2, 3$.

If $R_1 = R_2 = R_3 = R_Y$, there is

$$R_{12} = R_{23} = R_{31} = R_\Delta = 3R_Y \quad (2.3.8)$$

In a complex resistive network, circuit analysis can be simplified by using the equivalent transformation of the resistive network in Y connection and Δ connection. In the later discussion of the circuit analysis, such as three-phase circuit analysis, there are some important applications.

Example 2.3.1 For the circuit shown in Fig. 2.3.5a, calculate the total resistance R_{ab}.

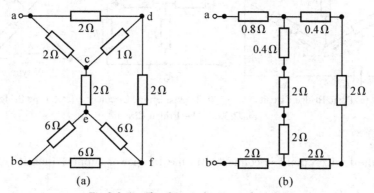

Fig.2.3.5 The Circuit for Example 2.3.8

Solution By observing the circuit shown in Fig.2.3.5a, it is not difficult to find that the circuit contains the resistance connections in Y and Δ, so this problem can be solved by applying the equivalent transformation of the resistive network in Y connection and Δ connection. There are two ways to solve the problem. One way is to transform Y→Δ, the second way is to transform Δ→Y. Here, transforming Δ→Y is selected to find the total resistance R_{ab}. First, two networks of acd and bef in delta are transformed into two resistive networks in Y, as shown in Fig.2.3.5b. Then, in the transformed circuit, there are only series and parallel connections, the total resistance can easily be found as

$$R_{ab} = 0.8 + 2 + (0.4 + 2 + 2) \parallel (0.4 + 2 + 2) = 2.8 + 2.2 = 5(\Omega)$$

2.3.3 The Bridge Circuit and Bridge Balance

2.3.3.1 The Bridge Circuit

The bridge circuit had been mentioned in the previous discussion, which is a special circuit without series and parallel connections. A common bridge circuit is shown in Fig.2.3.6a.

For the bridge Circuit shown in Fig.2.3.6a, R_1, R_2, R_3, R_4 branches are its four "arm", and R_0 branch is called "bridge" branch.

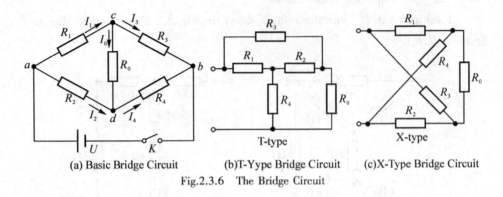

(a) Basic Bridge Circuit (b)T-Yype Bridge Circuit (c)X-Type Bridge Circuit

Fig.2.3.6 The Bridge Circuit

If the bridge circuit is connected to the DC power supply, then it is called a DC bridge.

The drawing of the bridge circuit is not unique, there are two common deformations of the drawing. T-type bridge circuit is shown in Fig. 2.3.6b and X-type bridge circuit is shown in Fig.2.3.6c.

Example 2.3.2 For the bridge circuit shown in Fig.2.3.7a, it is known that $R_1 = R_2 = R_4 = 2\Omega$, $R_3 = R_5 = R_6 = 1\Omega$. Find the total resistance R_{ab}.

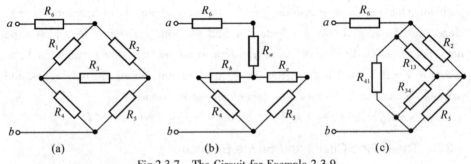

Fig.2.3.7 The Circuit for Example 2.3.9

Solution Both $Y \rightarrow \Delta$ or $\Delta \rightarrow Y$ methods can be applied to transform the bridge circuit. Now, let's discuss respectively.

(1) $\Delta \rightarrow Y$ method: the Δ connection of $R_1 R_2 R_3$ is transformed to Y connection, as shown in Fig.2.3.7b.

Due to $\sum R_\Delta = R_1 + R_2 + R_3 = 2 + 2 + 1 = 5$, then

$$R_a = \frac{2\times 2}{5} = 0.8\Omega, R_b = \frac{1\times 2}{5} = 0.4\Omega, R_c = \frac{1\times 2}{5} = 0.4\Omega$$

$$\therefore R_{ab} = R_6 + R_a + \frac{(R_b + R_4)(R_c + R_5)}{R_b + R_4 + R_c + R_5}$$

$$= 1 + 0.8 + \frac{(2+0.4)(1+0.4)}{3+0.8} = 2.684\Omega$$

(2) Y $\rightarrow \Delta$ method: the Y connection of $R_1 R_4 R_3$ is transformed to Δ connection, as shown in Fig.2.3.7c.

Due to $\sum R_Y = R_1 R_3 + R_3 R_4 + R_4 R_1 = 1\times 2 + 1\times 2 + 2\times 2 = 8$

$$\therefore R_{13} = \frac{8}{2} = 4\Omega, R_{34} = \frac{8}{2} = 4\Omega, R_{41} = \frac{8}{1} = 8\Omega$$

$$\therefore R_{ab} = 1 + \frac{8\left(\dfrac{2\times 4}{2+4} + \dfrac{1\times 4}{1+4}\right)}{8 + \dfrac{2\times 4}{2+4} + \dfrac{1\times 4}{1+4}} = 2.684\Omega$$

The results of two methods are the same.

2.3.3.2 Bridge Balance

In the bridge circuit shown in Fig.2.3.6, when the power is turned on, if there is no current flowing through the "bridge" branch, that is, $I_0 = 0$, it is called bridge balance.

The condition of the bridge balance will be deduced in the following.

Obviously, to make $I_0 = 0$, two potentials at node c and d must be same, namely: $U_{cd} = 0$. So there is

$$U_{ac} = U_{ad} \quad \text{or} \quad U_{cb} = U_{db}$$

Namely

$$I_1 R_1 = I_2 R_2 \quad \text{or} \quad I_3 R_3 = I_4 R_4$$

$$\therefore \frac{I_1 R_1}{I_3 R_3} = \frac{I_2 R_2}{I_4 R_4}$$

And as well, when $I_0 = 0$, $I_1 = I_3, I_2 = I_4$, then there is

$$\frac{R_1}{R_3} = \frac{R_2}{R_4} \quad \text{or} \quad R_1 R_4 = R_2 R_3 \qquad (2.3.9)$$

Thus, the condition for bridge balance can be summarize as:

(1) resistance ratio between two adjacent arms of bridge circuit is equal, that is

$$\frac{R_1}{R_3} = \frac{R_2}{R_4} \quad \text{or} \quad \frac{R_1}{R_2} = \frac{R_3}{R_4}$$

(2) the products of two face to face branch resistances in the bridge circuit are same, that is

$$R_1 R_4 = R_2 R_3$$

If bridge is balanced, because $I_0 = 0$ or $U_0 = 0$, potentials at c, d are equal. So, to reduce the circuit, the bridge branch can be regarded as an open circuit or a short circuit. It will not affect the voltages and currents of other resistors.

Example 2.3.3 For the circuit shown in Fig.2.3.6a, $R_1 = 10\Omega$, $R_2 = 3\Omega$, $R_3 = 20\Omega$, $R_4 = 6\Omega$, $R_0 = 10\Omega$, $U = 13\text{V}$, find the current of each branch.

Solution Duo to $R_1 R_4 = 10 \times 6 = 60\Omega$, $R_2 R_3 = 3 \times 20 = 60\Omega$, it can be seen that the bridge is balanced, so, $I_0 = 0\text{A}$. Then, by applying Ohm's law and KCL, there are

$$I_1 = I_3 = \frac{U}{R_1 + R_2} = \frac{13}{10+3} = \frac{13}{13}\text{A} = 1\text{A}$$

$$I_2 = I_4 = \frac{U}{R_3 + R_4} = \frac{13}{20+6} = \frac{13}{26}\text{A} = 0.5\text{A}$$

$$I = I_1 + I_2 = 1.5\text{A}$$

It should be noted that, if the bridge circuit is not balanced, $I_0 \neq 0$, then the above conclusion cannot be used. In this case, the circuit is neither in series, nor in parallel.

2.3.3.3 The application of bridge circuit

Bridge circuit is widely applied in electronic equipments, the most typical application is used to accurately measure the resistance of the resistor components. As shown in Fig.2.3.8a, it is a common QJ-23-type portable bridge circuit with single arm, Fig.2.3.8b shows its schematic.

Its simplified circuit is shown in Fig.2.3.9. It shows that it is a bridge circuit, four arms are R_1, R_2, R, R_X respectively. A zero center galvanometer G with high sensitivity is connected as the "bridge" branch. And R is an adjustable resistor, R_X is the measured resistance.

2.3 Delta-to-Wye Equivalent Circuits   67

 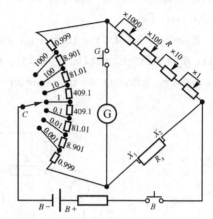

(a) QJ-23 Type Bridge Circuit with Single Arm   (b) Schematic of a Bridge Circuit with Single Arm
Fig.2.3.8   A Bridge Circuit with Single Arm

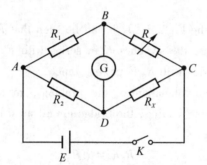

Fig.2.3.9   A bridge Circuit with Single Arm

When the bridge is unbalanced, there is a current flowing through the galvanometer, the stylus deviates from the zero. By adjusting R_1, R_2, R to make the stylus return to zero, bridge circuit is balanced. At this time:.

$$R_1 R_X = R_2 R$$

∴
$$R_X = \frac{R_2 R}{R_1} \qquad (2.3.10)$$

In this way, the value of resistance being measured can be derived. As the resistances of the bridge circuit can be selected very precisely, so the resistance value derived with this bridge circuit measurement is very precise. In addition to the DC resistance measurement, the bridge circuit can also be designed to measure the AC impedance.

Example 2.3.4 For the circuit shown in Fig.2.3.10, it is known that $R_1 = 1\text{k}\Omega$, $R_2 = 3\text{k}\Omega$, $R_3 = 2\text{k}\Omega$, $R_4 = 2\text{k}\Omega$, $R_6 = 500\Omega$. If it is known that switch ON/OFF have no influence on the ammeter reading, what should R_5 be?

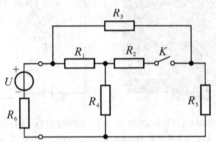

Fig.2.3.10 The Circuit for Example 2.3.11

Solution From the Fig.2.3.10, it can be seen that R_1, R_3, R_4, R_5 are the four arms of the bridge, the switches K in series with R_2 is bridge branch, and source voltage U in series with R_6 is power branch.

According to the explanation of the problem, to let switch ON/OFF no influence on the ammeter reading, the bridge circuit must be in a state of balance. Then, there should be

$$R_1 R_4 = R_5 R_3$$

∴
$$R_5 = \frac{R_1 R_4}{R_3} = \frac{1 \times 2}{2} = 1\text{K}\Omega$$

Example 2.3.5 For the DC circuit shown in Fig.2.3.11, ammeter resistance is supposed to be zero, the voltmeter resistance is supposed to be infinite. Find readings of ammeter, voltmeter.

Solution As the four resistors in the outside of circuit form four arms of a bridge circuit and it is balanced,

$$6 \times 4 = 3 \times 8$$

So two potentials at node B and C are same. By removing the BC branch and applying Ohm's law, the readings of ammeter can be derived as

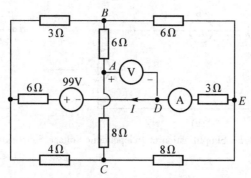

Fig.2.3.11 The Circuit for Example 2.3.12

$$I = \frac{99}{3+6+\frac{(3+6)(4+8)}{3+6+4+8}} = \frac{99}{9+\frac{36}{7}} = 7(A)$$

The readings of voltmeter is derived by applying KVL as

$$U_{AD} = U_{AB} + U_{BE} + U_{ED} = 0 + 6 \times \frac{4+8}{4+8+3+6} \times 7 + 3 \times 7 = 45(V)$$

2.4 Equivalent Simplification of Active One-Port Networks

In this section, the series-parallel equivalent transformation of active single-pot networks with independent sources branches will be discussed.

2.4.1 Equivalent Simplification of Series-Parallel Independent Source

2.4.1.1 Simplification of Independent Voltage Sources in Series

Fig.2.4.1a shows a single-port network with n independent voltage sources connected in series. In terms of port characteristics, it is equivalent to an independent voltage source, as shown in Fig.2.4.1b. According to KVL, the total voltage is equal to the algebraic sum of each voltage source.

$$u_S = \sum_{k=1}^{n} u_{Sk} \quad (2.4.1)$$

where, if the reference direction of source voltage u_{Sk} is same as u_S, it is taken positive. Otherwise, taken negative.

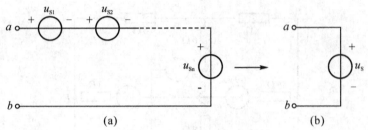

(a)   (b)

Fig.2.4.1 Simplification of Independent Voltage Source in Series

2.4.1.2 Simplification of Independent Current Sources in Parallel

A single-port network with n independent current sources in parallel is shown in Fig.2.4.2a. In terms of port characteristics, it is equivalent to an independent current source, as shown in Fig.2.4.2b. According to KCL, the total current is equal to the algebraic sum of all source currents, i.e.

$$i_s = i_{s1} + i_{s2} + \cdots + i_{sn} = \sum_{k=1}^{n} i_{sk} \quad (2.4.2)$$

In the above expression, the source current i_{Sk} with the same reference direction to i_S is positive, otherwise, negative.

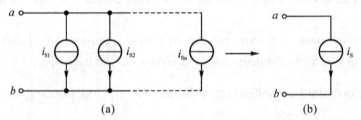

(a)   (b)

Fig.2.4.2 Simplification of Independent Voltage Sources in Parallel

Besides, it should be noted that, in terms of a circuit model, two voltage sources with exactly the same voltage cannot be connected in parallel, and two current sources with exactly the same current cannot be connected in series, otherwise it will violate the KCL, KVL and definitions of independent sources.

2.4.2 The Concept of Redundant Components

Since the equivalent circuit is in terms of external circuits, if a current source is connected in series with one or more voltage sources, it can be equivalently reduced to one current source, as shown in Fig.2.4.3a, where the voltage source is considered as redundant component and can be reduced. If a voltage source is in parallel with one current sources, it can be equivalently reduced to one voltage source, as shown in Fig.2.4.3b, that is, the current source is considered as redundant component and can be removed.

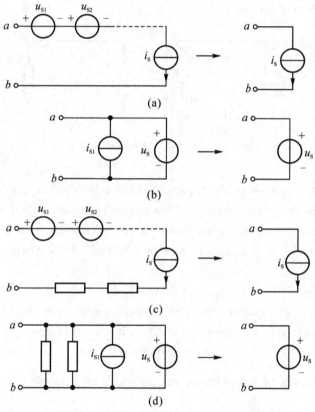

Fig.2.4.3 Redundant Component Reduction

Similarly, if a current source is connected in series with one or more voltage sources and resistors, it is equivalent to a current source, as shown in Fig.2.4.3c. In this case, the voltage sources and the resistors are considered as redundant components and can be reduced. If a voltage source is connected in parallel with multiple current sources and multiple resistors, it can also be equivalently reduced to a voltage source, as shown in Fig.2.4.3d. In this case, all the current source and the resistors are considered as redundant components and can be reduced.

It should be note that, equivalent is valid only for external circuit, the internal circuit is not equivalent. So if it is required to find voltages and currents of internal circuit, you should return back to the original circuit to find them.

Example 2.4.1 For the circuit shown in Fig.2.4.4a, find the voltage on the resistor and current source.

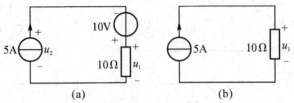

Fig.2.4.4 The Circuit for Example 2.4.13

Solution Let's assign the required voltage to be u_1 and u_2, as shown in Fig. 2.4.4a. Due to the current source and the voltage source are in series, so in terms of the resistance, only the current source should be considered, the voltage source is redundant and can be removed, as shown in Fig.2.4.4b. Therefore, u_1 can be derived as

$$u_1 = 5 \times 10 = 50 \text{V}$$

To find u_2, you cannot remove the voltage source, you should return to the original circuit to find u_2. According to KVL, it is derived that

$$u_2 = -10 + 50 = 40 \text{V}$$

2.4.3 Two Models of Actual Power Supply and Their Equivalent Transformation

In the circuit analysis, sometimes it is more convenient to apply the voltage source, and sometimes it is more convenient to apply the current source. So, it is required that the voltage source and the current source can be equivalently interchanged. But it is impossible to interchange a single voltage source and a single current source.

However, if the voltage source is connected in series with a resistor R_0, and the current source is connected in parallel with a resistor R_0, it can be proved

2.4 Equivalent Simplification of Active One-Port Networks

these two kind of sources can be transformed each other, as shown in Fig.2.4.5. Both two kind of sources are the model of actual power supply with internal resistance. They are also known as the accompanied source.

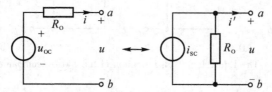

Fig.2.4.5 The Transformation of the Source with Companion

In the following, the equivalent conditions of the two sources will be discussed. To make the two sources to be equivalent, their external characteristics must be equal, that is, if the same voltage u is applied across the terminals a, b of two circuits at the same time, then the current flowing through the two circuits must also be same, namely $i = i'$. According to this condition, for voltage source circuit, there are

$$i = \frac{u_s - u}{R_0} = \frac{u_s}{R_0} - \frac{u}{R_0}$$

And for current source circuit, there are

$$i' = i_s - \frac{u}{R_0}$$

Let above two expression be equal, it is derived that: $i_s = \frac{u_s}{R_0}$, this is the equivalent conditions of the two sources, namely: $i_s = \frac{u_s}{R_0}$ or $u_s = i_s R_0$.

Note that in the process of equivalent transformation, the reference directions of the voltage source and the current source should be set as shown in the Fig., that is, the direction of the current source current flows out of the positive terminal of the corresponding voltage source.

The equivalent transformation of the two accompanied sources is shown in Fig.2.4.6. Fig.2.4.6a shows that the voltage source with companion can be transformed into a accompanied current source, and Fig.2.4.6b shows that the accompanied current source can be transformed into a accompanied voltage source.

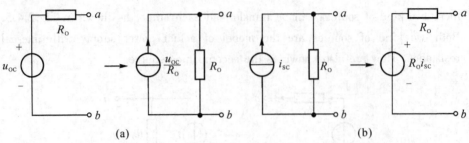

(a)   (b)

Fig.2.4.6 The Equivalent Transformation of the Two Accompanied Sources

In general, for two accompanied sources, their internal powers are not the same. In the accompanied voltage source as shown in Fig.2.4.7a, when port of a and b is open circuit, the current flowing through u_s is zero, the voltage source does not generate power, and the resistance does not absorb power. However, in the current source accompanied as shown in Fig.2.4.7b, if the port is open circuit, the power absorbed by the resistor is same as the power produced by the current source. It can be found that $P = Ri_s^2$, it is not zero. So, it can be seen that the internal powers for the two kind of accompanied sources are different.

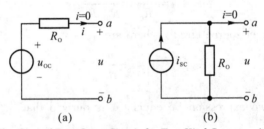

(a)   (b)

Fig.2.4.7 The Case of Port Open Circuit for Two Kind Sources with Companion

Example 2.4.2 Find equivalent circuit of single-port network in Fig.2.4.8a by applying equivalent transformation of two accompanied sources.

Solution By applying equivalent transformation method, the circuit can be reduced gradually into the simplest form, the steps are as follows:

(1) 2 voltage source in series with resistances are transformed into current source in parallel with resistance, as shown in Fig.2.4.8b;

(2) the two parallel current sources are equivalently reduced to a current source, the two parallel resistances are equivalently reduced to a resistance, as

shown in Fig.2.4.8c;

(3) the 4A current source in parallel with 2 Ohms resistance is transformed into 8V voltage source in series with 2 Ohms resistance, as shown in Fig.2.4.8d;

(4) two voltage sources in series are reduced to a 12V voltage source, two resistances in series are reduced to 3 Ohms resistance, as shown in Fig.2.4.8e, which is the simplest form of the equivalent circuit.

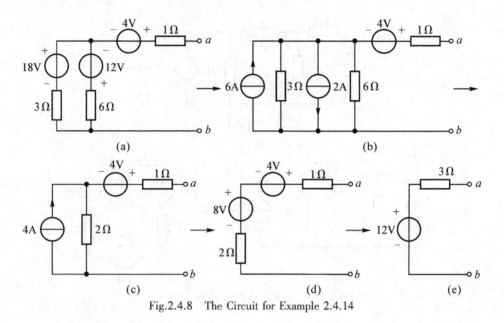

Fig.2.4.8 The Circuit for Example 2.4.14

Example 2.4.3 Find the current i of circuit in Fig.2.4.9a.

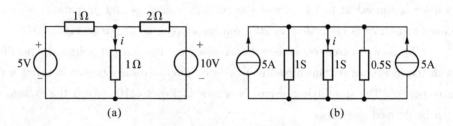

Fig.2.4.9 The Circuit for Example 2.4.15

Solution   First, the voltage source in series with the resistance is transformed equivalently into the current source in parallel with conductance, the circuit shown in Fig.2.4.9b is derived. By applying current division formula, the current i is derived as

$$i = \frac{1S}{(1+1+0.5)S}(5A+5A) = 4A$$

Example 2.4.4 Find the voltage u in the circuit shown in Fig.2.4.10a.

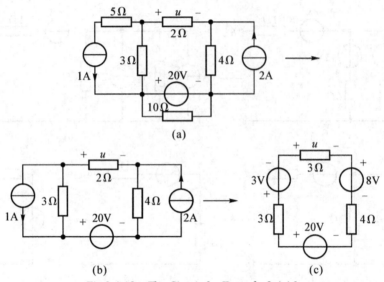

Fig.2.4.10 The Circuit for Example 2.4.16

Solution The analysis steps are as follows:

(1) remove redundant components: 1A current source in series with 5 Ohms resistor is equivalent to 1A current source. 20V voltage source in parallel with 10 Ohms resistance is equivalent to 20V voltage source, as shown in Fig.2.4.10b.

(2) apply source equivalent transformation: the current source in parallel with the resistance is transformed equivalently into the voltage source in series with a resistance. The simplifying circuit is shown in Fig.2.4.10c. Thus the voltage u can be derived as follows

$$u = \frac{(-3+20-8)V}{(2+3+4)\Omega} \times 2\Omega = 2V$$

2.4.4 Equivalent Simplification by Applying Source Shift Method

2.4.4.1 Transfer Method of Independent Voltage Source Without Companion

For an independent voltage source u_S in the circuit, if there is not any resistance connected in parallel with it, it is called an independent voltage source without companion. As shown in Fig. 2.4.11a, a separate voltage source u_S is located between nodes j and k, it is an independent voltage source without companion. It can be proved that, an independent voltage source u_S without companion can be transferred to all branches connected with node j and connected in series with each branches, as shown in Fig.2.4.11b. Similarly, voltage source u_S can also be transferred to all connected to node k and connected in series with each branches, as shown in Fig. 2.4.11c. The original independent voltage source between nodes j and k is replaced by short circuit. All the independent voltage sources after shift have the same polarity as the original independent voltage source.

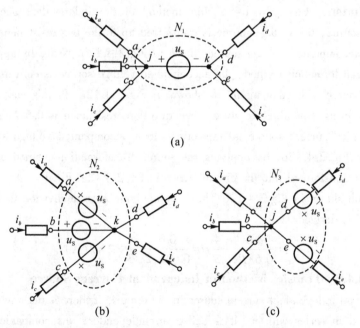

Fig.2.4.11 Transfer Method of Independent Voltage Source Without Companion

Example 2.4.5 For a T-type circuit shown in Fig.2.4.12a, it is given: $U = 2\text{V}$, $R = 0.2\Omega$, find: current i.

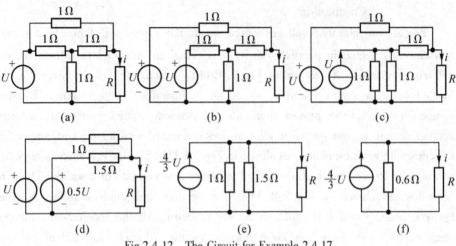

Fig.2.4.12 The Circuit for Example 2.4.17

Solution First, by using shift method of the independent accompanied voltage source, the voltage source is transferred up to the two resistances in series to form accompanied voltage source shown in Fig.2.4.12b. Next, by applying the source transformation method, the accompanied voltage source is converted with a current source with companion, as shown in Fig.2.4.12c. In this case, two 1Ω resistors forms a parallel structure, the equivalent resistance is 0.5Ω. Then, the accompanied current source is transformed to a accompanied voltage source, as shown in Fig.2.4.12d. By applying the source transformation method again, the circuit is transformed into the circuit shown in Fig.2.4.12e. Finally, it is reduce to the circuit shown in Fig.2.4.12f. Thus, by applying current division formula, the current i is derived as

$$i = \frac{0.6}{0.6+R} \cdot \frac{4}{3}U = \frac{0.6}{0.6+0.2} \times \frac{4}{3} \times 2 = 2(\text{A})$$

2.4.4.2 Transfer Method of Independent Current Source

For an independent current source in the circuit, if there is not any resistance connected in series with it, it is called an independent unaccompanied current source. As shown in Fig. 2.4.13a, the current source i_S is an independent unaccompanied current source. It can be proved that, an independent unaccompanied current source can be shifted to connected in parallel with every resistors along the any paths between node j and k, as shown in Fig. 2.4.13b, c. The original independent current source and all resistances along the path form a closed loop. If the direction of the original independent current source is in the clockwise (counter-clockwise), then the direction of the independent current source after shift should be in the counter-clockwise (clockwise) the direction of the loop.

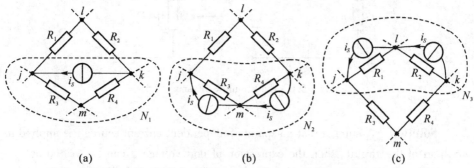

(a)   (b)   (c)

Fig.2.4.13 Transfer Method of Independent Current Source Without Companion

2.5 Equivalent Simplification of Controlled Source Circuit

In this section, the equivalent simplification of a single-port network with controlled sources will be discussed.

2.5.1 Equivalent Simplification of One-Port Networks with Controlled Sources

2.5.1.1 Simplification of single-port networks consisting of resistors and controlled sources

It has been pointed out in the first section of this chapter, a single-port network consisting of several linear two-terminal resistors can be equivalent to a linear two-terminal resistor in terms of port characteristics.

In terms of port characteristics, it can be proved that a single-port network consisting of linear two-terminal resistors and linear controlled sources can also be equivalent to a linear two-terminal resistor. By applying a separate independent source to the port of the circuit and then calculating via the single-port VCR equation, the equivalent resistance can be derive. Here is an example.

Example 2.5.1 Find the equivalent resistance of the single-port network shown in Fig.2.5.1a.

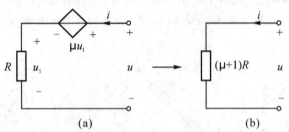

(a)   (b)

Fig.2.5.1 The Circuit for Example 2.5.1

Solution Assuming that a separate independent current source i is applied to the port of the circuit, then the expression of port voltage u can be written as

$$u = \mu u_1 + u_1 = (\mu+1) u_1 = (\mu+1) Ri = R_o i$$

So, the equivalent resistance of the single-port network can be derived as

$$R_o = \frac{u}{i} = (\mu+1) R$$

The equivalent circuit is shown in Fig.2.5.1b. Due to the presence of a controlled voltage source, the port voltage is increased to $\mu u_1 = \mu Ri$, it results in an increase $(\mu+1)$ times in the equivalent resistance of the port. If the control factor $\mu = -2$, the equivalent resistance of single port $R_o = -R$, which indicates that this circuit is capable of converting a positive resistance to a negative resistance.

Example 2.5.2 Find the input resistance of the port a, b in circuit shown in Fig.2.5.2a and draw its equivalent circuit.

Solution First, a voltage source u is applied to the port a, b, as shown in Fig.2.5.2b. Next, the circuit is reduced to the circuit shown in Fig.2.5.2c. Then, it can be derived that

$$u = (i-2.5) \times 1 = -1.5i$$

Thus, the input resistance of the port is

$$R_{in} = \frac{u}{i} = -1.5 \Omega$$

2.5 Equivalent Simplification of Controlled Source Circuit

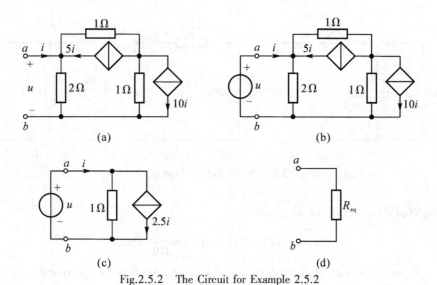

Fig.2.5.2   The Circuit for Example 2.5.2

From this example, It can be seen that the input resistance of the resistive circuit with controlled sources may be negative. Its equivalent circuit is shown in Fig.2.5.2d with an equivalent resistance value of $R_{eq} = R_{in} = -1.5\Omega$.

In general, in term of port characteristics, a one-port network consisting of linear controlled sources, linear resistors, and independent sources can be equivalent to an independent voltage source in series with a linear resistor, or an independent current source in parallel with a linear resistor.

Similarly, the equivalent circuit of the single-port network with resistors, independent sources and linear controlled sources can be derived from the VCR equation of the port by applying an external independent source.

Example 2.5.3   Find the equivalent circuit for the single-port network shown in Fig.2.5.3a.

Solution   By applying a external source, VCR equation of the port is derived as
$$u = 4u_1 + u_1 = 5u_1$$
where
$$u_1 = (2\Omega)(i+2A)$$
So
$$u = (10\Omega)i + 20V$$

Chapter 2 Equivalent Resistive Circuits

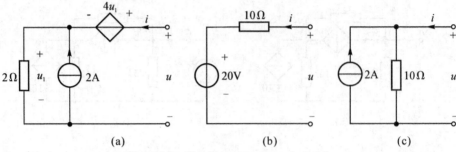

(a)   (b)   (c)

Fig.2.5.3 The Circuit for Example 2.5.3

The VCR equation of the port will be

$$u = (10\Omega)i + 20V \quad \text{or} \quad i = \frac{1}{10\Omega}u - 2A$$

From above two VCR expressions, it can be seen that its equivalent circuit is a 20V voltage source in series with a 10 Ohms resistor, as shown in Fig.2.5.3b, or a 2A current source in parallel with a 10 Ohms resistor, as shown in Fig.2.5.3c.

2.5.2 Equivalent Transformation of Two Kinds of Sources for One-Port Network with Controlled Sources

An independent voltage source in series with a resistor can be equivalently transformed into an independent current source in parallel with a resistor or vice versa. Similarly, a controlled voltage source (only its controlled branch, the same for the following) in series with a resistor can also be transformed into a controlled current source in parallel with a resistor, as shown in Fig.2.5.4.

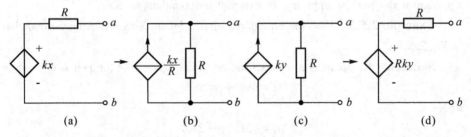

(a)   (b)   (c)   (d)

Fig.2.5.4 Equivalent Transformation of Two Kinds of Sources of Single-Port Network with Controlled Sources

Example 2.5.4 In the circuit as shown in Fig.2.5.5a, it is given: $r = 3\Omega$. Find the equivalent resistance of the single-port circuit.

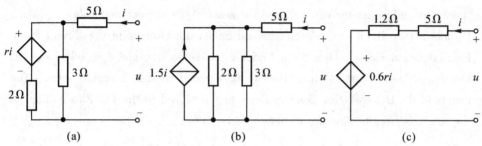

Fig.2.5.5 The Circuit for Example 2.5.4

Solution First, the controlled voltage source in series with 2Ω resistor is equivalently transformed into a controlled current source $0.5ri = 1.5i$ in parallel with 2Ω resistance, as shown in Fig.2.5.5b. Next, 2Ω resistance in parallel with 3Ω resistance is equivalently reduced to a 1.2Ω resistance. And then $1.5i$ control current source in parallel with 1.2Ω resistor is equivalently transformed into a controlled voltage source $0.6ri = 1.8i$ in series with 1.2Ω resistor, as shown in Fig.2.5.5c. Thus, with KVL, there is

$$u = (5\Omega + 1.2\Omega + 0.6r)i = (8\Omega)i$$

So, the equivalent resistance of the single-port circuit is

$$R_o = \frac{u}{i} = 8\Omega$$

2.6 Example of Computer-Aided Analys of Circuits

This section describes the application of EWB software and Matlab software to analyze simple DC circuits.

2.6.1 Analysis of Simple DC Circuits with EWB Software

For the circuit containing the current control voltage source shown in Fig.2.6.1, when the circuit is established, the controlled source element is connected to the corresponding position and the control element of the controlled source element is connected to the corresponding control branch, i.e., the current control element should be connected in series into the control branch, and the voltage control element should be connected in parallel with the control voltage. Ammeters and voltmeter can be used to measure the current and voltage of each branch in the circuit, or select command Schematic Options in the Circuit menu from command menu, select Show Nodes (display node), and then select the DC Operating Point command from the Analysis menu in the command menu. The results of the DC operating point analysis are displayed in the DC Bias column of the Analysis Graphs window, as shown in Fig.2.6.2.

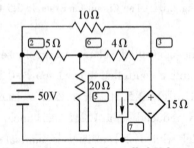

Fig.2.6.1 A Circuit with Controlled Voltage Source

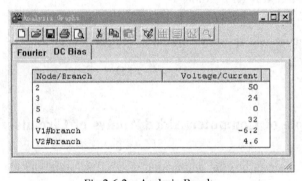

Fig.2.6.2 Analysis Results

2.6.2 Using Matlab Software to Analyze Simple DC Circuits

Here, Matlab / PSB tools is introduced to apply in analyzing the DC bridge circuit shown in Fig.2.6.3. The current i is required to find.

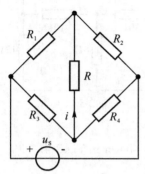
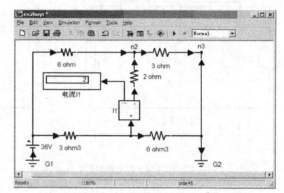

Fig.2.6.3   A Simple DC Circuit   Fig.2.6.4   Simulink Model

Simulink model designed by Matlab/PSB tool is shown in Fig.2.6.4. Assume that $R_1 = 6\Omega$, $R_2 = 3\Omega$, $R_3 = 3\Omega$, $R_4 = 6\Omega$, $R = 2\Omega$, $U_S = 36V$, the simulation results is shown in Fig.2.6.4, so the current i is 2A.

Problems

2-1   Find the input resistance R_{ab} of the single-port circuit as shown in Fig.2-1.

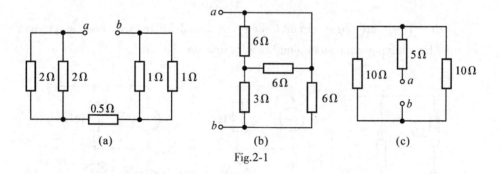

Fig.2-1

2-2   For the circuit shown in Fig.2-2, given: $R_1 = 5\Omega$, $R_3 = 15\Omega$, $R_4 = 10\Omega$, voltage for R_4 is $u = 18V$. Find the value of resistance R_2.

2-3   Find equivalent resistance R_{ab} of the circuit shown in Fig.2-3.

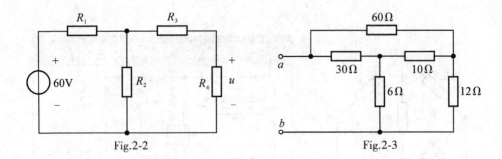

Fig.2-2   Fig.2-3

2-4 Find equivalent resistance R_{ab} of two circuits shown in Fig.2-4.

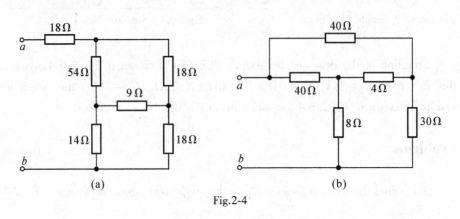

Fig.2-4

2-5 There are three circuits shown in Fig.2-5, reduce these single-port circuits by applying equivalent simplification transformation.

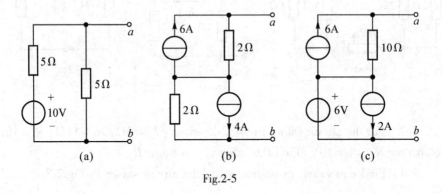

Fig.2-5

2-6 Reduce the single-port circuits as shown in Fig.2-6.

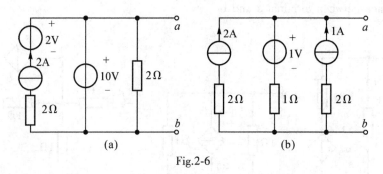

Fig.2-6

2-7 Reduce the single-port circuit as shown in Fig.2-7 by applying equivalent simplification transformation.

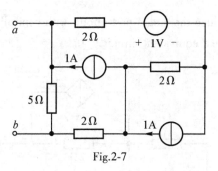

Fig.2-7

2-8 Find current i of the circuits shown in Fig.2-8 by applying equivalent simplification transformation.

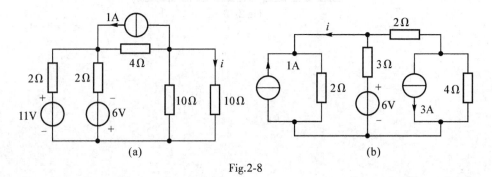

Fig.2-8

2-9 For the circuits with controlled sources shown in Fig. 2-9, find the resistance between terminal a and b.

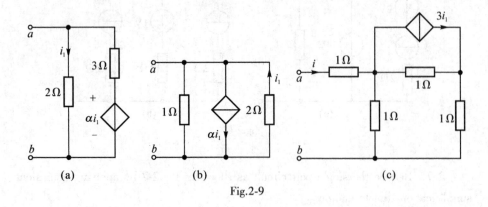

Fig.2-9

2-10 Try to reduce the single-port circuit with controlled source as shown in Fig.2-10 to the simplest equivalent circuit.

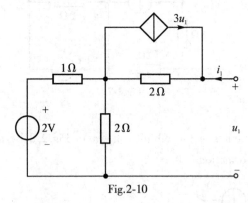

Fig.2-10

Chapter 3
Systematic Analysis of Circuits

The circuit consisting of resistive elements and independent sources is called a resistive circuit. In the resistive circuit, the independent sources play the role of input or excitation. And the voltages and currents in the every place of the circuit are generated by independent sources, they can be called the outputs or responses of the circuit. If all the independent sources in the circuit are DC sources, this type of circuit is often referred to as the DC circuit. A circuit composed of linear resistor elements and independent sources is called a linear resistive circuit and there is a linear relationship between its response and the excitation. With this linear relationship, the analysis and calculation of the circuit can be greatly simplified.

In this chapter, by choosing DC resistive circuit as the example, several systematic and universal analysis methods of linear resistive circuits are introduced. The so-called systematic means that the analysis steps are regular, easy to program, universal refers to the wide range of adaptations, it is applicable for any linear circuits.

In previous chapter, the equivalent transformation method is discussed, it is required to simplify the circuit and to change the circuit structure in the process of solving problems. Different from that, when systematic analysis methods are applied, it is not required to simplify the circuit, just in accordance with a fixed steps, the circuit can be analyzed step by step. Of course, maybe only some of the voltages and currents derived are what we need. Compared with the equivalent transformation method, these systematic methods are sometimes more cumbersome and not flexible, but they are particularly suitable for computer programming, their application are more extensive. In fact, almost all computer-aided circuit analysis software such as PSPICE, EWB generally apply systematic approaches to analyze the circuits.

The basic steps of the systematic analysis of the circuit are as follows:

1) Select the circuit variables (branch voltages, branch currents, node voltages or loop current);

2) Apply KCL, KVL and VCR to establish a group of equations with selected variables;

3) Solve the equations to find the solutions, and then find required circuit variables.

For the linear resistive circuits, the system equations derived with the systematic analysis method is a set of linear algebraic equations.

In this chapter, Some basic knowledge of electrical network graph theory will be introduced first, including the concept of connected graph, loop, mesh, tree and cut set. Then, some system analysis methods of linear DC resistive circuits are introduced, including 2b method, branch analysis method, mesh analysis method, loop analysis method, node analysis method and modified node analysis method. These methods are important methods of circuit analysis and should be mastered proficiently. Noted that, the systematic analysis method described in this chapter is not limited to apply in linear DC resistive circuit, it can also be applied to the AC circuit discussed in the subsequent chapters of the textbook.

3.1 The Basic Concept of Graph Theory

The concept of electrical network graph involves the knowledge of graph theory. Graph theory is also known as topology, it is a science studying the relationship between the line and point. Here only graph theory application in the electrical network is discussed and it is known as the graph theory of electrical network. Network graph theory is also called network topology. In order to systematically list the equations of a complex network for the computer analysis, it is necessary to apply the knowledge of network graph theory and linear algebra. With the development of computer, network graph theory has become a very important basic knowledge in computer aided analysis, it is also an indispensable tool for network analysis and synthesis.

In this section, only some relevant concepts of the network graph related to electrical network are introduced. It provides a theoretical basis for following circuit systematic analysis methods. To further understand the graph theory and computer-aided analysis, readers can refer to the relevant monographs.

3.1.1 Topology of the Circuit

From the previous chapter, it can be seen that Kirchhoff's law is the basic law of the lumped circuit, which stipulates the constraint relations between the currents and between the voltages in each part of circuit. The KCL and KVL equations of the circuit only depend on the geometrical structure of the circuit and independent of the characteristics of the components. Therefore, graph theory can be applied to study them. In writing KCL, KVL equations of the circuit, it can be omitted that what kind of element in the branch it is. So, the element in the branch can be abstracted into the line with direction, voltage and current. And the circuit can be abstracted into geometric graph consisting of lines with direction and nodes (points). It is called topological graph or line graph. Therefore, structural constraints are called topological constraints. By aiding of the topology graph, listing methods and its independence of KCL and KVL equations can be discussed.

3.1.1.1 Topological Branch, Topological Node and Topology Graph

In graph theory, each component (active or passive component) in the circuit can be replaced by a line segment (regardless of long or short, straight or twist), then each line is called a topology branch, referred to as a branch or edge. The terminal of each branch is called the topological node, or referred to as the node (vertex). The line graph of the network is consist of a set of the branches and nodes, for short, Graph, represented as G. For example, for the circuit shown in Fig.3.1.1a, its topological graph is shown in Fig.3.1.1b. There are four nodes and six branches in the graph. Noted that each branch must be connected and just connected to the two nodes, but it is not required that there is a branch existing between any two nodes. The topological graph of the network reflects the interconnection law of circuit elements, and is independent of the property of circuit elements.

It should be pointed out that, according to the demand to establish a complete theoretical system, the definition of the branch in the network graph theory is flexible. It may not be a single element. For example, the combination of the voltage source and the resistor in series, the combination of current source and resistor in parallel can be defined as a branch. Also, several resistors in series can

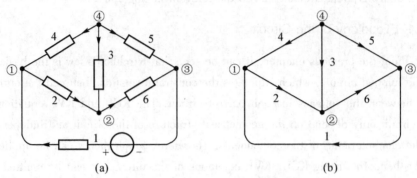

Fig.3.1.1 The Topological Graph of the Network

also be defined as a branch. However, several resistor in parallel is generally not regarded as a branch.

3.1.1.2 Connected and Disconnected Graph

Starting from a node in the graph, by moving continuously along some branches to reach another designated node (which can also be the original node), the passing branches form a path of the graph G. A path may be a branch. If there is at least one path between any two nodes in graph G, the graph G is called a connected graph, as shown in Fig.3.1.1. Otherwise it is called a non-connected graph or a disjoint graph. As shown in Fig.3.1.2a, it is a mutual inductance circuit, its topological graph is shown in Fig.3.1.2b, the left half of the figure is not connected with the right half, so it is a disconnected graph. In this chapter, we mainly study the connected graphs.

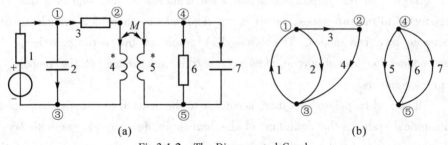

Fig.3.1.2 The Disconnected Graph

3.1.1.3 Subgraph and Generated Subgraph

If all the nodes and branches in graph G_1 are part of the nodes and branches in graph G, then G_1 is called the subgraph of graph G. If the subgraph contains all nodes of graph G, it is called generated subgraph of graph G. For example, for the graph G shown in Fig.3.1.3a, all graphs in Fig.3.1.3b, c, d, e are its subgraph, the graphs shown in Fig.3.1.3c, d, e are its generated subgraph, Fig.3.1.3b, c are its connected subgraphs, and Fig.3.1.3d, e are its disconnected subgraph.

The tree, cut set, and loop that are to be described later in this section are all subgraphs of a graph, where the tree is a generated subgraph. An isolated node (the node not connected to any branch) is also a subgraph, and nodes 2, 3 in Fig.3.1.3e are isolated nodes.

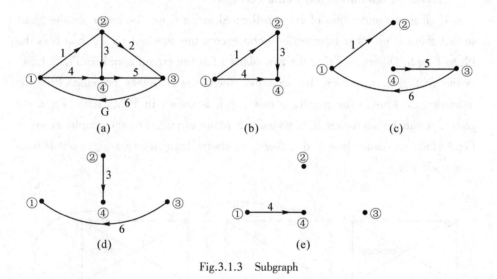

Fig.3.1.3 Subgraph

3.1.1.4 Directed and Disdirected Graphs

The graph which its each branch has been assigned a reference direction is called directed graph, otherwise it is called disconnected graph. As shown in Fig. 3.1.1-3.1.3, all graphs are directed graph. And the graph shown in Fig.3.1.4b is non-directed graph of the circuit shown in Fig3.1.4a.

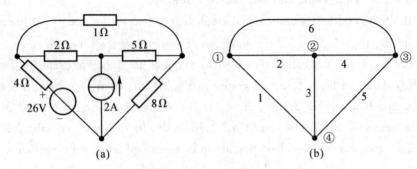

Fig.3.1.4   Non-Directed Graph

3.1.1.5 Plane and Non-Planar Graph

If all nodes and edges of an non-directed graph G can be drawn on the plane so that there is no other intersection point except the common node, then G is the Plane Graph. Otherwise, G is the non-planar. For the circuit shown in Fig.3.1.5a, in the first glance, it may be seen that there are branches crossing. But, by redrawing the line in the graph, a new graph is shown in Fig.3.1.5b. From the graph, it can be seen that it is actually a plane circuit. For the graph shown in Fig.3.1.5c, no matter how to do, there are always branches crossing, so it is non-planar circuit.

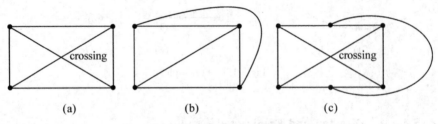

Fig.3.1.5   Plane and Non-Planar Graph

Fig.3.1.6a, c shows convex polyhedrons, if any of these faces is expanded, the other side can be wrapped in the inside and spread into a plane, as shown in Fig.3.1.6 b, d, so they are plane graphs.

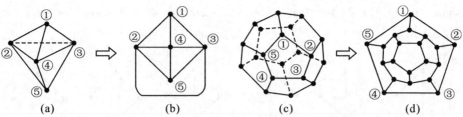

(a)   (b)   (c)   (d)

Fig.3.1.6   Convex Polyhedrons and Plane Graph

3.1.2   Tree, Tree Branch and Link

In the connected graph, a set of the least branches with which all the nodes are connected is called the tree of the connected graph, denoted by the letter T. In another word, the tree of the connected graph is a connected subgraph containing all the nodes without forming a loop. It can see that the tree has four characteristics: ① tree is a subgraph of connected graph G; ② tree contains all nodes of connected graph G; ③ in the tree, starting from any node, it is possible to reach any other node by passing through the tree branches, that is, the tree is connected; ④ tree does not contain any loop. For example, for the graph in Fig.3.1.7a, the graph in Fig.3.1.7b and Fig.3.1.7c are one of their trees. But, the graph in Fig.3.1.7d is not a tree, because there is a loop in the graph.

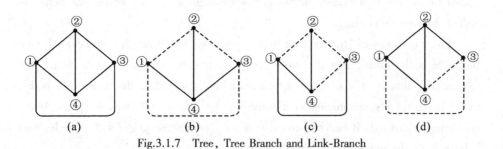

(a)   (b)   (c)   (d)

Fig.3.1.7   Tree, Tree Branch and Link-Branch

There are many different trees in the same graph. How many trees does a line graph has? It can be proved that, for a network with n nodes, if there is only one branch connected between each pair of nodes, then its graph is called the all connected graph, there are a total of n^{n-2} kinds of trees. For example, the graph shown in Fig.3.1.7a has four nodes, so there are $4^2 = 16$ trees, as shown in Fig.3.1.8.

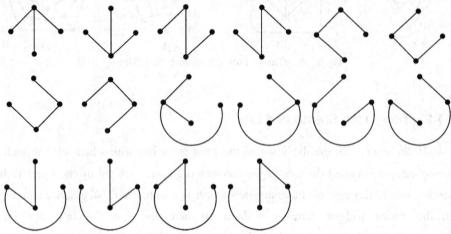

Fig.3.1.8 16 Trees of the Graph

When a tree is selected, the branches in the topology graph are divided into two categories: one is the branch of the tree, which is called the tree branch; the other is the branch that does not belong to the tree, which is called link-branch. The solid line in Fig.3.1.7b, c represents the corresponding tree branch, and the dotted line is the link-branch of the corresponding tree. A set of link-branches is called the tree remaining.

From the above 16 kinds of trees, we can see that the number of tree branches is the same, that is, there are three tree branches. The line graph has four nodes, that is, the number of tree branches is less than the number of nodes by 1. In fact, this conclusion is a universal law, it is determined by the tree's construction method. It can be proved that for a connected graph with n nodes and b branches, the number of tree branches is

$b_t = n - 1 =$ the number of independent nodes

The number of link-branches is

$$b_l = b - bt = b - n + 1$$

Above two expression can be simply proved as follows:

First, by removing all branches of graph G, then only its n nodes are left. In order to form a tree of graph G, connect any two nodes in these n nodes with a branch, and then every time by connecting with an additional branch, a new node is connected to the former graph and the number of tree branches increases by 1. In this way, in accordance with the definition of the tree, when all n nodes are connected together, it is just required $n-1$ branches to form a tree (the first branch is connected with two nodes), that is, the number of tree branches is equal to $n-1$, thereby, the number of link-branches is $b-n+1$.

3.1.3 Loop, Mesh and Fundamental Loop

3.1.3.1 Loop

Starting from a node in the figure, by passing through several branches and nodes (just passing by once) and returning to the starting node, a closed path is formed, it is called a loop. In another word, a loop is a closed path consisting of a set of branches. The loop in graph G has four characteristics:

① The loop is a subgraph of graph G;

② The loop is a connected graph;

③ There must be and can only be two branches connected to each node in the loop, in another word, the number of branches connected to the node in loop must be 2;

④ If any of the branches in the loop is removed, the rest of the branch can no longer constitute a closed path.

For example, in Fig.3.1.9a, the closed paths consisted by the branch sets (1,2,3,6), (1,2,4,5,10,12,11,8), (1,2,4,5,7, 6) respectively are all loops. However, the closed paths consisted by branch set (1,2,3,9,12,10,7,6) is not a loop, as shown in Fig.3.1.9b, because the number of branches connected with the node ⑤ is 4, greater than 2.

3.1.3.2 Mesh

The loop that does not contain an internal branch is called a mesh. As shown in Fig.3.1.9a, branch sets (1,2,3,6), (3,4,5,7), (7,9,10, 12), (6,8,9, 11) constitute the closed path respectively, so they are all meshes. Obviously the number of loops is generally more than the number of meshes, For example, for the connected graph shown in Fig.3.1.9a, the number of meshes is only 4, and the number of loops is up to 13. It is usually not an easy task to find all the loops.

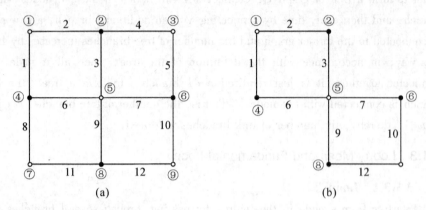

Fig.3.1.9 Loop and Mesh

3.1.3.3 The Fundamental Loop

It is already known that a tree of connected graphs does not contain any loops, and all nodes are connected by tree branches. Therefore, for any tree, by adding an additional branch, a loop with only one link will be formed, and the other branches of the loop are tree branches. For example, as shown in Fig.3.1.10a, the branch 1, 2, 3 is selected as a tree, as shown by the solid line in Fig.3.1.10a. If the link-branch 4 is added to the tree, (Fig.3.1.10a), a loop l_1 with single link-branch is constituted. If the link 5 is added to the tree, a loop l_2 with a single link-branch is constituted (Fig.3.1.10b). If the link-branch 6 is added to the tree, a loop l_3 with a single link-branch is constituted (Fig.3.1.10c). The loop with only one link is called a single link-branch loop or the basic loop. It can be seen from the graph theory that the single link-branch loop is unique and a group of single link-branch loops is a set of independent loops. Because each loop contains a link-branch that is not included by other loops, the number of single link-branch loops is equal to the number of link-branch in the graph.

It can be proved that the KVL equations written according to the fundamental loops are a set of independent equations. The number of independent equations is equal to the number of link-branch ($b-n+1$).

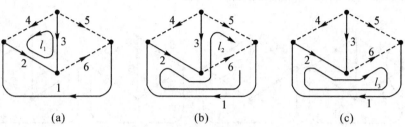

Fig.3.1.10 Single Link-Branch Loops(Basic Loop)

3.1.4 Cut Set and Fundamental Cut Set

3.1.4.1 Cut Set

The cut set of connected graphs is a set of branches and nodes, and it satisfies following conditions:

(1) If all the branches contained in the cut set are removed (all nodes are reserved), the remaining graph becomes two connected sub-graphs (the subgraph can also be an isolated node) that are separate from each other.

(2) If any of the branches in the set is left, the remaining graphs are still connected.

Condition (2) indicates that the cut set is the smallest branch set that satisfies condition (1).

It should be noted that the main points in the cut definition are:

① The graph is not connected if all the branches in the cut set are removed;

② The unconnected graph has two separate parts (rather than multiple);

③ Cut set is a minimum branch set to cut a graph into two parts (If any branch in the cut set is not removed, the graph is still connected).

For the connected graph as shown in Fig.3.1.11a, b, branch set (1,2,4), (1,3,4,6) form cut sets. However, branch set (2,3,5) is not a cut set, as shown in Fig.3.1.11c. The reason is that, if all branches in cut set are moved, the originals connected graph is not becoming two separate parts. Also, branch set (3, 4,5,6) is not a cut set, as shown in Fig.3.1.11d. It is because that, by leaving the branch 6, the remaining graph is still non-connected graph.

There are many different cut sets in a graph. The concept of the tree can be applied to find all of its independent cut sets.

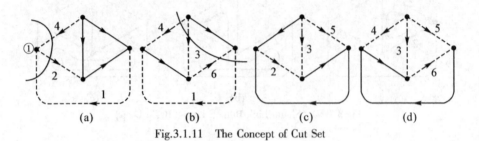

Fig.3.1.11 The Concept of Cut Set

3.1.4.2 Basic Cut Set

The cut set that only contains one tree branch, and the rest are the link-branch is called the basic cut set, also known as single tree cut set. Once the tree is selected, the basic cut sets can be uniquely determined.

As shown in Fig.3.1.1b, branch set (1, 2, 3) is selected as a tree. Then C_1 (1,5,6), C_2(2,4,5,6), C_3(3,4,5) are single tree branch cut set, as shown in Fig.3.1.12. If branch set (3,4,5) is selected as a tree, then C_1(2,3,6), C_2(1,2,4), C_3(1,5,6) forms single tree branch cut set. It is clear that if the tree selection is different, the single tree branch cut set is also different. It can be proved that the number of basic cut set is equal to the number of tree branches $(n-1)$.

The Kirchhoff current law can be applied to cut sets, i.e., algebraic sum of cut set currents equal zero. It can be proved that the KCL equations written in the basic cut set are a set of independent equations. The number of KCL independent equations is equal to the number of tree branches $(n-1)$.

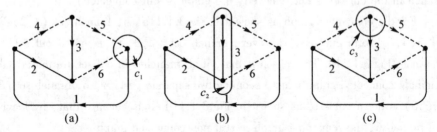

Fig.3.1.12 The Basic Cut Set

3.2 2b Method and Branch Analysis Method

In this section, the 2b method and the branch analysis methods will be discussed. The branch analysis methods includes the branch current method and the branch voltage method. They are the most basic circuit analysis methods. It is relatively simple to list their equations.

3.2.1 Two Types of Constraints and Circuit Equations

The lumped parameter circuit is constituted by interconnecting circuit elements. The currents of all branches in the circuit will be constrained by KCL. The voltages of all branches will also be constrained by KVL. These two constraints are related only to the interconnection of circuit elements, they are called topological constraints.

The voltages and currents of the lumping parameter circuit will also be constrained by the element characteristics (such as Ohm's law). This kind of constraint is only related to the VCR of the element, regardless of the element connection method, it is called element constraint.

Thus, the voltages and currents of any lumping parameter circuit must obey both types of constraints at the same time. The basic method of circuit analysis is to list enough independent KCL, KVL and VCR equations (known as the circuit equation) which reflect the two kinds of constraint relationships according to the structure and parameters of the circuit, and then solve the circuit equations to get the solution of each voltage and current.

3.2.2 2b Method

For a connected circuit with b branches and n nodes, the linear independent equations that can be listed are:
(1) $n-1$ KCL equations;
(2) $b-n+1$ KVL equations;
(3) b VCR equations.

Here, all branch circuits voltage and branch currents are selected as circuit variables. Since the number of all independent equations is $2b$, these equations is referred to as the $2b$ equations. These $2b$ equation are the most primitive circuit equations, which is the basic basis for analyzing the circuit. By solving the $2b$ equations, all branch voltages and currents of the circuit can be derived. So, the method that all branch voltages and branch currents are selected as variables and equations are listed by using KCL, KVL and VCR is called $2b$ method. Here's an example.

Example 3.2.1 A circuit is shown in Fig.3.2.1. It is a connected circuit with five branches and four nodes. Find the branch voltages and currents.

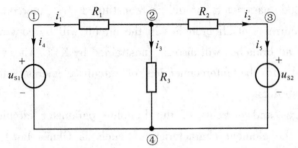

Fig.3.2.1 The Circuit for Illustrating 2b Method

Solution list all independent KCL equations for node ①,②,③ as follows

$$\begin{cases} i_1+i_4=0 \\ -i_1+i_2+i_3=0 \\ -i_2+i_5=0 \end{cases}$$

The voltage and current of each branch are assigned in the associated reference direction. And by passing along the two meshes in clockwise direction, the independent KVL equations of 2 meshes can be listed as

$$\begin{cases} u_1+u_3-u_4=0 \\ u_2+u_5-u_3=0 \end{cases}$$

VCR equations of b branches can be listed as:

$$\begin{cases} u_1=R_1i_1 \quad u_2=R_2i_2 \quad u_3=R_3i_3 \\ u_4=u_{S1} \quad u_5=u_{S2} \end{cases}$$

If it is given that $R_1=R_2=1\Omega$, $u_{S1}=5V$, $u_{S2}=10V$, by solving above 10 equations, all branch voltages and currents are derived as

$$\begin{cases} u_1 = 1\text{V} & i_1 = 1\text{A} \\ u_2 = -6\text{V} & i_2 = -3\text{A} \\ u_3 = 4\text{V} & i_3 = 4\text{A} \\ u_4 = 5\text{V} & i_4 = -1\text{A} \\ u_5 = 10\text{V} & i_5 = -3\text{A} \end{cases}$$

Example 3.2.2 For the circuit shown in Fig.3.2.2, it is given $i_1 = 3$A. Find all branches currents and the voltage u of current source.

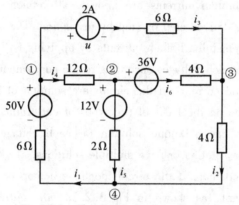

Fig.3.2.2 The Circuit for Example 3.2.2

Solution Note that the current $i_1 = 3$A and branch current $i_3 = 2$A of current source are known. By inspection, the current i_4 can be derived by applying KCL to the node ① as

$$i_4 = i_1 - i_3 = 3\text{A} - 2\text{A} = 1\text{A}$$

And the current i_5 can be derived by applying KVL and Ohm's Law as

$$i_5 = \frac{u_{R5}}{2\Omega} = \frac{-12\text{V} - 12\Omega \times 1\text{A} + 50\text{V} - 6\Omega \times 3\text{A}}{2\Omega} = 4\text{A}$$

By applying KCL to the node ② and ④, it is derived that

$$i_6 = i_4 - i_5 = 1\text{A} - 4\text{A} = -3\text{A}$$
$$i_2 = i_1 - i_5 = 3\text{A} - 4\text{A} = -1\text{A}$$

Finally, the voltage u of current source is derived by applying KVL as

$$u = 12\Omega \times 1\text{A} + 36\text{V} + 4\Omega \times (-3\text{A}) - 6\Omega \times 2\text{A} = 24\text{V}$$

It can be seen from this example that, if enough voltages or branch currents are known, the remaining branch voltages and branch currents can be derived via KCL and KVL and it is not necessary to solve $2b$ equations simultaneously.

In general, for a connected circuit with n nodes, if $n-1$ independent branch voltages are known, all branch voltages and branch currents can be derived step by step by inspection. The specific method is:

(1) Find all remaining branch voltages by applying KVL equations

(2) Find all branch currents according to the component characteristics

Again in general, for a connected circuit with n nodes and b branches, if $b-n+1$ independent branch currents are known, all branch voltages and branch currents can also be derived step by step by inspection. The specific method is:

(1) Find all remaining branch currents by applying KCL equations

(2) Find all branch voltages according to the component characteristics

The voltages and currents in the circuit are solution of the circuit equations which are established on the basis of two types of constraints. It should be noted that not all circuits has a unique solution for each voltage and current. Some circuits may have no solution or have multiple solutions.

It can be proved that, if the circuit contains a loop consisted only by pure voltage sources circuit, as shown in Fig. 3.2.3a, the current solution of these voltage sources will not be unique; if the circuit contains a node (or cut set) consisted only by pure current sources, as shown in Fig. 3.2.3b, the voltage solution of the current sources is not unique.

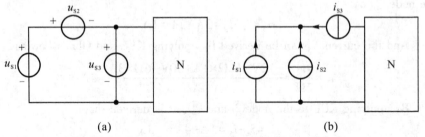

(a)   (b)

Fig.3.2.3　Example of the Circuit without Unique Solution

The disadvantage of the above $2b$ method is that the number of equations is too large and it is difficult to solve the simultaneous equations. How can the number of equations and variables be reduced? In the following, the branch analysis method will be introduced. For short, the branch analysis method is called the branch method. By applying the branch analysis method, only branch currents or branch voltages in the circuit are selected as equation variables. And the independent equations, which their the number is equal to the number of branch currents or branch voltages, are listed by applying KCL and KVL. Finally, all branch currents or branch voltages can be solved. There are two kind of branch analysis method. One is branch current method and another is branch voltage method.

3.2.3 Branch Current Analysis Method

If the circuit is composed of independent voltage sources and linear two-terminal resistors, by substituting the Ohm's law $u=Ri$ into the KVL equation, all resistor voltages can be eliminated and $b-n+1$ independent KVL equations with just branch currents as variables are derived. In addition of the $n-1$ independent KCL equations, total b linear independent equations with b branch currents as variables can be derived. These equations are also known as branch current equations. This method is called branch current analysis method, or for short, branch current method.

By applying this method, it is only required to solve b equations, and all the branch current can be derived. Then all the branch voltage can also be derived by using the VCR equations.

Now, let's take the circuit shown in Fig.3.2.4 as an example to illustrate how to establish the branch current equations.

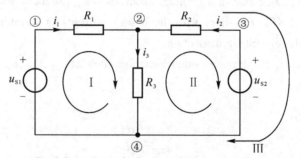

Fig.3.2.4   Example for Branch Current Method

There are three branches, two nodes, three loops in the circuit. First, branch current i_1, i_2, i_3 are selected as circuit variables, For node 2 and 4, by applying KCL, there are

$$-i_1-i_2+i_3=0 \qquad (3.2.1)$$
$$i_1+i_2-i_3=0 \qquad (3.2.2)$$

Obviously, for these two equations, only one equation is independent.

Next, the voltage and current of each branch are assigned in the associated reference direction. By selecting the loops I, II and III in the clockwise direction, as shown in Fig.3.2.4, the KVL equations of the three loops can be listed and VCR equations are applied into them. It is derived that

$$R_1i_1+R_3i_3-u_{s1}=0 \qquad (3.2.3)$$
$$-R_2i_2-R_3i_3+u_{s2}=0 \qquad (3.2.4)$$
$$R_1i_1-R_2i_2-u_{s1}+u_{s2}=0 \qquad (3.2.5)$$

By inspection, it is seen that only two of these three equations are independent.

In this way, according to KCL and KVL, a total of five equations can be listed, of which only three are independent. Since the number of circuit variables (i_1, i_2, i_3) is also three, the equations can be solved.

From equations (3.2.1), (3.2.3), (3.2.4):

$$\begin{cases} -i_1-i_2+i_3=0 \\ R_1i_1+R_3i_3=u_{S1} \\ R_2i_2+R_3i_3=u_{S2} \end{cases}$$

It can be seen that, the first equation is KCL equation, the next two equations can be regarded as that, the algebraic sum of all resistor voltages along the loop is equal to the algebraic sum of all voltages sources along the loop. With this method, in the later, all KCL equations with the branch currents as variables can be listed directly from the circuit by inspection.

After i_1, i_2, i_3 are derived, other variables such as u_{R1}, u_{R2}, u_{R3} can be derived via VCR easily.

Namely

$$u_{R1}=R_1i_1$$
$$u_{R2}=R_2i_2$$
$$u_{R3}=R_3i_3$$

Example 3.2.3 Find every branch current of the circuit shown in Fig.3.2.5.

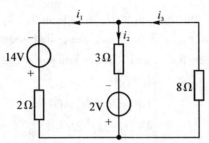

Fig.3.2.5 The Circuit for Example 3.2.3

Solution The reference direction of three currents i_1, i_2, i_3 are assigned first, as shown in Fig.3.2.5. Only one KCL equation needs to list, namely

$$i_1 + i_2 - i_3 = 0$$

By inspection, KVL equations of two meshes can be listed directly as follows

$$\begin{cases} (2\Omega)i_1 - (3\Omega)i_2 = 14V - 2V \\ (3\Omega)i_2 + (8\Omega)i_3 = 2V \end{cases}$$

By solving equations, the answers are

$$i_1 = 3A, \quad i_2 = -2A, \quad i_3 = 1A$$

When the branch current method is applied to analyze the circuit containing the controlled sources, the controlled sources can be handled in same way as the independent source. First, the branch current equations are listed in the same way as before, then the controlling quantities of the controlled sources must be expressed with branch currents. And then the equations can be solved.

Example 3.2.4 By applying the branch current method, try to find the current I_X of the controlled source in the circuit shown in Fig.3.2.6.

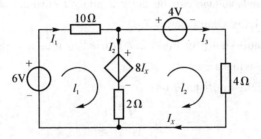

Fig.3.2.6 The Circuit for Example 3.2.4

Solution Assign the three branch currents as I_1, I_2, I_3 respectively, their directions are shown in Fig.3.2.6. First, controlled source is considered as an independent source, then the branch current equations can be listed as follows

$$\begin{cases} I_1 = I_2 + I_3 \\ 10I_1 + 2I_2 + 8I_X = 60 \\ 4 + 4I_X - 2I_2 - 8I_3 = 0 \end{cases}$$

Next, the controlling quantities I_X of the controlled sources is expressed with branch currents:

$$I_X = I_3$$

So, the current can be solved

$$I_X = 3\,\text{A}$$

3.2.4 Branch Voltage Analysis Method

Similar to the branch current method, for the circuits consisting of linear two-terminal resistors and independent current sources, circuit equations can be established by selecting branch voltages as variables. To do this, on the basis of the 2b-equation, the VCR equation $i = Gu$ of the resistive element is substituted into the KCL equations, then all branch currents is expressed with the branch voltages. The $n-1$ independent KCL equations with the branch voltage as the variables are derived. In addition of $b-n+1$ independent KVL equations, a total of b independent circuit equations can be constituted with b branch voltages as variables. This group of equations is called the branch voltage equations. For the circuits composed of linear two-terminal resistors and independent current sources, the equations can be listed directly by observing the circuit. By solving the equations, all branch voltage can be derived and all currents of resistors can also be derived by applying Ohm's law $i = Gu$.

Now, the circuit shown in Fig.3.2.7 is used to illustrate the establishment of the branch voltage equations.

2 KCL equations are listed first:

$$i_1 + i_3 = i_{S1}$$
$$i_2 - i_3 = -i_{S2}$$

By substituting following VCR equations of three resistors into above KCL equations.

$$i_1 = G_1 u_1, \quad i_2 = G_2 u_2, \quad i_3 = G_3 u_3$$

Then, the KCL equations with branch voltages u_1, u_2, and u_3 as variables can be derived as follows.

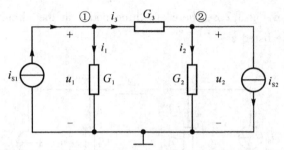

Fig.3.2.7 The Establishment of the Branch Voltage Equations

$$\left. \begin{array}{l} G_1 u_1 + G_3 u_3 = i_{S1} \\ G_2 u_2 - G_3 u_3 = -i_{S2} \end{array} \right\}$$

These two equations show that the sum of the resistance branch currents $G_k u_k$ flowing out of a node is equal to the sum of the source currents i_{Sk} flowing into the node. According to this understanding, these equations can be written directly by observing the circuit.

Next, a KVL equation can be listed, namely

$$u_1 - u_2 - u_3 = 0$$

After the three equations are listed, the circuit equations of the branch voltage method with three branch voltages as variables are obtained. It should be noted that, in practice, branch voltage method is rarely applied, instead branch current method is often used. So, in the following discussion, the branch analysis method only refers to the branch current method.

3.2.5 Selection of Independent Equations

It can be seen from the above discussion that the key to the branch analysis method is to list enough independent equations that their number is equal to the number of branch currents (or branch voltages), and these equations are derived from KCL and KVL only. So, for a general circuit with b branches and n nodes, according to KCL and KVL, how many independent equations can be listed? From the above example, it can be seen that the number of independent equations is just the same as the number of variables, then is this equality a coincidence, or is it necessary? To answer this question, a slightly more complicated example will be studied in the following.

As shown in Fig.3.2.8, there are three nodes in the circuit, so three KCL equations can be listed as:

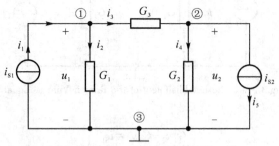

Fig.3.2.8 Selection of Independent Equations

$$-i_1-i_2+i_3=0$$
$$-i_3+i_4+i_5=0$$
$$i_1+i_2-i_4-i_5=0$$

In these equations, each branch current occurs twice, one is positive, anther is negative. This is obvious, because each branch must be connected between the two nodes, then each branch current flows into a node and must flow out of another node. And, in addition to the two nodes, the branch is no longer in contact with other nodes.

If the current flowing out of the node is defined as positive and the current flowing into the node is defined as negative, each current in the KCL equation must appear twice, that is, a positive and negative. So if all the equations are added together, there must be a $0=0$ equation. Therefore, the equations listed by KCL for all nodes are certainly not a set of independent equations.

But if we remove any one of these equations, it means that the branch variables of the nodes corresponding to the equation are removed. For the branch variables associated with that node can only occur once in other equations, the sum of all other equations is no longer equal to zero. It indicates that the rest of the set of equations should be independent (linearly independent). So, there are following conclusions and they can be proved by applying graph theory knowledge.

Conclusion 1 For a circuit with n nodes, only $n-1$ equations listed with KCL are independent.

Thus, for a circuit with n nodes, it is only required to list KCL equations for any $n-1$ nodes. The equations listed must be independent. The nodes corresponding to these independent equations are called independent nodes.

Conclusion 2 For a circuit with n nodes, only $n-1$ nodes are independent nodes.

Because of this, a reference node is often selected as the non-independent node and indicated as 0 node, or with a ground symbol.

Similarly, It can also be proved that there are only $l = b - n + 1$ KVL independent equations for circuits with b branches and n nodes.

For the circuit shown in Fig.3.2.9, $b=5$, $n=3$, So, $l=b-n+1=3$. So, there are three independent branch current equations.

The loop corresponding to the independent KVL equation is called independent loop.

Conclusion 3 For a the circuit with n branches and n nodes of, there are totally $b-n+1$ independent loops. That is, according to KVL, $b-n+1$ independent loop equations can be listed.

The following way can be applied to select the independent loops: while a new loop is selected, a new branch should be included in the loop, next loop can be selected in this way until all $b-n+1$ loops have been selected. Since each equation has a variable that is not presented in the other loop equation, the loops chosen in this way must be independent from each other and the sum of all equations cannot be equal to zero.

For the circuit shown in Fig.3.2.9, because $b-n+1=5-3+1=3$, so there are three independent loops need to be selected. As shown in Fig.3.2.9, the loop Ⅰ, Ⅱ, Ⅲ are selected as independent loops.

As shown in Fig.3.2.9, the single loops Ⅰ、Ⅱ、Ⅲ in circuits are also called the mesh. Obviously, a mesh is a independent loop. In fact, for planar circuits, it can be proved that the number of meshes is the number of independent loops. So, if you had to select the independent loops, you can simply select the meshes and

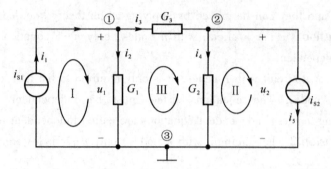

Fig.3.2.9 Selection of Independent Loops

then list the mesh equations directly. All planar circuits can be handled like this.

In short, for a circuit with n nodes and b branchs, $n-1$ independent KCL equations can be listed, and $b-n+1$ independent KVL equations can be listed. There are a total of b independent equations. The total number of independent equations is equal to the number of branches. And the solution can be derived by solving the equation.

3.2.6 Basic Steps of Branch Current Method

According to the above analysis, we can summarize the basic steps of the branch current method as follows:

1) specify the reference direction for each branch current;
2) list node KCL equations for $n-1$ nodes;
3) select $b-n+1$ independent loops (or meshes), list KVL equation for these independent loops;
4) solve the b equations to get all branch currents;
5) finally, find the desired circuit response.

Note 1: If the circuit contains current sources, the current source should be transformed to voltage source first and then it is easy to list equations.

Note 2: In applying the branch analysis method to solve the circuit, at least b equations had to be solved, so the amount of calculation is very large.

Example 3.2.5 For the circuit shown in Fig.3.2.10, it is given: $u_{S1} = 130\text{V}$, $u_{S2} = 117\text{V}$, $R_1 = 1\Omega$, $R_2 = 0.6\Omega$ $R_3 = 24\Omega$. Find:

(1) the currents i_1, i_2 flowing through two current sources;
(2) the power supplied by source.

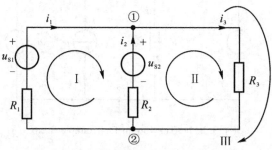

Fig.3.2.10 The Circuit for Example 3.2.5

Solution There are 2 nodes, 3 branches, 2 meshes in the circuit. So, there is only one independent KCL equation, two independent KVL equations.

With KCL, there is
$$i_1 + i_2 = i_3$$
With KVL, there are
$$\begin{cases} R_1 i_1 + R_2(-i_2) = u_{S1} - u_{S2} \\ R_2 i_2 + R_3 i_3 = u_{S2} \end{cases}$$
By solving above equations, it is derived that
$$i_1 = 10\text{A}, \quad i_2 = -5\text{A}$$
$$P_1 = i_1 u_{S1} = 10 \times 130 = 1300\text{W} \text{ (generating energy)}$$
$$P_2 = i_2 u_{S2} = (-5) \times 117 = -585\text{W} \text{ (absorbing energy)}$$

Example 3.2.6 For the circuit shown in Fig.3.2.11, it is given: $u_{S1} = 4\text{V}$, $u_{S2} = 2\text{V}$, $R_1 = R_2 = 10\Omega$, $R_3 = 20\Omega$, $I_S = 0.1\text{A}$. Find the each branch current and the powers generated by sources.

Solution There are 2 nodes, 4 branches, 3 meshes in the circuit. So, $b=4$, $n=2$, $\lambda=3$. KCL equation for node 1 can be listed as
$$-i_1 + i_2 + i_3 - i_4 = 0$$
KVL equation for 3 meshes are:
$$\begin{cases} R_1 i_1 + R_3 i_3 = u_{S1} \\ -R_3 i_3 + u = 0 \\ R_2 i_2 = u - u_{S2} \end{cases}$$

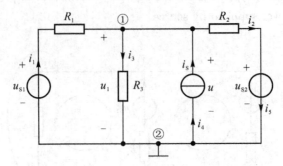

Fig.3.2.11 The Circuit for Example 3.2.6

Namely

$$\begin{cases} 10i_1 + 20i_3 = 4 \\ -20i_3 + u = 0 \\ 10i_2 = u - 2 \end{cases}$$

Supplement equation is:

$$i_4 = i_S = 0.1\text{A}$$

By solving above equations, the branch currents can be derived as follows

$$i_1 = 120\text{mA},\ i_2 = 80\text{mA},\ i_3 = 100\text{mA},\ i_4 = 100\text{mA},\ u = 2.8\text{V}$$

The powers absorbed by resistor is

$$P_R = P_{R1} + P_{R2} + P_{R3} = R_1 i_1^2 + R_2 i_2^2 + R_3 i_3^2 = 0.6\text{W}$$

The powers generated by sources are:

$$P_{u_{S1}} = u_{S1} i_1 = 4 \times 0.12 = 0.48\text{W} \ \text{(generating power)}$$

$$P_{u_{S2}} = -u_{S2} i_2 = -2 \times 0.08 = -0.16\text{W} \ \text{(absorbing power)}$$

$$P_{i_S} = u_{i_S} i_S = 0.1 \times 2.8 = 0.28\text{W} \ \text{(generating power)}$$

Then, total powers generated by sources is:

$$P_S = P_{u_{s1}} + P_{u_{S2}} + P_{i_S} = 0.48 - 0.16 + 0.28 = 0.6(\text{W})$$

3.3 Loop Analysis and Mesh Analysis

The branch current analysis discussed in the previous section is the most basic method of circuit analysis. In the branch analysis method, the circuit variables are the branch currents. So, for the circuit containing b branches, it is at least required to solve b independent equations and the amount of calculation is large.

In order to reduce the amount of calculation, on the basis of the branch analysis method, two new methods were developed: the loop analysis and the node analysis. The basic idea of the loop analysis is to introduce a new set of variables, namely the loop current. By assuming that there is a hypothetical loop current flowing through each loop, these loop currents can be selected as circuit variables. Then, by applying KVL, enough independent equations, which the number of equations is equal to the number of loops, are listed. Finally, according to the relationship between the loop current and branch current, all branch currents can be derived.

If all loops are meshes, the loop analysis is also called mesh analysis. The mesh analysis method is the special case of the loop analysis method. Since the mesh is easier to be found, so the mesh analysis method is more often used than the loop analysis method.

3.3.1 Mesh Current

What is mesh current? The mesh current is a hypothetical continuous current flowing along the mesh boundary of the planar network, and its flowing direction is generally defined as the same direction of the mesh. As shown in Fig.3.3.1, there are three meshes in the circuit. Assuming that there is a corresponding mesh current for each mesh, indicating as i_{l1}, i_{l2}, i_{l3}, as shown in Fig.3.3.1.

Obviously, if three meshes currents are known, every branch current can be derived by using KCL. That is

$$i_1 = -i_{l2}$$
$$i_2 = -i_{l3}$$
$$i_3 = i_{l2} - i_{l3}$$
$$i_4 = i_{l1} - i_{l2}$$
$$i_5 = i_{l1} - i_{l3}$$
$$i_6 = i_{l1}$$

Chapter 3 Systematic Analysis of Circuits

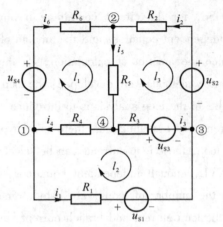

Fig.3.3.1 The Mesh Current

It can be proved that the mesh currents are a complete set of variables and a set of independent currents.

It can be also proved that the mesh currents satisfies KCL automatically. So, if the mesh currents are selected as variables to list equations, it is not required to list any KCL equations. It is only necessary to list a group of KVL equations, so, this method is called the mesh analysis method.

The key to applying the mesh analysis method is to list the circuit equations by use the mesh currents as the variables. These equations are known as the mesh current equations, or for short, mesh equations.

3.3.2 The Mesh Equations

In the following, how to list the mesh current equations will be discussed.

For example, there are 3 meshes in the circuit shown in Fig. 3.3.1, by applying KVL to these meshes respectively, there are:

$$\lambda_1 : R_6 i_{l1} + R_5 (i_{l1} - i_{l3}) + R_4 (i_{l1} - i_{l2}) = u_{S4}$$
$$\lambda_2 : R_1 i_{l2} + R_3 (i_{l2} - i_{l3}) + R_4 (i_{l2} - i_{l1}) = u_{S1} - u_{S3}$$
$$\lambda_3 : R_2 i_{l3} + R_3 (i_{l3} - i_{l2}) + R_5 (i_{l3} - i_{l1}) = u_{S3} - u_{S2}$$

Rewritten as:

3.3 Loop Analysis and Mesh Analysis

$$\begin{cases} (R_4+R_5+R_6)i_{l1} - R_4 i_{l2} - R_5 i_{l3} = u_{S4} \\ -R_4 i_{l1} + (R_1+R_3+R_4)i_{l2} - R_3 i_{l3} = u_{S1} - u_{S3} \\ -R_5 i_{l1} - R_3 i_{l2} + (R_2+R_3+R_5)i_{l3} = u_{S3} - u_{S2} \end{cases}$$

This is the mesh current equations of the circuit, where only the mesh currents i_{l1}, i_{l2}, i_{l3} are unknown variables, and the rest are known quantities. Since the number of unknown variables is equal to the number of equations, the equations can be solved.

Above mesh current equations are evaluated step by step on the base of the KVL equation. In fact, if you have mastered the law, you can list mesh current equations directly according to a given circuit.

Through observation, it can easily be found that the above equations have the following characteristics:

(1) the left hand side of the equation is sum of the voltage drops along the mesh, the right hand side of the equation is sum of the voltage rise (generally the source voltages);

For the equation of mesh λ_1, the preceding coefficient of i_{l1} is the sum of all resistances along mesh λ_1, and its sign is positive. Similarly, for the equations of mesh λ_2 and λ_3, the preceding coefficient of i_{l2}, i_{l3} are also the sum of all resistances along mesh λ_2 and λ_3, and their signs are also positive. These coefficients are called the self-resistance of the mesh, referred to as self-resistance, represented by R_{nn}. For the circuit shown in Fig. 3.3.1, the self-resistance of λ_1 is $R_{11}=R_4+R_5+R_6$, the self-resistances of λ_2 is $R_{22}=R_1+R_3+R_4$, the self-resistance of λ_3 is $R_{33}=R_2+R_3+R_5$;

(2) For the mesh λ_1, the preceding coefficient of i_{l2} or i_{l3} is the sum of the common resistance between λ_1 and λ_2, λ_3, and its sign is negative. It is similar for the meshes λ_2, λ_3. These coefficients are called the mutual-resistance of the meshes, referred to as mutual-resistance, represented with R_{nm}. For the circuit shown in Fig. 3.3.1, $R_{12}=-R_5$, $R_{21}=-R_4$, $R_{23}=-R_3$, $R_{31}=-R_5$, $R_{32}=-R_3$. Obviously, for this example, self-resistance is always positive, the mutual resistance is always negative.

The above characteristics can be described as follows:

(1) Since the direction of the mesh current is assumed to coincide with the direction of the mesh, the voltage drop generated by the mesh current in the mesh

resistor is always positive, so the sign of self-resistance is always positive;

(2) Since the directions of all meshes are the same (as shown in Fig.3.3.1, clockwise), the voltage drop generated by the mesh current in the other meshes is always negative, so the sign of mutual-resistance is always negative.

In this way, the above mesh current equations can be listed in a general form, as follows

$$R_{11}i_{l1}+R_{12}i_{l2}+R_{13}i_{l3}=u_{S11}$$
$$R_{21}i_{l1}+R_{22}i_{l2}+R_{23}i_{l3}=u_{S22}$$
$$R_{31}i_{l1}+R_{32}i_{l2}+R_{33}i_{l3}=u_{S33}$$

where, u_{S11}, u_{S22}, u_{S33} represent voltage rises of voltage sources in mesh λ_1, λ_2, λ_3, they are the algebraic sum of source voltages.

For circuits with only resistors and independent voltage sources, if there are n independent meshes and the directions of the mesh currents are assumed to be same, the general form of the mesh current equations will be listed as

$$R_{11}i_{l1}+R_{12}i_{l2}+\cdots+R_{1n}i_{ln}=u_{S11}$$
$$R_{21}i_{l1}+R_{22}i_{l2}+\cdots+R_{2n}i_{ln}=u_{S22}$$
$$\cdots\cdots\cdots\cdots\cdots\cdots\cdots\cdots\cdots\cdots$$
$$R_{k1}i_{l1}+R_{k2}i_{l2}+\cdots+R_{kn}i_{ln}=u_{Skk}$$
$$\cdots\cdots\cdots\cdots\cdots\cdots\cdots\cdots\cdots\cdots$$
$$R_{n1}i_{l1}+R_{n2}i_{l2}+\cdots+R_{nn}i_{ln}=u_{Snn}$$

where

R_{kk} is self-resistance of mesh k, it is equal the sum of all branch resistance along mesh k, its sign is always positive;

$R_{kj}(k\neq j)$ is the mutual resistance between the mesh k and the mesh j, which is equal to the sum of all the common resistances associated with the mesh k and the mesh j and its sign is always negative. If there is no common resistance between the two meshes, then the mutual resistance between the two meshes is equal to zero;

u_{Skk} is the equivalent voltage of the voltage sources for mesh k. It is the algebraic sum of the all the source voltages in mesh k. If the direction of the source voltage and the direction of the mesh are opposite, a positive sign is selected for u_{Skk}. Otherwise, a negative sign is selected.

The steps to solve the circuit by applying the mesh method can be summarized as follows:

(1) selecting n independent meshes, and specifying same mesh current direction with the mesh direction, normally clockwise.

(2) listing n mesh current equations directly. (Note that: self-resistance is positive, mutual-resistance is negative).

(3) solving the equations to find all mesh currents.

(4) finding the branch currents with the mesh currents. With specifying the reference direction of each branch current, the branch current is the algebraic sum of the mesh currents.

Example 3.3.1 For the circuit shown in Fig.3.3.2, $u_{S1} = u_{S2} = 17V$, $R_1 = 1$, $R_2 = 2$, $R_3 = 5$, find each branch current.

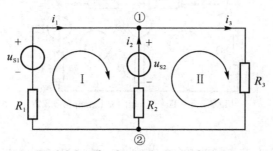

Fig.3.3.2 The Circuit for Example 3.3.1

Solution Two meshes I and II are selected as shown in Fig.3.3.2. Each self-resistances and mutual-resistances are

$$R_{11} = R_1 + R_2 = 1 + 2 = 3\Omega$$
$$R_{22} = R_2 + R_3 = 2 + 5 = 7\Omega$$
$$R_{12} = R_{21} = -R_2 = -2\Omega$$

The equivalent voltage of the voltage sources for two meshes are

$$u_{S11} = u_{S1} - u_{S2} = 17 - 17 = 0$$
$$u_{S22} = u_{S2} = 17V$$

Mesh equations can be listed as

$$\begin{cases} 3i_{I1} - 2i_{I2} = u_{S11} = u_{S1} - u_{S2} = 17 - 17 = 0 \\ -2i_{I1} + 7i_{I2} = u_{S22} = u_{S2} = 17 \end{cases}$$

By solving equations, there are

$$i_{l1} = 2\text{A}, \ i_{l2} = 3\text{A}$$

So, each branch current are

$$i_1 = i_{l1} = 2\text{A}$$
$$i_2 = i_{l2} - i_{l1} = 1\text{A}$$
$$i_3 = i_{l2} = 3\text{A}$$

Example 3.3.2 For the circuit shown in Fig. 3.3.3, all resistances and source voltages are given. Try to find all branch currents by applying mesh method.

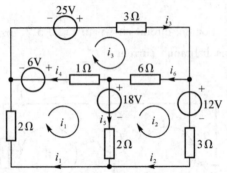

Fig.3.3.3 The Circuit for Example 3.3.2

Solution Select the reference direction for each mesh current, as shown in Fig.3.3.3. By inspection, the mesh equations can be listed directly as follows

$$\begin{cases} (2\Omega+1\Omega+2\Omega)i_1 - (2\Omega)i_2 - (1\Omega)i_3 = 6\text{V} - 18\text{V} \\ -(2\Omega)i_1 + (2\Omega+6\Omega+3\Omega)i_2 - (6\Omega)i_3 = 18\text{V} - 12\text{V} \\ -(1\Omega)i_1 - (6\Omega)i_2 + (3\Omega+6\Omega+1\Omega)i_3 = 25\text{V} - 6\text{V} \end{cases}$$

Namely

$$\begin{cases} 5i_1 - 2i_2 - i_3 = -12\text{A} \\ -2i_1 + 11i_2 - 6i_3 = 6\text{A} \\ -i_1 - 6i_2 + 10i_3 = 19\text{A} \end{cases}$$

By solving equations, there are

$$i_1 = -1\text{A} \quad i_2 = 2\text{A} \quad i_3 = 3\text{A}$$
$$i_4 = i_3 - i_1 = 4\text{A} \quad i_5 = i_1 - i_2 = -3\text{A} \quad i_6 = i_3 - i_2 = 1\text{A}$$

If the circuit contains current sources, there are two general methods of processing:

(1) one way is to set the voltage u of the current source as a new circuit variable, and treat this current source as a voltage source to list equations, and add an supplement equation for current source.

(2) Another way is to select only one mesh current passing through the current source and other the mesh currents not passing through that current source. In this way, the mesh current of the mesh is only determined by that current source. It is not need to list equation for the mesh with current source. Actually, by applying this method, mesh equations will be reduced.

Although the second method is more simple, it requires a clear concept to list equation. The first method is slightly more complicate, but it can be used to list equation according to the conventional steps, not easy to be error and can be applied flexible. Sometimes both methods are applied at the same time.

Example 3.3.3 Find the currents of each mesh in the circuit shown Fig.3.3.4.

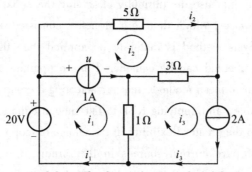

Fig.3.3.4　The Circuit for Example 3.3.3

Solution When the current source appears on the boundary of the circuit, the mesh current is determined by the current of source current which is in the mesh. This mesh current is given and it is not required to list the equation of that mesh. In this example, it can be seen that $i_3 = 2A$. The actual effect is equivalent to remove an equation and make analysis simple.

For 1A current source, as shown in Fig. 3.3.4, since there are two mesh currents flowing through it, it's voltage should be included into the listing equations. Two mesh equations and a supplementary equation can be listed as follows.

$$\begin{cases} (1\Omega)i_1-(1\Omega)i_3+u=20\text{V} \\ (5\Omega+3\Omega)i_2-(3\Omega)i_3-u=0 \\ i_1-i_2=1\text{A} \end{cases}$$

Substitute $i_3=2\text{A}$ into above equations and clear up, it is derived that

$$\begin{cases} i_1+8i_2=28\text{A} \\ i_1-i_2=1\text{A} \end{cases}$$

By solving them, the mesh currents are

$$i_1=4\text{A}, \quad i_2=3\text{A} \quad \text{and} \quad i_3=2\text{A}.$$

3.3.3 Loop Analysis

When the mesh method is applied, although it is convenient for selecting the mesh currents, there are also shortcomings. For example, in Example 3.3.3, it is required to set a new variable and add an supplement equation for pure current source branch. This increase the difficulty of solving the equations. For the circuit discussed in above case, which there are branches consisted only by pure current sources, loop analysis method is better to be applied than the mesh method. In fact, loop analysis method can be considered as an upgrade of mesh method. Its basic idea is similar to mesh method, that is, selecting a group of independent loop currents as a variable, and applying KVL to list enough equations and then solving for solution. Due to the greater flexibility in the choice of loop currents, so, if there are m branches of pure current sources in the circuit, the currents of current sources can be selected as loop current, then m corresponding loop equations will be not required to be listed. Therefore, the total number of loop equations is decreased.

Example 3.3.4 Applying the loop method to find the currents in the circuit shown in Fig.3.3.5.

Solution In order to decrease the number of simultaneous equations, the principle of selecting the loop currents is that each current source branch must be flowed through only by a loop current.

As shown in Fig.3.3.5, by selecting three loop currents i_1, i_3, i_4 shown in figure, then $i_3=2\text{A}$, $i_4=1\text{A}$ are given by current sources. So, it is only required to list the KVL equation for i_1 loop as follows.

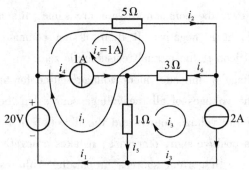

Fig.3.3.5 The Circuit for Example 3.3.4

$$(5\Omega+3\Omega+1\Omega)i_1-(1\Omega+3\Omega)i_3-(5\Omega+3\Omega)i_4=20\text{V}$$

Substitute $i_3 = 2\text{A}$ and $i_4 = 1\text{A}$ into above expression, each currents in the circuit can be derived as:

$$i_1=\frac{20\text{V}+8\text{V}+8\text{V}}{5\Omega+3\Omega+1\Omega}=4\text{A} \quad i_2=i_1-i_4=3\text{A}$$

$$i_5=i_1-i_3=2\text{A} \quad i_6=i_1-i_3-i_4=1\text{A}$$

Comparing with the solution in example 3.3.3, it is obvious that the number of equations with loop analysis method is less than that with mesh method, so, loop analysis is superior to mesh analysis.

In general, for the circuits that contain only resistors and independent voltage sources, if there are n independent loops, the general form of the loop equations can be listed as

$$R_{11}i_{l1}+R_{12}i_{l2}+\cdots+R_{1n}i_{ln}=u_{S11}$$
$$R_{21}i_{l1}+R_{22}i_{l2}+\cdots+R_{2n}i_{ln}=u_{S22}$$
$$\cdots\cdots\cdots\cdots\cdots\cdots\cdots\cdots\cdots$$
$$R_{k1}i_{l1}+R_{k2}i_{l2}+\cdots+R_{kn}i_{ln}=u_{Skk}$$
$$\cdots\cdots\cdots\cdots\cdots\cdots\cdots\cdots\cdots$$
$$R_{n1}i_{l1}+R_{n2}i_{l2}+\cdots+R_{nn}i_{ln}=u_{Snn}$$

where

R_{kk} is the self-resistance of loop k, it is equal to the sum of all resistances in the loop k, its sign is always positive.

$R_{kj}(k \neq j)$ is the mutual resistance between loop k and loop j, it is equal to sum of all common resistances between loop k and loop j. If passing directions of loop k and loop j over the common resistor are same, the mutual resistance is positive, otherwise, it is negative. If there is not common resistance existing between loop k and loop j, the mutual resistance is zero.

u_{Skk} is the voltage of the equivalent voltage source for the loop k, it is the algebraic sum of the voltages of all the voltage sources in the loop k. When the voltage direction of the voltage source and the direction of the loop bypassing is opposite, it takes a positive sign, otherwise, it takes a negative sign.

For the circuit with current sources in parallel with resistor, if conditions permitted, the source equivalent transformation method described in the previous chapter can be applied first. As shown in Fig.3.3.6, a current source in parallel a resistor is equivalent to a voltage source in series with a resistor. The equivalent circuit in Fig.3.3.6a has two advantages: (1) the number of loops can be decreased by 1; (2) it is easy to formulate the KVL equations directly.

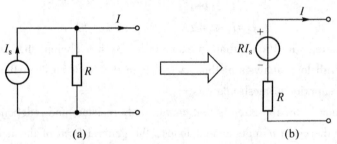

Fig.3.3.6 Source Equivalent Transformation

The shortcoming of the loop method is that selecting loops is not as convenient as selecting meshes. However, since the mesh method can only be applied to planar circuits, the loop method is a general method applying for any lumping circuit. So, the loop method is superior to the mesh method.

3.3.4 Loop Equations for Resistive Circuits with Controlled Sources

For a circuit containing a controlled source, to formulate its loop equations, the basic steps are similar to the steps in previous discussion, but the three points should be noted:

(1) the controlled source can be handled as independent source, that is, the contribution of controlled sources can be written in the right hand side of the loop equations;

(2) the controlling variables must be represented with the circuit variables, that is, the controlling voltage or current variables must be represented with the loop currents;

(3) the equations can be rewritten in a standard form, that is, the unknown quantities are put on the left hand side of the equations, the known quantities are put on the right hand side of the equations.

Example 3.3.5 For the circuit shown in Fig.3.3.7, try to write its loop current equations.

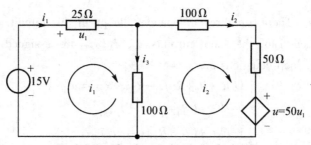

Fig.3.3.7 The Circuit for Example 3.3.5

Solution Choose meshes as the independent loops, the directions of mesh currents i_1, i_2 are shown in Fig.3.3.7. The mesh equations are as follows

$$\begin{cases} (25+100)i_1 - 100i_2 = 5 \\ -100i_1 + (50+100+100)i_2 = -u = -50u_1 = -50 \times 25 i_1 = -1250 i_1 \end{cases}$$

Supplement equation of controlling variable is

$$u_1 = 25i_1$$

Substituting above expression into mesh equations, gives

$$\begin{cases} 125i_1 - 100i_2 = 5 \\ 1350i_1 + 250i_2 = 0 \end{cases}$$

Obviously, $R_{12} \neq R_{21}$. This feature can be generalized to the general circuit, that is, if the circuit contains a controlled source, the coefficient of the equations will not be symmetrical.

Example 3.3.6 Write the loop current equations of the circuit shown in Fig.3.3.8.

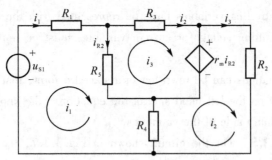

Fig.3.3.8 The Circuit for Example 3.3.6

Solution There are three independent loops in this circuit. Assuming the reference direction of the loop currents i_1, i_2, i_3 are assigned as shown in Fig.3.3.8, the loop equations are

$$\begin{cases} (R_1+R_2+R_4)i_1-R_4i_2-R_2i_3=u_{S1} \\ -R_4i_1+(R_4+R_5)i_2=r_m i_{R2} \\ -R_2i_1+(R_2+R_3)i_3=-r_m i_{R2} \end{cases}$$

∵ $$Qi_{R2}=i_1-i_3$$
∴ $$r_m i_{R2}=r_m i_1-r_m i_3$$

Substituting above expression into loop equations and rearranging gives the loop current equations as follows

$$\begin{cases} (R_1+R_2+R_4)i_1-R_4i_2-R_4i_3=u_{S1} \\ -(r_m+R_4)i_1+(R_4+R_5)i_2+r_m i_3=0 \\ (r_m-R_2)i_1+(R_2+R_3-r_m)i_3=0 \end{cases}$$

3.4 Node Analysis and Modified Node Analysis

Similar to establishing circuit equations with independent current variables, independent voltage variables can also be used to establish the circuit equations. For all the branch voltages in the circuit, only a part of them are independent, the

3.4 Node Analysis and Modified Node Analysis

other part of the branch voltage can be determined by these independent voltages according to KVL equation. So, if the circuit equations are established with these independent voltage variables, the total number of circuit equations can also be decreased. It can be proved that, for a connected circuit with n nodes, its $n-1$ node voltages relating to the n nodes voltage are a set of independent voltage variables. The circuit equations which are established by using these node voltages as variables are known as the node equations. In this way, by solving only $n-1$ node equations, all the node voltages can be derived. And then, according to KVL equation, all the branch voltages can also be derived. And finally, according to the VCR equation, all branch currents can be derived.

3.4.1 Node Voltages

In a connected circuit with n nodes, one of the nodes can be selected as a reference node. The voltages between other nodes relative to the reference node are called the node voltages. If the reference node is chosen as a potential reference point or zero potential point, then the node voltage is equal to the node potential. Because each node voltage cannot be represented by other node voltages, the node voltages must be a set of independent voltage variables. Since any branch voltage is the potentials difference or the node voltage difference between the two nodes connected by a branch, all branch voltages can be derived from the node voltages. Note that the reference polarity or direction of the node voltage always points to the reference node.

For the circuit shown in Fig.3.4.1, there are four nodes, namely, nodes ①, ②, ③ and ⓪. If the ⓪ node is selected as the reference node, the voltages between other nodes and the reference node ⓪ are the node voltages, represented as u_{n1}, u_{n2} and u_{n3} respectively.

If node voltages u_{10}, u_{20} and u_{30} are given, then each branch voltage can be derived:

$$u_1 = u_{10} = u_{n1} \qquad u_4 = u_{10} - u_{30} = u_{n1} - u_{n3}$$
$$u_2 = u_{20} = u_{n2} \qquad u_5 = u_{10} - u_{20} = u_{n1} - u_{n2}$$
$$u_3 = u_{30} = u_{n3} \qquad u_6 = u_{20} - u_{30} = u_{n2} - u_{n3}$$

With these branch voltages obtained, all branch currents can also be derived.

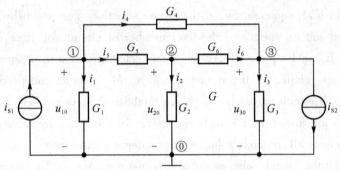

Fig.3.4.1 Explanation of Node Voltage

3.4.2 Node Analysis

Node analysis is a systematic method with the node voltages selected as circuit variables. First, by applying KCL, independent KCL equations whose number is equal to the number of node voltages are written. Next, the node voltages can be derived by solving these equations. Finally, the branch currents can also be derived by using VCR and KVL.

The key to the node analysis is to formulate enough independent circuit equations with the node voltage as a variable. These circuit equations are called the node voltage equations.

In the following, the circuit shown in Fig.3.4.1 is chosen as an example to discuss how to write the node voltage equation by inspection.

The KCL equations are written for the three independent nodes of the circuit as follows.

$$\begin{cases} i_1 + i_4 + i_5 = i_{S1} \\ i_2 - i_5 + i_6 = 0 \\ i_3 - i_4 - i_6 = -i_{S2} \end{cases}$$

VCR equations for all resistor are written in which the branch currents are expressed as the node voltages

$$i_1 = G_1 u_{n1} \quad i_2 = G_2 u_{n2} \quad i_3 = G_3 u_{n3}$$
$$i_4 = G_4(u_{n1} - u_{n3}) \quad i_5 = G_5(u_{n1} - u_{n2}) \quad i_6 = G_6(u_{n2} - u_{n3})$$

Substituting above VCR equations into KCL equations and making rearrangement, gives

$$\left.\begin{array}{r}(G_1+G_4+G_5)u_{n1}-G_5u_{n2}-G_4u_{n3}=i_{S1}\\ -G_5u_{n1}+(G_2+G_5+G_6)u_{n2}-G_6u_{n3}=0\\ -G_4u_{n1}-G_6u_{n2}+(G_3+G_4+G_6)u_{n3}=-i_{S2}\end{array}\right\}$$

The above equations are the required node voltage equations where the node voltage u_{n1}, u_{n2} and u_{n3} are the unknown variables.

There are two steps for writting node equation ① (1) write KCL equations; (2) substitute VCR equations into KCL. It seems that writing node equations is not a simple job. However, as long as the principle of writing equations is understood, the node equation can be directly and easily written by inspection based on the circuit.

By inspecting the above equations, it can be easily found that there are some characteristics in the node equations:

(1) The left-hand side of the equation is the current flowing out of the node, the right-hand side of the equation is the current flowing into the node, that is, the current of current sources connected to the node;

(2) For the equation of node ①, the coefficient of u_{n1} is the sum of the branch conductances associated with the node; the coefficients of u_{n2}, u_{n3} are the sum of the branch conductances connected between the node ① and adjacent nodes ② and ③ respectively. The same characteristics is true for the equations of node ② and node ③.

The sum of branch conductances associated with node i is called self-conductance and is represented as G_{ii}. For above example, they are G_{11}, G_{22}, G_{33}, the self-conductance of the node ① $G_{11}=G_1+G_4+G_5$, the self-conductance of node ② is $G_{22}=G_2+G_5+G_6$, and the self-conduction of node ③ is $G_{33}=G_3+G_4+G_6$. Since it has been assumed that the node voltage is directed from the node to the reference node, the current generated by each node voltage in the self-conductance always flows out of the node, and the sign in front of the self-conductance is always positive.

$G_{ij}(i\neq j)$ is called the mutual conductance of node i and node j, which is the negative value of the sum of the conductances between node i and node j. In above example, the mutual conductances are $G_{12}=G_{21}=-G_5$, $G_{13}=G_{31}=-G_4$, $G_{23}=G_{32}=-G_6$ respectively.

In terms of the node, because the current generated by the other node voltages across the mutual conductance always flows into the node, so the sign of mutual conductance is always negative.

In addition, the current i_{Sii} on the right-hand side of the equation is the algebraic sum of all currents of source currents flowing into node i. For the above example, they are $i_{S11}=i_{S1}$, $i_{S22}=0$ and $i_{S33}=-i_{S3}$. So the node voltage equation can be written in the following form

$$\begin{cases} G_{11}u_{n1}+G_{12}u_{n2}+G_{13}u_{n3}=i_{S11} \\ G_{21}u_{n1}+G_{22}u_{n2}+G_{23}u_{n3}=i_{S22} \\ G_{31}u_{n1}+G_{32}u_{n2}+G_{33}u_{n3}=i_{S33} \end{cases} \quad (3.4.1)$$

It can be seen that the coefficient and constant items in the nodal equation are very regular, so the nodal equation can be written directly by observing the circuit diagram.

In general, the node equations for a circuit with n nodes consisting of independent current sources and linear resistors, the node equations can be written as

$$\begin{cases} G_{11}u_{n1}+G_{12}u_{n2}+\cdots+G_{1(n-1)}u_{n(n-1)}=i_{S11} \\ G_{21}u_{n1}+G_{22}u_{n2}+\cdots+G_{2(n-1)}u_{n(n-1)}=i_{S22} \\ \cdots\cdots\cdots\cdots\cdots\cdots\cdots\cdots\cdots\cdots\cdots\cdots\cdots \\ G_{k1}u_{n1}+G_{k2}u_{n2}+\cdots+G_{kk}u_{n(n-1)}=i_{Skk} \\ \cdots\cdots\cdots\cdots\cdots\cdots\cdots\cdots\cdots\cdots\cdots\cdots\cdots \\ G_{(n-1)1}u_{n1}+G_{(n-1)2}u_{n2}+\cdots+G_{(n-1)(n-1)}u_{n(n-1)}=i_{S(n-1)(n-1)} \end{cases} \quad (3.4.2)$$

where: G_{kk} is the self-conductance of node k, it is the sum of all conductances of all branches connected to the node k, and is always positive;

$G_{kj}(k \neq j)$ is mutual-conductance between node k and node j, it is equal to the sum of conductances of all branches connected between the node k and the node j, and is always negative. If there is no branch connected between the node k and the node j, the mutual conductance is zero;

i_{Skk} is the current of the equivalent current source for node k. It is the algebraic sum of the all branches currents of the current sources connected to node k. If the current source is flowing into node k, i_{Skk} takes the positive sign, otherwise, takes the negative sign.

3.4 Node Analysis and Modified Node Analysis

The step-by-step procedure for the node equation can be summarized as follows:

(1) specify the reference node and label each node number;
(2) list node voltage equations of the circuit directly by inspection;
(3) find the node voltages by solving the node equations, and then find the branch voltages and the branch currents.

Example 3.4.1 List the node voltage equations of the circuit shown in Fig.3.4.2.

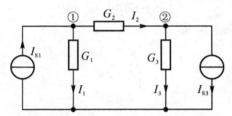

Fig.3.4.2 The Circuit for Example 3.4.1

Solution Select the reference node and label the node number as shown in Fig.3.4.2, the node voltage equations can be listed by inspection, as follows

$$\begin{cases} (G_1+G_2)U_1-G_2U_2=I_{s1} \\ -G_2U_1+(G_2+G_3)U_2=-I_{s3} \end{cases}$$

Example 3.4.2 Find each node voltage for the circuit shown in Fig.3.4.3.

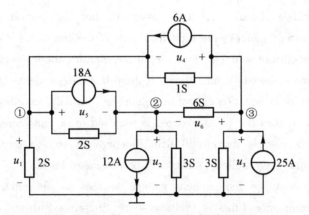

Fig.3.4.3 The Circuit for Example 3.4.2

Solution Select the reference node and label the node number as shown in Fig.3.4.3, the node voltage equations can be listed by inspection, as follows

$$\begin{cases} (2+2+1)u_1 - 2u_2 - u_3 = 6-18 \\ -2u_1 + (2+3+6)u_2 - 6u_3 = 18-12 \\ -u_1 - 6u_2 + (1+6+3)u_3 = 25-6 \end{cases}$$

By rearrangement, there are

$$\begin{cases} 5u_1 - 2u_2 - u_3 = -12 \\ -2u_1 + 11u_2 - 6u_3 = 6 \\ -u_1 - 6u_2 + 10u_3 = 19 \end{cases}$$

Three node voltages can be solved as

$$\begin{cases} u_1 = -1\text{V} \\ u_2 = 2\text{V} \\ u_3 = 3\text{V} \end{cases}$$

Then, three branch voltages can be derived as

$$u_4 = u_3 - u_1 = 4\text{V} \quad u_5 = u_1 - u_2 = -3\text{V} \quad u_6 = u_3 - u_2 = 1\text{V}$$

The power of controlled source is

$$p = u_3(gu_2) = 5 \times 2 \times 3\text{W} = 30\text{W}$$

From the above two examples, it can be seen that $G_{ij} = G_{ij}$. This feature can be generalized to the other similar circuits, that is, if there is not controlled sources in the circuit, the coefficient determinant of the node analysis is generally symmetrical.

In the above discussion, it is assumed that the circuit contains only independent current sources, the right-hand side of the equation is the algebra sum of independent current sources. However, if the circuit contains voltage sources or controlled sources, how to handle them? If there is a independent voltage source in the circuit, the node equation cannot be established directly according to (3.4.2), because the current of the voltage source is required to be considered.

Here, let's discuss the circuit with independent voltage sources first, the circuit that contains controlled sources will be discussed later.

Assuming that the independent voltage sources in the circuit are voltage sources with companion (that is, voltage source in series with resistor). For this kind of circuit, by applying source equivalent transformation first, voltage sources with companion (voltage source in series with resistor) are transformed into current sources with companion (current source in parallel with resistor). And then the node voltage equations can be listed.

Example 3.4.3 For the circuit shown in fig.3.4.4a, find the voltage u by applying the node analysis, and find branch currents i_1, i_2.

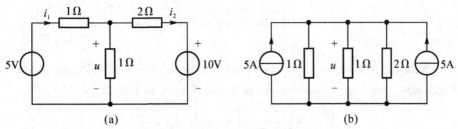

Fig.3.4.4 The Circuit for Example 3.4.3

Solution First, the voltage source in series with a resistance is equivalently transformed into the current source in parallel with a resistance, as shown in Fig.3.4.4b. In terms for the node voltage u, the circuit in Fig.3.4.4a is equivalent to the circuit in Fig.3.4.4b. Since there is only one independent node, it is only required to list one node equation, i.e.

$$(1+1+0.5)u = 5A + 5A$$

So it is derived that

$$u = \frac{10A}{2.5S} = 4V$$

Applying this node voltage to the circuit shown in Fig.3.4.4a, the currents i_1 and i_2 are

$$i_1 = \frac{5V - 4V}{1\Omega} = 1A \quad i_2 = \frac{4V - 10V}{2\Omega} = -3A$$

If the principle is understood well, node voltage equations can also be listed directly without the need to transform the voltage source in series with a resistor into the current source in parallel with a resistor.

Example 3.4.4 List the node voltage equation shown in Fig.3.4.5a and find the node voltages of nodes 1 and 2.

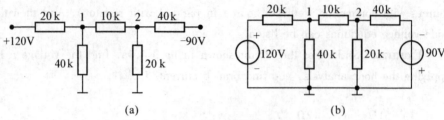

(a)　　　　　　　　　　　　　(b)

Fig.3.4.5　The Circuit for Example 3.4.4

Solution　Redraw the circuit and choose a reference node as shown in Fig.3.4.5b, the node equations can be listed directly as follows

$$\begin{cases} \left(\dfrac{1}{20k}+\dfrac{1}{40k}+\dfrac{1}{10k}\right)u_{n1}-\dfrac{1}{10k}u_{n2}=\dfrac{120}{20k} \\ -\dfrac{1}{10k}u_{n1}+\left(\dfrac{1}{20k}+\dfrac{1}{10k}+\dfrac{1}{40k}\right)u_{n2}=-\dfrac{90}{40k} \end{cases}$$

By solving the equations, the node voltages of nodes 1 and 2 are derived as follows

$$u_{n1}=40\text{V},\ u_{n2}=10\text{V}$$

3.4.3　Modified Node Analysis

For the circuit with unaccompanied independent voltage source branches, the voltage of these branches cannot be listed directly into the node equations. It is because that the node equations are essentially KCL equations and all terms in the equations must be currents. To applying node analysis to this kind of circuit, two modification should be done:

(1) If there is only one unaccompanied voltage source in the circuit, the negative side of the pure voltage source can be selected as a reference node. Then, the node voltage at positive polarity node of the pure voltage source is automatically equal to the voltage of the pure voltage source. It is not required to list the node equation at positive polarity node of the pure voltage source, thus the number of node equations can be decreased by 1.

(2) If there are more than two unaccompanied voltage sources in the circuit and there is no common node between them, it is clear that the above method

cannot be applied. In this case, the current I_{u_S} flowing through each unaccompanied voltage source u_S can be selected as a new circuit variable. Then, by considering the pure voltage source as a current source with current I_{u_S}, its contribution to the node equations can be listed on right hand side of the equations. Due to the number of circuit variables is increased, it is required to add a equation in which the voltage of unaccompanied voltage source is represented by node voltages.

Example 3.4.5 Apply the node method to find each node voltage of the circuit shown in Fig.3.4.6.

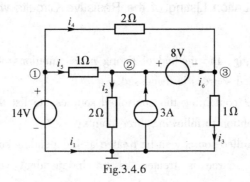

Fig.3.4.6

Solution There are two unaccompanied voltage source branches in the circuit. Since the 14V voltage source is connected between the node ① and the reference node, the node voltage of the node ① becomes a known quantity, $u_1 = 14\text{V}$, so the node equation of the node ① is not necessary to be listed. Because 8V voltage source is not connected to the reference node, its current i_6 should be selected as a new variable. By considering the 8V voltage source as a current source with current i_6, the node equations for node ② and node ③ can be listed as follows

$$\begin{cases} -(1\text{S})u_1 + (1\text{S}+0.5\text{S})u_2 = 3\text{A} - i_6 \\ -(0.5\text{S})u_1 + (1\text{S}+0.5\text{S})u_3 = 0 + i_6 \end{cases}$$

And supplement equation for 8V voltage source is

$$u_2 - u_3 = 8\text{V}$$

Substituting $u_1 = 14\text{V}$ into above node equations, there are:

$$\begin{cases} 1.5u_2+1.5u_3 = 24\text{V} \\ u_2-u_3 = 8\text{V} \end{cases}$$

By solving equations, all node voltages and current i can be derived.

$$u_2 = 12\text{V} \quad u_3 = 4\text{V} \quad i = -1\text{A}$$

This set of circuit equations, which is set up by adding the current flowing through pure voltage source as new variable, is called an modified node equation. The corresponding method is called modified node analysis. It extends the scope of the node analysis and had been applied by many computer circuit analysis programs.

3.4.4 Node Equation Listing of the Resistive Circuits with the Controlled Sources

In the following, the method of listing node equations of a resistive circuit containing controlled sources is discussed.

For the circuit containing the controlled sources, to list the node equations, we should pay attention to following three points:

(1) the controlled source can be treated as independent source, for example, controlled voltage source is treated as an independent voltage source, the controlled current source is treated as an independent current source. Its contribution can be listed on the right hand side of equation.

(2) the controlling quantity of the controlled source must be represented by the circuit variables, that is, the controlling voltage or current must be represented by node voltages.

(3) the equation is rearranged into a standard form, that is, the unknown quantities are listed on the left hand side of the equations, known quantities are listed on the right hand side of the equations.

Example 3.4.6 For the circuit shown in Fig.3.4.7, list its node equations.

Solution A reference node is selected as shown in Fig.3.4.7, there is only one independent node ① in the circuit, it's node voltage is defined as u_n. node equation is listed as follows

$$\left(\frac{1}{25}+\frac{1}{100}+\frac{1}{100+50}\right)u_n = \frac{15}{25}+\frac{u}{100+50}=\frac{3}{5}+\frac{50u_1}{150}$$

Controlling voltage is represent by node voltages as follows

3.4 Node Analysis and Modified Node Analysis 137

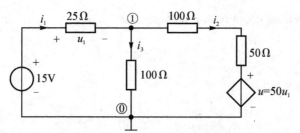

Fig.3.4.7 The Circuit for Example 3.4.6

$$u_1 = 15 - u_n$$

Then, there is

$$\left(\frac{1}{25} + \frac{1}{100} + \frac{1}{100+50}\right)u_n = \frac{3}{5} + \frac{15-u_n}{3}$$

Rearrangement, so, the node equation is derived as follows

$$\left(\frac{1}{25} + \frac{1}{100} + \frac{1}{100+50} + \frac{1}{3}\right)u_n = \frac{3}{5} + \frac{15}{3}$$

Example 3.4.7 List the node equations for the circuit shown in Fig.3.4.8.

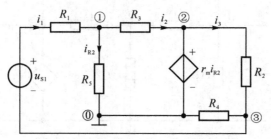

Fig.3.4.8 The Circuit for Example 3.4.7

Solution There are 4 nodes in the circuit. By selecting a reference node as shown in Fig.3.4.8 and assuming three independent node voltages are u_{n1}, u_{n2}, u_{n3} respectively, the node equations cab be listed as follows

$$\begin{cases} \left(\dfrac{1}{R_1} + \dfrac{1}{R_3} + \dfrac{1}{R_5}\right)u_{n1} - \dfrac{1}{R_3}u_{n2} - \dfrac{1}{R_1}u_{n3} = \dfrac{u_{S1}}{R_1} \\ u_{n2} = r_m i_{R2} \\ \left(\dfrac{1}{R_1} + \dfrac{1}{R_2} + \dfrac{1}{R_4}\right)u_{n3} - \dfrac{1}{R_1}u_{n1} - \dfrac{1}{R_2}u_{n2} = -\dfrac{u_{S1}}{R_1} \end{cases}$$

The controlling quantity is represented as

$$u_{n2} = \frac{u_{n1}}{R_5}$$

Thus, there are

$$\begin{cases} \left(\dfrac{1}{R_1}+\dfrac{1}{R_3}+\dfrac{1}{R_5}\right)u_{n1}-\dfrac{1}{R_3}u_{n2}-\dfrac{1}{R_1}u_{n3}=\dfrac{u_{S1}}{R_1} \\ u_{n2}=r_m\dfrac{u_{n1}}{R_5} \\ \left(\dfrac{1}{R_1}+\dfrac{1}{R_2}+\dfrac{1}{R_4}\right)u_{n3}-\dfrac{1}{R_1}u_{n1}-\dfrac{1}{R_2}u_{n2}=-\dfrac{u_{S1}}{R_1} \end{cases}$$

This is the required node equations.

Example 3.4.8 The circuit is shown in Fig.3.4.9. It is known that $g=2S$. Find each node voltage and the power of the controlled current source.

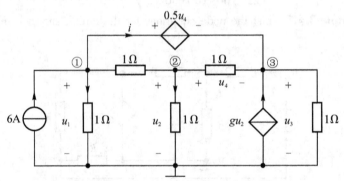

Fig.3.4.9 The Circuit for Example 3.4.8

Solution Since the circuit contains controlled voltage source, the current variable i in the controlled voltage source should be added to establish the nodal equations. By selecting the reference node and label the node number, as shown in Fig.3.4.9, the following node equations can be listed.

$$\begin{cases} (2S)u_1-(1S)u_2+i=6A \\ -(1S)u_1+(3S)u_2-(1S)u_3=0 \\ -(1S)u_2+(2S)u_3-i=gu_2 \end{cases}$$

Supplement equation is

$$u_1 - u_3 = 0.5u_4 = 0.5(u_2 - u_3)$$

Substitute $g = 2S$ into above node equations and cancelling current i, following node equations can be derived:

$$\begin{cases} 2u_1 - 4u_2 + 2u_3 = 6 \\ -u_1 + 3u_2 - u_3 = 0 \\ u_1 - 0.5u_2 - 0.5u_3 = 0 \end{cases}$$

By solving above equations, it is derived

$$u_1 = 4\text{V}, \ u_2 = 3\text{V}, \ u_3 = 5\text{V}.$$

Then, the power of the controlled current source is

$$p = u_3(gu_2) = 5 \times 2 \times 3 \text{W} = 30 \text{W}$$

For this example, if either terminal of the controlled voltage sources is selected as the reference node to list node equations, the number of equations can be reduced by one. In addition, it can be seen from this example that $G_{ij} \neq G_{ij}$. This feature can be generalized to the general circuit, that is, if there are controlled sources in the circuit, the coefficients determinant of the node equations is generally no longer symmetrical.

3.4.5 Comparison Between Node Analysis Method and Other Methods

For a circuit with n nodes and b branches, the number of independent nodes is $n-1$, the number of independent loops $l = b-n+1$. If $2b$ methods is applied, the number of independent equations listed is $2b$. If branch current method is applied, the number of independent equations listed is b. If loop or mesh method is applied, the number of independent equations listed is $b-n+1$. If node method is applied, the number of independent equations listed is $n-1$. Obviously, the number of equations with $2b$ method is maximum. Next is branch current analysis, branch voltage analysis. And less is mesh or loop analysis method, node analysis method. So, mesh or loop analysis method, node analysis method are better and more commonly applied. Branch analysis method is the most basic method and is applicable to any circuit, however, the number of independent equations is relatively large and is not easy to be solved. So their application is less. The following table lists the number of independent KVL and KVL equations listed by applying branch analysis method, loop analysis method, and node analysis method.

	KCL equations	KVL equations	total equations
branch method	$n-1$	$b-(n-1)$	b
loop method	0	$b-(n-1)$	$b-(n-1)$
node method	$n-1$	0	$n-1$

In order to choose a proper method from a variety of network analysis methods, pay attention to the following points:

(1) Mesh method is a special case of the loop method, it only applies to the plane circuit.

(2) Loop method is more flexible, it is suitable for any circuit, however the choice of loops for complex non-planar circuit is more difficult.

(3) For node voltage method, it is not difficult to select all independent nodes, so, it is applicable to any circuit and is most widely applied.

(4) If the number of independent nodes is less than the number of independent loops, the node method should be prefer to apply, and otherwise loop method is prefer to apply.

(5) Node analysis had been applied to a lot of computer-aided analysis software and can be used to analyze large-scale electrical networks.

3.5 Example of Computer-Aided Analysis of Circuits

3.5.1 Example of Computer Aided Circuit Analysis with Matlab

Matlab is a simple engineering computing language developed by MathWorks in the United States. As it operates with matrix or array as the data unit, so it can directly deal with matrix or array. MATLAB has a powerful graphic function and can easily draw two-dimensional, three-dimensional graphics. Its visual simulation environment Simulink provide users with a convenient graphical module Function and greatly simplify the design process. Because of these advantages, Matlab is particularly suitable for circuit analysis. The circuit equations written in the various circuit system analysis methods described in this chapter can be easily programmed by Matlab. In the following, typical examples of complex DC resistance circuit will be analyzed respectively by using MATLAB language programming and Simulink design block diagram.

3.5.1.1 Using Matlab Programming to Analyze Circuit

Example 3.5.1 As shown in Fig.3.5.1a, find the current on the R_B and the power of the voltage source.

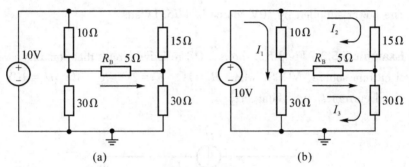

Fig.3.5.1 The Circuit for Example 3.5.1

Solution Modeling by loop method. As shown in Fig. 3.5.1b, select the three loops and set up the equations as follows

$$\begin{cases}(10+30)I_1-10I_2-30I_3=10\\-10I_1+(10+15+5)I_2-5I_3=0\\-30I_1-5I_2+(30+5+30)I_3=0\end{cases}$$

Note that the current of R_B is $I=I_3-I_2$, power of the source is $P=10I_1$.

Write the MATLAB program as follows

%This program determines the current flowing in a resistor RB and power supplied by source

%it computes the loop currents with the resistor matrix Z and voltage vector V

clear;   %clear all variables
Z=[40-10-30;-1030-5;-30-565]; %Z is the resistance matrix
V=[1000]';   %V is the voltage matrix
I=inv(Z)*V;   %solve for the loop currents
IRB=I(3)-I(2);   %current through RB is calculated
fprintf('the current through R is %8.3 fAmps\n', IRB)

PS=I(1) * 10;   %the power supplied by source is calculated
fprintf('the power supplied by 10V source is %8.4 fwatts\n', PS)

The calculation results are as follows:

The current through R is 0.037Amps.
The power supplied by 10V source is 4.7531Watts.

Example 3.5.2 Fig.3.5.2 shows a DC resistive circuit that contains a voltage control current source, VCCS, where $R_1 = 1\Omega$, $R_2 = 2\Omega$, $R_3 = 3\Omega$, $U_S = 10V$, $I_S = 15A$. Find current I_1 and voltage U_2.

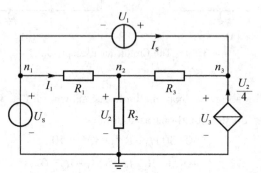

Fig.3.5.2 A DC Resistive Circuit that Contains VCCS

Solution First establish the mathematical model, apply node method to establish the following equations

$$\begin{cases} U_{n1} = U_S \\ -\frac{1}{R_1}U_{n1} + \left(\frac{1}{R_1} + \frac{1}{R_2} + \frac{1}{R_3}\right)U_{n2} - \frac{1}{R_3}U_{n3} = 0 \\ -\frac{1}{R_3}U_{n2} + \frac{1}{R_3}U_{n3} = I_S + \frac{U_2}{4} \\ U_2 = U_{n2} \end{cases}$$

Organize the above equation and write matrix equations in the form of AX = B, there are

$$\begin{bmatrix} 1 & 0 & 0 \\ -\dfrac{1}{R_1} & \dfrac{1}{R_1}+\dfrac{1}{R_2}+\dfrac{1}{R_3} & -\dfrac{1}{R_3} \\ 0 & -\dfrac{1}{R_3}-\dfrac{1}{4} & \dfrac{1}{R_3} \end{bmatrix} \begin{bmatrix} U_{n1} \\ U_{n2} \\ U_{n3} \end{bmatrix} = \begin{bmatrix} U_S \\ 0 \\ I_S \end{bmatrix}$$

Apply MATLAB language to program as follows:

```
clear;                                    %clear all variables
US=10;IS=15;R1=1;R2=2;R3=3;               %set parameter value
A=[100;-1/R11/R1+1/R2+1/R3-1/R3;
   0-1/R3-1/41/R3];                       %form matrix A
B=[US;0;IS];                              %form matrix B
X=A\B;                                    %find node voltage X
I1=(X(1)-X(2))/R1                         %find current I1
U2=X(2)                                   %find voltage U2
```

Results of Program Run:

I1=-10, U2=20

The results are correct, of course, the circuit equation of this example can also be established by using the loop method or branch method, and then calculates by Matlab programming, the reader can try it.

3.5.1.2 Simulation Based on Simulink Model

Using MATLAB's dynamic simulation toolbox Simulink environment for circuit analysis has a good visual effect, it does not require programming, so it is more convenient. When the circuit shown in Fig.3.5.2 is analyzed by this method, you can double-click the PowerSystemBlockset icon in Matlab to pop up the component library window used for circuit simulation. For circuit shown in Fig.3.5.2, its Simulink model diagram can be designed by selecting the corresponding components, as shown in Fig.3.5.3.

The design of this model will encounter how to deal with the problem of DC current source. Because the MATLAB power system toolbox only provide DC voltage source, AC voltage source, AC current source, there is no DC current source. However, we can treat AC current source as a DC current source, as long as the frequency of AC current source is set to 0 while the amplitude is set to 15, the initial phase is set to 90°, as shown in Fig.3.5.4.

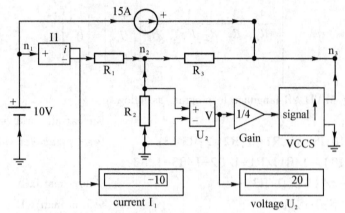

Fig.3.5.3 Simulink Model Diagram

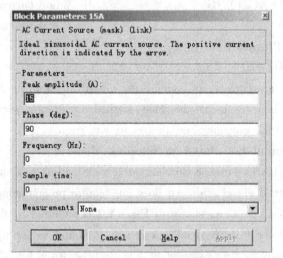

Fig.3.5.4 Treat AC Current Source as a DC Current Source

So with this set up, there is
$$I_S = I_m \sin(\omega t + \theta) = 15\sin(0 \times t + 90°) = 15(\text{A})$$

In the model shown in Fig. 3.5.3, DC current source is handled with this method.

In addition to the above method, another method is to use a controlled current source VCCS to achieve the required 15A DC current source. The Simulink model derived with this method is shown in Fig.3.5.5. A DC source is implemented with a controlled source and a constant module. A constant input module with a value of 15 is connected at the input of the controlled current source.

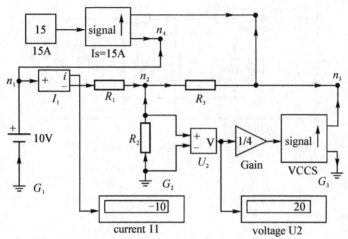

Fig.3.5.5　Using a VCCS to Achieve the DC Current Source

The current measurement module I1 is used to measure the branch current I_1. The voltage measurement module U2 is used to measure the branch voltage U_2. The corresponding reading is shown in these two modules. After simulation, for the two Simulink models shown in Fig.3.5.2 and Fig.3.5.4, both the results are I1 = −10A, U2 = 20V, and they are consistent with results derived from the above MATLAB programming.

3.5.2　Example of Using EWB to Analyze Circuits

EWB toolbox contains a wealth of components, a variety of components required in the circuit analysis can be easily found.

In the following, the circuit shown in Fig.3.5.2 is analyzed by using EWB software. First, the circuit diagram is drawn by using EWB toolbox components, as shown in Fig.3.5.6. Next, press the power button to start simulation. From the Fig.3.5.6, it can be seen that readings of voltmeter for measuring U2 is 20V, the readings of ammeter for measuring current I1 is-10A, these results are consistent with the previous calculation results in Matlab, so it is proved that the simulation is correct.

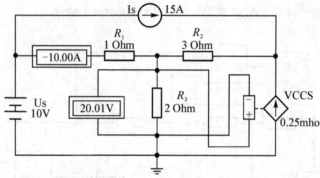

Fig.3.5.6 EWB Simulation Diagram

Problems

3-1 For the topological graph shown in Fig.3-1, draw four different trees. What is the number of tree? What is the number of branches?

3-2 In a topological graph as shown in Fig.3-2, a tree is indicated with the bold line. Try to find out all the basic loops and the basic cut sets. What is the number of independent nodes, the number of independent loops and the number of independent meshes?

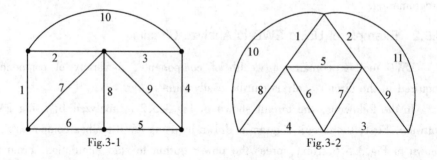

Fig.3-1   Fig.3-2

3-3 For the circuit shown in Fig.3-3, find all branch currents by using branch method.

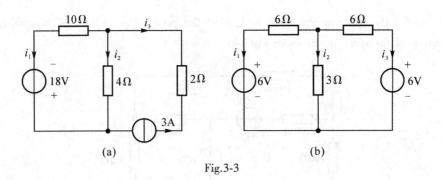

Fig.3-3

3-4 For the circuits shown in Fig. 3-4a, find the branch currents i_1 by applying branch method. Find the power of 1A current source in Fig.3-4b.

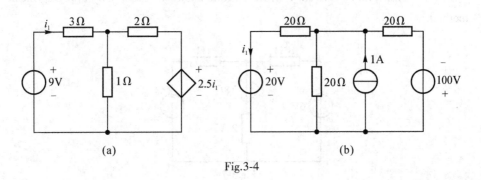

Fig.3-4

3-5 For the circuits shown in Fig.3-5, given: $U_{S1} = 10V$, $U_{S2} = 12V$, $U_{S3} = 16V$, $R_1 = 2\Omega$, $R_2 = 4\Omega$, $R_3 = 6\Omega$, find all branch currents by applying branch method and mesh method respectively.

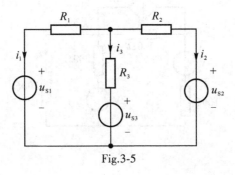

Fig.3-5

3-6 By applying mesh method, find the power P_{S1} and P_{S2} of two voltage sources of the circuits shown in Fig.3-6.

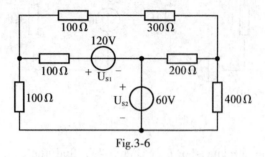

Fig.3-6

3-7 Find branch current i of the circuits shown in Fig.3-7 by applying mesh method.

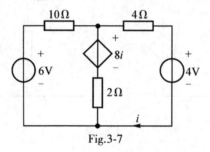

Fig.3-7

3-8 For the circuits shown in Fig.3-8, find branch current I_A by applying mesh method, and find the power of controlled source.

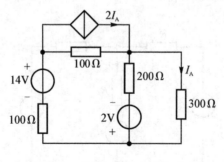

Fig.3-8

3-9 For the circuits shown in Fig. 3-9, find the power of 4Ω resistor by applying mesh method.

3-10 For the circuits shown in Fig. 3-10, find the voltage u of current source.

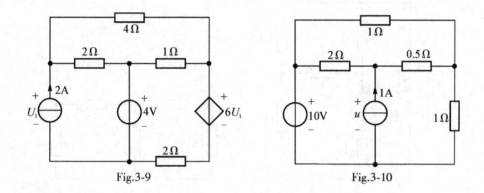

Fig.3-9   Fig.3-10

3-11 For the circuits shown in Fig. 3-11, list its mesh equations and loop equations respectively.

3-12 For the circuits shown in Fig.3-12, its mesh equations are given as:
$$\begin{cases} 2i_1+i_2=4\text{V} \\ 4i_2=8\text{V} \end{cases}$$

Find all element parameters and the power of two voltage sources.

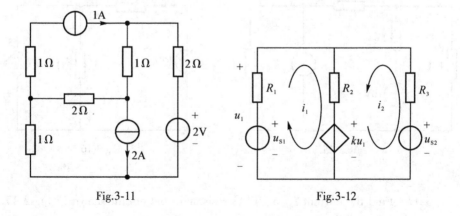

Fig.3-11   Fig.3-12

3-13 For the circuits shown in Fig.3-13, find all mesh currents.

3-14 For the circuits shown in Fig.3-14, find the power of current source by applying node analysis.

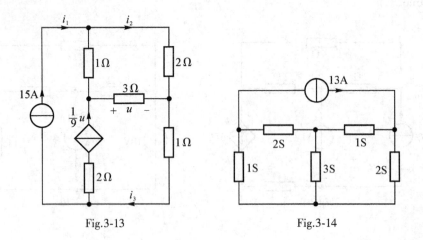

Fig.3-13 Fig.3-14

3-15 For the circuits shown in Fig.3-15, find u and i by applying node analysis.

3-16 For the circuits shown in Fig.3-16, find u_1 and i by applying node analysis.

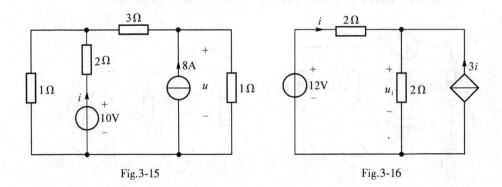

Fig.3-15 Fig.3-16

3-17 Find the current I_{AB} of 50kΩ resistor in the circuit shown in Fig.3-17.

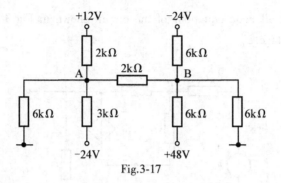

Fig.3-17

3-18 For the circuits shown in Fig.3-18, find the voltage u and the power of controlled source by applying node analysis.

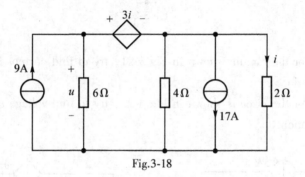

Fig.3-18

3-19 List node equations of the circuit shown in Fig.3-19 (S is Siemens).

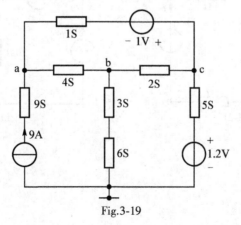

Fig.3-19

3-20 List all node equations of the circuit shown in Fig.3-20 which can be used to find voltage U_0.

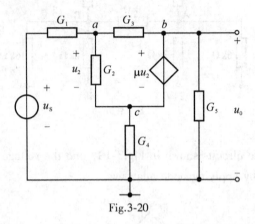

Fig.3-20

3-21 For the circuits shown in Fig.3-21, try to find current i just by listing only one equation.

3-22 For the circuits shown in Fig.3-22, try to find voltage u just by listing only one equation.

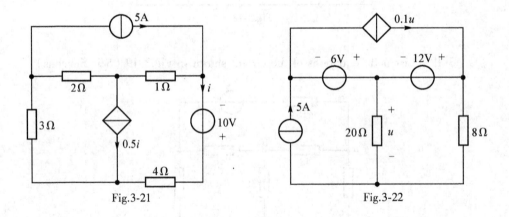

Fig.3-21   Fig.3-22

Chapter 4
Circuit Theorems

In previous chapters, equivalent circuits techniques and systematic analysis methods of circuit had been discussed. Equivalent circuits are very practical and can be applied to simplify the circuit and decrease the amount of computation. However, it is generally suitable for solving simpler circuits. And it is not convenient to apply in solving complex circuits or some special circuits. Systematic analysis methods are very powerful methods and can be applied to computer program. Its disadvantage is requiring to solve a set of simultaneous equations. If the number of network branch is more, the amount of computation will also be very large. So, It is a little difficult to solve these simultaneous equations.

In this chapter, some important network Theorems for linear resistance circuits will be discussed in order to further understand the properties of linear resistive circuits. They are superposition theorem and substitution theorem, thevenin's Theorem, Norton's Theorem, Tellegen's theorem and the reciprocity Theorem.

The theorems discussed in this chapter play an important role in circuit theory. These theorems can be applied not just to analyze the complex DC circuits, but also to analyze the AC circuits. Mastering these theorems is very important for learning the whole course of electric circuit and subsequent courses.

4.1 Superposition Theorem

Superposition Theorem discussed in this section is an important Theorem in circuit theory. It is the fundamental Theorem of linear circuits. Some other circuit Theorems introduced later can also be deduced based on Superposition Theorem.

4.1.1 Statement of Superposition Theorem

The circuits consisting of independent power sources and linear elements (linear resistors, linear controlled source etc) are called linear resistive circuits. The circuit equations which describes relationships between voltage and current of linear resistive circuits are a set of linear algebraic equations in which voltages and currents are selected as variables. Generally, the independent sources which are used as the input or excitation of circuits are often written in the right-hand side of the equations. By solving these equations, the voltage and current of each branch (also known as the output or responses) are derived and they are linear functions of all independent voltage sources u_S or current source i_S. Such linear relationship between circuit responses and excitations i_S are called superposition. It is an important basic properties of linear circuits.

Now, let's illustrate superposition with an example of a linear circuit shown in Fig.4.1.1a.

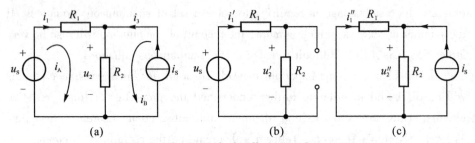

Fig.4.1.1 The Example for Illustrating Superposition

If current i_1 is selected as the response to be found, mesh method can be applied. First, two mesh currents i_A, i_B are assigned as shown in the Fig 4.1.1a. Then, the mesh equations of circuit can be listed as follows:

$$\left. \begin{array}{l} (R_1+R_2)i_A+R_2i_B=u_S \\ i_B=i_S \end{array} \right\} \quad (4.1.1)$$

By solving above equations, the current i_1 is

$$i_1=i_A=\frac{u_s}{R_1+R_2}-\frac{R_2}{R_1+R_2}i_s$$

Let

$$i_1'=i_1\big|_{i_S=0}=\frac{1}{R_1+R_2}u_S$$

4.1 Superposition Theorem

to be the current of resistor R_1 contributed by the voltage source u_S only. and let

$$i_1'' = i_1 \big|_{u_S=0} = \frac{-R_2}{R_1+R_2} i_S$$

to be the current of resistor R_1 contributed by the current source i_S only. Then, the total current i_1 can be derived by Superposition as

$$i_1 = i_1' + i_1''$$

It indicates that current i_1 can be derived by superposition.

Similarly, the voltage u_2 can also be derived by superposition, as follows

$$u_2 = \frac{R_2}{R_1+R_2} u_S + \frac{R_1 R_2}{R_1+R_2} i_S = u_2' + u_2''$$

where,

$$u_2' = u_2 \big|_{i_S=0} = \frac{R_2}{R_1+R_2} u_S$$

$$u_2'' = u_2 \big|_{u_S=0} = \frac{R_1 R_2}{R_1+R_2} i_S$$

From the evaluation above, it can be see that both current i_1 and voltage u_2 are superimposed by two terms.

The first term i_1' and u_1' is obtained by setting the independent voltage source to 0 ($u_s = 0$), it is the contribution generated by single independent current source only.

The second term i_1'' and u_1'' is obtained by setting the independent current source to 0 ($i_s = 0$), it is the contribution generated by single independent voltage source only.

So, it shows that the responses produced by the two independent sources at the time is equal to sum of the individual responses contributed by each independent source. This additive property of linear circuits is known as superposition theorem.

In General, the superposition theorem states that the voltage across (or current through) an element in a linear circuit is the algebraic sum of the voltages across (or currents through) that element due to each independent source acting alone.

In other words, as long as a unique solution exists in the circuit, any node voltages, branch voltages and branch currents in a linear resistive circuit can be expressed as

$$y = H_1 u_{S1} + H_2 u_{S2} + \cdots + H_m u_{Sm} + K_1 i_{S1} + K_2 i_{S2} + \cdots + K_n i_{Sn} \quad (4.1.2)$$

where $u_{sk}(k=1,2,\cdots,m)$ represents voltage of independent voltage source in the circuit; $i_{sk}(k=1,2,\cdots,n)$ represents current of independent current source in the circuit. $H_k(k=1,2,\cdots,m)$ and $K_k(k=1,2,\cdots,n)$ are constants and they are determined by circuit parameters, circuit structure. They have nothing to do with independent power sources.

When calculating voltages or currents contributed only by one independent source, the other independent voltage sources must be treated as short circuits ($u_s = 0$), and other independent current sources must be treated as open circuit($i_s = 0$).

Every term $y(u_{sk}) = H_k u_{sk}$ or $y(i_{sk}) = K_k i_{sk}$ in the expression (4.1.2) is the response contributed only by one independent power source and all other independent power sources are set to zero. It can be seen that this response is proportional to the input or source. It embodies a homogeneous property of linear circuit.

Expression (4.1.2) also shows that, the responses generated by the interaction of several independent sources in linear resistive circuits, is equal to sum of individual responses contributed by each independent power source. It embodies an additive property of a linear circuit. superposition theorem is the reflection of these fundamental natures of linear circuits. It is widely applied to simplify the analysis and calculation of linear circuits.

It needs to note that: the power of linear circuits does not obey superposition theorem. It is not a linear function of voltage or current. So, total power of an element contributed by all independent source is not equal to the sum of power contributed by each independent source. For example, the power of an element in a linear circuit excited by two sources can be written as the following expressions.

$$p = ui = (u' + u'')(i' + i'') = u'i' + u'i'' + u''i' + u''i'' \neq u'i' + u''i'' = p_1 + p_2$$

4.1.2 The Application of the Superposition Theorem

By applying the basic property of linear networks embodied in superposition theorem, the analysis and calculation of linear circuits can be simplified.

When superposition theorem is applied, the following points should be noted:

(1) Superposition theorem can only be applied to the linear circuits with unique solutions. It can be applied to find voltages or currents and cannot be applied to find power. Because power is not a linear function of voltage or current.

(2) For a linear circuit containing only one independent source, the voltage or current is proportional to the source.

(3) When superimpose, pay attention to the reference directions of the voltages and currents. It is actually a algebraic sum.

(4) When applying superposition, each circuit structure cannot be changed except the sources is replaced by short circuit or open circuit.

(5) If there is a controlled source in the circuit, it cannot be treated as independent source and cannot be set to zero. In fact, it must be kept in the circuit and treated it as a special kind of resistor.

(6) By applying the superposition theorem to find voltages and currents of linear circuits consisting of several independent power sources, you can find the individual component contributed by each source. You can also divide sources into several groups, calculate the component contributed by each groups of sources, then add them to find total result.

Example 4.1.1 The circuit is shown in Fig.4.1.2a. Given:

(1) $u_{S1} = 5V, u_{S2} = 10V$

(2) $u_{S1} = 10V, u_{S2} = 5V$

(3) $u_{S1} = 20\cos\omega t V, u_{S2} = 15\sin 2\omega t V$

Find voltage u by applying Superposition.

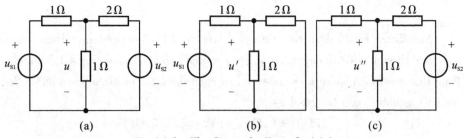

Fig.4.1.2 The Circuit for Example 4.1.1

Solution First, drawing the circuits driven by each source u_{S1} and u_{S2}, as shown in Fig.4.1.2b and c. Next, find two components of u contributed each source u_{S1} and u_{S2} as follows

$$u' = H_1 u_{S1} = \frac{2/3}{1+2/3} u_{S1} = 0.4 u_{S1}$$

$$u'' = H_2 u_{S2} = \frac{0.5}{2+0.5} u_{S2} = 0.2 u_{S2}$$

Finally, based on Superposition Theorem, the total voltage can be derived as

$$u = u' + u'' = 0.4 u_{S1} + 0.2 u_{S2}$$

For three given cases, substituting the value of u_{S1} and u_{S2} in the given conditions into above expression, there are:

(1) $u = 0.4 \times 5\text{V} + 0.2 \times 10\text{V} = 4\text{V}$

(2) $u = 0.4 \times 10\text{V} + 0.2 \times 5\text{V} = 5\text{V}$

(3) $u = [0.4 \times 20\cos\omega t + 0.2 \times 15\sin 2\omega t]\text{V} = [8\cos\omega t + 3\sin 2\omega t]\text{V}$

Example 4.1.2 The circuit is shown in Fig.4.1.3, it is given: $r = 2$, find the current i and voltage u by applying Superposition Theorem.

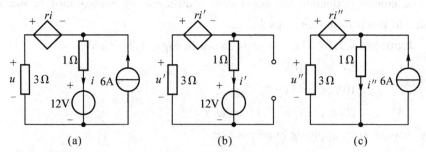

Fig.4.1.3 The Circuit for Example 4.1.2

Solution First, draw two circuits driven by 12V independent voltage source only and driven by 6A independent current source only, as shown Fig.4.1.3 b and c. Note that controlled sources are reserved in each circuit. For circuit in Fig.4.1.3b, its KVL equation can be listed as

$$(2\Omega)i' + (1\Omega)i' + 12\text{V} + (3\Omega)i' = 0$$

It can be derived that

$$i' = -2\text{A}$$

$$u' = -(3\Omega)i' = 6\text{V}$$

For circuit in Fig.4.1.3C, it's KVL equation can be listed as follows

$$(2\Omega)i'' + (1\Omega)i'' + (3\Omega)(i''-6\text{A}) = 0$$

It can be derived that

$$i'' = 3\text{A}$$
$$u'' = (3\Omega)(6\text{A}-i'') = 9\text{V}$$

Finally, total current and voltage are derived based on Superposition Theorem as

$$i = i' + i'' = -2\text{A} + 3\text{A} = 1\text{A}$$
$$u = u' + u'' = 6\text{V} + 9\text{V} = 15\text{V}$$

Example 4.1.3 Applying Superposition Theorem to find voltage u showing in the circuit in the Fig.4.1.4a.

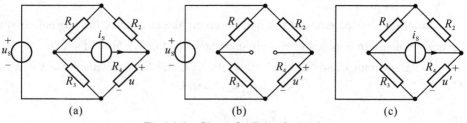

Fig.4.1.4 Circuit for Example 4.1.3

Solution First, draw the circuits driven by independent voltage source u_S and independent current source i_S respectively, as shown in Fig.4.1.4b, c. Next, find u' and u'' respectively.

$$u' = \frac{R_4}{R_2 + R_4} u_S$$

$$u'' = \frac{R_2 R_4}{R_2 + R_4} i_S$$

And finally superimpose u' and u'' to derive the sum of voltages based on Superposition Theorem as follows.

$$u = u' + u'' = \frac{R_4}{R_2 + R_4}(u_S + R_2 i_S)$$

Example 4.1.4 The circuit shown in Fig.4.1.5a is a circuit containing controlled sources. It is given: $u_s = 10\text{V}$, $i_s = 2\text{A}$, try to find node voltages u_{n1} and branch currents i_1 and i_2.

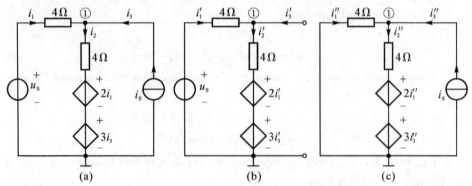

Fig.4.1.5 The Circuit Diagram for Example 4.1.4

Solution Based on Superposition Theorem, the analysis of the original circuit is transformed into analysis of two circuits shown in Fig.4.1.5b and 4.1.5c.

For the circuit shown in Fig.4.1.5b, its KVL and KCL equations are listed as
$$4i'_1 + 4i'_2 + 2i'_1 - 10 = 0$$
$$i'_1 = i'_2$$
By solving above two equations, it is derived that
$$i'_1 = i'_2 = 1\text{A}$$
Then, from the branch KVL equation
$$u'_{n1} = u_s - 4i'_1$$
It can be derived that
$$u'_{n1} = 10 - 4 \times 1 = 6\text{V}$$
For the circuit shown in Fig.4.1.5c, its node equation is listed as
$$\left(\frac{1}{4} + \frac{1}{4}\right) u''_{n1} = i_s + \frac{1}{4}(2i''_1 + 3i''_3)$$
And
$$i''_3 = i_s, \quad i''_1 = -\frac{u''_{n1}}{4}$$
Substituting them into above node equations, it is derived that
$$u''_{n1} = 5.6\text{V}$$

$$i_1'' = -1.4\text{A}$$

According to the KCL, it is known that
$$i_2'' = i_1'' + i_3''$$

Substituted given i_1'' and i_3'' into the above expression, it is derived that
$$i_2'' = -1.4 + 2 = 0.6(\text{A})$$

Finally, by superimposing, it is derived that
$$u_{n1} = u_{n1}' + u_{n1}'' = 6 + 5.6 = 11.6(\text{V})$$
$$i_1 = i_1' + i_1'' = 1 - 1.4 = -0.4(\text{A})$$
$$i_2 = i_2' + i_2'' = 1 + 0.6 = 1.6(\text{A})$$

4.1.3 Homogenous Theorem

Homogenous Theorem can be stated as: In linear circuits, if all excitations (voltage sources and current sources) increase or decrease k times (k is the real constant), the responses (voltages and currents) will also increase or decrease k times.

It should be noted that all excitations must increase or decrease k times in the same time, otherwise it will result in erroneous results. Homogenous Theorem can be proved easily by applying Superposition Theorem.

Homogeneous Theorem is especially effective to analyze a ladder circuit.

Example 4.1.5 A ladder circuit is shown in Fig.4.1.6. (1) Given: $I_5 = 1\text{A}$, find each branch current and source voltage U_S; (2) if U_S is changed to 120V, find each branch current again.

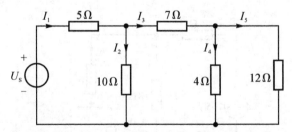

Fig.4.1.6 The Circuit Diagram for Example 4.1.5

Solution (1) Applying KCL and KVL backward from I_5 to calculate each branch current:

$$I_4 = 12I_5/4 = 3(A)$$
$$I_3 = I_4 + I_5 = 4A$$
$$I_2 = (7I_3 + 12I_5)/10 = 4(A)$$
$$I_1 = I_2 + I_3 = 8A$$

So
$$U_S = 5I_1 + 10I_2 = 80(V)$$

(2) Due to $U_S = 120V$, it is 1.5 times of the original voltage 80V. According to homogeneous Theorem of linear circuits, it can be asserted that all voltages and currents in the circuit will be increased to 1.5 times of original value, i.e.,

$$I_1 = 1.5 \times 8A = 12A$$
$$I_2 = I_3 = 1.5 \times 4A = 6A$$
$$I_4 = 1.5 \times 3A = 4.5A$$
$$I_5 = 1.5 \times 1A = 1.5A$$

The above method of applying homogeneous Theorem in a ladder circuits is also called "backward method" or "Mountain climbing method". Calculation is starting from the most far away from the power source, and then it is gradually evaluating back to the voltage source. By finding the ratio of source voltage to actual source values, finally, the actual value of voltages and currents can be derived. In order to facilitate the calculation, the branch current can be selected as a relatively simple values such as $I_5 = 1A$ and to begin analysis.

Example 4.1.6 Find all currents and voltages marked in circuit as shown in Fig.4.1.7.

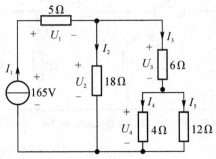

Fig.4.1.7 The Circuit for Example 4.1.6

Solution Applying the Homogeneous Theorem. Set a fixed value to I_5 first, and then calculate backward.

Let $I_5 = 1\text{A}$, by applying KCL and KVL, there are
$$U_4 = 12I_5 = 12\text{V}$$
$$I_4 = 12/4 = 3\text{A}, \quad I_3 = I_4 + I_5 = 4\text{A},$$
$$U_3 = 6I_3 = 24\text{V}, \quad U_2 = U_3 + U_4 = 36\text{V},$$
$$I_2 = 36/18 = 2\text{A}, \quad I_1 = I_2 + I_3 = 4 + 2 = 6\text{A},$$
$$U_1 = 5I_1 = 6 \times 5 = 30\text{V}$$

So, the source viltage is
$$U_s = U_1 + U_2 = 66\text{V}$$

Since the given source voltage $U_s = 165\text{V}$ is 2.5 times to the derived value 66V, according to Homogenous Theorem, the voltages and currents in the circuit will increase 2.5 times, that is,
$$I_1 = 15\text{A}, \ I_2 = 5\text{A}, \ I_3 = 10\text{A}, \ I_4 = 7.5\text{A}, \ I_5 = 2.5\text{A},$$
$$U_1 = 75\text{V}, \ U_3 = 24\text{V}, \ U_2 = 90\text{V}.$$

4.2 Substitution Theorem

4.2.1 Statement of Substitution Theorem

For any branch k in a circuit, if the branch voltage u_k and current i_k are given, that the branch k can be substituted by an independent voltage source with voltage u_k, or an independent current source with current i_k. After substitution, all voltage and current in the circuit maintain the original value and will not be changed.

Substitution Theorem can also be stated as follows:

For a network N consisting of a one-port resistive network N_R and an arbitrary one-port network N_L, as shown in Fig.4.2.1a.

(1) If there is a unique solution for port voltage u, a voltage source with voltage u can be used to replace one-port network N_L, only if there is still a unique solution for the network replaced [as shown in Fig.4.2.1b], and all voltages and currents in the one-port network N_R will not be affected.

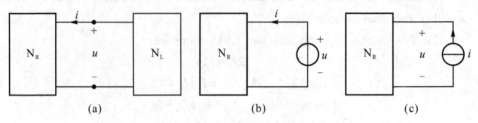

Fig.4.2.1 Substitution Theorem

(2) If there is a unique solution for the port current I, the one-port network N_L can be replaced by a current source with current I, only if there is still the a unique solution for network replaced [as shown in Fig.4.2.1c], and all voltages and currents in the one-port N_R will not be affected.

Value of the Substitution Theorem is that if a branch voltage or a branch current in a network is given, an independent source can used to replace that branch or port network N_L to simplify the analysis and calculation of circuit.

Substitution theorem has no special requirements on one-port network N_L. For example, it may be nonlinear resistor one-port network and non-resistive one-port network.

Example 4.2.1 For the circuit shown in Fig.4.2.2A, $I = 2A$. Find power supplied by 20V voltage source.

Solution Since $I = 2A$. the part of circuit including the resistor R_X and single-port network N_2 in Fig.4.2.2a can be replaced by a 2A current source, as shown in Fig.4.2.2b. The mesh equations of this circuit can be listed as follows

$$(4\Omega)I_1 - (2\Omega) \times 2A = -20V$$

So, it is derived that

$$I_1 = -4A$$

Then, the power supplied by 20V voltage sources is

$$P = -20V \times (-4A) = 80W.$$

A few points to be noted:

(1) The k branch mentioned in the Theorem can be passive element, such as a resistive element. It can also be a active element, such as a voltage source in series with a resistor.

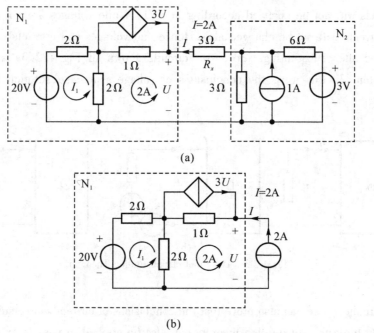

Fig.4.2.2 The Circuit for Example 4.2.1

(2) It is not allowed that the branch being substituted includes controlling variable of a controlled source which is placed on non-substituted part of the circuit, or vice versa, i.e., the substituted part must not be coupled with no-substituted part.

4.2.2 Proof of Substitution Theorem

Now, let's prove the conclusions of voltage source substitution. As shown in Fig.4.2.3a, suppose that voltage of the resistive branch k of circuit is given, then, two voltage sources can be connected in series with the resistive branch k, as shown in Fig.4.2.3b. Two voltage sources have same voltage U_k and opposite direction. Since the voltage U_k of the resistive branch k offsets with the voltage source U_k, the original circuit is equivalent to the circuit shown in Fig.4.2.3c.

Because the constraint relationships of all branches in two circuits shown in Fig.4.2.3a and c are exactly the same except the branch k, and the voltage of the branch k in the substituted circuit is also fixed as U_k, thus, the voltage of all other branches will not be changed according to KVL. While voltages are not changed, the currents will not be changed also. Hence, all voltages and currents will not be changed after substituting. i.e., two circuits shown in Fig.4.2.3a and c are equivalent. In this way, the conclusions of voltage source substitution had been proved.

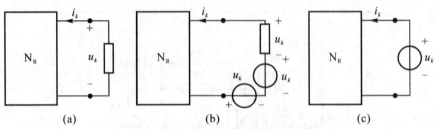

Fig.4.2.3 The Proof of Substitution Theorem

Similarly, we can also prove that the conclusions of current source substitution.

By the way, substitution theorem can also be applied to non-linear and time-varying circuit.

Example 4.2.2 For the circuit shown in Fig.4.2.4a, capacitor current is given: $i_C(t) = 2.5e^{-t}$ A. Find $i_1(t)$ and $i_2(t)$ by applying Substitution Theorem.

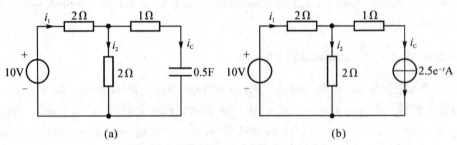

Fig.4.2.4 The Circuit for Example 4.2.2

Solution Although the circuit is not a linear resistive circuit, due to $i_C(t)$ is given, a current source with current $i_C(t) = 2.5e^{-t}$ A can be used to substitute the capacitor in the circuit of Fig.4.2.4a, then a linear resistive circuit is obtained, as shown in Fig.4.2.4b. Finally, by applying Superposition Theorem, currents are derived as follows:

$$i_1(t) = \frac{10}{2+2}A + \frac{2}{2+2} \times 2.5e^{-t}A = (2.5 + 1.25e^{-t})A$$

$$i_2(t) = \frac{10}{2+2}A - \frac{2}{2+2} \times 2.5e^{-t}A = (2.5 - 1.25e^{-t})A$$

Example 4.2.3 For the circuit shown in Fig.4.2.5a, $g = 2S$. Find current I.

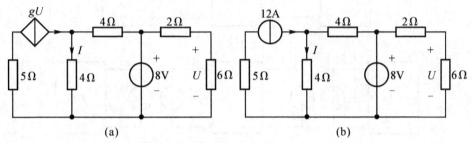

Fig.4.2.5 The Circuit for Example 4.2.3

Solution First, by applying voltage division formula, the controlling voltage u of controlled source can be derived as

$$U = \frac{6}{2+6} \times 8V = 6V$$

Since the current of controlled current source $gU = 12A$ is given, a 12A current source can be used to replace the controlled current source, as shown in fig 4.2.5b. Now there is no controlled source in the circuit. So, it is easy to find current I by applying Superposition Theorem.

$$I = \left(\frac{4}{4+4} \times 12 + \frac{8}{4+4}\right)A = 7A$$

By applying substitution theorem (or complemented by the source transfer), a large network can be torn into several smaller networks. Here is a example.

Example 4.2.4 A large linear resistive network is consist of 3 sub-network a, b and c, as shown in Fig.4.2.6a. Divide it into three small sub-networks.

Solution Assume that u_1 and u_2 are given, according to Substitution Theorem, for sub-network a, the combination of sub-network b and c can be replaced by a voltage source u_1. For sub-network b, the sub-network b and c can be replaced by two voltage sources u_1 and u_2 respectively. For sub-network c, the combination of sub-network a and b can be replaced by a voltage source u_2. So, the original large network can be torn into three small sub-networks, as shown in Fig.4.2.6b.

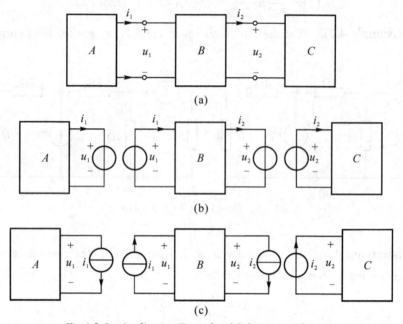

Fig.4.2.6 Application Example of Substitution Theorem

Likewise, this large network can also be torn as another kind of three small sub-networks, as shown in Fig.4.2.6c.

4.3 Thevenin's Theorem and Norton's Theorem

To analyze a electric network in practical engineering, it is normally not required to find all voltages or currents of the network. Most of time, it is often only required to find the voltage or current of one branch or one component in the network. In this case, a better way to solve problem is to apply Thevenin's Theorem or Norton's Theorem which will be discussed in this chapter. Thevenin's Theorem and Norton's Theorem provide a general method for finding the equivalent circuit of active one-port network. They are very useful tools to simplify the analysis and calculation of circuit. We will discuss Thevenin's Theorem first and then Norton's Theorem.

4.3.1 Thevenin's Theorem

4.3.1.1 The Statement of Thevenin's Theorem

In terms of the port characteristics, a linear resistive one-port network N with independent sources is equivalent to one-port network consisting of a voltage source u_{oc} in series with a resistor R_o, as shown in Fig.4.3.1a. The source voltage u_{oc} is equal to the open circuit voltage u_{oc} when port of network is open circuit. The resistance R_o is the equivalent resistance of the passive network N_o which is derived by setting all independent sources inside the original network to zero, as shown in Fig.4.3.1b.

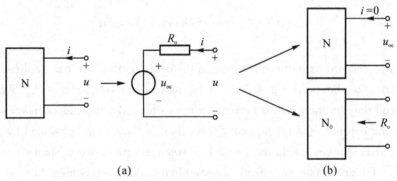

(a)　　　　　　　　　　　(b)

Fig.4.3.1　The Illustration for Thevenin's Theorem

R_o is called Thevenin's equivalent resistance. In the electronic circuits, if a one-port network is considered as a power source, this resistance is often referred to as the output resistance, written as R_o. If the one-port network is considered as a load, it is called the input resistance and written as R_i.

4.3.1.2 Proof of Thevenin's Theorem

Thevenin's Theorem can be proved by applying substitution theorem and superposition theorem.

Considering the circuit shown in Fig.4.3.2a, N is an active one-port network which is connected to the external circuit or load. It is assumed that port current i is given. Then, by applying substitution theorem, the external circuit or load can be replaced by a current source i, and it's voltage is u, as shown in Fig.4.3.2b.

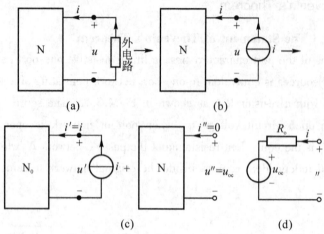

Fig.4.3.2 Proof of Thevenin's Theorem

Also, according to the superposition theorem, port voltage can be divided into two parts, as shown in Fig.4.3.2c. First part is the voltage $u' = R_o i$ Which is produced only by the external current source i when all independent power sources inside the network N is set to zero. Second part is the voltage produced by all the independent sources inside the network N when external current source i is set to zero ($i=0$) or the port of network is open circuit. Obviously, this voltage is known as open circuit voltage and can be represented as $u''=u_{oc}$. Then, by add them, it is derived that

$$u = u' + u'' = R_o i + u_{oc} \qquad (4.3.1)$$

This expression is the same as the characteristic equation of the circuit shown in Fig.4.3.2d. So, it had been proved that a linear resistive one-port network is equivalent to a voltage source u_{oc} in series with a resistor R_o. The condition of applying Thevenin's theorem is that there must be a unique solution to the circuits when it's port is driven by an external current source.

Therefore, if the open circuit voltage u_{oc} and equivalent resistance R_o of the network N_o, which is obtained by setting all independent power sources inside the network to zero (replaced independent voltage sources with short circuits and independent current sources with open circuit instead), are found, Thevenin equivalent circuit of the one-port network can be derived.

Thevenin's Theorem is very useful and widely applied in network analysis.

Example 4.3.1 Find the Thevenin's equivalent circuit of the circuit shown in Fig.4.3.3a.

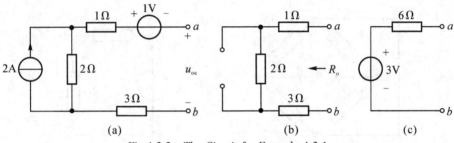

Fig.4.3.3 The Circuit for Example 4.3.1

Solution First, set a reference direction for open circuit voltage u_{oc} on port of the circuit as shown in the Fig 4.3.3a. Note that $i=0$, so open circuit voltage u_{oc} can be derived as

$$u_{oc} = -1\text{V} + (2\Omega) \times 2\text{A} = 3\text{V}$$

Next, by replacing 1V voltage source in the circuit by a short circuit and replacing 2A current source by an open circuit, as shown in Fig.4.3.3b. Then, resistance R_o can be derived as

$$R_o = 1\Omega + 2\Omega + 3\Omega = 6\Omega$$

Finally, according to the reference direction of the u_{oc}, Thevenin equivalent circuit can be drawn as shown in Fig.4.3.3c.

Example 4.3.2 Find the current i flowing through resistor R_L in the bridge circuit shown in Fig.4.3.4a.

Solution First, disconnect the load resistor R_L, as shown in Fig.4.3.4b circuits. By applying voltage division formula, open circuit voltage u_{oc} can be derived as

$$u_{oc} = \left(\frac{R_2}{R_1 + R_2} - \frac{R_4}{R_3 + R_4} \right) u_S \quad (4.3.2)$$

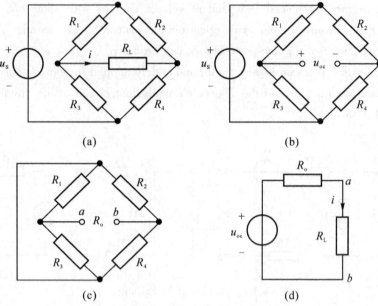

Fig.4.3.4 The Circuit for Example 4.3.2

Next, independent voltage source is replaced by short circuit, as shown in Fig.4.3.4c, then resistance R_o can be derived

$$R_o = \left(\frac{R_1 R_2}{R_1 + R_2} + \frac{R_3 R_4}{R_3 + R_4}\right) \tag{4.3.3}$$

Finally, by replacing the single-port network with its Thevenin's equivalent circuit, as shown in Fig.4.3.4d. The current I can be derived by using Ohm's Law

$$i = \frac{u_{oc}}{R_o + R_L} \tag{4.3.4}$$

4.3.1.3 Two Ways to Find Resistance R_o

(1) Testing-probe method: sets all independent sources in network N to zero, keeps all controlled sources, connects a voltage source to the port of the network N, as shown in Fig.4.3.5.

After the port current i is found, R_o can be derived by applying Ohm's law

$$R_o = u/i$$

Attention: A current source i can also be connected to the port of network N_0. Then, After finding port voltage u is found, R_o can also be found by using Ohm's law.

4.3 Thevenin's Theorem and Norton's Theorem

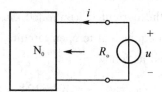

Fig.4.3.5 Test-Probe Method

(2) Open-short circuit method.

From Thevenin equivalent circuit, there are

$$u = u_{oc} - R_o i$$

Let port of network N_0 to be short circuit, i.e., set $u = 0$, then:

$$u_{oc} - R_o i_{SC} = 0$$

or,

$$R_o = u_{oc} / i_{SC}$$

It can be seen that if open circuit voltage u_{oc} and short circuit current i_{SC} are known, the equivalent resistance R_o can be derived by applying Ohm's law.

Example 4.3.3 Find the Thevenin's equivalent circuit for the circuit shown in Fig.4.3.6a.

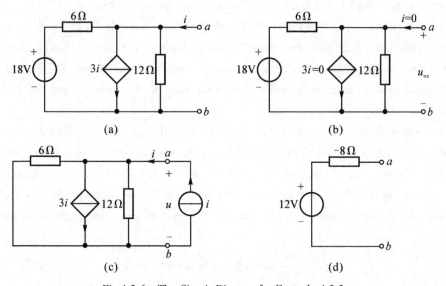

Fig.4.3.6 The Circuit Diagram for Example 4.3.3

Solution The reference direction of voltage u_{oc} is assigned as shown in Fig.4.3.6b. Due to $i = 0$, the current of controlled current source $3i = 0$. So, the controlled current source is equivalent to open circuit. By applying voltage division formula, U_{OC} can be derived as follows

$$u_{oc} = \frac{12}{12+6} \times 18\text{V} = 12\text{V}$$

To find resistance R_o, first, 18V independent voltage source is replaced by short circuit and controlled sources is reserved. Next, an external current source I is connected between terminal a and b of the port, as shown in Fig.4.3.6c. Finally, by evaluating from the expression of port voltage, the resistance R_o can be found as follows.

$$u = \frac{(6 \times 12)\,\Omega}{6+12}(i-3i) = (-8\Omega)i$$

$$R_o = u/i = -8\Omega$$

So, Thevenin equivalent circuit obtained is shown in Fig.4.3.6d.

Thevenin's theorem requires that the elements inside the load network N_L does not coupled with the elements outside the network N_L. Besides, it is also required that there is an unique solution for the whole network. As for the property of network N_L, there is not limitation. It can be nonlinear or linear.

Example 4.3.4 Find currents I_1 and I_2 of the circuit shown in Fig.4.3.7a.

Solution Note that the circuit in this problem is a nonlinear resistor circuit. It cannot be solved by mesh/node analysis or Superposition. However, Thevenin's Theorem can be used to simplify the linear part of the circuit, and then this problem can be solved.

Although the circuit in Fig.4.3.7a is a nonlinear resistive circuit, if two branches with ideal diodes are removed, the remaining circuit becomes an active linear resistive single port circuit, as shown in Fig.4.3.7b. It can be reduced by applying Thevenin's Theorem. Now, let's find this Thevenin's equivalent circuit. First, for the circuit shown in Fig.4.3.7b, its open circuit voltage can be derived as

$$U_{oc} = \frac{6}{3+6} \times 9\text{V} + 5\text{V} - (2\Omega) \times (4\text{A}) = 3\text{V}$$

Next, by setting all independent sources to zero, circuit shown in Fig.4.3.7c is derived. Its equivalent resistance can be derived as

$$R_o = \frac{3\times 6}{3+6}\Omega + 4\Omega + 2\Omega = 8\Omega$$

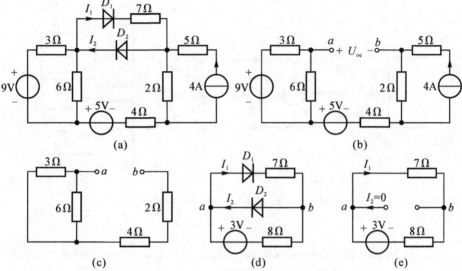

Fig.4.3.7 The Circuit for Example 4.3.4

Next, by replacing the linear resistive single-port circuit with its Thevenin's equivalent circuit of 3V voltage source in series with a 8 Ohms, a simplifying circuit is obtained, as shown in Fig.4.3.7d. Due to the ideal diode D_2 is reverse biased, it is equivalent to open circuit, namely $I_2 = 0$. And ideal diode D_1 is forward-biased, it is equivalent to short circuits, so, the circuit in Fig.4.3.7d can be reduced to a very simple equivalent circuit, as shown in Fig.4.3.10e. Hence, it is easy to find current I_1 in the circuit of Fig.4.3.7e by applying Ohm's law.

$$I_1 = \frac{3}{8+7}A = 0.3A.$$

4.3.2 Norton's Theorem

Norton's Theorem can be stated as follows:

In terms of the port characteristics, any linear resistive one-port network N with independent sources is equivalent to a current source i_{sc} in parallel with a resistor R_o, as shown in Fig.4.3.8a. The current i_{sc} of independent source is equal to the short circuit current of port in one-port network; The resistance R_o is an equivalent resistance of the network N_0 in which all the independent sources inside the N are set to zero, as shown in Fig.4.3.8b.

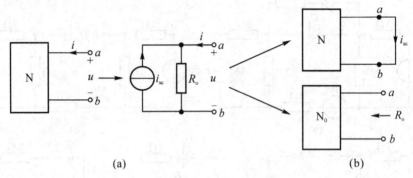

(a)   (b)

Fig.4.3.8   The Illustration for Norton's Theorem

i_{sc} is called the short-circuit current. R_o is also called Norton equivalent resistance and it is exactly the same as Thevenin equivalent resistance. The parallel circuit of current sources i_{sc} and resistor R_o is known as the Norton equivalent circuit of one-port network.

If the standard reference directions of port voltage and current are adopted, VCR equation of the port can be expressed as

$$i = \frac{1}{R_o} u - i_{sc} \qquad (4.3.5)$$

Proof of Norton's Theorem is similar to that of Thevenin's theorem.

It can be proved by using Substitution Theorem and superposition theorem.

First, assume that the voltage u is known. Based on substitution theorem, the external circuit or load of the network in Fig.4.3.9a can be replaced by a voltage source u, as shown in fig.4.3.9b.

Then, according to superposition theorem, the current of port will be the sum of two items contributed by each source.

$$i = i' + i'' = \frac{1}{R_o} u - i_{sc}$$

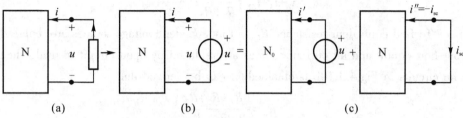

Fig.4.3.9 The Proof of Norton's Theorem

This expression shows the relationships between port voltage and port current. It is exactly the same as the expression 4.3.6. So, it can be seen that any linear resistive one-port network is equivalent to a current source i_{SC} in parallel with resistance R_0, provided by a unique solution existing in the circuit where an external voltage source is connected

Similar to Thevenin's theorem, Norton's theorem is also often applied in circuit analysis to find a voltage across and current through one branch. It is not suitable for finding all voltages and currents of a circuit.

Example 4.3.5 Find the Norton equivalent circuit for the circuit shown in Fig.4.3.13a.

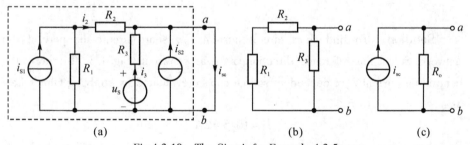

Fig.4.3.10 The Circuit for Example 4.3.5

Solution To find short circuit current i_{SC}, the single-port network is shorted from the external port. The reference direction of short-circuit current i_{SC} is marked as shown in Fig.4.3.10a. By applying KCL and VCR, short circuit current i_{SC} can be derived as

$$i_{sc} = i_2 + i_3 + i_{S2} = \frac{R_1}{R_1+R_2}i_{S1} + \frac{u_S}{R_3} + i_{S2}$$

To find equivalent resistance R_0, all independent voltage sources are replaced by short circuit and all current sources are replaced by open circuit instead, then the circuits in Fig.4.3.10b is obtained. It can be derived that

$$R_0 = \frac{(R_1+R_2)R_3}{R_1+R_2+R_3}$$

According to the reference direction of the i_{SC}, Norton equivalent circuit can be drawn as shown in Fig.4.3.3c.

Example 4.3.6 Find the Norton equivalent circuit for the circuit shown in Fig.4.3.11a.

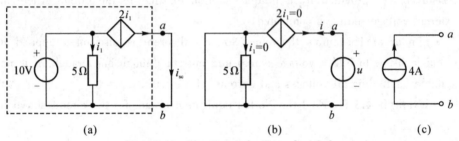

Fig.4.3.11 The Circuit for Example 4.3.6

Solution To find short circuit current i_{sc}, short circuit the port of the network. Select the reference direction of i_{sc} as shown in Fig.4.3.11, then, the controlling current i_1 of dependent source can be evaluated by applying Ohm's Law as

$$i_1 = 10/5 = 2\text{A}$$

So, short circuit current is

$$i_{sc} = 2i_1 = 4\text{A}$$

To find R_0, replace 10V voltage source with short circuit, applied a voltage source u to the port, as shown in Fig.4.3.11b. For $i_1 = 0$, so $i = -2i_1 = 0$. It is derived that

$$G_0 = i/u = 0 \quad \text{or} \quad R_0 = 1/G_0 = \infty$$

It can be seen that the single-port network is equivalent to 4A current source only, its Norton equivalent circuit can be drawn as shown in Fig.4.3.11c. Because it is not possible to find open circuit voltage u_{oc}, so there are not Thevenin's equivalent circuit existing for this circuit.

4.3.3 The Equivalent Circuit of Active Linear Resistive One-Port Network

It is known from Thevenin's theorem and Norton's theorem that an active linear resistive one-port network (as Fig.4.3.12a) is equivalent to a voltage source in series with a resistor (as Fig.4.3.12b), or a current source in parallel with a resistor (as Fig.4.3.12c). So, if u_{oc}, i_{sc} and R_o can be found, as shown in Fig.4.3.12 d, e, f, its Thevenin equivalent circuit or Norton equivalent circuit can be derived.

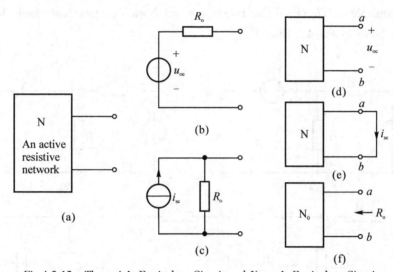

Fig.4.3.12 Thevenin's Equivalent Circuit and Norton's Equivalent Circuit

The main points of finding two equivalent circuits can be summarized as follows:

(1) General method for finding the open circuit voltage u_{oc}: first, disconnecting the load from the network, as shown in Fig.4.3.12d, next, find the open circuit voltage u_{oc} of the port with any method of network analysis.

(2) General method for finding the short circuit current i_{sc}: first, replace the

load with short circuit, as shown in Fig. 4.3.12e, then, find the short circuit current i_{sc} with any method of network analysis.

(3) General method for finding the Thevenin's equivalent resistance R_o: first, by replacing all independent voltage sources in the single-port network with short circuit and all independent current sources with open circuit, a passive single-port network N_0 is obtained, as shown in Fig.4.3.12f. Next, applying a external source to the port to drive the current to flow through the circuit. Then, evaluating the resistance R_0 by any method of circuit analysis. For a simple circuit, the resistance R_0 can be easily calculated just by using series-parallel reduction technique.

Otherwise, if any two quantities of the u_{oc}, i_{sc}, and R_0 are given, the third quantity can be derived with the following formulas.

$$R_o = u_{oc}/i_{sc} \quad u_{oc} = R_o i_{sc} \quad i_{sc} = u_{oc}/R_o \tag{4.3.6}$$

Example 4.3.7 Find the Thevenin's and Norton's equivalent circuit for the circuit shown in Fig.4.3.13a.

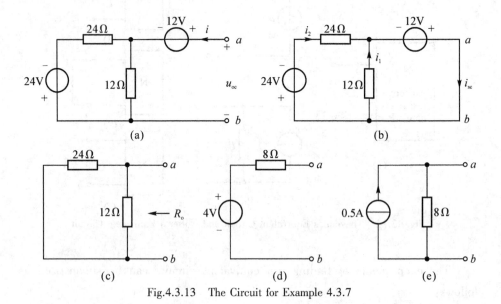

Fig.4.3.13 The Circuit for Example 4.3.7

Solution To find u_{oc}, assume that the reference direction of open circuit voltage u_{oc} is from a to b, as shown in Fig.4.3.13a. Then, by applying KVL, there are

4.3 Thevenin's Theorem and Norton's Theorem

$$u_{oc} = 12V + \frac{12}{12+24} \times (-24V) = 4V$$

To find i_{sc}, short circuit the port, and assume reference direction of the i_{sc} is from a to b, as shown in Fig.4.3.13b. Then, by applying KCL, there are

$$i_{sc} = i_1 + i_2 = \frac{12V}{12\Omega} + \frac{(-24+12)V}{24\Omega} = 0.5A$$

To find Thevenin's resistance R_o, replace all voltage sources inside the single-port network with short circuit, as shown in Fig.4.3.13c. Then, by applying the formula of paralleling resistor, Thevenin's resistance R_o can be derived as

$$R_o = \frac{12 \times 24}{12+24}\Omega = 8\Omega$$

Finally, with the results of $u_{oc} = 4V$, $i_{sc} = 0.5A$, $R_o = 8\Omega$ and directions of u_{oc} and i_{sc}, Thevenin's equivalent circuit and Norton's equivalent circuit can be drawn, as shown in Fig.4.3.13d and 4.3.16e.

For this example, if any two quantities among u_{oc}, i_{sc} and R_o are given, then another quantity can be calculated from them with the expression (4.3.7). Such as, $u_{oc} = R_o i_{sc} = 8 \times 0.5V = 4V$, $i_{sc} = u_{oc}/R_o = 4V/8\Omega = 0.5A$, $R_o = u_{oc}/i_{sc} = 4V/0.5A = 8\Omega$.

It needs to be mentioned that Thevenin's or Norton's equivalent circuits do not always exist for all active linear resistor single-port network.

Generally speaking, if there is a unique solution existing for the single-port network where a current source is connected to the port to drive the current to flow, it's Thevenin's equivalent circuit is available.

Some single-port networks containing controlled source have no unique solution (no solution, or infinite solutions) when the voltage source or current source is applied. They have neither the Thevenin equivalent circuit, nor Norton equivalent circuit. For example, for the one-port network shown in Fig.4.3.14, both the port voltage and current are zero, namely $u = i = 0$, its characteristic is the origin in the $u-i$ plane, as shown in Fig.4.3.14b. So, neither Thevenin equivalent circuit, nor Norton equivalent circuit exists for this circuit.

For maximum power and sensitivity of voltage and current to change of some circuit elements, Norton's theorem and Thevenin's theorem are also very effective.

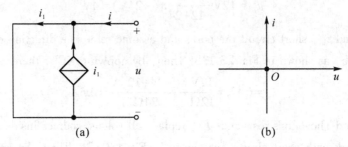

(a) (b)

Fig.4.3.14 The Case That the Thevenin's Equivalent Circuit and Norton's Equivalent Circuit Does Not Exist

4.3.4 Maximum Power Transfer

In this section, an important application of Thevenin's and Norton's theorem will be discussed.

In electronic engineering, a problem is often encountered that how a resistive load can get maximum power from the source circuit. This kind of problem can be analyzed with the circuit model shown in Fig.4.3.15a.

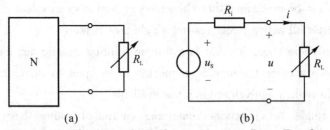

(a) (b)

Fig.4.3.15 The Circuit for Explaining Maximum Power Transfer

Network N in Fig.4.3.15a is an active linear resistive one-port network which supplies energy to a resistive load R_L. It can be replaced by its Thevenin's equivalent circuit, as shown in Fig.4.3.15b. R_L is resistive load dissipating the energy.

Suppose that load resistance R_L is variable. Now, let us analyze how the load can get the maximum power from the power supply.

Notice that the changing of R_L does not affect the Thevenin equivalent circuit, so the power expression of the load R_L can be written as

$$p = R_L i^2 = \frac{R_L u_{oc}^2}{(R_o + R_L)^2}$$

To find the maximum value of power p, the condition $dp/dR_L = 0$ must be satisfied, namely

$$\frac{dp}{dR_L} = \frac{u_{oc}^2}{(R_o + R_L)^2} + \frac{-2R_L u_{oc}^2}{(R_o + R_L)^3} = \frac{(R_o - R_L) u_{oc}^2}{(R_o + R_L)^3} = 0$$

From this expression, the condition that p is maximum is

$$R_L = R_o \qquad (4.3.7)$$

Because

$$\left.\frac{d^2 p}{dR_L^2}\right|_{R_L = R_o} = -\left.\frac{u_{oc}^2}{8 R_o^3}\right|_{R_o > 0} < 0$$

It can be seen that if $R_0 > 0$, and $R_L = R_0$, load resistor can get the maximum power from one-port network N. And then, it is easy to find that the maximum power is

$$P_{R_L, \max} = R_i \cdot \left(\frac{u_S}{2R_i}\right)^2 = \frac{u_s^2}{4R_i}$$

This formula is a very important conclusion and can be used directly to find the maximum power.

So, maximum power transfer states that maximum power is transferred to the load when the load resistance equals Thevenin resistance as seen from the load ($R_L = R_0$).

When load resistance R_L is equal to Thevenin resistance R_0, it is said that the network is matched in maximum power. The maximum power of load resistor is

$$P_{\max} = \frac{u_{oc}^2}{4R_o} \qquad (4.3.8)$$

When the maximum power matching conditions is met ($R_L = R_0 > 0$), the power absorbed by R_0 is equal to the power absorbed by R_L, so, the efficiency of energy transfer for voltage source u_S is just 50%, it is very low. For the independent sources inside the one-port network N, their efficiency of power transfer may be lower.

For power transmission systems, it is required to improve efficiency as much as possible. To make better use of energy, the maximum power matching cannot be applied. However, for measurement, electronic and information engineering, it is often focused on getting the maximum power from weak signals, and power transfer efficiency is not considered. So, the maximum power matching is often applied.

Example 4.3.8 For the circuit shown in Fig.4.3.16a, it is known that R_L gets the maximum power. (1) find value of R_L; (2) find the power transfer efficiency for 10V voltage source.

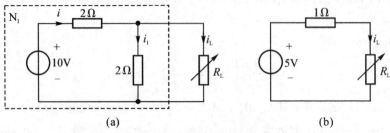

Fig.4.3.16 The Circuit for Example 4.3.8

Solution (1) Find Thevenin's equivalent circuit of single-port network N_1 first.

To find u_{oc}, disconnect the load, and by applying voltage division, there are

$$u_{oc} = \frac{2}{2+2} \times 10V = 5V$$

To find R_o, all independent sources inside the N_1 are set to zero, and there are

$$R_o = \frac{2 \times 2}{2+2}\Omega = 1\Omega$$

Equivalent circuit is derived as shown in Fig.4.3.16b. According to Maximum power transfer theorem, the maximum power can be obtained if $R_L = R_0 = 1\Omega$.

(2) From the expression 4.3.9, the maximum power of R_L can be derived as

$$P_{max} = \frac{u_{oc}^2}{4R_o} = \frac{25}{4 \times 1}W = 6.25W$$

(3) To find the efficiency, let's find the power produced by 10V voltage source first.

If $R_L = 1\Omega$, there are

$$i_L = \frac{u_{oc}}{R_o + R_L} = \frac{5}{2}A = 2.5$$

$$u_L = R_L i_L = 2.5V$$

$$i = i_1 + i_2 = \left(\frac{2.5}{2} + 2.5\right)A = 3.75A$$

$$P = 10V \times 3.75A = 37.5W$$

Since the power produced by 10V voltage source is 37.5W, the power dissipated by resistor is 6.25W. So, the power transfer efficiency is

$$\eta = \frac{6.25}{37.5} \approx 16.7\%$$

Obviously, it is very low.

Example 4.3.9 Find the maximum power that the single-port network shown in Fig.4.3.17a can transfer to load.

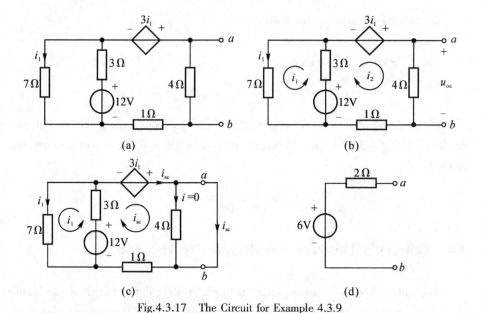

Fig.4.3.17 The Circuit for Example 4.3.9

Solution Let's find u_{oc} first. Assign the reference direction of mesh currents as shown in Fig.4.3.17b, lists all mesh equations as follows

$$\begin{cases}(10\Omega)i_1+(3\Omega)i_2=12\text{V}\\(3\Omega)i_1+(8\Omega)i_2=12\text{V}+(3\Omega)i_1\end{cases}$$

By Rearrangement, there are

$$\begin{cases}10i_1+3i_2=12\text{A}\\8i_2=12\text{A}\end{cases}$$

By Solving equations, the results of u_{oc} is derived as

$$i_2=1.5\text{A}$$
$$u_{oc}=(4\Omega)i_2=6\text{V}$$

Next, let's find i_{sc}. Assign the reference direction of mesh currents as shown in Fig.b 4.3.17c, list all mesh equations as follows

$$(10\Omega)i_1+(3\Omega)i_{sc}=12\text{V}$$
$$(3\Omega)i_1+(4\Omega)i_{sc}=12\text{V}+(3\Omega)i_1$$

Rearrangement, there are

$$10i_1+3i_{sc}=12\text{A}$$
$$4i_{sc}=12\text{A}$$

By Solving equations, the results are

$$i_{sc}=3\text{A}$$

Then Thevenin's resistance is

$$R_0=\frac{u_{oc}}{i_{sc}}=\frac{6}{3}=2\Omega$$

Finally, Thevenin's equivalent circuit of the single-port network can be obtained as shown in Fig.4.3.17d. So, the maximum power that the single-port network can generate is

$$P_{max}=\frac{u_{oc}^2}{4R_0}=\frac{6^2}{4\times 2}=4.5\text{W}$$

4.4 Tellegen's Theorem and Reciprocity Theorem

Tellegen's Theorem is an important network theorem derived from of Kirchhoff's laws. Because it has nothing to do with the characteristics of the network elements, it is widely applied. For example, it can be applied to the networks with the nonlinear and time-varying elements. Reciprocity theorem is a special case of Tellegen's theorem.

4.4.1 Tellegen's Theorem

There are two statements for Tellegen's theorem.

4.4.1.1 Tellegen's Theorem 1

Tellegen's theorem 1 can be stated as follows:

For a circuit with n nodes and b branches, if the voltage and current in each branch are assigned in the standard reference directions and $(i_1, i_2, \cdots, i_b)$, $(u_1, u_2, \cdots, u_b)$ are currents and voltages of b branches respectively, then, we have

$$\sum_{k=1}^{b} u_k i_k = 0, \quad \forall t \qquad (4.4.1)$$

To help better understand this theorem, now let's explain Tellegen's theorem with an example as follows.

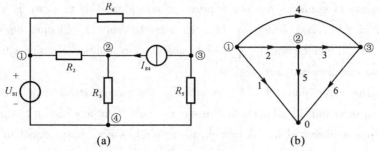

Fig.4.4.1 A Graph with 4 Nodes and 6 Branches

For the circuit shown in Fig.4.4.1a, there are 4 nodes and 6 branch in its graph, as shown in Fig.4.4.1b. Assume branch voltages are expressed as $(i_1, i_2, \cdots, i_6)$ and branch currents are $(u_1, u_2, \cdots, u_6)$ respectively. Then following KVL equations can be listed.

$$\begin{cases} u_1 = u_{n1} \\ u_2 = u_{n1} - u_{n2} \\ u_3 = u_{n2} - u_{n3} \\ u_4 = u_{n1} - u_{n3} \\ u_5 = u_{n2} \\ u_6 = u_{n3} \end{cases}$$

By applying KCL, the following equations can be listed.
$$\begin{cases} i_1+i_2+i_4=0 \\ -i_2+i_3+i_5=0 \\ -i_3-i_4+i_6=0 \end{cases}$$
Then, we hvae
$$\begin{aligned}\sum_{k=1}^{6} u_k i_k &= u_1 i_1 + u_2 i_2 + u_3 i_3 + u_4 i_4 + u_5 i_5 + u_6 i_6 \\ &= u_{n1} i_1 + (u_{n1}-u_{n2}) i_2 + (u_{n2}-u_{n3}) i_3 + (u_{n1}-u_{n3}) i_4 + u_{n2} i_5 + u_{n3} i_6 \\ &= u_{n1}(i_1+i_2+i_4) + u_{n2}(-i_2+i_3+i_5) + u_{n3}(-i_3-i_4+i_6) \\ &= 0\end{aligned}$$

From above analysis, it can be seen that:

① Since only circuit topologies, KCL, KVL and the relationships between node voltages and branch voltages in the circuit are considered in the analysis and the property of elements are not required to consider. This property is similar to KCL an d KVL. So, Tellegen's Theorem has the same application limitation as KCL/KVL, it can be widely applied to analyze any lumped circuits with linear, nonlinear and time-varying elements.

②The expression (4.4.1) is actually the mathematical expression of the power conservation. It indicates that in any network N, at any instant t, the algebra sum of power absorbed by all branch of the circuits are always equal to zero. In other words, this theorem essentially embodies power conservation.

4.4.1.2 Tellegen's Theorem 2

Tellegen's theorem 2 can be stated as follows:

If there are two different networks N and $\hat{N}$ with same topology structure, both have n nodes and b branches. All branches are labeled in same number and their reference directions are also same. Assume that currents and voltages of b branches are represented as $(i_1, i_2, \cdots, i_b)$, $(u_1, u_2, \cdots, u_b)$ and $(\hat{i}_1, \hat{i}_2, \cdots, \hat{i}_b)$, $(\hat{u}_1, \hat{u}_2, \cdots, \hat{u}_b)$ respectively, then, we have

$$\sum_{k=1}^{b} u_k \hat{i}_k = 0 \quad \text{and} \quad \sum_{k=1}^{b} \hat{u}_k i_k = 0 \tag{4.4.2}$$

Let's explain theorem with the Network shown in Fig.4.4.2a, b. Obviously, topology of two networks are same, or their graph are same, as shown in Fig.4.4.2c. Assume that the branch voltages and branch currents in the network shown in

Fig.4.4.2b are $(\hat{i}_1, \hat{i}_2, \cdots, \hat{i}_6)$ and $(\hat{u}_1, \hat{u}_2, \cdots, \hat{u}_6)$ respectively.

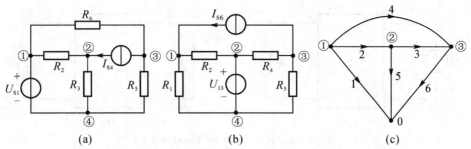

(a)   (b)   (c)

Fig.4.4.2 Two Different Graphs with 4 Nodes and 6 Branches

Then, for the circuit shown in Fig.4.4.2b, their KVL equations are

$$\begin{cases} \hat{i}_1 + \hat{i}_2 + \hat{i}_4 = 0 \\ -\hat{i}_2 + \hat{i}_3 + \hat{i}_5 = 0 \\ -\hat{i}_3 - \hat{i}_4 + \hat{i}_6 = 0 \end{cases}$$

So

$$\sum_{k=1}^{6} u_k \hat{i}_k = u_{n1}(\hat{i}_1 + \hat{i}_2 + \hat{i}_4) + u_{n2}(-\hat{i}_2 + \hat{i}_3 + \hat{i}_5) + u_{n3}(-\hat{i}_3 - \hat{i}_4 + \hat{i}_6) = 0$$

Tellegen's theorem 2 shows that, for any two different networks N and $\hat{N}$ with the same directed graph, at any instant t, the algebraic sum of product of branch voltages in one network with branch currents in another network are always equal to zero.

① Tellegen's theorem 2 shows that for two different circuits with same topological structures must follow a mathematical relationship between the branch voltages in one circuit and the branch currents in another circuit;

② Because the voltages and currents used in expression 4.42 come from two different circuits, their product has not physical meaning. So, Tellegen's theorem 2 cannot be explained with the power conservation, it is sometimes also known as "similar-power conservation theorem".

Example 4.4.1 For the circuit shown in Fig.4.4.3a, the network N is a linear passive network. Given: if $R_2 = 2\Omega$, $U_1 = 6V$, it is measured that $I_1 = 2A$, $U_2 = 2V$, as shown in Fig.4.4.3a. if $R_2 = 4\Omega$, $\hat{U}_1 = 10V$, it is measured that $\hat{I}_1 = $

3A, as shown in Fig.4.4.3b. Find $\hat{U}_2 = ?$

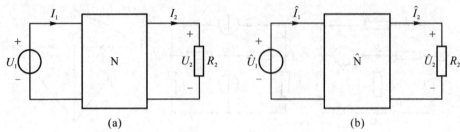

Fig.4.4.3 The Circuit for Example 4.4.1

Solution Assume that there are b branches inside the network N. Then, by applying Tellegen's theorem 2, there are

$$-U_1\hat{I}_1 + U_2\hat{I}_2 + \sum_{k=1}^{b} U_k\hat{I}_k = 0 \qquad (4.4.3a)$$

$$-\hat{U}_1 I_1 + \hat{U}_2 I_2 + \sum_{k=1}^{b} \hat{U}_k I_k = 0 \qquad (4.4.3b)$$

Since the structure and resistance parameters of network N shown in Fig.4.4.3a, b are same, so there are

$$\sum_{k=1}^{b} U_k\hat{I}_k = \sum_{k=1}^{b} R_k I_k \hat{I}_k = \sum_{k=1}^{b} (R_k \hat{I}_k) I_k = \sum_{k=1}^{b} \hat{U}_k I_k$$

Then, by subtracting (4.4.3a) with (4.4.3b), it can be derived that

$$-U_1\hat{I}_1 + U_2\hat{I}_2 = -\hat{U}_1 I_1 + \hat{U}_2 I_2 \qquad (4.4.3c)$$

So it can be derived that

$$\hat{U}_2 = 4V$$

This example shows that expression (4.4.3c) is an important. When we had to find the voltage or current of the port only, this expression can be used simply and it is not necessary to apply the expression (4.4.3a) and (4.4.3b) in Tellegen's theorem 2. When applying this formula, pay attention to the reference directions of the port voltage and current. They must be associated with each other or same directions.

Example 4.4.2 A linear resistive two-port network is shown in Fig.4.4.4a. A 10V voltage source u_S is connected to the input port and output port is short circuit, it is measured that input current is 5A and output current is 1A. If this voltage source u_s is moved to output port and a 2Ω resistor is connected to the input port, as shown in Fig.4.4.4b, what is the voltage of 2Ω resistor?

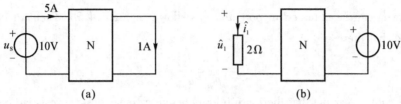

(a)　　　　　　　　　　　(b)

Fig.4.4.4　The Circuit Diagram for Example 4.4.2

Solution　According to the expression (4.4.2c) obtained from Tellegen's theorem 2, there are

$$u_1 \hat{i}_1 + u_2 \hat{i}_2 = \hat{u}_1 i_1 + \hat{u}_2 i_2$$

And because

$$u_1 = 10\text{V}, \ i_1 = -5A, \ u_2 = 0, \ i_2 = 1A, \ \hat{u}_1 = 2\hat{i}_1, \ \hat{u}_2 = 10\text{V}$$

∴

$$10 \hat{i}_1 + 0 \times \hat{i}_2 = 2\hat{i}_1 \times (-5) + 10 \times 1$$

$$20 \hat{i}_1 = 10 \Rightarrow \hat{i}_1 = 0.5A$$

So the voltage of 2Ω resistor is

$$\hat{u}_1 = 2\hat{i} = 1\text{V}$$

4.4.2　The Reciprocity Theorem

Reciprocity is the summary of the reciprocal nature of the network. Namely: For a linear time-invariant resistive circuits with single excitation, if the excitation and responses are exchanged, their responses generated by the same excitation will not be changed.

Not all networks obey reciprocity. Generally speaking, only those linear time-invariant networks without controlled sources, independent voltage sources, current sources and gyrators possess this property. Therefore, the application of the reciprocity is relatively limited.

The reciprocity theorem can be stated in three forms.

4.4.2.1　First Statement form of Reciprocity Theorem

The reciprocity theorem 1

For a time-invariant resistive network N without independent sources and controlled sources, there are two ports $\alpha\alpha'$ and $\beta\beta'$ being considered. If an input voltage u_{sa} is applied the port $\alpha\alpha'$, output current i_β can be obtained in Port $\beta\beta'$, as shown in Fig.4.4.5a. Instead, the input voltage $\hat{u}_{s\beta}$ is applied to port $\beta\beta'$, output current $\hat{i}_\alpha$ can be obtained in port $\alpha\alpha'$, as shown in Fig.4.4.5b. Then, it can be proved that there is

$$\frac{\hat{i}_\alpha}{\hat{u}_{s\beta}} = \frac{i_\beta}{u_{sa}}$$

Proof Assume that there are b branches in a linear passive resistive network N as shown in Fig.4.4.5. Their branch voltages are $u_k(k=1,2,\cdots,b)$ and branch currents are $i_k(k=1,2,\cdots,b)$. The branch voltages and branch currents of port $\alpha\alpha'$ and $\beta\beta'$ are u_α, i_α and u_β, i_β respectively, and the reference directions of all branch currents and branch voltages are standard. Likewise, for the linear passive resistive networks N in Fig.4.4.5b, it's branch voltage is $\hat{u}_k(k=1,2,\cdots,b)$, branch currents is $\hat{i}_k(k=1,2,\cdots,b)$, and port voltages and currents are $\hat{u}_\alpha, \hat{i}_\alpha$ and $\hat{u}_\beta, \hat{i}_\beta$ respectively, and the reference direction of all branch voltages and branch currents are standard.

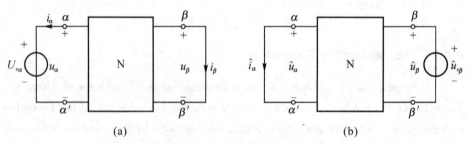

Fig.4.4.5 First Statement of Reciprocity Theorem

According to the reference direction gives in the Fig.4.4.5, applying the expression (4.4.2c)

$$u_\alpha \hat{i}_\alpha + u_\beta \hat{i}_\beta + \sum_{k=3}^{b} u_k \hat{i}_k = 0 \qquad (4.4.4)$$

$$\hat{u}_\alpha i_\alpha + \hat{u}_\beta i_\beta + \sum_{k=3}^{b} \hat{u}_k i_k = 0 \qquad (4.4.5)$$

Because the topology of the network N in Fig.4.4.5a is the same as such that of the network N in Fig.4.4.5b. And both networks consist of same linear time-invariant resistors.

$$u_k = R_k i_k, \quad k = 1, 2, \cdots, b$$
$$\hat{u}_k = R_k \hat{i}_k, \quad k = 1, 2, \cdots, b$$

Then, expression (4.4.4) can be rewritten as

$$u_\alpha \hat{i}_\alpha + u_\beta \hat{i}_\beta = -\sum_{k=3}^{b} R_k i_k \hat{i}_k \quad (4.4.6)$$

The expression (4.4.5) can be rewritten as

$$\hat{u}_\alpha i_\alpha + \hat{u}_\beta i_\beta = -\sum_{k=3}^{b} R_k \hat{i}_k i_k \quad (4.4.7)$$

Since right hand side of expression (4.4.6) and (4.4.7) are equal, we have

$$u_\alpha \hat{i}_\alpha + u_\beta \hat{i}_\beta = \hat{u}_\alpha i_\alpha + \hat{u}_\beta i_\beta \quad (4.4.8)$$

In Fig.4.4.4a, $u_\alpha = u_{s\alpha}$, $u_\beta = 0$, In Fig.4.4.4b, $\hat{u}_\alpha = 0$, $\hat{u}_\beta = \hat{u}_{s\beta}$. Substituting them into expression (4.4.8), yields

$$u_{s\alpha} \hat{i}_\alpha = \hat{u}_{s\beta} i_\beta$$

So,

$$\frac{\hat{i}_\alpha}{\hat{u}_{s\beta}} = \frac{i_\beta}{u_{s\alpha}}$$

Example 4.4.3 Find current I in the network shown in Fig.4.4.6a.

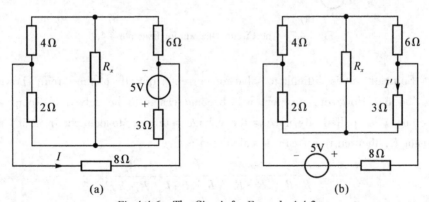

Fig.4.4.6 The Circuit for Example 4.4.3

Solution The network shown in Fig.4.4.6a is a bridge circuit. Because the resistance Rx is unknown, it is difficult to solve for current I. However, by applying Reciprocity Theorem 1, 5V voltage source can be moved to connect in series with 8 Ohm resistors, as shown in Fig.4.4.6b. So, if I' can be found, then according to Reciprocity Theorem, $I=I'$.

Since the circuit in Fig.4.4.6b is a balanced bridge circuits, there are not current flowing through Rx. Rx can be replaced by open circuit to reduce the circuit. Then I' can be derived by applying current division and KCL as follows.

$$I' = \frac{5}{17}A$$

Therefore,

$$I = I' = \frac{5}{17}A$$

Example 4.4.4 Find current i in the circuit shown in Fig.4.4.7a.

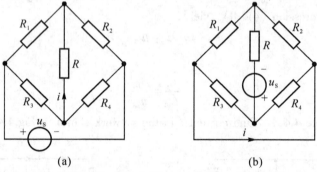

Fig.4.4.7 The Circuit Diagram for Example 4.4.4

Solution It is difficult to solve for current i directly of the circuit shown in Fig.4.4.6a. However, problem will become easier to be solved if Reciprocity theorems 1 is applied. By moving the voltage source u_S to connect in series with resistor R, then current i can be calculated easily as

$$i = \frac{u_S}{R+R_1 /\!/ R_2 + R_3 /\!/ R_4} \left(\frac{R_4}{R_3+R_4} - \frac{R_2}{R_1+R_2} \right).$$

4.4.2.2 Second Statement form of Reciprocity Theorems
The reciprocity theorem 2

For a linear resistive network N without independent sources and controlled sources, there are two ports $\alpha\alpha'$ and $\beta\beta'$ to be considered, if a current source i_{sa} is applied to input port $\alpha\alpha'$, the output voltage of port $\beta\beta'$ is obtained to be u_β, as shown in Fig.4.4.8a. Instead, a current source $\hat{i}_{s\beta}$ is applied to output port $\beta\beta'$, output voltage of port $\alpha\alpha'$ is obtained to be $\hat{u}_\alpha$, as shown in Fig.4.4.8b. Then, we have

$$\frac{\hat{u}_\alpha}{\hat{i}_{s\beta}} = \frac{u_\beta}{i_{s\alpha}}$$

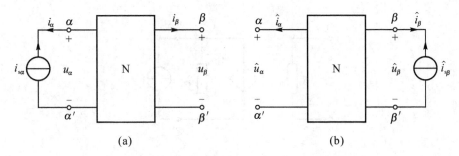

Fig.4.4.8 Second Statement of Reciprocity Theorem

Proof Similar to the proof of Reciprocity Theorem 1. Based on the expression (4.4.3) derived from Tellegen's theorem

$$u_\alpha \hat{i}_\alpha + u_\beta \hat{i}_\beta = \hat{u}_\alpha i_\alpha + \hat{u}_\beta i_\beta$$

For Fig.4.4.8a, $i_\alpha = -i_{s\alpha}$, $i_\beta = 0$. For Fig.4.4.8b. $\hat{i}_\beta = -\hat{i}_{s\beta}$, $\hat{i}_\alpha = 0$. Substituting them into the expression above, gives

$$-u_\beta \hat{i}_{s\beta} = -\hat{u}_\alpha i_{s\alpha}$$

Therefore,

$$\frac{\hat{u}_\alpha}{\hat{i}_{s\beta}} = \frac{u_\beta}{i_{s\alpha}}$$

Application of reciprocity theorem is relatively limited. It can only be applied to linear time-invariant networks without any sources. If the network have the sources (independent or non-independent), nonlinear elements, time-varying elements, Reciprocity theorem is not necessarily met. Here is an example as follows.

Example 4.4.5 The circuit in Fig.4.4.9A contains controlled source. Is this circuit a reciprocal network?

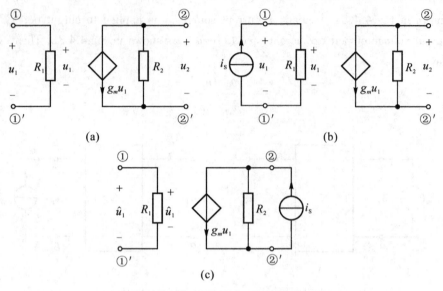

Fig.4.4.9 The Circuit for Example 4.4.5

Solution First, a current source i_s is connected to port ①①', as shown in Fig.4.4.9b. Excited by i_s, the response on port ②②' will be

$$u_2 = -g_m u_1 R_2 = -g_m R_1 R_2 i_s$$

Next, this current source i_s is moved to port ②②', as shown in Fig.4.4.9c. Excited by this i_s, the response on the port ①①' will obviously be $\hat{u}_1 = 0$. Due to $\hat{u}_2 \neq \hat{u}_1$, so the given network is not a reciprocal network.

This example indicates that network with controlled source is non-reciprocal network. However, under certain conditions, individual network with controlled source may be a reciprocal network. Here is an example.

Example 4.4.6 For a network shown in Fig.4.4.10a, to make it become a reciprocity network, what kind of relationship between α and μ should be?

Solution Because a reciprocal network obeys Reciprocity Theorem, so if given network obeys reciprocity, then according to the Reciprocity theorem 2, u_2 obtained from Fig.4.4.10b must equal to the $\hat{u}_1$ obtained from Fig.4.4.10c.

From the circuit in Fig.4.4.10b, there is

$$u_2 = u + R_3 i + \mu u = (1+\mu)u + R_3 i$$

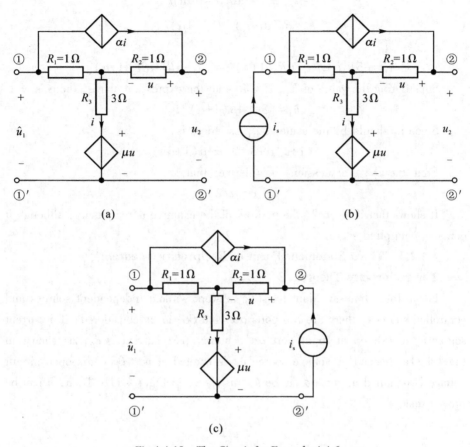

Fig.4.4.10 The Circuit for Example 4.4.6

and
$$i = i_s, \quad u = \alpha R_2 i = \alpha R_2 i_s$$
So, there are
$$u_2 = [(1+\mu)\alpha R_2 + R_3] i_s$$
Substituting the value of R_2, R_3 into the expression above, there is
$$u_2 = [(1+\mu)\alpha + 3] i_s$$
From Fig.4.4.10c, there is
$$\hat{u}_1 = \hat{u}_{R_1} + R_3 \hat{i} + \mu \hat{u}$$
Because

$$\hat{i} = \hat{i}_s, \quad \hat{u}_{R_1} = -\alpha R_1 \hat{i} = -\alpha R_1 \hat{i}_s,$$
$$\hat{u} = R_2(\alpha\hat{i} + i_s) = R_2(1+\alpha)i_s$$

So,
$$\hat{u}_1 = -\alpha R_1 i_s + R_3 i_s + \mu R_2(1+\alpha)i_s = [R_3 - \alpha R_1 + \mu R_2(1+\alpha)]i_s$$

Substituting the value of R_1, R_2, R_3 into the expression above, there is
$$\hat{u}_1 = [3 - \alpha + \mu(1+\alpha)]i_s$$

Since u_2 should be the same as $\hat{u}_1$, so there is
$$(1+\mu)\alpha + 3 = 3 - \alpha + \mu(1+\alpha)$$

From the above expression, it is derived that
$$\alpha = \mu/2$$

It shows that if $\alpha = \mu/2$, the network of the example is reciprocity, although it contains controlled sources.

4.4.2.3 Third Statement Form of Reciprocity Theorem

The reciprocity Theorem 3

For a linear time-invariant resistive network without independent sources and controlled sources, there are two ports $\alpha\alpha'$ and $\beta\beta'$ to be considered, if a current source i_{sa} is excited at input port $\alpha\alpha'$, output port current is i_β, as shown in Fig.4.4.11a. Instead, a voltage source $\hat{u}_{s\beta}$ is excited at port $\beta\beta'$, the open circuit voltage is obtained at port $\alpha\alpha'$ to be $\hat{u}_\alpha$, as shown in Fig.4.4.11b. Then, it can be proved that

$$\frac{\hat{u}_\alpha}{\hat{u}_{s\beta}} = \frac{i_\beta}{i_{sa}}$$

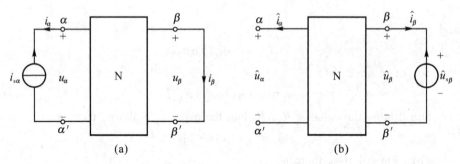

Fig.4.4.11 Third Statement of Reciprocity Theorem

Numerically, if $i_{s\alpha} = \hat{u}_{s\beta}$, then $i_\beta = \hat{u}_\alpha$.

Proof of Reciprocity theorem 3 is similar to proof of Reciprocity Theorem 1, 2 and It is omitted here.

When Reciprocity Theorem is applied to network analysis, it is required not only to pay attention to the values of the variables, but also their reference directions.

4.5 Computer-Aided Analysis of Circuits

Here Matlab / PSB tools is introduced in applying to verify the Reciprocity Theorem. According to the Reciprocity Theorem, the calculation of the current in the circuit shown in Fig.4.5.1a can be converted into the calculation of the current i in the circuit shown in Fig.4.5.1b. Now let's use the Matlab / PSB tool to verify that the current of the two circuits is the same.

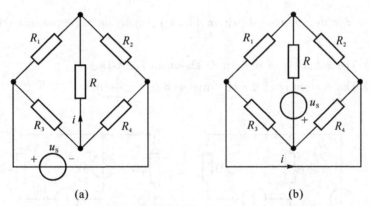

Fig.4.5.1 Applying Matlab to Verify the Reciprocity Theorem

The Simulink model designed by Matlab/PSB tool is shown in Fig.4.5.2, it is given that $R_1 = 6\Omega$, $R_2 = 3\Omega$, $R_3 = 3\Omega$, $R_4 = 6\Omega$, $R = 2\Omega$, $U_S = 36V$, The simulation results are shown in Fig.4.5.2, it can be seen that the readings of two ammeter are same, 2A. Therefore, Reciprocity Theorem has been verified.

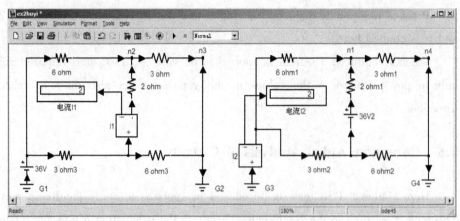

Fig.4.5.2　Simulink Model of the Circuit

Exercise

4-1　For the circuits shown in Fig.4-1, applying Superposition theorem to find:

(1) The voltage u of the circuit shown in Fig.4-1a;

(2) The current i_X of the circuit shown in Fig.4-1b.

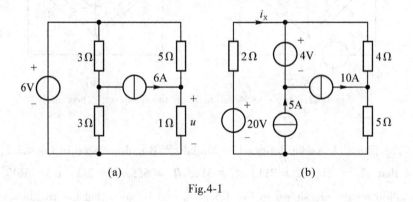

Fig.4-1

4-2　For the circuit shown in Fig.4-2, $R_2 = R_3$. If $I_S = 0$, it is known that $I_1 =$

2A, $I_2 = I_3 = 4$A. Find: I_1, I_2 and I_3 if $I_S = 10$A.

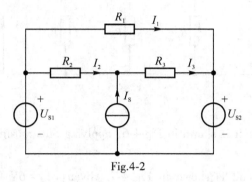

Fig.4-2

4-3 For the circuit shown in Fig.4-3, If $u_s = 10$V, $i_s = 2$A, $u_{ab} = 5$V; If $u_s = 10$V, $i_s = 1$A, $u_{ab} = 3$V. Find u_{ab} if $u_s = 1$V, $i_s = 0$A.

4-4 For the circuit shown in Fig.4-4, if 2A current source is not connected (open), 3A current source provides 54W power for network and $u_2 = 12$V. If 3A current source is not connected (open), 2A current source provides 28W power for network and $u_3 = 8$V. Find the power of two current sources when both current sources are connected.

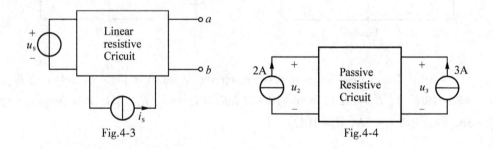

Fig.4-3   Fig.4-4

4-5 For the circuit shown in Fig.4-5, given: $R_1 = 2\Omega$, $R_2 = 20\Omega$, $i_7 = 1$A, find:

(1) The voltage of the resistance R_2;

(2) The current of resistance R_1;

(3) The voltage of power source;

(4) Find the value of current i_7 if $u = 100$V.

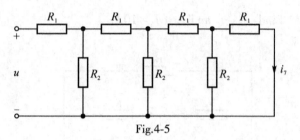

Fig.4-5

4-6 The circuit is shown in Fig.4-6, applying Superposition Theorem to find u_X:

4-7 The circuit is shown in Fig.4-7. Given: $u_S = 6V$, $i_S = 3A$. Applying Superposition Theorem to find i_X.

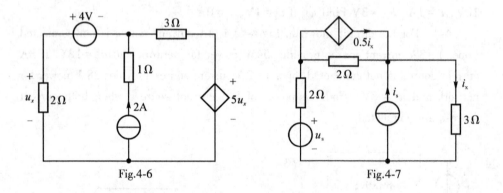

Fig.4-6   Fig.4-7

4-8 A linear time invariant resistive circuit is shown in Fig.4-8. Given: if $i_S = 2\cos10t(A)$, $R_L = 2\Omega$, $i_L = 4\cos10t + 2(A)$, if $i_S = 4A$, $R_L = 4\Omega$, it is given $i_L = 8A$. Find i_L if $i_S = 5A$, $R_L = 10\Omega$.

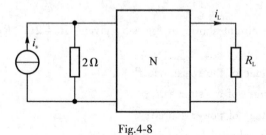

Fig.4-8

4-9 Find Thevenin's equivalent circuit and Norton's equivalent circuit for the circuit shown in Fig.4-9.

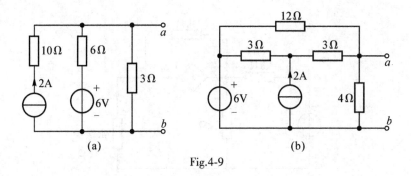

Fig.4-9

4-10 Find Thevenin's equivalent circuit and Norton's equivalent circuit for the circuit shown in Fig.4-10.

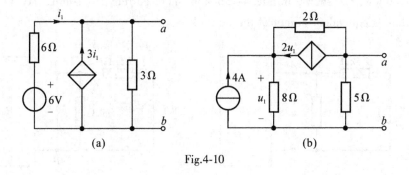

Fig.4-10

4-11 What is the resistor current in the circuit shown in Fig.4-11 if R is 3Ω or 7Ω respectively?

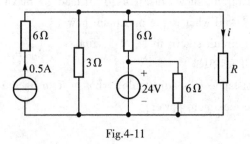

Fig.4-11

4-12 Try to find current i of the circuit shown in Fig. 4-22 by applying Thevenin's theorem.

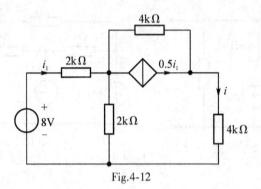

Fig.4-12

4-13 For the circuit in Fig.4-13a, $u_2 = 12.5$V. If the A, B two terminals are short circuit, as shown in Fig. 4-13b and short current $i = 10$mA. Try to find Thevenin's equivalent circuit of the network N.

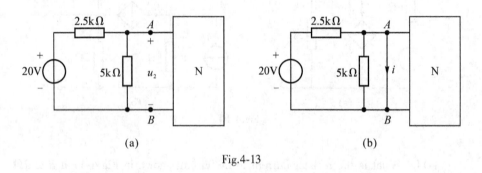

Fig.4-13

4-14 For the circuit shown in Fig.4-14, if load get maximum power, what is the load resistance? And what is the maximum power?

4-15 For the circuit shown in Fig.4-5, find:

(1) I and P_R if $R = 5\Omega$.

(2) if the resistance R is adjustable, what is R to let the load get maximum power? What is the maximum power?

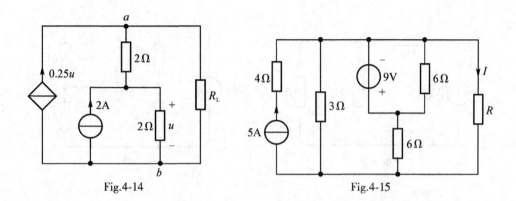

Fig.4-14   Fig.4-15

4-16 For the circuit shown in Fig.4-16. What is the load resistance if load get maximum power? What is the maximum power?

4-17 For the circuit shown in Fig.4-17. What is the load resistance R_L if load get maximum power? What is the maximum power?

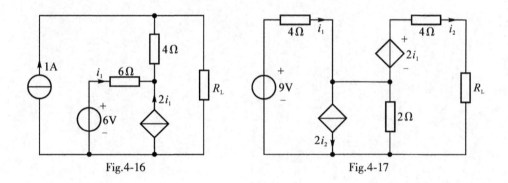

Fig.4-16   Fig.4-17

4-18 For the circuit shown in Fig.4-18, it is known that load R gets the maximum power. (1) Find the value of load R; (2) find the power transmission efficiency of load in the original circuit; (3) find the power transmission efficiency η of load in the Thevenin's equivalent circuit.

4-19 For the circuit shown in Fig.4-19, find current i of 8Ω resistor by applying Reciprocity theorem.

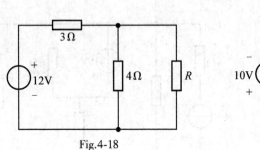
Fig.4-18

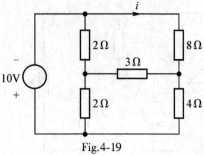
Fig.4-19

Chapter 5
Sinusoidal Steady-State Analysis

For a the linear circuit, if its excitation is a sinusoidal quantity, the response is also a sinusoidal quantity with the same frequency, this kind of circuit is called sinusoidal AC circuit. The steady-state response of a linear time-invariant circuit with sinusoidal excitation is called sinusoidal steady-state analysis. Sinusoidal AC circuit has many advantages, so it is widely used in daily life, engineering technology and theoretical research. For example, the voltage generated by a three-phase alternator is a sinusoidal waveform, and most of the problems in the power system can be analyzed by sinusoidal AC circuits. The non-sinusoidal periodic signal in communication and automatic control system, according to Fourier theory, can be decomposed into several sinusoidal components, and then the system analysis is converted into the analysis of the sinusoidal quantity. Therefore, it is of great value and theoretical significance to study the theory of AC circuit and master its analytical method. In this chapter, the basic concept of sinusoidal steady-state AC circuit, the phasor analysis method of sinusoidal steady-state AC circuit, the power of sinusoidal AC circuit, the maximum power transfer, etc, will be discussed.

5.1 The Basic Concept of Sinusoidal Quantity

5.1.1 Sinusoidal Quantity

A voltage or current that varies sinusoidally with time is called sinusoidal voltage or current, or collectively called sinusoidal quantity. Either the sine function or the cosine function can be used to express a sinusoidal quantity. The cosine function is used throughout the textbook.

The magnitude and direction of the sinusoidal voltage and current change over time, and its value at any time is called the instantaneous value. Its time function expression is called the instantaneous value expression. For example, for a sinusoidal AC circuit shown in Fig.5.1.1, if the reference direction of current and voltage are assigned as shown in the Fig.5.1.1, its instantaneous value of the sinusoidal can be expressed as

$$i(t) = I_m \cos(\omega t + \psi_i) \qquad (5.1.1)$$
$$u(t) = U_m \cos(\omega t + \psi_u) \qquad (5.1.2)$$

where U_m (or I_m) is peak value, ω is its angular frequency and ψ_u (or ψ_i) is initial phase angle. They are called three elements of a sinusoidal quantity. The waveform of a sinusoidal current is shown in Fig.5.1.2.

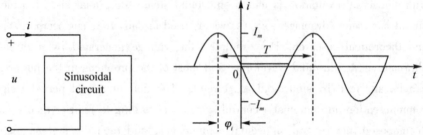

Fig.5.1.1 A Part of a Sinusoidal Circuit   Fig.5.1.2 Waveform of Sinusoidal Quantity

Three elements are very important for a sinusoidal quantity. If three elements are known, a sinusoidal quantity can be written. To write the expression of a sinusoidal quantity, its three elements have to be found first.

5.1.1.1 Peak value U_m (or I_m)

Peak value is the maximum instantaneous value of a time function. For sinusoidal voltage (or current), its peak value is denoted by U_m (or I_m). If $\cos(\omega t + \psi_u) = 1$, then $u_{max} = U_m$. If $\cos(\omega t + \psi_u) = -1$, then $u_{min} = -U_m$. So, there are $u_{max} - u_{min} = 2U_m$, it is called peak-to-peak voltage and is denoted by U_{p-p}. The peak-to-peak current is denoted by I_{p-p}.

5.1.1.2 Angular frequency ω

Angular frequency is known as the velocity of phase angle and is denoted by Greek letter ω. In the expression (5.1.1) and (5.1.2), $\omega t + \psi_u$ (or ψ_i) is called phase angle. The unit of phase angle is radian (rad) or degree (°). So, the relationship between phase angle and angular frequency can be written as

5.1 The Basic Concept of Sinusoidal Quantity

$$\omega = \frac{d}{dt}(\omega t + \psi_u) \quad \text{or} \quad \omega = \frac{d}{dt}(\omega t + \psi_i)$$

The unit of angular frequency is radian per second (rad/s). The relationships among angular frequency and period (T), angular frequency and frequency (f) are

$$\omega T = 2\pi$$
$$\omega = 2\pi f$$
$$f = 1/T$$

where, the unit of frequency is Hertz(Hz) and the unit of period is second(s). In China, the frequency of industrial and residential electricity is 50Hz, so the period is 0.02s and the angular frequency is 314rad/s.

5.1.1.3 Initial phase angle

Initial phase angle is the phase angle of voltage (or current) at the instant $t = 0$, and is denoted by ψ_u (or ψ_i), that is

$$\psi_u = (\omega t + \psi_u)|_{t=0}$$
$$\psi_i = (\omega t + \psi_i)|_{t=0}$$

where the unit of initial phase angle is radian (rad) or degree (°). Usually the value of initial phase angle is derived within the principle range $(-\pi, \pi]$. The initial phase angle is related to the initial instant or starting instant. If the positive maximum point of a sinusoidal quantity occurs at the instant prior to origin instant ($t=0$), then ψ_u (or ψ_i) >0, as shown in Fig.5.1.3a; If the positive maximum point of a sinusoidal quantity occurs at the origin instant ($t=0$), then ψ_u (or ψ_i) $= 0$, as shown in Fig.5.1.3b; If the positive maximum point of a sinusoidal quantity occurs at the instant after origin instant ($t=0$), then ψ_u (or ψ_i) <0, as shown in

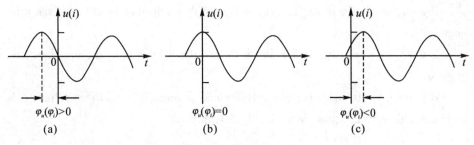

Fig.5.1.3　Initial Phase Angel

Fig.5.1.3c.

5.1.2 Phase Difference of Sinusoidal Quantities

The difference of phase angle between any two sinusoidal quantities is called phase difference. For example, assuming that there are two sinusoidal quantities with the same frequency as follow:

$$\left.\begin{array}{l} u(t) = U_m \cos(\omega t + \psi_u) \\ i(t) = I_m \cos(\omega t + \psi_i) \end{array}\right\}$$

The phase difference (denoted by φ) between them is

$$\varphi = (\omega t - \psi_u) - (\omega t - \psi_i) = \psi_u - \psi_i \qquad (5.1.3)$$

It indicates that the phase difference between two sinusoidal quantities with the same frequency is a constant. Note that: the value of phase difference must also be derived within principle range $[-\pi, \pi]$. The unit of phase difference is radian (or rad) or degree (°).

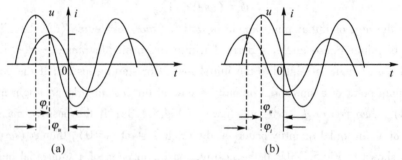

Fig.5.1.4 Phase Difference

If $\varphi > 0$, as shown in Fig.5.1.4a, it is said that u leads i by φ, or i lags u by angle φ.

If $\varphi < 0$, as shown in Fig.5.1.4b, it is said that i leads u by φ, or u lags i by angle φ.

If $\varphi = \psi_u - \psi_i = 0$, namely, phase difference is zero, it is said that voltage u is in phase with current i, as shown in Fig.5.1.5a.

If $\varphi = \psi_u - \psi_i = \pm \dfrac{\pi}{2}$, it is said that voltage u is orthogonal in phase with current

i, as shown in Fig.5.1.5b.

If $\varphi = \psi_u - \psi_i = \pm\pi$, it is said that voltage u is opposite in phase with current i, as shown in Fig.5.1.5c.

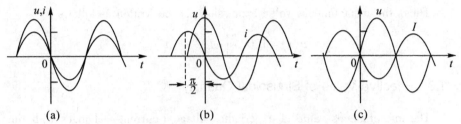

Fig.5.1.5 In Phase, Orthogonal in Phase and Opposite in Phase

The phase difference between two sinusoidal quantities with different frequencies is a time-dependent quantity, not a constant, it has no physical meaning. So, only the phase difference between two sinusoidal quantities with same frequency will be discussed in the textbook.

Example 5.1.1 A sinusoidal voltage waveform is given as shown in Fig.5.1.6. Find its three elements and write down its instantaneous value expression.

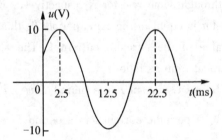

Fig.5.1.6 Figure for Example 5.1.1

Solutions: By inspecting the waveform, its three elements can be found.

Maximum value is $U_m = 100(V)$

Due to
$$T = 22.5 - 2.5 = 20 (ms)$$
$$f = 1/T = 50 (Hz)$$

So, angular frequency is

$$\omega = 2\pi f = 100\pi \,(\text{rad/s})$$

Initial phase angle is

$$\psi_u = -\omega t\big|_{t=2.5\text{ms}} = -\frac{\pi}{4}$$

Thus, the instantaneous value expression can be written as follows

$$u(t) = 100\cos\left(\omega t - \frac{\pi}{4}\right)(\text{V}).$$

5.1.3 Effective Value of Sinusoidal Quantity

The instantaneous value of a periodic voltage (current) changes with time. Normally, it is not required to know its value at any instant. For example, if a thermal insulation harm, which is caused by a sinusoidal voltage u in an electro-thermal device, is considered, only its maximum voltage (U_m) is required to be considered.

In order to measure and compare the size of the periodic quantity, the concept of effective value is introduced in engineering calculations. It is defined by comparing the thermal effect of the periodic current (voltage) with the thermal effect of the DC current (voltage). That is, let the sinusoidal current i and the direct current I flow through same resistor R respectively, if two kind of energies consumed by the resistor is equal in the same period T, then the value of I is said to be the effective value of the periodic current i. The above concepts can be expressed in mathematical form as follows.

Resistor Energy by a DC current I in a period $T: w_- = I^2 R T$

Resistor Energy by a periodic current i in a period $T: w_\sim = \int_0^T i^2 R dt$

If $w_- = w_\sim$, that is

$$I^2 R T = \int_0^T i^2 R dt$$

Then

$$I = \sqrt{\frac{1}{T}\int_0^T i^2 dt} \tag{5.1.4}$$

Above expression is used to define the effective value of a periodic current. In a similar way, the effective value of a periodic voltage is

$$U = \sqrt{\frac{1}{T}\int_0^T u^2 dt} \qquad (5.1.5)$$

In a AC circuit, the current is a sinusoidal quantity, namely $i(t) = I_m \cos(\omega t + \varphi_i)$, then the effective value of a sinusoidal current can be derived as follows,

$$I = \sqrt{\frac{1}{T}\int_0^T I_m^2 \cos^2(\omega t + \psi_i) dt} = \sqrt{\frac{1}{T}\int_0^T \frac{1 + \cos^2(\omega t + \psi_i)}{2} dt}$$

$$= \sqrt{\frac{1}{T}I_m^2 \times \frac{T}{2}} = \frac{I_m}{\sqrt{2}} \approx 0.707 I_m \qquad (5.1.6)$$

In a similar way, the effective value of a sinusoidal voltage is

$$U = \frac{1}{\sqrt{2}} U_m \approx 0.707 U_m \qquad (5.1.7)$$

So, the effective value of a sinusoidal voltage or current or voltage is 0.707 times its maximum value. Due to this relationship, effective value can be used as one of three elements of sinusoidal quantity by replacing maximum value. Therefore, the sinusoidal voltage and current can be expressed as

$$u(t) = \sqrt{2} U \cos(\omega t + \psi_u)$$
$$i(t) = \sqrt{2} I \cos(\omega t + \psi_i) \qquad (5.1.8)$$

Usually, the value of sinusoidal AC voltage or current refers to effective value, such as AC voltage 220V for civil use, industrial voltage 380V, the readings of AC instruments, rated value of electrical equipment, etc.. However, the voltage-withstanding value of various devices and electrical equipment generally refer to the maximum value.

5.2 Phasor Representation of Sinusoidal Quantity

In this section, to facilitate the analysis of AC circuits, the complex number is introduced to express sinusoidal quantity and called phasor. Let's review some concepts of complex number first.

5.2.1 Complex Number and Its Operations

Assume that A is a complex number, its real part is a and its imaginary part is b. A can be expressed in rectangular form as follows

$$A = a + jb \tag{5.2.1}$$

where j is the unit of imaginary number.

A complex number can also be expressed in the trigonometry form:

$$A = |A|\cos\theta + j|A|\sin\theta$$

or exponential form:

$$A = |A|e^{j\theta}$$

or polar form:

$$A = |A| \angle \theta$$

where, $|A|$ is the magnitude of A, θ is the argument of A, the value range of θ is $[-\pi \quad \pi]$.

According to Euler's formula

$$|A|e^{j\theta} = |A|\cos\theta + j|A|\sin\theta \tag{5.2.2}$$

where the magnitude and angle are determined by

$$|A| = \sqrt{a^2 + b^2}, \theta = \arctan\frac{b}{a} \tag{5.2.3}$$

A complex number can be expressed as a line with an arrow on a complex plane, as shown in Fig.5.2.1a. Its projection on the horizontal axis will be the real part and projection on the vertical axis is the imaginary part. The angle is measured counterclockwise from the positive real axis to the line. Sometimes, the horizontal and vertical axis can be omitted, so the complex number can be as shown in Fig.5.2.1b.

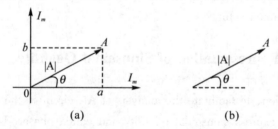

Fig.5.2.1 A Complex Number on a Complex-Number Plane

Let's discuss the operations of complex numbers.

If two complex numbers are given as follows:

$$A = a_1 + ja_2 = |A|e^{j\theta_a} = |A| \angle \theta_a \\ B = b_1 + jb_2 = |B|e^{j\theta_b} = |B| \angle \theta_b \Bigg\} \quad (5.2.4)$$

Their operations are as follows:

(1) Equality. If two complex numbers are equal, then their real parts are equal, the imaginary parts are also equal, and vice versa. That is

$$A = B \iff a_1 = b_1, \ a_2 = b_2 \quad (5.2.5)$$

(2) Addition (or Subtraction). To add (or subtract) two complex numbers, they must be expressed in rectangular form. Then, the real part of the result is equal to sum of the real parts of two complex numbers, and the imaginary part of the result is equal to sum of the imaginary parts of two complex numbers. That is,

$$A \pm B = (a_1 \pm a_2) + j(b_1 \pm b_2) \quad (5.2.6)$$

(3) Multiplication (or division). It's more convenient to multiply two complex numbers in the polar form or exponential form. To multiply two complex numbers in polar form, the magnitude of the result can be derived by multiplying magnitudes of two complex numbers, and the argument of the result can be derived by adding arguments of two complex numbers. That is,

$$AB = |A| \angle \theta_a |B| \angle \theta_b = |A||B| \angle (\theta_a + \theta_b) \quad (5.2.7)$$

$$\frac{A}{B} = \frac{|A| \angle \theta_a}{|B| \angle \theta_b} = \frac{|A|}{|B|} \angle (\theta_a - \theta_b) \quad (5.2.8)$$

Multiplication of complex numbers can also be carried out in rectangular form, but it is a little complicate to find the result.

(4) Conjugate complex numbers and its operation. The conjugate complex number of A is denoted by A^*. The real part of the conjugate complex number A^* is same as the real part of A, and the imaginary part of A^* is opposite to the imaginary part of A. That is, if

$$A = a + jb$$

then

$$A^* = a - jb \quad (5.2.9)$$

Obviously, both A and A^* possess same magnitude, however their arguments are opposite.

The addition and subtraction for A and A^* are

$$A + A^* = 2a, \quad A - A^* = -2jb$$

And the product of A and A^* is
$$AA^* = \sqrt{a^2+b^2} = |A|^2$$
Euler's formula is often used in complex number operation.
$$|A|e^{j\theta} = |A|\cos\theta + j|A|\sin\theta$$
It can be applied to transform complex number between rectangular form and polar form. $e^{j\theta}$ is called, its magnitude is 1 and argument is θ.

Euler's formula indicates that, a complex number A with real part $|A|\cos\theta$ and imaginary part $|A|\sin\theta$ can be expressed as a vector with its length $|A|$ and intersection angle θ with respect to real axis. So, it can be seen that Euler's formula relates a complex number or vector to a sinusoidal quantity.

5.2.2 Sinusoidal Quantity and Its Phasor

Suppose that there is a sinusoidal voltage
$$u(t) = U_m \cos(\omega t + \psi_u)$$
and a complex number function
$$U_m e^{j(\omega t + \psi_u)}$$
According to Euler's formula, there is
$$u(t) = U_m \cos(\omega t + \psi_u) = \text{Re}[U_m e^{j(\omega t + \psi_u)}] = \text{Re}[U_m e^{j\omega t} \cdot e^{j\psi_u}] \quad (5.2.10)$$
Note that the quantity $U_m e^{j\psi_u}$ is a complex number with the same amplitude and phase angle relative to the given sinusoidal quantity. This complex number can be derived by transforming the given sinusoidal quantity. It is defined as the maximum phasor of the given sinusoidal voltage and is indicated with symbol $\dot{U}_m$. That is
$$\dot{U}_m = U_m e^{j\psi_u} = U_m \angle \psi_u \quad (5.2.11)$$
By introducing the concept of phasor, a sinusoidal quantity is related to a complex number, and there are a lot of advantages in AC circuit analysis. It provide a good way to analyze the AC circuit.

It has been seen that a phasor is a complex number. It can be represented by a oriented straight line or an arrow on the complex plane, and this is phasor diagram. The length of arrow is corresponding to the modulus of phasor and the angle relative to real axis is corresponding to the argument of phasor. For example, the phasor diagram of $\dot{U}_m$ can be drawn as shown in Fig.5.2.2.

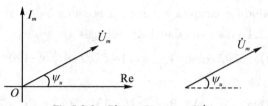

Fig.5.2.2 Phasor Diagram of $\dot{U}_m$

Because the sinusoidal voltage can also be expressed by the effective value, that is

$$u(t) = \sqrt{2}\,U\cos(\omega t + \psi_u) = \mathrm{Re}[\sqrt{2}\,\dot{U}e^{j\omega t}]$$

where

$$\dot{U} = Ue^{j\psi_u} = U\angle\psi_u \tag{5.2.12}$$

is called effective value phasor, for short, phasor.

The relationship between effective phasor and maximum phasor as follows

$$\dot{U} = \frac{1}{\sqrt{2}}\dot{U}_m \tag{5.2.13}$$

Similarly, a sinusoidal AC current can be written as

$$i(t) = I_m\cos(\omega t + \psi_i) = \mathrm{Re}[\dot{I}_m e^{j\omega t}] = \sqrt{2}\,I\cos(\omega t + \psi_i) = \mathrm{Re}[\sqrt{2}\,\dot{I}e^{j\omega t}]$$

where

$$\dot{I}_m = I_m e^{j\psi_i} = I_m \angle\psi_i \tag{5.2.14}$$

$$\dot{I} = Ie^{j\psi_i} = I\angle\psi_i \tag{5.2.15}$$

and

$$\dot{I} = \frac{1}{\sqrt{2}}\dot{I}_m \tag{5.2.16}$$

The effective value phasor is used throughout the textbook, unless other wise stated.

5.2.3 Operations of Sinusoidal Quantities with Phasor

In electric circuit analysis, it is often necessary to add, subtract, multiply and divide sinusoidal AC voltages or currents. If these operations are conducted in time-domain, it may be required to carry out trigonometric operations, differential or integral operations, so it is difficult. However, by introducing phasor and conducting operations in complex number, it becomes more convenient.

Example 5.2.1 Two sinusoidal AC voltages are given:
$$u_1(t) = 22\sqrt{2}\cos\omega t \, (\text{V}), \quad u_2(t) = 22\sqrt{2}\cos(\omega t - 120°) \, (\text{V})$$
Find: $u_1 + u_2, u_1 - u_2$.

Solution Due to $u_1(t) = \text{Re}[\sqrt{2}\dot{U}_1 e^{j\omega t}]$, $u_2(t) = \text{Re}[\sqrt{2}\dot{U}_2 e^{j\omega t}]$, so their phasors are
$$\dot{U}_1 = 22\angle 0°\,(\text{V}), \quad \dot{U}_2 = 22\angle -120°\,(\text{V})$$
Then,
$$u_1 \pm u_2 = \text{Re}[\sqrt{2}\dot{U}_2 e^{j\omega t}] \pm \text{Re}[\sqrt{2}\dot{U}_2 e^{j\omega t}] = \text{Re}[\sqrt{2}(\dot{U}_1 \pm \dot{U}_2)e^{j\omega t}]$$
And there are
$$\dot{U}_1 + \dot{U}_2 = 22\angle 0° + 22\angle -120° = 22 + j0 - 11 - j11\sqrt{3} = 22\angle -60°\,(\text{V})$$
$$\dot{U}_1 - \dot{U}_2 = 11\angle 0° - 11\angle -120° = 22 + j0 + 11 + j11\sqrt{3} = 38\angle 30°\,(\text{V})$$
Based on the result of phasors, their sinusoidal AC voltages can be derived as
$$u_1 + u_2 = 22\sqrt{2}\cos(\omega t - 60°)\,(\text{V})$$
$$u_1 - u_2 = 38\sqrt{2}\cos(\omega t + 30°)\,(\text{V})$$
The phasor diagram can be shown in Fig.5.2.3.

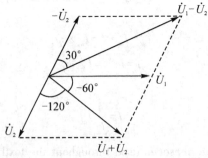

Fig.5.2.3 Phasor Diagram for Example 5.2.1

Example 5.2.2 Two sinusoidal AC currents are given as follows:
$$i_1(t) = 4\sqrt{2}\sin(314t + 120°)\,(\text{A}), \quad i_2(t) = -3\sqrt{2}\cos(314t + 120°)\,(\text{A})$$
Draw the phasor diagram and find the phase difference between them.

Solution First, convert the sine function expression into the cosine function expression in standard form, that is

$$i_1(t) = 4\sqrt{2}\sin(314t+120°) = 4\sqrt{2}\cos(314t+30°)$$
$$i_2(t) = -3\sqrt{2}\cos(314t+120°) = 3\sqrt{2}\cos(314t-60°)$$

Next, the phasors of i_1 and i_2 can be derived as follows:

$$\dot{I}_1 = 4\angle 30°(A)$$
$$\dot{I}_2 = 3\angle -60°(A)$$

So, their phase difference is

$$\varphi = \varphi_1 - \varphi_2 = 30° - (-60°) = 90°$$

The phasor diagram is drawn as shown in Fig.5.2.4. It can be seen that the current i_1 leads the current i_2 by 90°.

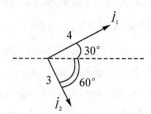

Fig.5.2.4 Phasor Diagram for Example 5.2.2

5.3 Kirchhoff's Laws and VCR in Phasor Form

5.3.1 Kirchhoff's Laws in Phasor Form

By applying the concept of phasor, KCL and KVL can be expressed in phasor form.

KCL in the time domain can be expressed as

$$\sum i(t) = 0 \quad \forall t \tag{5.3.1}$$

By representing $i(t)$ with its corresponding phasor, KCL in phasor form can be derived as follows

$$\sum \dot{I} = 0 \tag{5.3.2}$$

All the rules used to express the terms of the KCL expression in phasor form are similar as that in the time domain.

Similarly, for KVL in the time domain

$$\sum u(t) = 0 \quad \forall t \tag{5.3.3}$$

By representing $u(t)$ with its corresponding phasor, KVL in phasor form can also be derived as follows

$$\sum \dot{U} = 0 \tag{5.3.4}$$

All the rules used to express the terms of the KVL expression in phasor form are similar as that in the time domain.

Example 5.3.1 As shown in Fig. 5.3.1, the three AC currents are given: $i_1(t) = 10\sqrt{2}\cos 314t$ A, $i_2(t) = 10\sqrt{2}\cos(314t - 120°)$ A, $i_3(t) = 10\sqrt{2}\cos(314t + 120°)$ A. Write down their KCL expression $i_1 + i_2 + i_3$ in the time domain and the phasor domain respectively.

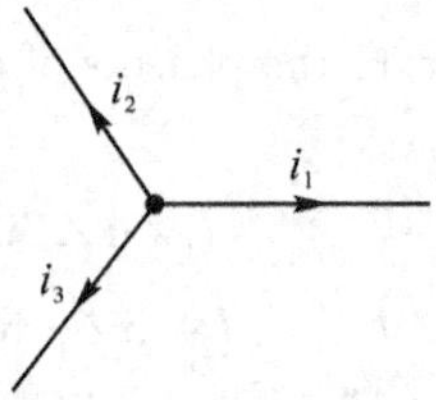

Fig.5.3.1 The Circuit for Example 5.3.1

Solution The KCL expression in the time domain can be written as follows

$$\begin{aligned}\sum_{k=1}^{3} i_k &= i_1 + i_2 + i_3 \\ &= 10\sqrt{2}\cos 314t + 10\sqrt{2}\cos(314t - 120°) + 10\sqrt{2}\cos(314t + 120°) \\ &= 10\sqrt{2}[\cos(314t) + \cos(314t)\cos(120°) + \sin(314t)\sin(120°) + \\ &\quad \cos(314t)\cos(120°) - \sin(314t)\sin(120°)] \\ &= 10\sqrt{2}\left[\cos 314t - \frac{1}{2}\cos 314t - \frac{1}{2}\cos 314t\right] \\ &= 0\end{aligned}$$

The KCL expression in the phasor domain is,

$$\begin{aligned}\sum_{k=1}^{3} \dot{I}_k &= \dot{I}_1 + \dot{I}_2 + \dot{I}_3 = 10\angle 0° + 10\angle -120° + 10\angle 120° \\ &= 10 - 5 - j8.66 - 5 + j8.66 = 0\end{aligned}$$

From this example, It can be seen that it is easier to add sinusoidal quantities in the phasor domain than in the time domain.

Example 5.3.2 For the circuit shown in Fig.5.3.2, the voltages for elements A, B and C are: $u_A(t) = 80\sqrt{2}\cos 50t$ V, $u_B(t) = 120\sqrt{2}\cos(50t+90°)$ V, $u_C(t) = 60\sqrt{2}\cos(50t-90°)$ V respectively, find the port voltage u.

Solution Applying phasor to find the result. With given conditions, three voltage phasors are

$$\dot{U}_A = 80\angle 0°\text{V},\ \dot{U}_B = 120\angle 90°\text{V},\ \dot{U}_C = 60\angle -90°\text{V}$$

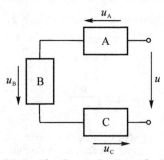

Fig.5.3.2 The Circuit for Example 5.3.2

By applying KVL, the port voltage phasor can be derived as follows.

$$\dot{U} = \dot{U}_A + \dot{U}_B + \dot{U}_C = 80\angle 0° + 120\angle 90° + 60\angle -90°$$
$$= 80 + j120 + j(-60) = 80 + j60 = 100\angle 36.9°(\text{V})$$

Then the port voltage expression in the time domain is

$$u(t) = 100\sqrt{2}\cos(50t + 36.9°)\ (\text{V})$$

It can be seen that, $\dot{U} = \dot{U}_A + \dot{U}_B + \dot{U}_C$, but $U \neq U_A + U_B + U_C$. This characteristic of AC circuits is different from that of DC circuit.

5.3.2 VCR in Phasor Form

5.3.2.1 VCR of Resistor

According to Ohm's law, if the voltage and current are in standard reference directions, as shown in Fig.5.3.3a, VCR of a resistor can be expressed as

$$u(t) = Ri(t)$$

So, if a sinusoidal current $i(t) = \sqrt{2}I\cos(\omega t + \varphi_i)$ flows through a resistor, the voltage across the resister can be written as

$$u = \sqrt{2}U\cos(\omega t + \psi_u) = R\sqrt{2}I\cos(\omega t + \psi_i)$$

It can be rewritten as

$$u = \text{Re}[\sqrt{2}\dot{U}e^{j\omega t}] = \text{Re}[\sqrt{2}R\dot{I}e^{j\omega t}]$$

So, VCR of resistor in phasor form can be expressed as

$$\dot{U} = R\dot{I} \tag{5.3.5}$$

This expression can be regarded as Ohm's law in phasor form. It states that the voltage phasor of a resistor is proportional to its current phasor. Circuit diagram for a resistor in the phasor domain is shown in Fig.5.3.3b. The phasor diagram for the voltage phasor and current phasor is shown in Fig.5.3.3c.

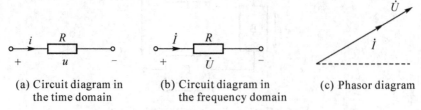

(a) Circuit diagram in the time domain

(b) Circuit diagram in the frequency domain

(c) Phasor diagram

Fig.5.3.3 A Resistive Element Caring a Sinusoidal Current

Assuming that
$$\dot{U}=Ue^{j\psi_u}, \dot{I}=Ie^{j\psi_i} \qquad (5.3.6)$$
and applying (5.3.5), gives
$$\dot{U}=R\dot{I}, \psi_u=\psi_i \qquad (5.3.7)$$

It can bee seen from (5.3.7) the effective voltage across a resistor is equal to the product of the resistance and the effective current in the phasor domain.

5.3.2.2 VCR of Inductor

If the voltage and current are in the standard reference directions, as shown in Fig.5.3.4a, the relationship between the current and the voltage of an inductor in the time domain can be written as

$$u(t)=L\frac{di(t)}{dt}$$

So, if the current $i(t)=\sqrt{2}I\cos(\omega t+\varphi_i)$ flows through the inductor, the corresponding voltage will be

$$u=\sqrt{2}U\cos(\omega t+\psi_u)=L\frac{d}{dt}[\sqrt{2}I\cos(\omega t+\psi_i)]$$
$$=-\sqrt{2}\omega LI\sin(\omega t+\psi_i)=\sqrt{2}\omega LI\cos\left(\omega t+\psi_i+\frac{\pi}{2}\right)$$

The above equation can also be expressed as
$$u=\mathrm{Re}[\sqrt{2}\dot{U}e^{j\omega t}]=L\frac{d}{dt}\mathrm{Re}[\sqrt{2}\dot{I}e^{j\omega t}]=\mathrm{Re}[\frac{d}{dt}(\sqrt{2}L\dot{I}e^{j\omega t})]=\mathrm{Re}[\sqrt{2}j\omega L\dot{I}e^{j\omega t}]$$

So, the VCR of the inductor in phasor form can be derived as follows

$$\dot{U}=j\omega L\dot{I} \tag{5.3.8}$$

If
$$\dot{U}=Ue^{j\psi_u},\ \dot{I}=Ie^{j\psi_i} \tag{5.3.9}$$

Then
$$Ue^{j\psi_u}=j\omega LIe^{j\psi_i}=\omega LIe^{j(\psi_i+\frac{\pi}{2})}$$

It is derived that
$$U=\omega LI \quad \psi_u=\psi_i+\frac{\pi}{2} \tag{5.3.10}$$

It can been seen from (5.3.10) the voltage across the inductor is equal to ωL times its current in the phasor domain. ωL is called inductive reactance, measured in ohm. The circuit diagram of an inductor is shown in Fig.5.3.4b. Its phasor diagram is shown in Fig.5.3.4c. It can be seen that the voltage leads the current by 90°.

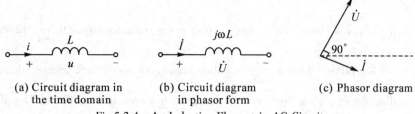

(a) Circuit diagram in the time domain
(b) Circuit diagram in phasor form
(c) Phasor diagram

Fig.5.3.4 An Inductive Element in AC Circuit

5.3.2.3 VCR of Capacitor

If the voltage and current of a capacitor are in the standard reference directions, as shown in Fig.5.3.5a, the relationship between the current and the voltage in the time domain can be written as

$$i(t)=C\frac{du(t)}{dt}$$

So, if a voltage $u(t)=\sqrt{2}U\cos(\omega t+\varphi_u)$ is applied to the capacitor, the corresponding current will be

$$i=\sqrt{2}I\cos(\omega t+\psi_i)=C\frac{d}{dt}[\sqrt{2}U\cos(\omega t+\psi_u)]$$
$$=-\sqrt{2}\omega CU\sin(\omega t+\psi_u)=\sqrt{2}\omega CU\cos\left(\omega t+\psi_u+\frac{\pi}{2}\right)$$

It can also be expressed as:

$$\text{Re}[\sqrt{2}\dot{I}e^{j\omega t}] = C\frac{d}{dt}\text{Re}[\sqrt{2}\dot{U}e^{j\omega t}] = \text{Re}[\sqrt{2}j\omega C\dot{U}e^{j\omega t}]$$

So, the relationship between the current phasor and the voltage phasor of an capacitor can be derived as follows

$$\dot{I} = j\omega C\dot{U} \quad \text{or} \quad \dot{U} = \frac{1}{j\omega C}\dot{I} \tag{5.3.11}$$

If

$$\dot{U} = Ue^{j\varphi_u}, \dot{I} = Ie^{j\psi_i}$$

then

$$Ue^{j\psi_u} = \frac{1}{j\omega C}Ie^{j\psi_i} = \frac{1}{\omega C}Ie^{j\left(\psi_i - \frac{\pi}{2}\right)}$$

So, we have

$$U = \frac{1}{\omega C}I, \psi_u = \psi_i - \frac{\pi}{2} \tag{5.3.12}$$

Eg.(5.3.12) shows the voltage across a capacitor is equal to $\frac{1}{\omega C}$ times the current in the phasor domain. $\frac{1}{\omega C}$ is called capacitive reactance, measured in ohm circuit diagram in phasor domain for a capacitor is shown in Fig.5.3.5b. The phasor diagram for a capacitor is shown in Fig.5.3.5c. It can be seen that the voltage lags the current by 90°.

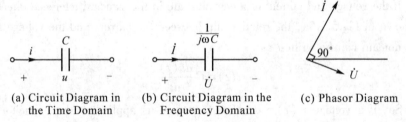

(a) Circuit Diagram in the Time Domain   (b) Circuit Diagram in the Frequency Domain   (c) Phasor Diagram

Fig.5.3.5 A Capacitive Element Caring a Sinusoidal Current

Example 5.3.3 As shown in Fig.5.3.6a, R, L and C are connected in parallel. $I_1 = 2A$, $I_2 = 1A$, $I_3 = 3A$, find current I.

Solution Note that both the current and the voltage are given in RMS, not phasors.

Assume that the initial phase angle of voltage phasor $\dot{U}$ is 0, namely, $\dot{U} = U \angle 0°$ (V). By applying the VCR in phasor form for resistor, inductor and capacitor, it is derived that

$$\dot{I}_1 = \frac{\dot{U}}{R} = I_1 \angle 0° = 2 \angle 0° (\text{A})$$

$$\dot{I}_2 = \frac{\dot{U}}{j\omega L} = I_2 \angle -90° = 1 \angle -90° (\text{A})$$

$$\dot{I}_3 = j\omega C \dot{U} = I_3 \angle 90° = 3 \angle 90° (\text{A})$$

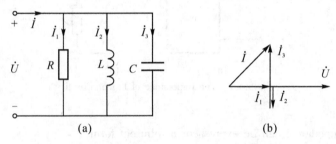

Fig.5.3.6 The Circuit for Example 5.3.3

According to the KCL in phasor form, current phasor $\dot{I}$ can be derived as follows

$$\dot{I} = \dot{I}_1 + \dot{I}_2 + \dot{I}_3 = 2 - j1 + j3 = 2 + j2 = 2\sqrt{2} \angle 45° (\text{A})$$

So, the effective current is 2.828A. The phasor diagram of the currents is shown in Fig.5.3.6b.

5.4 Impedance and Admittance

5.4.1 Impedance

As shown in Fig.5.4.1a, N is a linear network without independent sources, the voltage phasor and current phasor is assumed to be

$$\left.\begin{array}{l}\dot{U}=Ue^{j\varphi_u}\\ \dot{I}=Ie^{j\varphi_i}\end{array}\right\} \qquad (5.4.1)$$

So, if the voltage phasor and current phasor are in the standard reference directions, the impedance of N is defined as the ratio of the voltage phasor to its current phasor

$$Z=\frac{\dot{U}}{\dot{I}} \qquad (5.4.2)$$

where Z is a complex number measured in Ohms. Note that impedance is a complex number, not a phasor. The circuit symbol for impedance is shown in Fig.5.4.1b.

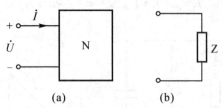

(a) (b)

Fig.5.4.1 The Impedance of Linear Circuit

The impedance can be expressed in different forms,

$$Z=R+jX=|Z|e^{j\varphi_z}=|Z|\angle\varphi_z \qquad (5.4.3)$$

where, R is the real part of impedance and is called resistance. X is the imaginary part of impedance and is called reactance. $|Z|$ is the magnitude of impedance and φ_z is the angle of impedance. Obviously, φ_z is also the argument difference between voltage phasor and current phasor.

The relationships among them are

$$\left.\begin{array}{l}R=|Z|=\cos\varphi_z\\ X=|Z|=\sin\varphi_z\end{array}\right\} \qquad (5.4.4)$$

$$\left.\begin{array}{l}|Z|=\sqrt{R^2+X^2}\\ \varphi_z=\arctan\dfrac{X}{R}\end{array}\right\} \qquad (5.4.5)$$

The above relationships among R, X, $|Z|$ and φ_z can be shown with an impedance triangle, as shown in Fig.5.4.2.

The impedance for a single resistor, inductor or capacitor can be written as follows

$$\left.\begin{array}{l}Z_R=\dfrac{\dot{U}}{\dot{I}}=R\\[6pt]Z_C=\dfrac{\dot{U}}{\dot{I}}=\dfrac{1}{j\omega C}=-jX_C\\[6pt]Z_L=\dfrac{\dot{U}}{\dot{I}}=j\omega L=jX_L\end{array}\right\} \quad (5.4.6)$$

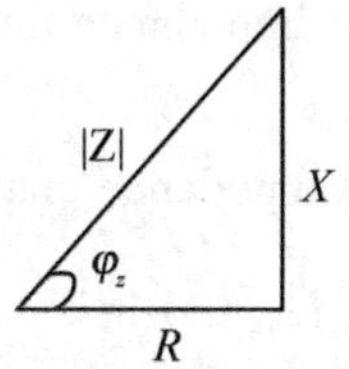

Fig.5.4.2 Impedance Triangle

So, all the relationships can be expressed in the following form

$$\dot{U}=Z\dot{I} \quad (5.4.7)$$

The above expression can be regarded as Ohm's law in phasor form. Here, the voltage phasor and current phasor are in the standard reference directions.

By introducing the concept of impedance, it is convenient to handle the series connection of multiple impedances. It can be proved that the equivalent impedance of multiple impedances in series is equal to the sum of each impedance. This is similar to resistances in series in the time domain.

The multiple impedances in series, as shown in Fig.5.4.3a can be reduced to an equivalent impedance shown in Fig.5.4.3b. The equivalent impedance can be derived simply by adding all individual impedance.

$$Z_{eq}=\sum_{m=1}^{k}Z_m \quad (5.4.8)$$

The voltage drops across each impedance can also be derived as follows

$$\dot{U}_m=\dfrac{Z_m}{Z_{eq}}\dot{U} \quad (5.4.9)$$

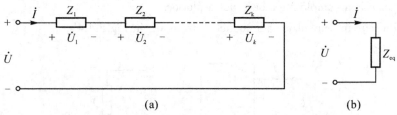

Fig.5.4.3 Impedances in Series

It is the voltage division formula in the phasor form.

For circuits containing only the linear elements R, L, and C, it can be proved that the impedance angle is satisfied with the condition $-\dfrac{\pi}{2} \leqslant \varphi_z \leqslant \dfrac{\pi}{2}$.

If impedance angle is satisfied with $-\dfrac{\pi}{2} \leqslant \varphi_z \leqslant 0$, then the current $\dot{I}$ leads the voltage $\dot{U}$, and it is said that the circuit is capacitive;

If impedance angle is satisfied with $\varphi_z = 0$, then the current $\dot{I}$ and voltage $\dot{U}$ are in phase, and it is said that the circuit is resistive;

If impedance angle is satisfied with $0 \leqslant \varphi_z \leqslant \dfrac{\pi}{2}$, then the voltage $\dot{U}$ leads the current $\dot{I}$, and it is said that the circuit is inductive.

5.4.2 Admittance

As shown in Fig.5.4.4a, N represents a linear circuit without independent sources.

Its voltage phasor and current phasor is assumed to be

$$\left. \begin{array}{l} \dot{U} = U e^{j\varphi_u} \\ \dot{I} = I e^{j\varphi_i} \end{array} \right\} \quad (5.4.10)$$

If the voltage phasor and current phasor are in the standard reference directions, the admittance can be defined as the ratio of the current phasor to its voltage phasor,

$$Y = \dfrac{\dot{I}}{\dot{U}} \quad (5.4.11)$$

where Y represents the admittance of the circuit, measured in Simence. Note that admittance is a complex number, not a phasor.

The circuit symbol for admittance Y is shown in Fig.5.4.4b.

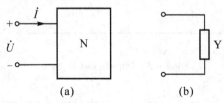

(a)   (b)

Fig.5.4.4 The Admittance of Linear Circuit

The admittance can be expressed in different forms.
$$Y = G + jB = |Y|e^{j\varphi_Y} = |Y|\angle\varphi_Y \tag{5.4.12}$$
where G is the real part of admittance and is called conductance. X is the imaginary part of admittance and is called susceptance. $|Y|$ is the magnitude and φ_Y is the angle of admittance. Obviously, φ_Y is the phase difference between current phasor and voltage phasor and there is $\varphi_Y = -\varphi_Z$. The relationships among them are

$$\left. \begin{array}{l} G = |Y|\cos\varphi_Y \\ B = |Y|\sin\varphi_Y \end{array} \right\} \tag{5.4.13}$$

$$\left. \begin{array}{l} |Y| = \sqrt{G^2 + B^2} \\ \varphi_Y = \arctan\dfrac{B}{G} \end{array} \right\} \tag{5.4.14}$$

These relationships among G, B, $|Y|$ and φ_Y can be indicated by an admittance triangle, as shown in Fig.5.4.5.

The admittances for single resistor, inductor or capacitor are

$$\left. \begin{array}{l} Y_G = \dfrac{\dot{I}}{\dot{U}} = G \\ Y_C = \dfrac{\dot{I}}{\dot{U}} = j\omega C = jB_C \\ Y_L = \dfrac{\dot{I}}{\dot{U}} = \dfrac{1}{j\omega L} = jB_L \end{array} \right\} \tag{5.4.15}$$

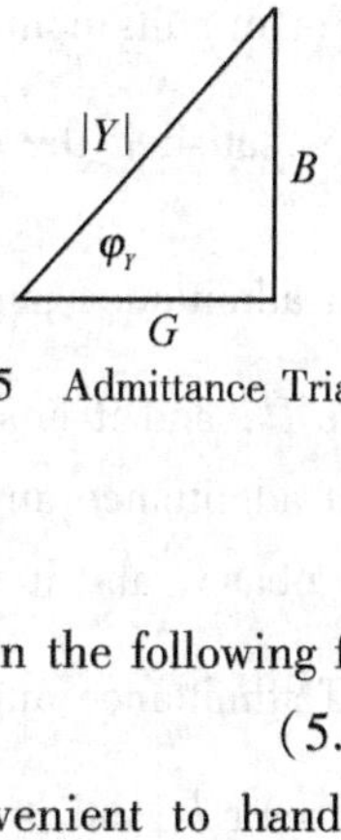

Fig.5.4.5 Admittance Triangle

In can be seen that all relationships can be expressed in the following form
$$\dot{I} = Y\dot{U} \tag{5.4.16}$$

By introducing the concept of admittance, it is convenient to handle the parallel connection of multiple admittances. It can be proved that the equivalent impedance of multiple impedances in parallel is equal to the sum of each admittance. This is similar to resistances in parallel in the time domain. The multiple admittances in parallel, as shown in Fig.5.4.6a can be reduced to an equivalent admittance shown in Fig.5.4.6b. The equivalent admittance can be derived by simply adding all individual admittance.

$$Y_{eq} = \sum_{m=1}^{k} Y_m \qquad (5.4.17)$$

The current flowing through each admittance can be derived as follows

$$\dot{I}_m = \frac{Y_m}{Y_{eq}} \dot{I} \qquad (5.4.18)$$

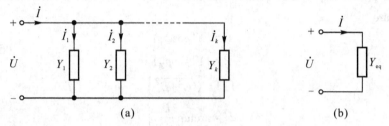

Fig.5.4.6 Admittances in Parallel

This formula is the current division formula in the phasor form.

For circuits containing only the linear elements R, L, and C, the admittance angle is satisfied the condition $-\frac{\pi}{2} \leq \varphi_Y \leq \frac{\pi}{2}$.

If admittance angle is satisfied with $0 \leq \varphi_Y \leq \frac{\pi}{2}$, then the current $\dot{I}$ leads the voltage $\dot{U}$, and it is said that the circuit is capacitive;

If admittance angle is satisfied with $\varphi_Z = 0$, then the current $\dot{I}$ and voltage $\dot{U}$ are in phase, and it is said that the circuit is resistive;

If admittance angle is satisfied with $-\frac{\pi}{2} \leq \varphi_Y \leq 0$, then the voltage $\dot{U}$ leads the current $\dot{I}$, and it is said that the circuit is inductive.

5.4.3 The Relationship between Impedance and Admittance

For a passive two-terminal circuit consisting of resistors, inductors and capacitors, it can be reduced to an equivalent impedance, or an equivalent admittance, as shown in Fig.5.4.7.

If equivalent impedance and equivalent admittance are written as

5.4 Impedance and Admittance

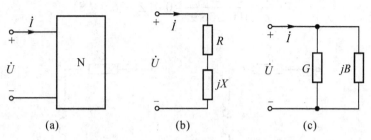

Fig.5.4.7 Impedance and Admittance

$$Z = R + jX$$
$$Y = G + jB$$

Then, the relationship between impedance and admittance will be

$$Z = \frac{1}{Y}$$

So

$$Y = \frac{1}{Z} = \frac{1}{R+jx} = \frac{R-jx}{R^2+x^2} = \frac{R}{R^2+x^2} - j\frac{x}{R^2+x^2} = G+jB$$

$$G = \frac{R}{R^2+x^2}, B = -\frac{x}{R^2+x^2}$$

(5.4.19)

It can be seen that, for any given circuit, its equivalent circuit can be expressed not only as a resistance in series with a reactance, but also as an conductance in parallel with a susceptance

Example 5.4.1 As shown in Fig.5.4.8, the resistor, inductor and capacitor are connected in series. The source angular frequency is $\omega = 100\text{rad/s}$, $r = 80\Omega$, $L = 0.4\text{H}$, $C = 100\mu\text{F}$, find the equivalent impedance and the equivalent admittance.

Solution The reactances for inductor and capacitor are

$$X_L = \omega L = 100 \times 0.4 = 40\Omega$$

$$X_C = \frac{1}{\omega C} = \frac{1}{100 \times 100 \times 10^{-6}} = 100\Omega$$

The equivalent impedance can be derived as

$$Z = r + jX_L - jX_C = 80 + j40 - j100 = 80 + j60 = 100\angle 36.9°\Omega$$

The equivalent admittance can be derived as

$$Y = \frac{1}{Z} = \frac{1}{100\angle 36.9°} = 0.01\angle -36.9°(\text{S})$$

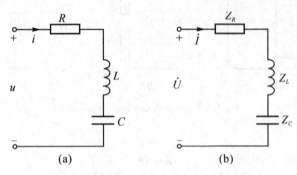

Fig.5.4.8 Circuit for Example 5.4.1

Example 5.4.2 In circuit shown in Fig.5.4.9, the resistor and capacitor are in series, $R = 50\Omega$, $L = 50\mu\text{H}$, and the source angular frequency is $\omega = 10^6\text{rad/s}$. If the circuit shown in Fig.5.4.9a is equivalent to the circuit shown in Fig.5.4.9b, what are R', L'?

Solution The inductive reactance and equivalent impedance of the circuit shown in Fig.5.4.9a is

$$X_L = \omega L = 10^6 \times 50 \times 10^{-6} = 5\Omega$$

$$Z = R + jX_L = 50 + j50 = 70.7\angle 45°\Omega$$

Then, the equivalent admittance the circuit shown in Fig.5.4.9a is

$$Y_a = \frac{1}{Z} = \frac{1}{70.7\angle 45°} = 0.01 - j0.01(\text{S})$$

Because the circuit shown in Fig.5.4.9a is equivalent to the circuit shown in Fig.5.4.9b, the admittance of the circuit shown in Fig.5.4.9b is

$$Y_b = G' + jB' = \frac{1}{R'} - j\frac{1}{\omega L'}$$

Obviously, by comparison, it can be derived that

$$G' = \frac{1}{R'} = 0.01\text{S}, B' = -\frac{1}{\omega L'} = -0.01\text{S}$$

So

$$R' = 100\Omega, L' = 100\mu\text{H}$$

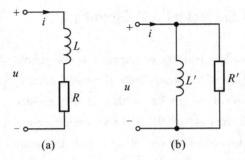

Fig.5.4.9 The Circuit for Example 5.4.2

Example 5.4.3 In the circuit shown in Fig.5.4.10, $r=10\Omega, L=20\mathrm{mH}, C=10\mu\mathrm{F}, R=50\Omega$ and the source angular frequency $\omega=10^3\mathrm{rad/s}$, find the equivalent impedance.

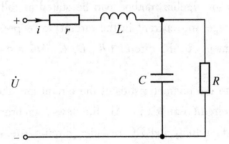

Fig.5.4.10 The Circuit for Example 5.4.3

Solution

The reactances for inductor and capacitor is
$$X_L=\omega L=10^3\times20\times10^{-3}=20\Omega$$
$$X_C=\frac{1}{\omega C}=\frac{1}{10^3\times20\times10^{-6}}=100\Omega$$

The equivalent impedance can be derived as
$$Z=r+jX_L+\frac{R(-jX_C)}{R-jX_C}=10+j20+\frac{50(-j100)}{50-j100}$$
$$=10+j20+40-j20=50\Omega$$

5.5 Analysis of Sinusoidal AC Circuit

After introducing the concept of impedance and admittance, phasor method can be used for analysis of the steady-state sinusoidal circuit. Since the phasor form of KCL, KVL and VCR is similar to that in DC resistive circuit, the circuit theorem and analysis method of DC resistive circuit can also be applied to the analysis of sinusoidal steady-state circuits. To apply this phasor method, the circuit model in the time domain should be transformed into corresponding phasor model first, and then AC circuit can be analyzed with following steps similar to the linear resistance circuit analysis.

There are two kind of phasor methods, they are phasor algebra and phasor diagram respectively. Phasor algebra method is a method by phasor equations via KCL/KVL/VCR and solving these algebraic equations to find answers.

The steps of phasor algebra method can be stated as follows:

(1) All the voltage and current in the circuit are expressed in phasor form.

(2) All the elements in the circuit (R, L, C, M) are expressed in the form of impedance.

(3) According to the characteristics of the circuit and the quantities required, write and solve the circuit equations. All the laws, theorems, and the analysis methods that are used in analyzing DC resistive circuits are suitable for sinusoidal AC circuits, such as KCL, KVL, superposition law, substitution theorem, Thevenin's theorem, loop current method, node voltage method, etc..

(4) Transform the solution voltage and current phasors into the corresponding the time domain form.

Phasor diagram is a special kind of method in AC circuit analysis. It applies the phasor diagram to solve AC circuit problem. First, the given current phasors and the voltage phasors are drawn in the complex plane. Next, by applying the geometrical relationship of the phasor diagram, the required phasors can be derived. And finally, the phasors is transformed to its sinusoidal quantities.

Steps of phasor diagram method can be stated as follows:

(1) Select a reference phasor. In general, the current phasor in series-connected circuit and the voltage phasor in parallel-connected circuit are selected as the

reference phasor.

(2) Draw these phasors one by one according to the phase relationship between the other phasors and the reference phasor. Either parallelogram method or polygon method can be used to draw phasor diagram. If number of phasors is more than two, polygonal method is more suitable in use.

(3) Find the solution using the geometric relationship in the phasor diagram.

Example 5.5.1 For circuit shown in Fig.5.5.1, R, L and C are connected in series, and $R=15\Omega$, $L=12\text{mH}$, $C=5\mu\text{F}$, $u=100\sqrt{2}\cos 5000t$, find: I and u_R, u_L, u_C.

Solution By applying the phasor method, the circuit is transformed into the phasor form as shown in Fig.5.5.1b. There are

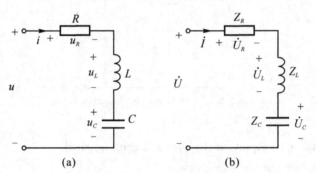

Fig.5.5.1 The Circuit for Example 5.5.1

$$\dot{U} = 100\angle 0°(\text{V})$$
$$Z_R = R = 15(\Omega)$$
$$Z_L = j\omega L = j\times 5000\times 12\times 10^{-3} = j60(\Omega)$$
$$Z_C = \frac{1}{j\omega C} = -j\frac{1}{5000\times 5\times 10^{-6}} = -j40(\Omega)$$
$$Z = Z_R + Z_L + Z_C = 15+j20 = 25\angle 53.1°(\Omega)$$

Then

$$\dot{I} = \frac{\dot{U}}{Z} = \frac{100\angle 0°}{25\angle 53.1°} = 4\angle -53.1°(\text{A})$$
$$I = 4(\text{A})$$

The phasor voltages across the resistor, capacitor and inductor are as follows:

$$\dot{U}_R = Z_R \dot{I} = 60 \angle -53.1°(\text{V})$$
$$\dot{U}_L = Z_L \dot{I} = 240 \angle 36.9°(\text{V})$$
$$\dot{U}_C = Z_C \dot{I} = 160 \angle -143.1°(\text{V})$$

Transforming phasor form into sinusoidal quantities gives
$$u_R = 60\sqrt{2}\cos(5000t - 53.1°)\ (\text{V})$$
$$u_L = 240\sqrt{2}\cos(5000t + 36.9°)\ (\text{V})$$
$$u_C = 160\sqrt{2}\cos(5000t - 143.1°)\ (\text{V})$$

Example 5.5.2 There is a sinusoidal AC voltage source in the circuit, as shown in Fig.5.5.2. $R = 3\text{k}\Omega$, $\omega = 1000\text{rad/s}$ and u_2 lags u_1 by 30°. Find C.

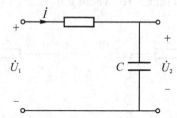

Fig.5.5.2 The Circuit for Example 5.5.2

Solution (1) Applying the phasor algebra method.
Applying voltage division gives
$$\dot{U}_2 = \frac{\dot{U}_1}{R + \dfrac{1}{j\omega c}} \cdot \frac{1}{j\omega c} = \frac{\dot{U}_1}{1 + j\omega Rc}$$

So, we have
$$\frac{\dot{U}_2}{\dot{U}_1} = \frac{1}{\sqrt{1+(\omega RC)^2}\ \angle \tan^{-1}\omega RC} = \frac{1}{\sqrt{1+(\omega RC)^2}} \angle -\tan^{-1}\omega RC$$

Since $\dot{U}_2$ lags by $\dot{U}_1$ 30°, we get
$$\tan^{-1}\omega RC = 30°$$
$$\omega RC = \tan 30° = \frac{\sqrt{3}}{3}$$

$\therefore$
$$C = \frac{1}{\omega R} \cdot \frac{\sqrt{3}}{3} = \frac{\sqrt{3}}{10^3 \times 3 \times 10^3 \times 3} = 0.19\ \mu\text{F}$$

(2) Applying the phasor diagram method.

The voltage phasors $\dot{U}_1$, $\dot{U}_2$ and the current phasor $\dot{I}$ are drawn in phasor diagram, as shown in Fig.5.5.3. Then, by inspecting triangle in the phasor diagram, we have

$$\frac{\dot{U}_R}{\dot{U}_2} = \frac{RI}{\frac{1}{\omega C} \cdot I} = R\omega C = \tan 30°$$

So,

$$C = \frac{1}{\omega R} \cdot \tan 30° = 0.19 \mu F$$

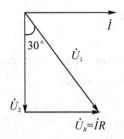

Fig.5.5.3 Phasor Diagram for Ex.5.5.2

Example 5.5.3 In the circuit shown in Fig.5.5.4, $\dot{U} = 70.7\text{V}$, $\dot{U}$ and $\dot{I}_L$ are in phase. Find R, X_L, X_C.

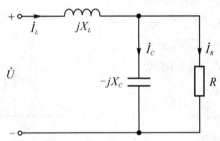

Fig.5.5.4 The Circuit for Example 5.5.3

Method 1 Applying the phasor algebra method.

Assume $\dot{I}_R = 5\angle 0°\text{A}$, then $\dot{I}_C = 5\angle 90°\text{A}$

Applying KCL, gives

$$\dot{I}_L = \dot{I}_R + \dot{I}_C = 5 + 5j = 5\sqrt{2}\angle 45°\text{A}$$

Since $\dot{U}$ and $\dot{I}_L$ are in phase, so

$$\dot{U} = 70.7\angle 45° = 50 + j50(\text{V})$$

Applying KVL, yields

$$\dot{U} = jX_L\dot{I}_L + R\dot{I}_R = jX_L(5+5j) + 5R = 5(R - X_L) + j5X_L = 50 + j50(\text{V})$$

By comparing above two expressions with phasor $\dot{U}$, two equations can be derived as follows

$$5(R-X_L) = 50$$
$$5X_L = 50$$

So
$$X_L = 10\Omega, \ R = 20\Omega.$$

Again, since the capacitor and the resistor R are in series, their voltage must be same, namely
$$RI_R = I_C X_C$$

So,
$$X_C = \frac{RI_R}{I_C} = 20(\Omega)$$

Method 2 Applying the phasor diagram method

Assuming that the phase angle of voltage $\dot{U}_R$ is zero, the phasor diagram can be drawn, as shown in Fig.5.5.5. Since to $\dot{I}_R = \dot{I}_C = 5\text{A}$, the Pythagorean formula can be used to find the total current

$$\dot{I}_L = \sqrt{I_R^2 + I_C^2} = 5\sqrt{2}\,\text{A}, \ \theta = 45°$$

Again, using $U = 70.7\text{V}$, gives
$$\dot{U}_L = \dot{U} = 70.7\text{V}, \ \dot{U}_R = 100\text{V}$$

$$\therefore \ X_L = \frac{\dot{U}_L}{\dot{I}_L} = \frac{70.7}{5\sqrt{2}} = 10\Omega$$

$$X_C = \frac{\dot{U}_C}{\dot{I}_C} = \frac{100}{5} = 20\Omega$$

$$R = \frac{\dot{U}_R}{\dot{I}_R} = \frac{100}{5} = 20\Omega$$

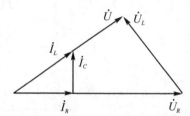

Fig.5.5.5 The Circuit for Example 5.5.3

Example 5.5.4 As shown in Fig.5.5.6a, $R = 2\Omega$, $C = 100\mu\text{F}$, $L = 5\text{mH}$, $u_{s1} = 120\sqrt{2}\cos 1000t\,\text{V}$ and $u_{s2} = 100\sqrt{2}\cos(1000t - 30°)\,\text{V}$. Find each branch current.

Solution The reference directions for each branch current are shown in Fig.5.5.6a and the current phasors are shown in Fig.5.5.6b. The voltages of sources are
$$\dot{U}_{S1} = 120\angle 0°(\text{V}), \ \dot{U}_{S2} = 100\angle -30°(\text{V}).$$

Method 1 Applying the mesh-current method

The reference directions of mesh current are assigned as shown in Fig.5.5.6b and the mesh current equations can be written as follows

$$\begin{cases}\left(R+\dfrac{1}{j\omega c}\right)\dot{I}_a-\dfrac{1}{j\omega c}\dot{I}_b=\dot{U}_{s1}\\-\dfrac{1}{j\omega c}\dot{I}_a+\left(j\omega L+\dfrac{1}{j\omega c}\right)\dot{I}_b=\dot{U}_{s2}\end{cases}$$

Substituting the parameters into equations gives

$$\begin{cases}(2-j10)\dot{I}_a+j10\dot{I}_b=120\\j10\dot{I}_a+j(5-10)\dot{I}_b=100\angle-30°\end{cases}$$

Solving the equations yields

$$\dot{I}_a=11.1\angle39.3°(\text{A}),\ \dot{I}_b=7.88\angle-24.4°(\text{A})$$

∴
$$\dot{I}_1=\dot{I}_a=11.1\angle39.3°(\text{A})$$
$$\dot{I}_2=\dot{I}_b=7.88\angle-24.4°(\text{A})$$
$$\dot{I}_3=\dot{I}_a-\dot{I}_b=11.1\angle39.3°-7.88\angle-24.4°=10.4\angle82.3°(\text{A})$$

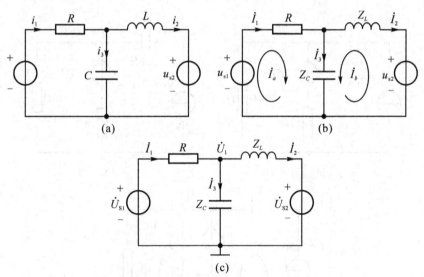

Fig.5.5.6 The Circuit for Example 5.5.4

Method 2 Applying the node voltage method

For the circuit shown in Fig.5.5.6c, the node voltage equation can be written as follows

$$\left(\frac{1}{R}+j\omega C+\frac{1}{j\omega L}\right)\dot{U}_1 = \frac{\dot{U}_{S1}}{R}+\frac{\dot{U}_{S2}}{j\omega L}$$

So, we have

$$\dot{U}_1 = \frac{\dfrac{\dot{U}_{S1}}{R}+\dfrac{\dot{U}_{n1}}{j\omega L}}{\dfrac{1}{R}+j\omega C+\dfrac{1}{j\omega L}} = 137.08-j14.06(\text{V})$$

$\dot{I}_1$、$\dot{I}_2$ and $\dot{I}_3$ are

$$\dot{I}_1 = \frac{\dot{U}_{S1}-\dot{U}_1}{R} = 11.1\angle 39.3°(\text{A})$$

$$\dot{I}_2 = \frac{\dot{U}_1-\dot{U}_{S2}}{j\omega L} = 7.88\angle -24.4°(\text{A})$$

$$\dot{I}_3 = j\omega C\dot{U}_1 = 10.4\angle 82.3°(\text{A})$$

Example 5.5.5 Find the voltage $\dot{U}$ in the circuit shown in Fig.5.5.7a.

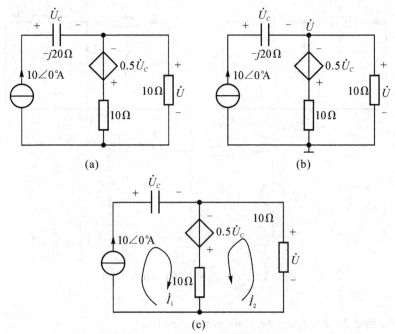

Fig.5.5.7 The Circuit for Example 5.5.5

Solution Three methods are applied to solve this problem.

Method 1 Applying the node voltage method

The reference node is chosen as shown in Fig.5.5.7b and the node voltage equation can be written as follows

$$\dot{U}(10+10) = 10\angle 0° + \frac{-0.5\dot{U}_C}{10}$$

Then, the voltage across the capacitor can be solved as follows

$$\dot{U}_C = -j20 \times 10\angle 0°(\text{V})$$

So

$$\dot{U} = 50 + 50j = 50\sqrt{2}\angle 45°(\text{V})$$

Method 2 Applying the mesh current method

The reference directions of mesh currents are assigned as shown in Fig.5.5.7c and the mesh equations can be written as follows:

$$\left.\begin{array}{l} \dot{I}_1 = 10\angle 0° \\ \dot{I}_2(10+10) - \dot{I}_1 \times 10 = -0.5\dot{U}_C \end{array}\right\}$$

Then, the voltage across the capacitor can be solved as follows

$$\dot{U}_C = -j20 \times 10\angle 0°(\text{V})$$

So

$$\dot{I}_1 = 10\angle 0°(\text{A})$$
$$\dot{I}_2 = 5 + 5j = 5\sqrt{2}\angle 45°(\text{A})$$

and

$$\dot{U} = 50 + 50j = 50\sqrt{2}\angle 45°(\text{V})$$

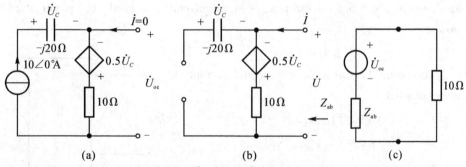

Fig.5.5.8 The Circuit for Example 5.5.5

Method 3 Applying the Thevenin's theorem

As shown in Fig.5.5.8a, the open circuit voltage between the two terminals is
$$\dot{U}_{oc} = -0.5\dot{U}_c + 10 \times 10 \angle 0° = -0.5 \times (-j20) \times 10 \angle 0° + 100 = 100 + j100 \text{ (V)}$$

Killing the independent current source, as shown in Fig. 5.5.8b, the Thevenin's equivalent impedance can be derived as follows
$$Z_{ab} = 10 \text{ (}\Omega\text{)}.$$

From Thevenin's equivalent circuit shown in Fig.5.5.8c, the phasor voltage $\dot{U}$ can be derived as follows
$$\dot{U} = \frac{10}{10+10}\dot{U}_{oc} = 50 + j50 = 50\sqrt{2} \angle 45° \text{ (V)}.$$

5.6 Power in Sinusoidal AC Circuit

Power in sinusoidal AC circuit is more complicate than that in DC circuit. The power used in DC circuit is equal to the product of voltage and current. However, because this power is always changed with time in sinusoidal AC circuit, it is of no use. Due to this reason, some different kind of powers are introduced to describe the power in sinusoidal AC circuit. In this section, average power, reactive power, apparent power and complex power will be discussed. Besides, an important parameter associated with power, namely power factor, will also be discussed.

5.6.1 Power in Sinusoidal AC Circuit

For a passive AC circuit, it is assumed that its voltage is u and current is i, as shown in Fig.5.6.1. If the passive sign convention is used, the power at any instant is
$$p = ui$$

Assuming the sinusoidal voltage and current are expressed as
$$u = \sqrt{2}U\cos(\omega t)$$
$$i = \sqrt{2}I\cos(\omega t - \varphi)$$

The instantaneous power is
$$p = ui = \sqrt{2}U\cos\omega t \cdot \sqrt{2}I\cos(\omega t - \varphi)$$

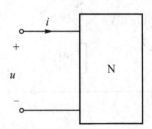

Fig.5.6.1 A Passive Network

$$= 2UI\left[\frac{1}{2}\cos(2\omega t-\varphi)+\frac{1}{2}\cos\varphi\right]$$
$$= UI\cos\varphi + UI\cos(2\omega t-\varphi) \quad (5.6.1)$$

(5.6.1) can be rewritten as follows

$$p = ui = UI\cos\varphi[1+\cos(2\omega t)]+UI\sin\varphi\sin(2\omega t) \quad (5.6.2)$$

From (5.6.1), it can be seen that the instantaneous power of the circuit consists of two parts: the constant ($UI\cos\varphi$) and ($UI\cos(2\omega t-\varphi)$) whose frequency is twice source frequency. So, it may be said that the frequency of the instantaneous power is twice the frequency of the voltage or current, as shown in Fig.5.6.2.

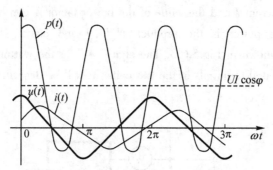

Fig.5.6.2 The Waveform of Instantaneous Power

It can be seen from Fig.5.6.2, that three are three cases:

If signs of u and i are same, $p>0$, the circuit absorbs power;

If signs of u and i are opposite, $p<0$, the circuit produces power;

If one of u and i are zero, $p=0$, the circuit neither produce nor absorb power.

Because the instantaneous power always changes with time, it cannot be used to indicate the power status of a sinusoidal AC circuit. So, there is not much practical significance for Instantaneous power.

To indicate the power status and exchange of a sinusoidal AC circuit, the following powers are introduced:

5.6.1.1 Average Power (Active Power)

Average power is also called active power. The average power is the average value of the instantaneous power over one period and is denoted by P.

$$P = \frac{1}{T}\int_0^T pdt = \frac{1}{T}\int_0^T uidt = \frac{1}{T}\int_0^T UI[\cos\varphi + \cos(2\omega t - \varphi)]dt$$

$$= \frac{1}{T}\int_0^T UI\cos\varphi dt + \frac{1}{T}\int_0^T UI\cos(2\omega t - \varphi)dt \tag{5.6.3}$$

Since the integral of Sine function over a cycle must be zero, we get

$$P = UI\cos\varphi \tag{5.6.4}$$

where $\cos\varphi$ is called the power factor and is denoted by λ, namely $\lambda = \cos\varphi$.

It can be seen from equation (5.6.1) that the average power consumed by the circuit is the constant component of the instantaneous power, measured in watts.

The average power can be measured with a wattmeter. The internal structure of the wattmeter consists of a voltage coil and a current coil. The rules of the voltage U and current I and the value of the power factor λ can be measured, and then the average power is the product of U, I and $\cos\varphi$. The wiring of the measurement is shown in Fig.5.6.3. The sign " * " in the wattmeter indicates the concept of the dotted terminals of the two coils, it will be described in detail in the next chapter.

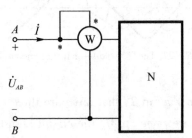

Fig.5.6.3 the Measure of Average Power

5.6.1.2 Reactive Power

Reactive power is defined as

$$Q = UI\sin\varphi = \frac{1}{2}U_m I_m \sin\varphi \tag{5.6.5}$$

Reactive power reflects the maximum size of energy exchanging between internal and external circuit of one-port circuit. Reactive power is only a calculating quantity, it does not mean the work done by the circuit. In order to distinguish it with average power, Var is used as the unit of reactive power.

If one-port circuit is a passive network, power factor angle φ will be the impedance angle φ_z. Then, average power can be written as

$$P = UI\cos\varphi_z = \frac{1}{2}U_m I_m \cos\varphi_z$$

$$Q = UI\sin\varphi_z = \frac{1}{2}U_m I_m \sin\varphi_z$$

To better understand the average and reactive power, let's discuss them for purely resistive, purely capacitive, or purely inductive circuits.

(1) purely resistive circuit

$$\varphi_z = 0, \quad \cos\varphi_z = 1$$

$$\therefore \quad P = UI, \quad Q = 0$$

It indicates that a resistor only dissipates energy only and its reactive power is zero.

(2) purely inductive circuit

$$\varphi_z = \frac{\pi}{2}, \quad \cos\varphi_z = 0 > 0$$

$$\therefore \quad P = 0, \quad Q = UI = I^2 X_L = \frac{U^2}{X_L} > 0$$

(3) purely capacitive circuit

$$\varphi_z = -\frac{\pi}{2}, \quad \cos\varphi_z = 0$$

$$\therefore \quad P = 0, \quad Q = -UI = -I^2 X_c = -\frac{U^2}{X_c} < 0$$

It indicates that the average power of the inductor and the capacitor is zero, both the inductor and the capacitor do not consume energy, however, they exchange energy with the external circuit. The reactive power of an inductor is always positive, the reactive power of a capacitor is always negative.

5.6.1.3 Apparent Power

For some electrical equipment, such as generators, transformers and others, the power factor depends on the loads, so the apparent power is usually used to express its capacity of power. The apparent power is defined as

$$S = UI = \frac{1}{2}U_m I_m \tag{5.6.6}$$

The apparent power is measured in VA.

5.6.1.4 Complex Power

The complex power is denoted by $\tilde{S}$. Its real part is active power and imaginary part is reactive power.

$$\tilde{S} = P + jQ \tag{5.6.7}$$

Assuming that $\varphi = \varphi_u - \varphi_i$, $\tilde{S}$ can be expressed as

$$\tilde{S} = P + jQ = UI\cos\varphi + jUI\sin\varphi = UIe^{j\varphi} = UIe^{j(\varphi_u - \varphi_i)} = Ue^{j\varphi_u} \cdot Ie^{-j\varphi_i} = \dot{U}\dot{I} = Se^{j\varphi} \tag{5.6.8}$$

The complex power is measured in in VA.

It is seen that apparent power is the magnitude of complex power.

In a sinusoidal AC circuit, it can be proved that

$$\sum \tilde{S} = 0 \tag{5.6.9a}$$

$$\sum P = 0 \tag{5.6.9b}$$

$$\sum Q = 0 \tag{5.6.9c}$$

Eq.(5.6.9) shows that in a sinusoidal AC circuit, the algebraic sum of the complex power is zero, the algebraic sum of the active powers is zero and the algebraic sum of the reactive power is zero too.

Example 5.6.1 As shown in Fig.5.6.4, $U_c = 10\text{V}$, $R = 3\Omega$, $X_c = X_L = 4\Omega$. Find P, Q, S, λ.

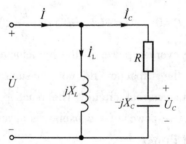

Fig.5.6.4   The Circuit for Example 5.6.1

Solution   Assume $\dot{U}_c = 10\angle 0°\text{V}$,

Then
$$\dot{I}_c = \frac{\dot{U}_c}{-jX_c} = \frac{10\angle 0°}{-j4} = 2.5\angle 90°\text{A}$$

$$\dot{U} = (R-jX_C)\dot{I}_C = (3-j4) \times 2.5\angle 90° = 12.5\angle 36.9°\text{V}$$

$$Z = \frac{jX_L(R-jX_C)}{jX_L+(R-jX_C)} = \frac{j4(3-j4)}{3} = \frac{20}{3}\angle 36.9°\Omega$$

$$\dot{I} = \frac{\dot{U}}{Z} = \frac{12.5\angle 36.9°}{\frac{20}{3}\angle 36.9°} = \frac{15}{8}\text{A}$$

So, it can be derived that

$$P = UI\cos\theta = 12.5 \times \frac{15}{8}\cos 36.9° = \frac{75}{4}\text{W}$$

$$Q = UI\sin\theta 12.5 \times \frac{15}{8}\sin 36.9° = \frac{225}{16}\text{Var}$$

$$S = UI = 12.5 \times \frac{15}{8} = \frac{375}{16}\text{VA}$$

$$\lambda = \cos\theta = \cos 36.9° = 0.8$$

For this problem, the total active and reactive power can also be found by adding active and reactive power of each element.

In the following, with an *RLC* series circuit as an example, as shown in Fig.5.6.5, the specific meaning of *P* and *Q* will be discussed.

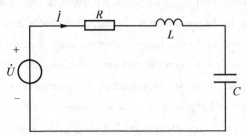

Fig.5.6.5 *RLC* Series Circuit

It can be derived from the circuit that

$$P = UI\cos\varphi = |Z|I^2\cos\phi = I^2|Z|\cos\varphi = RI^2 \quad (5.6.10\text{a})$$
$$Q = UI\sin\varphi = |Z|I^2\sin\varphi = XI^2 = (X_L-X_C)I^2 \quad (5.6.10\text{b})$$
$$S = UI \quad (5.6.10\text{c})$$

It can be seen that since *L* and *C* do not dissipate active power, the active power dissipated by the whole circuit is actually the power dissipated by *R*. Since *R* dissipates no reactive power, the reactive power of the whole circuit is the result of reactance X. Therefore, it is equal to the algebraic sum of the reactive power absorbed by L and the reactive power produced by C

$$Q = X_L I^2 - X_C I^2 = Q_L + Q_C$$

The relationship among the average power, the reactive power and the apparent power are

$$P = UI\cos\varphi = S\cos\varphi$$
$$Q = UI\sin\varphi = S\sin\varphi$$
$$S = \sqrt{P^2 + Q^2}$$
$$\text{tg}\varphi = \frac{P}{Q} \qquad (5.6.11)$$

This relationship can be expressed with a power triangle, as shown in Fig.5.6.6.

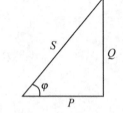

Fig.5.6.6   Power Triangle

It is not difficult to know that the power triangle and the impedance triangle are similar triangles.

5.6.2 Power Factor Correction

The design of any power transmission system is very sensitive to the magnitude of the current on the transmission lines, this current is determined by loads. Due to the resistance of the transmission lines, increased currents result in increased power losses on the transmission lines. Larger currents also require larger conductors for transmission lines, so it will increase the amount of copper or aluminum needed for the system, and also increase requirement of generator capacities. Therefore, efforts must be made to keep line current at a proper level.

From the average power expression (5.6.4), the current can be derived as follows

$$I = \frac{P}{U\cos\varphi} \qquad (5.6.12)$$

For a given load, P is a constant. Since the line voltage U of a transmission system is also fixed value, the method to reduce the current is to increase the power factor as large as possible. Since the largest power factor is I, power factor angle should be made to approach zero degree. In particular, it can be achieved by connecting a reactance element at both terminals of the circuit to correct or improve power factor.

Most loads in our daily life are inductive. So, in order to improve the power factor, the general method is connecting a capacitor in parallel with the load. Although the power factor can also be improved by connecting a capacitor in series with the load, the load may not work normally on account of change in rated voltage caused by the capacitor. Therefore, the capacitor should be connected in parallel with the load to ensure that the load can normally operate at the rated voltage.

Example 5.6.2 In the circuit shown in Fig.5.6.7a, the frequency of the source is $f = 50\text{Hz}$, the terminal voltage of the source is $U = 380\text{V}$. The average power and power factor of the inductive load is respectively $P = 20\text{kW}, \cos\varphi_1 = 0.6$. If a capacitor be connected in parallel with the load to correct the power factor to $\cos\varphi_2 = 0.9$, determine the value of capacitance.

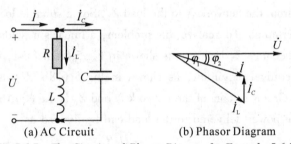

(a) AC Circuit   (b) Phasor Diagram

Fig.5.6.7 The Circuit and Phasor Diagram for Example 5.6.2

Solution For the circuit shown in Fig.5.6.7a, its phasor diagram can be drawn as shown in Fig.5.6.7b. Before capacitor is connected, the total current is same as the inductor current and can be derived as follows

$$I_L = \frac{P}{U\cos\varphi_1} = \frac{20 \times 10^3}{380 \times 0.6} = 87.72\text{A}$$

$$\varphi_1 = \cos^{-1} 0.6 = 53.13°$$

To correct the power factor $\cos\varphi_1$, a capacitor is connected in parallel with the inductive load.

And assume the current flowing through the capacitor is $\dot{I}_C$, then the total current is

$$\dot{I} = \dot{I}_L + \dot{I}_C$$

After the capacitor is connected, power factor $\cos\varphi_1$ is promoted to $\cos\varphi_2$, but the total active power will be changed. So, there is

$$I = \frac{P}{U\cos\varphi_2} = \frac{20\times 10^3}{380\times 0.9} = 58.48\text{A}$$

$$\varphi_2 = \cos^{-1} 0.9 = 25.84°$$

From the phasor diagram, it can be seen that

$$I_C = I_L \sin\varphi_1 - I\sin\varphi_2 = 87.72\sin 53.13° - 58.48\sin 25.84° = 44.7\text{A}$$

Thus, capacitance can be derived as follows

$$C = \frac{I_C}{\omega U} = \frac{44.7}{314\times 380} = 375\mu\text{F}$$

5.6.3 Maximum Power Transfer

For the circuit shown in Fig.5.6.8, it is required that the maximum power can be transferred from the network N to the load Z_L. So, a suitable load impedance Z_L have to be determined. To analyze this problem, a linear sinusoidal AC network N with a load impedance Z_L is used, as shown in Fig.5.6.8a. First, it is replaced by its Thevenin's equivalent circuit, as shown in Fig.5.6.8b. U_{oC} is the equivalent source or open circuit voltage of the network N and Z_0 is the equivalent impedance. So, the average power delivered to the load can be derived as

$$P = I^2 R_L = \frac{U_s^2 R_L}{(R_0 + R_L)^2 + (X_0 + X_L)^2} \tag{5.6.13}$$

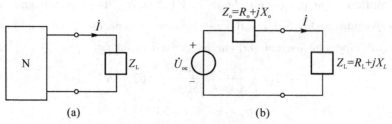

Fig.5.6.8 Circuit for Maximum Power Transfer

Usually R_0 and X_0 are fixed but R_L and X_L are adjustable. Therefore, to maximize power P, the values of R_L and X_L must satisfy the following conditions.

$$\frac{\partial P}{\partial X_L}=0 \quad \text{and} \quad \frac{\partial P}{\partial R_L}=0 \qquad (5.6.14)$$

It can be derived that

$$X_L = -X_0$$
$$R_L = R_0 \qquad (5.6.15)$$

That is

$$Z_L = R_0 - X_0 = Z_0^* \qquad (5.6.16)$$

Eq.(5.6.15) shows that when R_L and X_L are adjustable, the condition that the load Z_L obtain the maximum average power from the network N is that Z_L is equal to the conjugate of Z_0. This is called maximum power matching condition or conjugate matching. And the maximum average power delivered to the load can be derived as

$$P_{L\max} = \frac{U_s^2}{4R_i} \qquad (5.6.17)$$

For the case that R_L and X_L cannot be adjustable, namely argument of Z_L is fixed and it amplitude is changeable, it can be proved that the condition of load to obtain the maximum power is that the impedance magnitude of load is equal to the impedance magnitude of the internal impedance of source.

$$|Z_L| = |Z_i| \qquad (5.6.18)$$

This condition is called magnitude matching. In this case, the maximum power obtained by the load is smaller than that obtained by conjugate matching.

In power system, it is not allowed to work in the state of conjugate matching. On the one hand the efficiency is too low, on the other hand, because the internal impedance of the power supply is very small, the matching current is large, it will damage the power supply and load. The conjugate matching problem is only considered in the communication system and some electronic circuits.

Example 5.6.3 As shown in Fig.5.6.9, $\dot{U}_S = 10\angle 0°\text{V}$, $Z_C = -j3\Omega$, $R = 4\Omega$. If it is known that the maximum average power is transferred to Z_L, what is the value of Z_L? And what is the maximum power?

Solution First, the left part seen from a, b of the circuit is replaced by its Thevenin's equivalent circuit, as shown in Fig.5.6.9b. The Thevenin's voltage and impedance can be derived as follows:

$$\dot{U}_{oc} = \frac{4}{4-j3} \times 10\angle 0° = 8\angle 36.9°\,\text{V}$$

$$Z_0 = \frac{4(-j3)}{4-j3} = 2.4\angle -53.1°\,\Omega$$

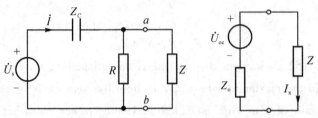

Fig.5.6.9 The Circuit of Example 5.6.4

Next, according to maximum power transfer Theorem, if there are no restrictions on the load, R_L and X_L can be derived as follows

$$Z_L = Z_0^* = 2.4\angle 53.1° = 1.44+j1.92\,\Omega$$

Or

$$R_0 = 1.44\,\Omega, \quad X_0 = j1.92\,\Omega$$

And the maximum average power is

$$P_{L\max} = \frac{U_{oc}^2}{4R_o} = \frac{8^2}{4\times 1.44} = 11.1\,\text{W}$$

5.7 Examples of Computer-Aided Analysis of Circuits

In the following, analyzing an sinusoidal AC example by applying computer-aided circuit analysis software EWB will be discussed.

For the AC circuit, to find RMS value of the node voltage and branch current, similar to the DC circuit, the ammeter is connected in series with branch in which current is measured, the voltmeter in connected in parallel with the part which is required to measure. The ammeter and voltmeter should be set to AC range. Then activate the simulation switch, current and voltage values can be read from the meter. Fig.5.7.1 shows a AC phase-shifting circuit, in which a AC ammeter and a voltmeter can be used to measure the current and voltage across resistor of the circuit. And from the oscilloscope waveform, it can also be observed that the resistor voltage (i.e. current phase) leads the supply voltage by 60°, as shown in Fig.5.8.2.

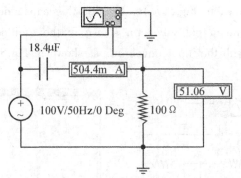

Fig.5.7.1　AC Phase-Shifting Circuit

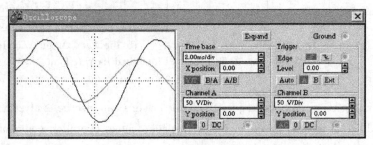

Fig.5.7.2　Oscilloscope Waveform

Fig.5.7.3 shows an AC trapezoidal circuit. It is known that resistance $R =$

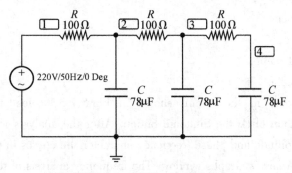

Fig.5.7.3　An AC Trapezoidal Circuit

100Ω. If the output voltage is opposite to the input voltage, it is required to find the capacitance C. For this purpose, an oscilloscope is connected to the circuit, its two channels A、B were connected to the node 1 (input) and node 4 (output) respectively, as shown in Fig.5.7.4a. By adjusting capacitor C, it is found that when $C = 78\mu F$, the output waveform shown in the oscilloscope is exactly the opposite in phase with the input waveform, as shown in Fig.5.7.4b.

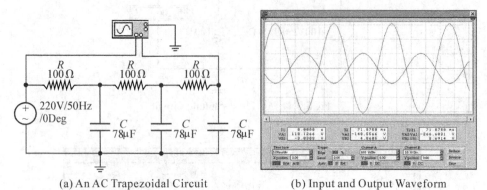

(a) An AC Trapezoidal Circuit (b) Input and Output Waveform

Fig.5.7.4 An AC Trapezoidal Circuit and Its Waveform

For the AC circuit, its frequency characteristics can also be analyzed. After the circuit diagram is established in the workspace, select operation command of AC frequency analysis from Analysis menu on the command menu. Then in the pop-up dialog box, you need to set some parameters as follows:

Nodes for Analysis,

Start Frequency,

End Frequency,

Sweep type,

Number of point,

Vertical scale.

For example, in the circuit shown in Fig.5.7.3, select the node 4 for analysis, and then click the Simulate button. After the analysis is complete, you can see the amplitude and phase frequency characteristic curves in the AC Analysis column of the Analysis Graphs window. The frequency analysis of the circuit shown in Fig.5.7.3 is shown in Fig.5.7.5.

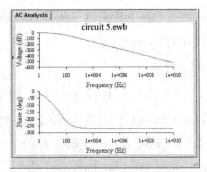

Fig 5.7.5 The Amplitude and Phase Frequency Characteristic Curves

Problems

5-1 The instantaneous expressions of voltage or current are given as follows:
(1) $u(t) = 30\cos(314t+60°)$ (V)
(2) $i(t) = 10\cos(3140t-120°)$ (A)
(3) $u(t) = 15\cos(628t+90°)$ (V)

Draw their waveforms and find their amplitude, frequency and initial phase angle for each sinusoidal quantity.

5-2 The amplitude of a sinusoidal current is $I_m = 8$mA, the angle frequency is $\omega = 10^3$ rad/s and the initial phase angle is $\varphi = 45°$. Find its the instantaneous expression and effective value.

5-3 Calculate the effective value of the periodic voltage and current shown in Fig.5-3.

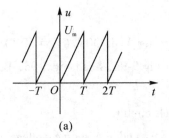
(a)

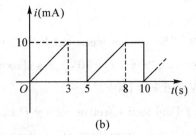
(b)

Fig.5-3

5-4 Find the phasors for the following voltages or currents.

(1) $u(t) = 150\sqrt{2}\cos(314t-45°)$ (V)

(2) $i(t) = 14.14\cos(1000t+60°)$ (A)

(3) $i(t) = 5\sqrt{2}\cos(314t+36.9°) + 10\sqrt{2}\cos(314t-53.1°)$ (A)

(4) $u(t) = 300\sqrt{2}\cos(100t+45°) + 100\sqrt{2}\cos(100t-45°)$ (V)

5-5 It is given: $\dot{I}_1 = 6+j8$ A, $\dot{I}_2 = -6+j8$ A, $\dot{I}_3 = -6-j8$ A, $\dot{I}_4 = 6-j8$ A, find their corresponding expressions in polar form and the instantaneous expressions (assume the frequency is ω).

5-6 For the circuit shown in Fig.5-6, $R = 200\Omega$, $L = 0.1$ mH, the voltage drops across the resistance is $u_R = \sqrt{2}\cos10^6 t$ (V). Find the source voltage u_S and draw the phasor diagram.

5-7 For the circuit shown in Fig.5-7, $R = 10$kΩ, $C = 0.2\mu$F, $i_C = \sqrt{2}\cos(10^6 t + 30°)$ (V). Find the current source i_S and draw the phasor diagram.

5-8 For the circuit shown in Fig.5-8, $i_S = 10\sqrt{2}\cos(2t-36.9°)$ A, $u = 50\sqrt{2}\cos2t$ V. Find the value of R and L.

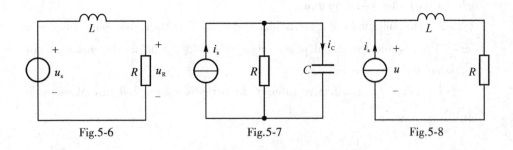

Fig.5-6　　　　　　Fig.5-7　　　　　　Fig.5-8

5-9 The voltage measured by AC voltmeter V_1 is 30V ($V_1 = 30$V) and by voltmeter V_2 is 60V ($V_2 = 30$V), as shown in Fig.5-9a, b. In Fig.5-9c, $V_1 = 15$V, $V_2 = 80$V and $V_3 = 100$V.

(1) Find total effective voltage U in each circuit.

(2) If the sources are DC voltage sources and the source voltage is 12V, determine the reading of each AC voltmeter.

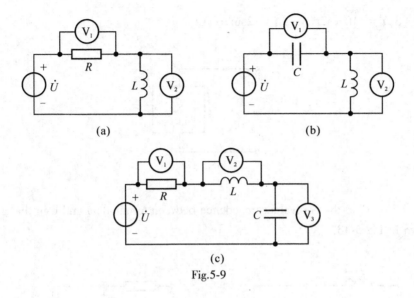

(a) (b)

(c)

Fig.5-9

5-10 As shown in Fig.5-10, the reading of ammeter A_1 is 3A, the reading of ammeter A_2 is 4A, find the reading of ammeter A. If the reading of the voltmeter V is 100V, find the value of the resistance R and the reactance of the capacitor C.

5-11 For the circuit shown in Fig.5-1, $R=50\Omega$, $L=2.5\text{mH}$, $C=5\mu\text{F}$, $U=10\angle 0°\text{V}$ and $\omega=10^4\text{rad/s}$, find I_R, I_L, I_C, I, and draw the phasor diagram.

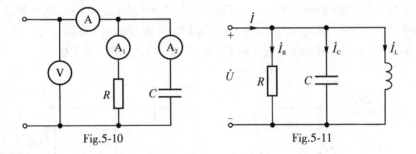

Fig.5-10 Fig.5-11

5-12 For the circuit in Fig.5-12, each of the following cases of voltage and current are given. What should the element N may be? What is it's element parameter?

(1) $u=10\sqrt{2}\sin 5t(\text{V})$, $i=\sqrt{2}\cos 5t(\text{A})$

(2) $u=100\cos(10t+45°)(\text{V})$, $i=10\sin(10t+135°)(\text{A})$

(3) $u = -10\cos 2t$ (V), $i = -2\sin 2t$ (A)

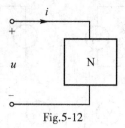

Fig.5-12

5-13 Find the equivalent impedance between terminals a and b in the circuit shown in Fig.5-13.

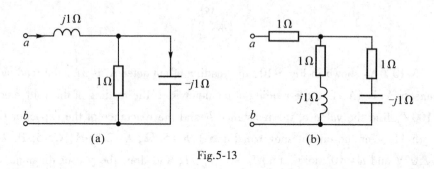

Fig.5-13

5-14 For the circuit shown in Fig.5-14, $Y_1 = 0.16 + j0.12$ (S), $Z_2 = 25\Omega$, $Z_3 = 3 + j4$ (Ω), the reading of the ammeter is 1A, find effective voltage U.

5-15 For the circuit shown in Fig.5-15, $\dot{I}_L = 1\angle 0°$A. Find $\dot{U}_S$.

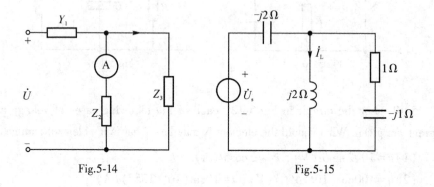

Fig.5-14   Fig.5-15

5-16 For the circuit shown in Fig.5-16, $R = 10\Omega$, $f = 50\text{Hz}$, $I = 4\text{A}$, $I_1 = 3.5\text{A}$, $I_2 = 1\text{A}$. Find R_L and L.

5-17 For the circuit shown in Fig.5-17, $U = 50\text{V}$, $I_C = I_R = 5\text{A}$, the voltage $\dot{U}$ is in phase with the current $\dot{I}$ find I, R, X_L and X_C.

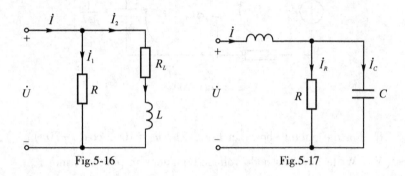

Fig.5-16   Fig.5-17

5-18 For the circuit shown in Fig.5-18, $U = 100\text{V}$, $I = 100\text{mA}$, $X_{L1} = 1.25\text{k}\Omega$, $x_C = 0.75\text{k}\Omega$, the average power delivered to the circuit is 6W. If the circuit is inductive, find r and X_L.

5-19 For the circuit shown in Fig.5-19, $U = 10\text{V}$, $\omega = 10^4 \text{rad/s}$, $r = 3\text{k}\Omega$. By adjusting variable resistor to make the reading of the voltmeter approaching to minimum, and it is known that $r_1 = 900\Omega$, $r_2 = 1600\Omega$. Find the minimum reading of the voltage meter and the capacitance C.

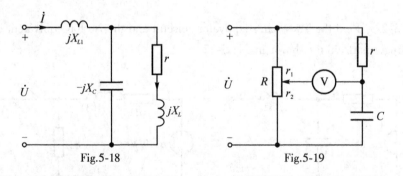

Fig.5-18   Fig.5-19

5-20 Write down the mesh current equations in phasor form for the circuit shown in Fig.5-20.

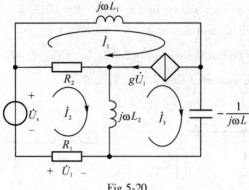

Fig.5-20

5-21 For the circuit shown in Fig.5-21, $u_S = 10\sqrt{2}\cos(t+30°)$ (V), $i_S = \sqrt{2}\cos t$ (V). Write down its node voltage equations in phasor form.

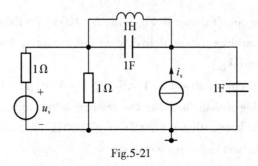

Fig.5-21

5-22 Find the Thevenin's equivalent circuit and the Norton equivalent circuit the single-port circuit shown in Fig.5-22.

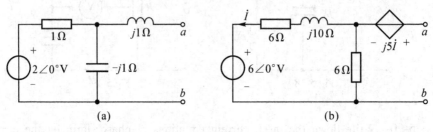

(a)   (b)

Fig.5-22

5-23 For circuit shown in Fig.5-23, $u = 10\sqrt{2}\cos 314t (\text{V})$, $i = 2\sqrt{2}\cos(314t + 53.1°)$ A. Find the average power, reactive power, apparent power and power factor.

5-24 For circuit shown in Fig.5-24, $\dot{U} = 10\angle 0°\text{V}$. Find the average power, reactive power, apparent power and power factor.

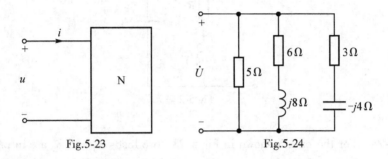

Fig.5-23　　　　　　　　　　Fig.5-24

5-25 For the circuit shown in Fig.5-25, $P = 880\text{W}$, $Q = 160\text{var}$, $R_1 = 60\Omega$, $C = 1.25\mu\text{F}$ and $u = 200\sqrt{2}\cos 1000t (\text{V})$. Find R_L and L.

5-26 For the circuit shown in Fig.5-26, $U = 20\text{V}$, the average power of the capacitive branch is $P_1 = 24\text{W}$ and its power factor $\cos\theta_{Z1} = 0.6$; the average power of the inductive branch is $P_2 = 16\text{W}$, and its power factor $\cos\theta_{Z2} = 0.8$. Find I, U_{ab} and the complex power of the circuit.

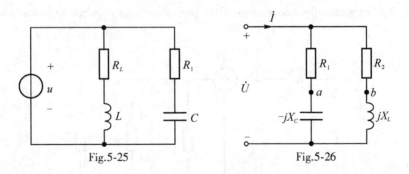

Fig.5-25　　　　　　　　　　Fig.5-26

5-27 The circuit shown in Fig. 2-27 is a fluorescent lamp circuit. The resistance and inductance of the fluorescent lamp are R and L respectively. The frequency of the power source is 50Hz and the voltage of the source is 220V. The current flowing through the fluorescent lamp is 410mA and its power factor is 0.5. Determine the required capacitance with which the power factor can be promoted to 0.9.

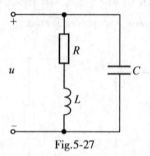

Fig.5-27

5-28 For the circuit shown in Fig.5-28, two loads Z_1 and Z_2 are in parallel, the current flowing through the loads are $I_1 = 10A$ and $I_2 = 20A$ respectively. The power factors are $\lambda_1 = \cos\phi_1 = 0.8\,(\phi_1<0)$, $\lambda_2 = \cos\phi_2 = 0.6\,(\phi_2>0)$ respectively. The port voltage $U = 100V$. The source frequency $\omega = 1000 \text{rad/s}$.

(1) Find the readings of the ammeter and voltmeter. Calculate the power factor;

(2) If the rated current of the source is 30A, determine the maximum resistor that can be connected in parallel with the loads? Find the reading of the wattmeter and the power factor after parallel the resistor.

(3) Determine the capacitance if the power factor is required to promote to 0.9.

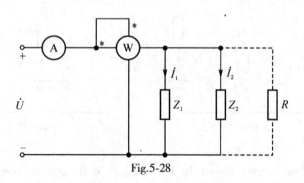

Fig.5-28

5-29 The circuit is shown in Fig.5-29.

(1) What is Z_L if Z_L obtains the maximum power from the source?

(2) What is the maximum power?

5-30 For the circuit shown in Fig.5-30, $\dot{I}_S = 2\angle 0°$, what is Z_L if Z_L obtains the maximum power from the source? And what is the maximum power?

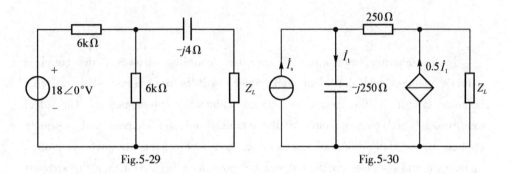

Fig.5-29   Fig.5-30

5-31 For the circuit in Fig.5-31, $\dot{I}_S = 2\angle 0°$, what is Z_L if Z_L obtains the maximum power from the source? And what is the maximum power?

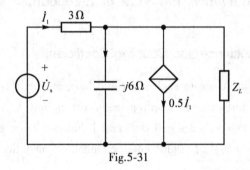

Fig.5-31

Chapter 6
Magnetically Coupled Circuits

In this chapter, two kinds of important coupling elements, the coupling inductor element and the ideal transformer, will be introduced. The coupling inductor circuit is the result of mutual inductance phenomenon. The ideal transformer is a typical example of the coupling inductor element and is widely applied in our daily life and engineering. Some new concepts such as mutual inductance and coupling coefficient will be introduced first. And then the analysis method of the circuit with these two kinds of ideal coupling elements will also be discussed.

6.1 Mutual Inductance and VCR of the Coupled Inductor

6.1.1 Mutual Inductance and Coupling Coefficient

Two coils that are close to each other and have magnetic coupling phenomena are called mutual inductance coupling coils or mutual inductance coils. For convenience, these two coils are called as coil 1 and coil 2, respectively, as shown in Fig. 6.1.1. The coupling inductance element is modelled from the mutual inductance coil.

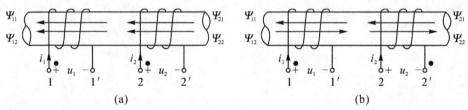

Fig.6.1.1 Mutual Inductance Coil

6.1 Mutual Inductance and VCR of the Coupled Inductor

For the circuit shown In Fig.6.1.1a, Ψ_{11} is the magnetic flux generated by the current i_1 in its own coil 1 and its flux linkage is $\Psi_{11} = N_1 \Psi_{11}$. Obviously, a part of the magnetic flux Ψ_{11} will pass through the coil 2, and this magnetic flux that is generated by current i_1 and passes through the coil 2 is assumed to be Ψ_{21} so its flux linkage in the coil 2 is $\Psi_{21} = N_2 \Psi_{21}$, where N_2 is the turns number of the coil 2. If the voltage and current are in standard reference direction, the self-inductance voltage u_{11} generated by the current i_1 in the coil 1 can be written as

$$u_{11} = \frac{d\Psi_{11}}{dt} = N_1 \frac{d\Psi_{11}}{dt} \qquad (6.1.1\text{ a})$$

The mutual inductance voltage u_{21} generated in coil 2 can be written as

$$u_{21} = \frac{d\Psi_{21}}{dt} = N_2 \frac{d\Psi_{21}}{dt} \qquad (6.1.1\text{ b})$$

Although the voltage u_{21} is shown in coil 2, it is related to the magnetic flux Ψ_{21} which is generated by current i_1 flowing through coil 1, so u_{21} is related to both coils. Ψ_{21} is called mutual inductance flux linkage and u_{21} is called mutual voltage.

Similarly, the part of magnetic flux generated by current i_2 and passing through the coil 1 is denoted as Ψ_{12} and its flux linkage is $\Psi_{12} = N_1 \Psi_{12}$, where N_1 is the turns number of the coil 1. When the voltage and current are in the standard reference direction, the self-inductance voltage u_{22} generated by the current i_2 in the coil 2 can be written as

$$u_{22} = \frac{d\Psi_{22}}{dt} = N_2 \frac{d\Psi_{22}}{dt} \qquad (6.1.2\text{ a})$$

The mutual inductance voltage u_{12} generated in coil 1 can be written as

$$u_{12} = \frac{d\Psi_{12}}{dt} = N_1 \frac{d\Psi_{12}}{dt} \qquad (6.1.2\text{b})$$

In the above discussion, two subscripts are used. The first subscript indicates the numbering of the coil in which the quantity is located, and the second subscript indicates the numbering of the coil where the quantity is generated. For example, Ψ_{12} indicates that the mutual inductance flux linkage is in coil 1 but is generated by the current i_2 flowing through the coil 2.

If the currents flow through the coil 1 and coil 2 respectively, total flux linkage in each coil can be derived as follows:

For coil 1: $\Psi_1 = \Psi_{11} + \Psi_{12}$

For coil 2: $\Psi_2 = \Psi_{21} + \Psi_{22}$

It is known that the self-inductance coefficient of the linear inductor $L_1 = \dfrac{\Psi_{11}}{i_1}$ or $L_2 = \dfrac{\Psi_{22}}{i_2}$ are constant. Accordingly, the magnetic flux generated by the unit current flowing through the other coil is called mutual inductance coefficient, and is denoted as M. If there is no ferromagnetic material around the coil, the relationship between magnetic flux Ψ_{21} and current i_1 is linear, and the relationship between flux linkage Ψ_{12} and current i_2 is also linear. So, the mutual inductance coefficient between coil 1 and coil 2 can be defined as

$$M_{21} = \left| \dfrac{\Psi_{21}}{i_1} \right| \tag{6.1.3}$$

$$M_{12} = \left| \dfrac{\Psi_{12}}{i_2} \right| \tag{6.1.4}$$

where M_{12} is called the mutual inductance of coil 1 with respect to coil 2, and M_{21} is called the mutual inductance of coil 2 with respect to coil 1.

It can be proved from electromagnetic field theory that

$$M_{12} = M_{21} = M$$

The coefficient M, just like L, is related to the changing rate of flux and has nothing to do with the value of the current. The unit of M is also Henry(H). According to the formula (6.1.3) and (6.1.4), the mutual voltages u_{21} induced in coil 2 in (6.1.1b) and the mutual voltage u_{12} induced in coil 1 in (6.1.2b) can be written as follows

$$\begin{aligned} u_{21} &= \dfrac{d\Psi_{21}}{dt} = M \dfrac{di_1}{dt} \\ u_{12} &= \dfrac{d\Psi_{12}}{dt} = M \dfrac{di_2}{dt} \end{aligned} \tag{6.1.5}$$

The mutual coefficient M between two mutual coils is related to the coil structure, surrounding medium and position of the two coils. In order to quantitatively describe the coupling degree between two coupling coils, the geometric mean value of the ratio between the mutual inductance flux linkage and the self inductance flux linkage of the two coils is defined as coefficient of coupling k of the mutual inductance, that is,

$$k \stackrel{def}{=\!=\!=} \sqrt{\frac{\Psi_{12}\Psi_{21}}{\Psi_{11}\Psi_{22}}} = \sqrt{\frac{\Psi_{12}\Psi_{21}}{\Psi_{11}\Psi_{22}}} \quad (6.1.6)$$

Given $\Psi_{11} = L_1 i_1$, $\Psi_{12} = M i_2$, $\Psi_{21} = M i_1$, $\Psi_{22} = L_2 i_2$, so

$$k \triangleq \frac{M}{\sqrt{L_1 L_2}} \quad (6.1.7)$$

Due to leakage flux in the coils, it is not possible that all flux generated by the coil 1 can pass through the coil 2. Namely, only part of the magnetic flux generated by the coil 1 will pass through the coil 2. Similarly, only part of the magnetic flux generated by the coil 2 will pass through the coil 1. So,

$$0 \leqslant k \leqslant 1$$

It can be proved that, the closer two coils are placed, the higher their coupling degree is. For two overlapping coils, its coupling degree is highest or $k=1$. For two vertically-placed coils, its coupling degree is lowest or $k=0$. If $k=1$, it is said that two coils are perfectly coupled. And if $k=0$, it is said that there is no coupling between two coils.

If the coil winding direction and current reference direction is assigned as shown in Fig.6.1.1a, the flux linkage passing through coils 1 and 2 is

$$\Psi_1 = \Psi_{11} + \Psi_{12}$$
$$\Psi_2 = \Psi_{21} + \Psi_{22}$$

So the total voltage of each coil can be derived by applying Lenz's Law as follows:

$$u_1 = \frac{d\Psi_1}{dt} = \frac{d(\Psi_{11} + \Psi_{12})}{dt} = L_1 \frac{di_1}{dt} + M \frac{di_2}{dt} = u_{11} + u_{12}$$
$$u_2 = \frac{d\Psi_2}{dt} = \frac{d(\Psi_{21} + \Psi_{22})}{dt} = M \frac{di_1}{dt} + L_2 \frac{di_2}{dt} = u_{21} + u_{22} \quad (6.1.8)$$

It shows that the voltage of each coil consist of two parts. One part is self-induced voltage u_{11} or u_{22}, and another part is mutual voltage or induced voltage u_{12} or u_{21}. Noted that, above expressions are derived according to the winding direction of the coil aid the direction of the current shown in Fig 6.1.1a. In this case, the magnetic fluxes in two coils aid each other, and it is known as flux-aiding, so the signs in front of mutual inductance voltage and mutual flux linkage are positive.

If the winding direction of the coil and the direction of the current are assigned as shown in Fig.6.1.1b, the magnetic flux in two coils oppose each other, which is called flux-opposing. So the signs in front of mutual inductance voltage and mutual flux linkage are negative. In this case, the flux linkage passing through each coil is

For coil 1: $\Psi_1 = \Psi_{11} - \Psi_{12}$

For coil 2: $\Psi_2 = \Psi_{22} - \Psi_{21}$

Then the total voltage across each coil can be written as follows:

$$u_1 = L_1 \frac{di_1}{dt} - M \frac{di_2}{dt}$$
$$u_2 = -M \frac{di_1}{dt} + L_2 \frac{di_2}{dt}$$
(6.1.9)

In summary, the mutual voltage is related to the direction of the current and the winding direction of the coil. If the fluxes generated by the currents in the respective aid each other, mutual voltage is positive otherwise it is negative.

6.1.2 Dotted Convention and the VCR of Coupled Inductor

In general, the actual winding of the coil cannot be seen from the outside, nor easy to draw on the circuit. Therefor a concept called dotted terminal is introduced. If the dotted terminal and current reference direction is given, whether the flux is to aid or oppose with each other the polarity of mutual voltage can be determined.

(1) Dotted terminal. If a current enters the dotted terminal of one coil, the reference polarity of the mutual voltage in the second coil is positive at the dotted terminal of the second coil.

(2) Un-dotted terminal. Alternatively, if a current leaves the dotted terminal of one coil, the reference polarity of the mutual voltage in the second coil is negative at the dotted terminal of the second coil.

For the coupled inductor shown in Fig 6.1.1a, it can be seen that terminal 1 and 2 are dotted terminal, 1 and 2' are a pair of un-dotted terminal.

By introducing the concept of dotted terminal, the coupled inductor can be modeled as the circuit symbol shown in Fig.6.1.2, where, the winding direction of coils is indicated by dotted terminal. And two coil are expressed by two inductor symbols.

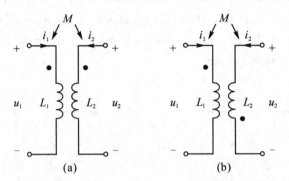

Fig.6.1.2 Circuit Symbol for Coupled Inductors

If the port voltage and current are in the associated reference direction and both currents flow into the dotted terminal of two coils, as shown in Fig.6.1.2a, then it can be found that the polarity of mutual voltage is the same as the self-induced voltage. Therefore, there is

$$u_1 = L_1 \frac{di_1}{dt} + M \frac{di_2}{dt}$$

$$u_2 = M \frac{di_1}{dt} + L_2 \frac{di_2}{dt}$$

If the currents flow into the un-dotted terminals of two coils, as shown in Fig. 6.1.2b, the polarity of mutual voltage is opposite to the polarity of self-induced voltage, so

$$u_1 = L_1 \frac{di_1}{dt} - M \frac{di_2}{dt}$$

$$u_2 = M \frac{di_1}{dt} - L_2 \frac{di_2}{dt}$$

Another physical meaning of the dotted terminal can be described as: The positive polarity terminal of the mutual voltage and the corresponding terminal where the current reference direction for generating mutual voltage, are a pair of dotted-terminals.

Obviously, the mutual inductance coupling effect can also be expressed by current controlled voltage source model. For example, the circuit shown in Fig.6.1.2

can be modeled as the equivalent circuit shown in Fig.6.1.3. It can be seen that both circuit models have the same VCR equations. In the equivalent circuit models shown in Fig. 6. 1. 3, L_1, L_2 are self-inductances, so there is no inductance coupling element in the circuit.

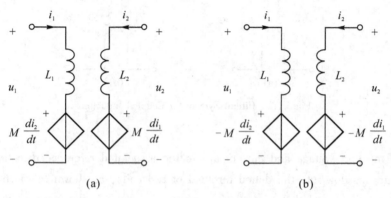

(a)　　　　　　　　　　(b)

Fig.6.1.3　Equivalent Circuit Model of Coupled Inductor

6.1.3　VCR of Coupled Inductor in the Sinusoidal AC Circuit

If sinusoidal currents i_1 and i_2 with the same frequency flow through a coupled inductor, its voltage will also be sinusoidal voltage with the same frequency. The currents phasors can be expressed as $\dot{I}_1$, $\dot{I}_2$. And their voltage phasors are expressed as $\dot{U}_1$, $\dot{U}_2$. If the voltage and current phasor of each port are in the standard reference direction, then VCR of the coupled inductor can be written as follows

$$\begin{cases} \dot{U}_1 = j\omega L_1 \dot{I}_1 \pm j\omega M \dot{I}_2 \\ \dot{U}_2 = j\omega L_2 \dot{I}_2 \pm j\omega M \dot{I}_1 \end{cases} \quad (6.1.10)$$

The phasor model for Eq.(6.1.10) is shown in Fig.6.1.4.

If both currents flow into the dotted terminals, as shown in Fig.6.1.4a, the mutual voltages are positive. If both currents flow into the un-dotted terminals, as shown in Fig.6.1.4b, mutual voltages are negative. In formula (6.1.10), ωM is called mutual inductance reactance.

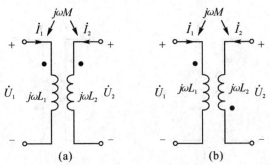

Fig.6.1.4 Coupling Inductor Symbol

Example 6.1.1 Try to find dotted terminals of the coupling coils shown in Fig.6.1.5.

Solution According to the definition of the dotted terminals, considering winding direction of two coils around, if both currents flow into the terminals 1 and 2′, self-inductance flux of each coil is enhanced by the mutual flux, therefore, terminals 1 and 2′ are the dotted terminals, and 2 and 1′ are also the dotted terminals.

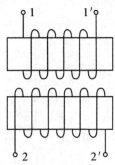

Fig.6.1.5 The Circuit for Example 6.1.1

Example 6.1.2 The port voltage and current direction of the coupled inductor element is assigned as shown in Fig.6.1.6a, and writes down VCR characteristics expression of coupled inductor.

Solution To write VCR expression of the coupled inductor, first, the voltage and current in each port are assumed in the associated reference direction, then the inductance voltage takes positive sign. The sign of mutual voltages is related to the terminals that currents flow into. If currents flow into the dotted terminals, mutual voltage are positive. If the currents flow into the un-dotted terminals, mutual inductance voltage negative sign.

For this problem, as the reference direction of right port voltage and current are not in associated with each other, so, it is transformed into the standard direction, as shown in Fig.6.1.6b. Obviously, currents i_1 and i_2 flows into the un-dotted terminals. So

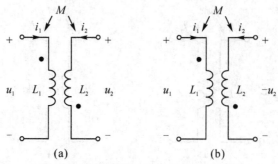

Fig.6.1.6 The Circuit for Example 6.1.2

$$u_1 = L_1 \frac{di_1}{dt} - M \frac{di_2}{dt}$$

$$-u_2 = L_2 \frac{di_2}{dt} - M \frac{di_1}{dt}$$

Or is rewritten as

$$u_1 = L_1 \frac{di_1}{dt} - M \frac{di_2}{dt}$$

$$u_2 = -L_2 \frac{di_2}{dt} + M \frac{di_1}{dt}$$

This is the VCR characteristics expression of coupled inductor.

Example 6.1.3 The circuit shown in Fig.6.1.7 can be used to determine the dotted terminals of the coupled inductor in laboratory. Try to explain its principle.

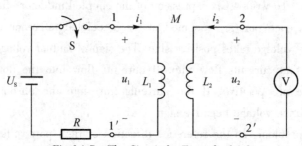

Fig.6.1.7 The Circuit for Example 6.1.3

Solution In Fig.6.1.7, U_s is DC power supply, such as 1.5V battery. Since

V is a high impedance DC voltmeter, there is no current flowing along the right loop of the circuit. Thus the readings of voltmeter is equal to mutual voltage $u_2 = M\dfrac{di_1}{dt}$. And this mutual voltage is related to the dotted terminals. When the switch is closed, as the impedance of the left loop is small, the current i_1 will increase from zero to a certain value, then the changing rate of current versus time is greater than zero, that is $\dfrac{di_1}{dt}>0$. If the voltmeter pointer is found to forward deflected, it indicates $u_2 = M\dfrac{di_1}{dt}>0$, so it can be concluded that terminal 1 and 2 are dotted terminals.

6.2 Analysis of Coupled Inductor Circuit

The analysis of the coupled inductor circuit is basically the same as that of the general inductive AC circuit. Phasor analysis method is commonly applied. It should be noted that, to list phasor equations, it is required not only to consider the self-induced voltage, but also consider the mutual voltage. Self-induced voltage is generated by the current flowing through the coil itself, the mutual voltage is produced by the other coil current and shown in the coil. It can be seen that the key of the coupling inductance circuit analysis is to deal with the problem of mutual inductance coupling. For this purpose, the analysis of simple mutual inductance circuit will be discussed first.

6.2.1 Coupled Inductors in Series

If two mutual inductance coils are connected in series, according to the different connecting position, their connection can be divided into two types: series-aiding connection and series-opposing connection, as shown in Fig.6.2.1.

For the circuit shown in Fig.6.2.1a, the two mutual inductance coils are connected with un-dotted terminals, this kind of connection is called series-aiding connection. In this case, both currents will flow into dotted terminals of two coils. For the circuit shown in Fig.6.2.1b, the two mutual inductance coils are connected with dotted terminals. This kind of connection is called series-opposing connection and currents will flow into un-dotted terminals of two coils.

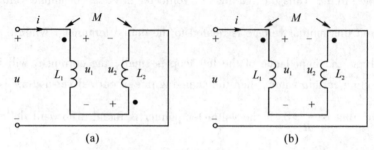

Fig.6.2.1 Mutual Inductance Coil in Series(a) Series-aiding Connection and (b) Series-opposing Connection

For series-aiding connection, its VCR expression can be written as follows

$$u = L_1 \frac{di}{dt} + M \frac{di}{dt} + L_2 \frac{di}{dt} + M \frac{di}{dt} = (L_1 + L_2 + 2M) \frac{di}{dt} \qquad (6.2.1)$$

So, the equivalent inductance is

$$L_{eq} = L_1 + L_2 + 2M \qquad (6.2.2)$$

For series-opposing connection, its VCR expression can be written as follows

$$u = L_1 \frac{di}{dt} - M \frac{di}{dt} + L_2 \frac{di}{dt} - M \frac{di}{dt} = (L_1 + L_2 - 2M) \frac{di}{dt} \qquad (6.2.3)$$

So, equivalent inductance is

$$L_{eq} = L_1 + L_2 - 2M \qquad (6.2.4)$$

Therefore, in the analysis of a complex circuit, if there are two coils with mutual inductance connected in series, it can be reduced to single equivalent inductor. In this way, mutual inductance is removed.

Example 6.2.1 For the circuit shown in Fig.6.2.2, $\dot{U}_{ab} = 220 \angle 0°$ V, $L_1 = 8$H, $L_2 = 10$H, $M = 2$H. Find the phasor current $\dot{I}$ that flowing through the circuit.

Solution As it can be seen from the circuit diagram, the mutual inductance coils are in series-aiding connection, so the circuit current can be derived as follows

$$\dot{I} = \frac{\dot{U}}{j\omega L_{eq}} = \frac{\dot{U}}{j\omega(L_1 + L_2 + 2M)} = \frac{220}{j\omega \times 22} = -j \frac{10}{\omega} A$$

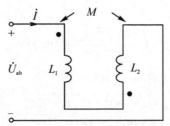

Fig.6.2.2 The Circuit for Example 6.2.1

Example 6.2.2 The circuit is shown in Fig.6.2.3a, $\dot{I} = 10\angle 0°$A, $L_1 = 5$H, $L_2 = 7$H, $M = 2$H, $R = 10\Omega$, $C = 1$F and $\omega = 1$rad/s. Find phasor voltage $\dot{U}$.

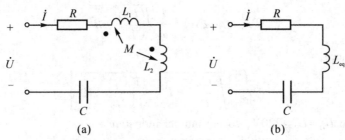

Fig.6.2.3 The Circuit for Example 6.2.2

Solution Since the mutual inductance coils are in series-aiding connection, the original circuit can be reduced to equivalent circuit shown in Fig.6.2.3b. Then, there is

$$L_{eq} = L_1 + L_2 + 2M = 16\text{H}.$$

$$\dot{U} = j\omega L_{eq}\dot{I} + R\dot{I} + \frac{1}{j\omega C}\dot{I} = \left(j\omega L_{eq} + R - j\frac{1}{\omega C}\right)\dot{I}$$

$$= [10 + j15] \times 10 = 180.3\angle 56.3°(\text{V})$$

Example 6.2.3 Two coupled coils is connected in series. And they are driven by a 50Hz/220V sinusoidal voltage source. When connected in series-aiding connection series, $I_O = 2.7$A, $P = 218.7$W. When connected in series-aiding connection, $I_I = 7$A. Find the mutual inductance M.

Solution Because the ideal inductor does not consume power, the power is consumed only the self internal resistance R of the coils. Since the connection way of coils does not affect internal resistance of the coils, therefore, it can be derived that

$$R = \frac{P}{I_0^2} = \frac{218.7}{2.7^2} = 30(\Omega)$$

For series-aiding connection, there is

$$U_O = \sqrt{R^2 + \omega^2 (L_1 + L_2 + 2M)^2} \cdot I_O$$

For series-opposing connection, there is

$$U_I = \sqrt{R^2 + \omega^2 (L_1 + L_2 - 2M)^2} \cdot I_I$$

So,

$$(L_1 + L_2 + 2M) = \frac{1}{\omega}\sqrt{\left(\frac{U_O}{I_O}\right)^2 - R^2}$$

$$(L_1 + L_2 - 2M) = \frac{1}{\omega}\sqrt{\left(\frac{U_I}{I_I}\right)^2 - R^2}$$

Therefore,

$$M = \frac{1}{4\omega}\left[\sqrt{\left(\frac{U_O}{I_O}\right)^2 - R^2} - \sqrt{\left(\frac{U_I}{I_I}\right)^2 - R^2}\right]$$

Due to $U_O = U_I = 220V$, so the mutual inductance is

$$M = 52.86 mH$$

6.2.2 Coupled Inductors in Parallel

The parallel connection of mutual inductor is also divided into two kinds. If the two mutual inductance coils are connected with terminals, it is called the same-side parallel connection, as shown in Fig.6.2.4a. If the two mutual inductance coils are connected with by un-dotted terminals, it is called the opposite-side parallel connection, as shown in Fig.6.2.4b.

For the dotted terminal parallel connection, according to the direction of the mesh currents shown in Fig.6.2.4a, the mesh current equations can be written as follows

$$L_1 \frac{di_1}{dt} - L_1 \frac{di_2}{dt} + M \frac{di_2}{dt} = u_1$$

$$-L_1 \frac{di_1}{dt} + M \frac{di_1}{dt} + (L_1 + L_2 - 2M) \frac{di_2}{dt} = 0$$

(6.2.5)

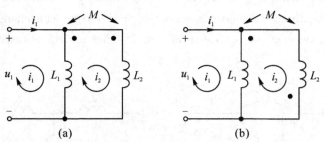

Fig.6.2.4 Coupled Inductor in Parallel

By solving the above equations, it can be derived that

$$u_1 = \left(\frac{L_1 L_2 - M^2}{L_1 + L_2 - 2M}\right)\frac{di_1}{dt} = L_{eq}\frac{di_1}{dt}$$

It is seen that coupled inductor in the dotted terminal parallel connection is equivalent to a single inductor, its equivalent inductance is

$$L_{eq} = \frac{L_1 L_2 - M^2}{L_1 + L_2 - 2M} \qquad (6.2.6)$$

Similarly, coupled inductor in the undotted terminal parallel connection is also equivalent to a single inductor, its equivalent inductance L_{eq} is

$$L_{eq} = \frac{L_1 L_2 - M^2}{L_1 + L_2 + 2M} \qquad (6.2.7)$$

By comparing expression (6.2.6) with (6.2.7), it is obvious that the equivalent inductance undotted terminal parallel connection is smaller than the equivalent inductance in the dotted terminal parallel. Similar to the coupled inductor in series, when the coupled inductor are connected in parallel, it can be replaced by the equivalent inductor.

6.2.3 T-type Equivalent of Coupled Inductor

For a circuit with coupled inductor, if mutual inductance coils are connected to a common terminal, as shown in Fig.6.2.5a, it forms a T-type connection. This kind of connection is neither series nor parallel connection. It can be proved that the circuit of Fig.6.2.5a is equivalent to the circuit shown in Fig.6.2.5b by using T-type equivalent method. Here, the dotted terminals of coupled inductor are connected to a common node, as shown in Fig.6.2.5a. For equivalent circuit shown in Fig.6.2.5b, three inductors are connected in a T-type connection, there is not mutual inductance in the equivalent circuit. In other words, mutual inductance is opposited.

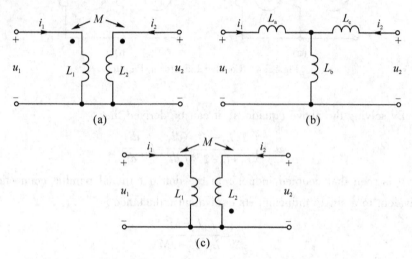

Fig.6.2.5 Equivalent Circuit of Coupled Inductor with a Common Terminal

For the circuit shown in Fig.6.2.5a, its port VCR equations are

$$u_1 = L_1 \frac{di_1}{dt} + M \frac{di_2}{dt}$$
$$u_2 = M \frac{di_1}{dt} + L_2 \frac{di_2}{dt}$$
(6.2.8)

Rewritten as

$$u_1 = (L_1 - M) \frac{di_1}{dt} + M \left(\frac{di_1}{dt} + \frac{di_2}{dt} \right)$$
$$u_2 = M \left(\frac{di_1}{dt} + \frac{di_2}{dt} \right) + (L_2 - M) \frac{di_2}{dt}$$
(6.2.9)

For the circuit shown in 6.2.5b, its port VCR equations are

$$u_1 = L_a \frac{di_1}{dt} + L_b \left(\frac{di_1}{dt} + \frac{di_2}{dt} \right)$$

$$u_2 = L_b \left(\frac{di_1}{dt} + \frac{di_2}{dt} \right) + L_c \frac{di_2}{dt}$$

Due to the circuit of Fig.6.2.5a is equivalent to the circuit shown in Fig.6.2.5b, their port VCR equations must be same. So, by comparing their port VCR equations, the value of three inductance can be derived as follows

$$L_a = L_1 - M$$
$$L_b = M \qquad\qquad (6.2.10)$$
$$L_c = L_2 - M$$

Similarly, for circuit shown in Fig.6.2.5c, the un-dotted terminals of coupled inductor are connected to a common node, the three inductance in its equivalent T-type circuit can also be derived as follows

$$L_a = L_1 + M$$
$$L_b = -M \qquad\qquad (6.2.11)$$
$$L_c = L_2 + M$$

6.2.4 Analysis of Circuit with Coupled Inductor

For a circuit with coupled inductors, if coupled inductor is connected in series, in parallel or has a common terminal, it is usually analyzed by the decoupling equivalent method, or dependent source equivalent method. For the general circuit with coupled inductors, it can be analyzed by applying the general network analysis methods, such as branch analysis, loop analysis, Thevenin's theorem or Superposition. However, generally speaking, node analysis cannot be applied directly.

Example 6.2.4 Find the input impedance Z_i of the circuit shown in Fig.6.2.6a.

Solution Since there is a common node in the coupled inductor, so the T-type equivalent method can be applied to remove the mutual inductance. Its equivalent circuit can be derived as shown in Fig.6.2.6b, then input impedance Z_i can be derived as follows

$$Z_i = -j\omega M + \frac{[R_1 + j\omega(L_1 + M)][R_2 + j\omega(L_2 + M)]}{R_1 + j\omega(L_1 + M) + R_2 + j\omega(L_2 + M)}$$

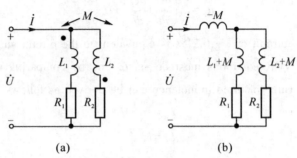

(a)　　　　　　　　　　(b)

Fig.6.2.6　The Circuit for Example 6.2.4

Example 6.2.5　A circuit is shown in Fig.6.2.7a, list its loop equations.

Solution 1　Select the reference direction of loop current as shown in the Fig. 6.2.7a. Then its loop equations can be listed directly as follows

$$(R_1+j\omega L_1)\dot{I}_1-(j\omega M+R_1)\dot{I}_2=\dot{U}_{S1}$$

$$-(R_1+j\omega M)\dot{I}_1+(R_1+j\omega L_2)\dot{I}_2=-\dot{U}_{S2}$$

Solution 2　Applying T type equivalent method, the mutual inductance is removed, as shown in Fig.6.2.7b. Then, its loop equations the equations can be listed as follows

$$[R_1+j\omega L_1]\dot{I}_1-(R_1+j\omega M)\dot{I}_2=\dot{U}_{S1}$$

$$-(R_1+j\omega M)\dot{I}_1+(R_1+j\omega L_2)\dot{I}_2=-\dot{U}_{S2}$$

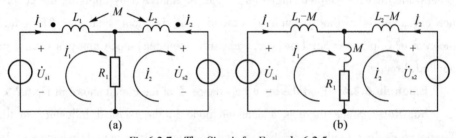

(a)　　　　　　　　　　(b)

Fig.6.2.7　The Circuit for Example 6.2.5

6.2.5　Application Electrical Instrument with Inductance

Usually, if an ammeter is used to measure the current of the circuit, it needs to cut off the circuit, then the can be connected in series into the measured circuit. However, if a clamp ammeter to used to measure the current of the circuit, it need not to cut off the circuit and the current of the circuit can be measured directly. This is because that there is a coupled inductor inside the clamp ammeter. Mutual inductance coupling is applied to measure mutual current without the need to cut off the circuit. According to the difference of structure, the clamp ammeters are commonly divided into the transformer-type clamp ammeter and electromagnetic clamp ammeter. Combined with the previous knowledge, the structure and working principle of transformer-type clamp ammeter will be described in the following.

For transformer-type clamp ammeters, its outline structure is shown in Fig.6.2.8. It mainly consists of "cross-center" current transformer and magnetoelectric Ammeter with rectifier device, as shown in Fig.6.2.9.

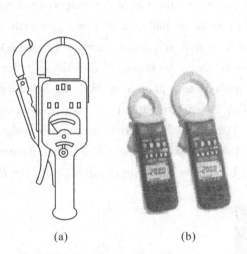
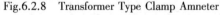
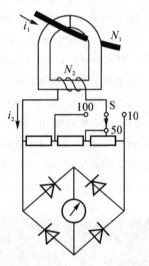

Fig.6.2.8 Transformer Type Clamp Amneter   Fig.6.2.9 Transformer Type Clamp Current Meter Circuit

The shape of the iron core in the transformer-type clamp ammeter is a clamp mouth. If wrench is pinched, iron can be opened, so that the wires carrying measured current can be put into the open gap of the clamp core without the need to cut off the wire. Then the wrench is loosen, the core will be closed. In this way, the wire with measured current becomes a primary N_1 of the current transformer. The flux is generated by the current of measured wire in the closed iron core, and mutual electromotive force will be generated around the secondary N_2. Then there is a induced current I_2 flowing through measured circuit to form a coupling inductance. Being rectified to a direct current through the rectification equipment and converted through the switch S according to the different shunt ratio, the inductive current i_2 make the ammeter pointer deflection. Due to the meter is scaled based on primary current i_1 scale, so that the readings of ammeter is the value of the AC current in the measured wire.

Here is another example in the ship by applying mutual inductance to measure the current. Due to the existence of the corrosion phenomenon in the seawater, the corrosion protection is required. It is known that the current of ship corrosion and corrosion resistance the ship will form a large electric field in the sea water. So, by measuring these currents, it helps to understand the size of the underwater electric field. The most feasible method is to measure the current flowing through the spindle. However, as the spindle can be broken and ammeter cannot be connected in series into the spindle, so the current cannot be measured directly. In order to solve this problem, the principle of mutual inductance is applied. By installing a current transformer in the ship spindle, the spindle current can be measured. then the spindle current can be measured. The shape of the current transformer is shown in Fig.6.2.10a, and its working principle is shown in Fig.6.2.10b. I_e is the current of the shaft to be measured, the coil between a, b is the excitation coil, the coil

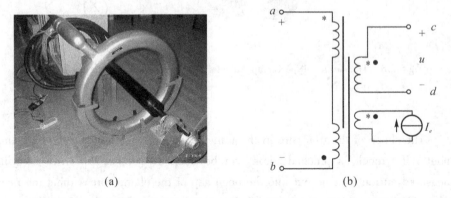

Fig.6.2.10 Application of Mutual Inductance to Measure the Current in the Ship

between c, d is the detection coil, The excitation coil has a mutual inductance coupling with the detection coil and the measured current, respectively, so that the magnitude of spindle current can be indirectly obtained from the coupling current.

6.3 Air-Core Transformer and Ideal Transformer

Most basic function of transformers is to step-up or down voltage. In addition, it can also play the role of power matching and conversion impedance. No matter what the transformer, its basic structure is the same: that is, consists of the two coils with mutual inductance.

A coil connected to the input power source is called the primary winding of the transformer. The other the coil connected to the load is called secondary coil of the transformer. Accordingly, the circuit where the primary coils locates is called the primary winding (or primary loop), the circuit where the secondary coil locates is called the secondary winding(or secondary loop).

There is only magnetic coupling between primary and secondary coils, without direct electrical connection. By magnetic coupling, the input power source transfers energy from the primary winding to the secondary winding. And by utilizing the turns difference in the original and secondary coil, voltage transformation can be achieved by transformer. However, the transformer does not work for DC.

6.3.1 Air-Core Transformer

Coupled inductance components before the, followed by the load structure of the circuit called the air-core transformer circuit, with its circuit model shown in Fig.6.3.1a.

A hollow transformer is a specific form of a circuit with a coupling inductance, which is discussed below.

A coupled coil that does not contain an iron core (or magnetic core) is called an air-core transformer, which is widely used in electronic and communication engineering and measuring instruments. By connecting a signal source to the primary coil and connecting a load to the secondary coil, a typical air-core transformer circuit is derived, as shown in Fig.6.3.1a. It is a kind of mutual inductance circuit and will be discussed in the following.

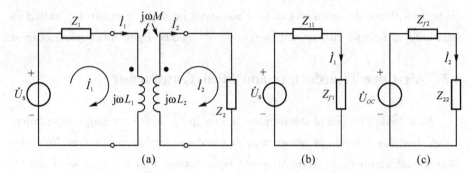

Fig.6.3.1 Air-Core Transformer Circuit and Its Equivalent Circuit

The loop equations of the circuit shown in Fig.6.3.1a can be written as

$$\begin{cases} Z_{11}\dot{I}_1 - Z_M\dot{I}_2 = \dot{U}_s \\ -Z_M\dot{I}_1 + Z_{22}\dot{I}_2 = 0 \end{cases} \quad (6.3.1)$$

where, $Z_{11} = Z_1 + j\omega L_1$ is called self-impedance of primary loop, $Z_{22} = Z_2 + j\omega L_2$ is called self-impedance of secondary loop, $Z_M = j\omega M$ is called mutual impedance.

The above equation can be solved that

$$\dot{I}_1 = \frac{\dot{U}_s}{Z_{11} - \frac{Z_M^2}{Z_{22}}} = \frac{\dot{U}_s}{Z_{11} + \frac{\omega^2 M^2}{Z_{22}}} = \frac{\dot{U}_s}{Z_{11} + Z_{f1}} \quad (6.3.2)$$

According to the expression (6.3.2), a equivalent circuit can be drawn as shown in Fig.6.3.1b, which is called the primary equivalent circuit of the air-core transformer circuit.

In Eq. (6.3.2),

$$Z_{f1} = \frac{\omega^2 M^2}{Z_{22}} \quad (6.3.3)$$

It is called the reflected impedance secondary loop to primary loop.

The current of secondary loop can be solved from Eq.(6.3.1) as follows

$$\dot{I}_2 = \frac{Z_M}{Z_{22}}\dot{I}_1 \quad (6.3.4)$$

Substituting expression (6.3.2) to (6.3.4), it is derived that

6.3 Air-Core Transformer and Ideal Transformer

$$\dot{I}_2 = \frac{Z_M \dot{U}_s}{Z_{11}Z_{22}-Z_M^2} = \frac{\dfrac{Z_M}{Z_{11}}\dot{U}_s}{Z_{22}+\dfrac{\omega^2 M^2}{Z_{11}}} = \frac{\dfrac{Z_M}{Z_{11}}\dot{U}_s}{Z_{22}+Z_{f2}} \quad (6.3.5)$$

where Z_{f2} is called the reflected impedance primary loop relative to secondary loop.

According to the expression (6.3.5), an equivalent circuit can be drawn as shown in Fig.6.3.1c, it is called the secondary equivalent circuit of the air-core transformer circuit. For this circuit, the voltage of source is

$$\dot{U}_{OC} = \frac{Z_M}{Z_{11}}\dot{U}_s \quad (6.3.6)$$

Easy to verify, $\dot{U}_{OC}$ is open-circuit voltage of the secondary loop. Therefore, the secondary equivalent circuit is actually the Thevenin's equivalent circuit looking from the port of the secondary winding.

Example 6.3.1 For the circuit shown in Fig.6.3.2a, $u_s(t)=10\sqrt{2}\cos 10t$ V. Try to find:

(1) the currents $i_1(t)$, $i_2(t)$;

(2) the power absorbed by the load resistance 1.6Ω.

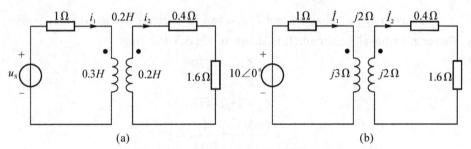

Fig.6.3.2 The Circuit for Example 6.3.1

Solution The phasor model of the circuit is drawn first, as shown in Fig.6.3.2b.

(1) draw its primary equivalent circuit, as shown in Fig.6.3.3a. Then, there are

$$Z_{11} = 1+j3(\Omega)$$
$$Z_{22} = 2+j2(\Omega)$$

$$Z_{f1} = \frac{(\omega M)^2}{Z_{22}} = \frac{4}{2+j2} = 1-j1(\Omega)$$

Primary current and secondary current are derived as follows

$$\dot{I}_1 = \frac{\dot{U}_1}{Z_{11}+Z_{f1}} = \frac{10\angle 0°}{1+j3+1-j1} = 2.5\sqrt{2}\angle -45°(A)$$

$$\dot{I}_2 = \frac{Z_M}{Z_{22}}\dot{I}_1 = \frac{j2}{2+j2}\times 2.5\sqrt{2}\angle -45° = 2.5(A)$$

So,

$$i_1 = 5\cos(10t-45°)A, \quad i_2 = 2.5\sqrt{2}\cos 10tA$$

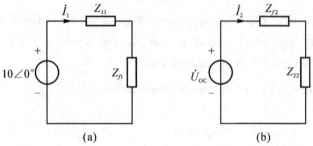

Fig.6.3.3 The Circuit for Example 6.3.1

In this example, phasor $\dot{I}_1$ and $\dot{I}_2$ also can be analyzed by using the secondary Thevenin's equivalent circuit. It is shown in Fig.6.3.3b. Then

$$\dot{U}_{OC} = \frac{Z_M}{Z_{11}}\dot{U}_s = \frac{j20}{1+j3}V$$

$$Z_{22} = 2+j2(\Omega)$$

$$Z_{f2} = \frac{(\omega M)^2}{Z_{11}} = \frac{4}{1+j3}(\Omega)$$

So, secondary current is

$$\dot{I}_2 = \frac{\dot{U}_{OC}}{Z_{f2}+Z_{22}} = 2.5\angle 0°A$$

And primary current is

$$\dot{I}_1 = \frac{Z_{22}}{Z_M}\dot{I}_2 = 2.5\sqrt{2}\angle -45°A$$

(2) The active power absorbed by the load resistance can be derived as

follows
$$P = R_L I_2^2 = 1.6 \times 2.5^2 = 10(\text{W})$$

Example 6.3.2 The circuit is shown in Fig.6.3.4a. It is known that Z_L can get the maximum power from the source. Find the value of the load impedance Z_L and the value of the maximum power?

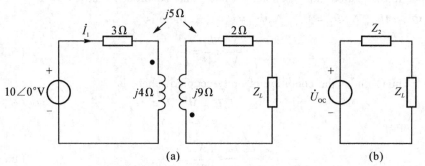

Fig.6.3.4 The Circuit for Example 6.3.2

Solution Usually, Thevenin's equivalent method is applied to solve the problem of maximum power transfer. The secondary Thevenin's equivalent circuit is drawn as shown in Fig.6.3.4b. Note that the location of the dotted terminal is different from that in Fig.6.3.1c, so there are

$$Z_2 = 2 + j9 + \frac{5^2}{3 + j4} = 2 + j9 + 3 - j4 = 5 + j5(\Omega)$$

$$\dot{U}_{OC} = -\frac{Z_M}{Z_{11}} \dot{U}_s = -\frac{j5}{3 + j4} \times 10\angle 0° = \frac{50\angle -90°}{5\angle 53.1°} = 10\angle -143.1°(\text{V})$$

Therefore, when $Z_L = 5 - j5\Omega$, the maximum power is transferred, and the maximum power is

$$P_{max} = \frac{10^2}{4 \times 5} = 5(\text{W})$$

6.3.2 Derfectly Coupled Transformer

If two coils are wound around the magnetic core which is made of ferromagnetic material with high permeability, the two coils can be tightly coupled. Ideally, the flux Φ_{11} generated by the primary coils can fully passed through the secondary coils, that is $\Phi_{11} = \Phi_{21}$. And the flux Φ_{22} generated by the secondary coils can fully passed through the primary coils, that is $\Phi_{22} = \Phi_{12}$. Then, the coupling coefficient will be

$$K = \sqrt{\frac{\Phi_{21}\Phi_{12}}{\Phi_{11}\Phi_{22}}} = 1$$

This is called unity-coupled. Under this condition, due to $N_1\Phi_{11} = L_1 i_1$, $N_1\Phi_{12} = Mi_2$, $N_2\Phi_{21} = Mi_1$, $N_2\Phi_{22} = L_2 i_2$, so there is

$$\frac{N_1}{N_2} = \frac{L_1}{M} = \frac{M}{L_2} \qquad (6.3.7)$$

Thus, under the condition of unity-coupled, there is

$$L_1 L_2 = M^2 \qquad (6.3.8)$$

and

$$\frac{L_1}{L_2} = \left(\frac{N_1}{N_2}\right)^2 \qquad (6.3.9)$$

Fig.6.3.5a shows a $K=1$ coupling inductance, which is also called the unity-coupled transformer. Assume that N_1 and N_2 are the turns number of the primary and secondary coils respectively, then VCR of two coils can be written as

$$u_1 = L_1 \frac{di_1}{dt} + M \frac{di_2}{dt} = \sqrt{L_1}\left(\sqrt{L_1}\frac{di_1}{dt} + \sqrt{L_2}\frac{di_2}{dt}\right) \qquad (6.3.10)$$

$$u_2 = M \frac{di_1}{dt} + L_2 \frac{di_2}{dt} = \sqrt{L_2}\left(\sqrt{L_1}\frac{di_1}{dt} + \sqrt{L_2}\frac{di_2}{dt}\right) \qquad (6.3.11)$$

Divided two expressions and taking into account of the expression (6.3.9), it is derived that

$$\frac{u_1}{u_2} = \sqrt{\frac{L_1}{L_2}} = \frac{N_1}{N_2} \qquad (6.3.12)$$

Expression (6.3.10) can be rewritten as

$$L_1 \frac{di_1}{dt} = u_1 - M \frac{di_2}{dt}$$

or rewritten as

$$\frac{di_1}{dt} = \frac{u_1}{L_1} - \frac{M}{L_1}\frac{di_2}{dt} = \frac{u_1}{L_1} - \frac{N_2}{N_1}\frac{di_2}{dt}$$

That is

$$di_1(t) = \frac{u_1(t)}{L_1}dt - \frac{N_2}{N_1}di_2(t)$$

Take Integral for the above expression from $t = -\infty$ to the t and set $i_1(-\infty) = 0$, $i_2(-\infty) = 0$, there is

$$i_1(t) = \frac{1}{L_1}\int_{-\infty}^{t} u_1(\xi)d\xi - \frac{N_2}{N_1}i_2(t) = i_\Phi(t) + i_1'(t) \quad \forall t \quad (6.3.13)$$

where

$$i_\Phi(t) = \frac{1}{L_1}\int_{-\infty}^{t} u_1(\xi)d\xi \quad (6.3.14)$$

$$i_1'(t) = -\frac{N_2}{N_1}i_2(t) \quad (6.3.15)$$

Expression (6.3.13) shows that the input current $i_1(t)$ of the unity-coupled transformer consists of two parts. First component is the $i_\Phi(t)$ which is presented due to the existence of primary self inductance L_1. It has nothing to do with the secondary coils and is called the excitation current. The second component is current $i_1'(t)$ which is a reflection of the secondary current in the primary loop, it indicates the interaction relationship between the primary loop and the secondary loop.

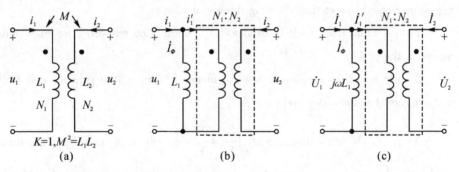

Fig.6.3.5 Fully-Coupled Transformer and Its Equivalent Circuit

According to the expression (6.3.12) and (6.3.13), an equivalent circuit can be drawn for unity-coupled transformer, as shown in Fig.6.3.5b. VCR of the circuit in the dashed box can be written according to expression (6.3.12) and (6.3.15), i.e.

$$u_1(t) = \frac{N_1}{N_2} u_2(t)$$

$$i_1'(t) = -\frac{N_2}{N_1} i_2(t)$$

In sinusoidal steady-state, its corresponding phasor circuit model is shown in Fig.6.3.5c, and the VCR can be expressed as

$$\dot{U}_1 = \frac{N_1}{N_2} \dot{U}_2$$

$$\dot{I}_1' = -\frac{N_2}{N_1} \dot{I}_2$$

And the excitation current is

$$\dot{I}_\Phi = \frac{\dot{U}_1}{j\omega L_1} \tag{6.3.16}$$

6.3.3 Ideal Transformer

The ideal transformer is a special lossless, perfectly coupled transformer. It is an ideal transformer abstracted out of the actual transformer model. The ideal transformer should meet the following three conditions:

(1) the transformer itself is no loss (i.e., there is no resistance for consuming energy in the coil);

(2) the coupling coefficient $K = 1$ (magnetic flux in the primary coil fully pass through the secondary coil);

(3) L_1, L_2, M are infinite, and $\sqrt{\frac{L_1}{L_2}} = \frac{N_1}{N_2} = n$, where N_1 and N_2 is the turns number for the primary and secondary windings, n is the turns ratio for the primary windings versus secondary windings.

The circuit symbols for the ideal transformer with two different dotted-terminals are shown in Fig.6.3.6.

The VCR of the ideal transformer in time domain and phasor form can be written respectively as follows:

$$\left.\begin{array}{l}\dfrac{u_1}{u_2}=\pm\dfrac{N_1}{N_2}=\pm n\\[2mm]\dfrac{i_1}{i_2}=\mp\dfrac{N_2}{N_1}=\mp\dfrac{1}{n}\end{array}\right\} \qquad (6.3.17)$$

$$\left.\begin{array}{l}\dfrac{\dot U_1}{\dot U_2}=\pm\dfrac{N_1}{N_2}=\pm n\\[2mm]\dfrac{\dot I_1}{\dot I_2}=\mp\dfrac{N_2}{N_1}=\mp\dfrac{1}{n}\end{array}\right\} \qquad (6.3.18)$$

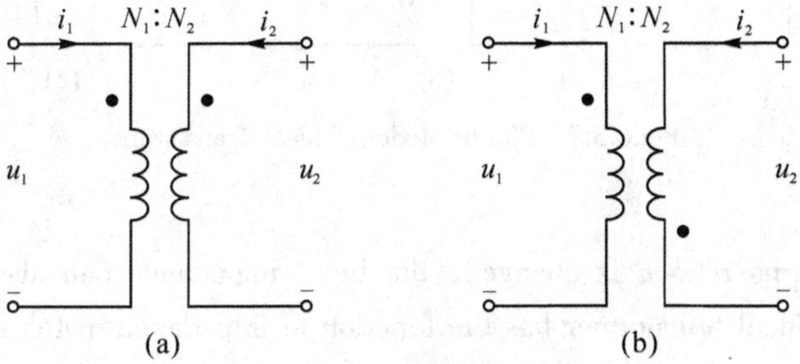

Fig.6.3.6 Ideal Transformer

The sign in above expressions of the ideal transformer is related to the dotted terminals. If the positive polarity of primary and secondary voltage u_1, u_2 are consistent with the dotted terminals, the voltage ratio takes plus sign, otherwise, it takes negative sign. On the contrary, if both primary and secondary current i_1, i_2 flow into the dotted terminals, the current ratio is positive, otherwise, it is negative.

Besides, ideal transformer has the following characteristics:

(1) Ideal transformer does not consume power. Because $R_1 = R_2 = 0$, so its power is

$$p = u_1 i_1 + u_2 i_2 = u_1 i_1 + \dfrac{u_1}{n}\cdot(-n i_1) = 0 \qquad (6.3.19)$$

(2) The ideal transformer can be used to change the voltage and current, it can also be used to change the impedance. As shown in Fig.6.3.7c, if load impedance Z_L is connected to the secondary coil, the input impedance (conversion

impedance) of the primary port in the ideal transformer can be derived as follows

$$Z_i = \frac{\dot{U}_1}{\dot{I}_1} = \frac{n\dot{U}_2}{-\frac{1}{n}\dot{I}_2} = n^2 Z_L \qquad (6.3.20)$$

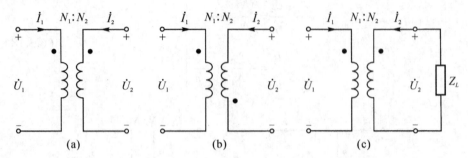

Fig.6.3.7 Phasor Model of Ideal Transformer

So, if turns ratio n is changed, the input impedance can also be changed. That is, the ideal transformer has the function of impedance matching.

When the circuit with ideal transformer is analyzed, both methods of primary equivalent circuit and secondary equivalent circuit can be adopted.

Example 6.3.3 An ideal transformer circuit is shown in Fig.6.3.8. Try the primary input resistance when the switch K is turned on or closed.

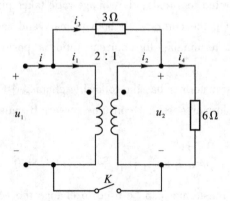

Fig.6.3.8 The Circuit for Example 6.3.3

Solution

(1) When K is open, $i_3 = 0$, $i = i_1$, according to the VCR of ideal transformer, there are

$$i_1 = \frac{1}{2}i_2 = \frac{1}{2} \times \frac{u_2}{6} = \frac{u_2}{12}$$

$$u_1 = 2u_2$$

Therefore, the primary input resistance is

$$R_i = \frac{u_1}{i} = 24\Omega$$

(2) When K is closed, there are

$$i = i_1 + i_3 = \frac{1}{2}i_2 + i_3 = \frac{1}{2}(i_4 - i_3) + i_3 = \frac{1}{2}(i_3 + i_4)$$

$$i_3 = \frac{u_1 - u_2}{3} = \frac{u_1 - \frac{1}{2}u_1}{3} = \frac{1}{6}u_1$$

$$i_4 = \frac{u_2}{6} = \frac{1}{2} \cdot \frac{1}{6}u_1 = \frac{1}{12}u_1$$

$$i = \frac{1}{2}\left(\frac{1}{12}u_1 + \frac{1}{6}u_1\right) = \frac{1}{2} \times \frac{1}{4}u_1 = \frac{1}{8}u_1$$

$$R_i = \frac{u_1}{i} = 8\Omega$$

Example 6.3.4 Fig. 6.3.9 shows an equivalent circuit for the final-stage power amplifier of the transistor radio. Source voltage $u = 6V$ and the internal resistance $R_i = 200\Omega$.

(1) If the circuit is connected with $R = 8\Omega$ speaker as load, try to find the power of the load?

(2) In order to match the maximum power for the load, a transformer is connected between the source and the load, try to find the turns ratio of the transformer and the value of power.

Solution

(1) If the speaker is connected to source directly, as shown in Fig.6.3.9a, there are

$$i = \frac{u}{R + R_i} = \frac{6}{200 + 8} = 28.8(\text{mA})$$

$$P = i^2 R = (^28.8 \times 10^{-3})^2 \times 8 = 6.6 (\text{mW})$$

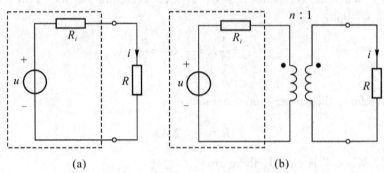

Fig.6.3.9 The Circuit for Example 6.3.4

(2) After the transformer is connected, as shown in Fig.6.3.9b, it is required to match the maximum power, so $R_i = n^2 R$, the turns ratio of the transformer can be derived as follows

$$n = \sqrt{\frac{R_i}{R}} = \sqrt{\frac{200}{8}} = 5$$

And the maximum power of the speaker is

$$p_{\max} = \frac{u^2}{4R_i} = \frac{36}{4 \times 200} = 45 (\text{mW})$$

It can be seen that after the transformer is connected, the power received by the speaker load is much larger than that directly connected to the load.

Example 6.3.5 For the circuit shown in Fig.6.3.10a, find current flowing through 4Ω resistance load.

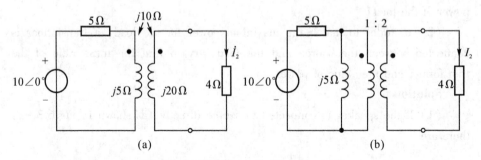

Fig.6.3.10 The Circuit for Example 6.3.5

Solution Due to the mutual inductance coupling coefficient is

$$K = \frac{M}{\sqrt{L_1 L_2}} = \frac{\omega M}{\sqrt{\omega L_1 \omega L_2}} = \frac{10}{\sqrt{5 \times 20}} = 1$$

So, the circuit contains a unity-coupled transformer. Based on the knowledge in the section 6.3.2, the unity-coupled transformer is equivalent to a primary inductance in parallel with the ideal transformer, then its equivalent circuit can be drawn as shown in Fig.6.3.10b.

Turns ratio of ideal transformer is

$$\frac{N_1}{N_2} = \sqrt{\frac{L_1}{L_2}} = \sqrt{\frac{\omega L_1}{\omega L_2}} = \sqrt{\frac{5}{20}} = \frac{1}{2}$$

Then, Thevenin's equivalent method can be used to find the current of secondary loop.

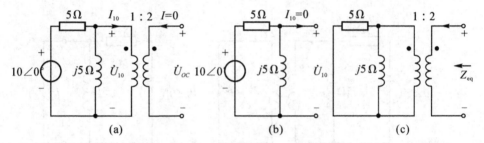

Fig.6.3.11 The Circuit for Example 6.3.5

First, let's find the open circuit voltage of the secondary port. As shown in Fig.6.3.11a, In this case, the load can be considered as an infinite impedance, so, there is no current flowing through secondary coil. According to expression (6.3.20), it can be seen that there is also not current flowing through primary coil or the input impedance of the ideal transformer looking from primary side is infinite too. The output voltage of the primary circuit as shown in Fig.6.3.11b is derived as follows

$$\dot{U}_{10} = \frac{j5}{5+j5} \times 10 \angle 0° = 5\sqrt{2} \angle 45° (\text{V})$$

Then

$$\frac{\dot{U}_{10}}{\dot{U}_{OC}} = \frac{1}{2}$$

$$\dot{U}_{OC} = 2\dot{U}_{10} = 10\sqrt{2}\angle 45°\text{V}$$

Next, find Thevenin's equivalent impedance, there are two ways

Method 1 Setting the independent source to zero, the equivalent circuit is shown in Fig.6.3.11c, the equivalent impedance of the secondary port is derived as follows

$$Z_{eq} = \left(\frac{2}{1}\right)^2 \times \frac{5\times j5}{5+j5} = 10\sqrt{2}\angle 45°(\Omega)$$

Method 2 Open circuit and short circuit method. As shown in Fig.6.3.12a, when secondary circuit is short circuited in port, according to expression (6.3.20), it shows that primary side circuit of the ideal transformer is equivalent to short circuit too, as shown in Fig.6.3.12b.

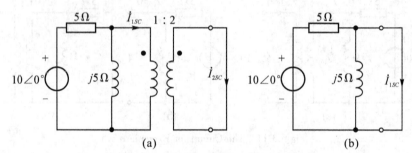

(a)   (b)

Fig.6.3.12 The Circuit for Example 6.3.5

So short-circuit current in primary coil can be derived:

$$\dot{I}_{1SC} = \frac{10\angle 0°}{5} = 2\angle 0°(\text{A})$$

And due to

$$\frac{\dot{I}_{1SC}}{\dot{I}_{2SC}} = \frac{2}{1}$$

So there is

$$\dot{I}_{2SC} = \frac{\dot{I}_{1SC}}{2} = 1\angle 0°\text{A}$$

Therefore, the Thevenin's equivalent impedance is

$$Z_{eq} = \frac{\dot{U}_{OC}}{\dot{I}_{2SC}} = \frac{10\sqrt{2}\angle 45°}{1} = 10\sqrt{2}\angle 45°(\Omega)$$

Now, Thevenin's equivalent circuit can be derived as shown in Fig.6.3.11c. So, it is easy to calculate the load resistance current as follows

$$\dot{I}_2 = \frac{\dot{U}_{OC}}{R+Z_{eq}} = \frac{10\sqrt{2}\angle 45°}{4+10\sqrt{2}\angle 45°} = 0.822\angle 9.5°(A)$$

The primary or secondary equivalent circuit can also applied to analyze the example.

6.4 Examples of Computer-Aided Circuit Analysis with Matlab

For the circuit with mutual inductance shown in Fig.6.4.1, the reference direction of the phasor voltages and currents are assigned as shown in the circuit. In the following, Matlab is applied to analyze the circuit.

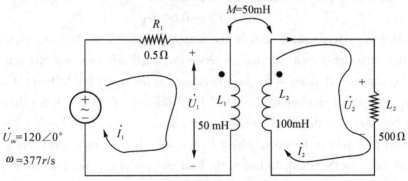

Fig.6.4.1   Mutual Inductance Circuit

Its mesh current equations can be listed as follows

$$R_1\dot{I}_1 + j\omega L_1 \dot{I}_1 - j\omega M \dot{I}_2 = \dot{U}_{in}$$
$$-j\omega M \dot{I}_1 + R_L \dot{I}_2 + j\omega L_2 \dot{I}_2 = 0$$
(6.4.1)

Take the parameter into the expression (6.4.1), there are

$$(0.5+j18.85)\dot{I}_1 - j18.85\dot{I}_2 = 120\angle 0°$$
$$-j18.85\dot{I}_1 + (1000+j37.7)\dot{I}_2 = 0$$

In MATLAB workspace, enter the following code
```
Z=[0.5+18.85j   18.85j 18.85j 500+37.7j];
V=[120 0]';
I=Z\V;
fprintf(' \n');
fprintf('V1=%7.3f V \t', abs(18.85j * I(1)));
fprintf('V2=%7.3f V \t', abs(500 * I(2)));
fprintf('Ratio V2/V1=%7.3f \t',abs((500 * I(2))/(18.85j * I(1))))
```
Run MATLAB program, results will be

    V1 = 120.093 V   V2 = 119.753 V   Ratio V2/V1 = 0.997

It is seen that voltage ratio is

$$\frac{U_2}{U_{in}} = \frac{119.753}{120} = 0.998$$

By adding a sentence in the program

    fprintf('Phase V2=%6.2f deg', angle(500 * I(2)) * 180/pi)

Run Matlab program again, it is obtained that

$$\text{Phase V2} = -0.64 \text{ deg}$$

That is, voltage phase shift in the output port is -0.64 degrees. It indicates that the output amplitude and output phase are small different from the amplitude and input phase. If value of the load resistance is increased to $1K$Ohms, it will be found, the output port voltage $\dot{U}_2$ is still little difference from the input voltage $\dot{U}_{in}$. It can be seen that the coupling inductor in the circuit shown in Fig.6.4.1 can be regarded as a voltage follower, which is also called 1 : 1 transformer. Its work is characterized by the ability to isolate the load and power supply, even if the output load changes, the output voltage will not change. Generally, the transformer in which output voltage is higher than the input voltage is called a step-up transformer; the transformer in which the output voltage is less than the input voltage called step-down transformer.

Exercises

6-1   Write out the VCR equations of the coupling inductance shown in Fig.6-1.

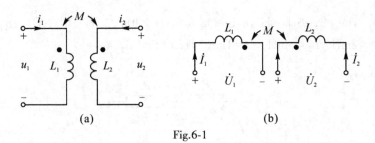

Fig.6-1

6-2 Write out the equivalent inductance coefficient of the circuit shown in Fig.6-2.

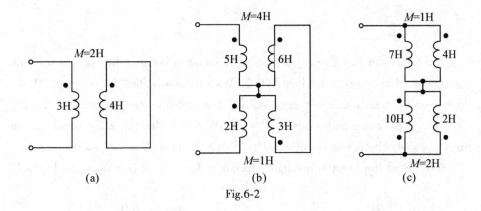

Fig.6-2

6-3 The circuit is shown in Fig.6-3, write out voltage u_{ab}, u_{bc} and u_{ca}.

6-4 When the circuit shown in Fig.6-4 is connected to a sinusoidal power supply with a frequency of 500Hz, the ammeter reading is 1A, the voltmeter reading is 31.4V, find mutual inductance M.

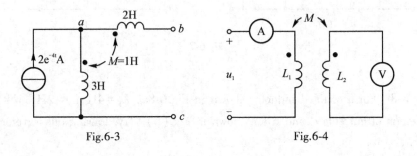

Fig.6-3 Fig.6-4

6-5 The circuit is shown in Fig.6-5, $u = 200\sqrt{2}\cos 10^4 t\ (\text{V})$, $R_1 = R_2 = 20\Omega$, $L_1 = 2\text{mH}$, $L_2 = 3\text{mH}$, $M = 1\text{mH}$. Try to find u_1, u_2.

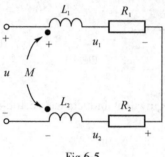

Fig.6-5

6-6 In order to measure the mutual inductance between two coils, two coils are connected in series and driven by a 220V/50Hz sinusoidal power source. When the two coils connected in sequence series, it is measured the current $I = 2.5\text{A}$ and the average power of both coils is $P = 62.5\text{W}$. When the two coils connected in reverse series, the power of coils is $P = 250\text{W}$. Try to find mutual inductance M.

6-7 Find the input equivalent impedance for each circuit shown in Fig.6-7.

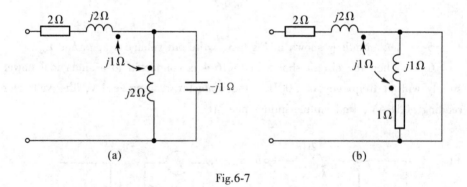

Fig.6-7

6-8 For a coupled inductor shown in Fig.6-8a, $L_1 = 4\text{H}$, $L_2 = 2\text{H}$, $M = 1\text{H}$, waveform of currents i_1 and i_2 are shown in Fig.(b). Try drawing out waveform of u_1, u_2.

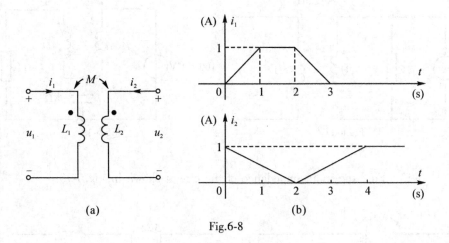

Fig.6-8

6-9 For the circuit shown in Fig. 6-9, find the voltage $\dot{U}$ across 10Ω resistance load. If the current source is replaced by a voltage source $\dot{U}_S = 2\angle 0°\text{V}$, find the voltage again.

6-10 The circuit is shown in Fig.6-10, $u_S = 150\sqrt{2}\cos 100t\,\text{V}$, $R_1 = 5\Omega, R_2 = 15\Omega, R_L = 5\Omega$, $L_1 = 0.1\text{H}$, $L_2 = 0.2\text{H}$, $M = 0.1\text{H}$. Find the current i_1, i_2.

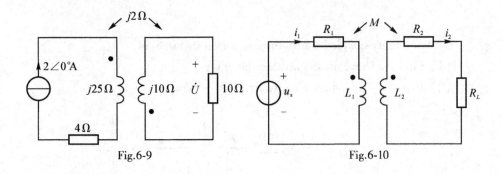

Fig.6-9   Fig.6-10

6-11 The circuit shown in Fig.6-11, given: $i_S = 5\sqrt{2}\cos 2t$ A, find open-circuit voltage u_{OC}.

6-12 For the circuit shown in Fig.6-12, the coupling coefficient $k = 0.5$. Please find amplitude and phase of the output voltage $\dot{U}_2$.

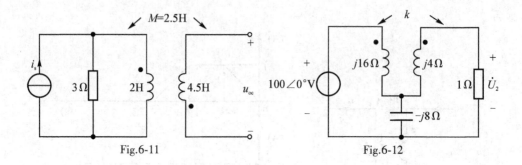

Fig.6-11 Fig.6-12

6-13 Find the input impedance of the circuit shown in Fig.6-13.

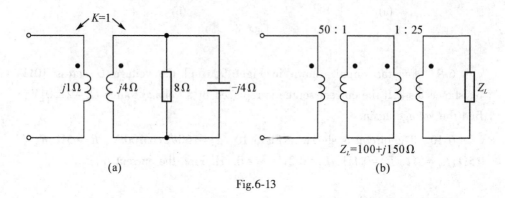

(a) (b)

Fig.6-13

6-14 A unity-coupled transformer is shown in Fig.6-14.
(1) Find its Thevenin's equivalent circuit ;
(2) If port a, b is short circuit, find the current $\dot{I}_1$.

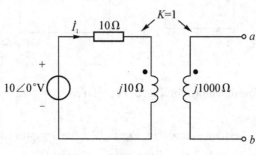

Fig.6-14

6-15 As shown in Fig. 6-15, calculate the input resistance of R_{ab} when switch K is switched on or off.

6-16 The circuit is shown in Fig.6-16, find the current $\dot{I}$.

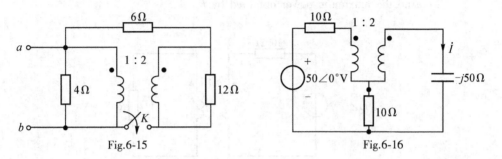

Fig.6-15   Fig.6-16

6-17 The circuit is shown in Fig.6-17, find the power of the 5Ω resistance and the power of the voltage source.

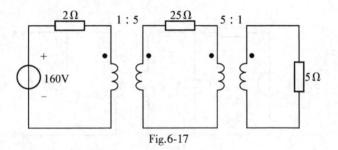

Fig.6-17

6-18 The circuit is shown in Fig.6-18, in order to get the maximum power, find the value of the load impedance (Applying Thevenin's Theorem).

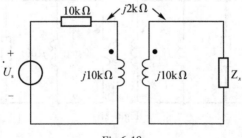

Fig.6-18

6-19 The circuit is shown in Fig.6-19:

(1) Find the ratio of turns when the load resistance R obtains the maximum power;

(2) Find the maximum power obtained by R.

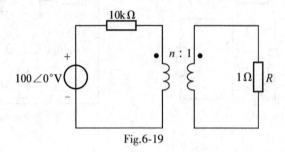

Fig.6-19

6-20 The circuit is shown in Fig.6-20. Find its Thevenin's equivalent circuit.

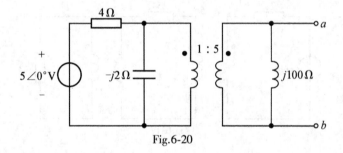

Fig.6-20

6-21 The circuit is shown in Fig.6-21. Find the voltage $\dot{U}_1$ and $\dot{U}_2$.

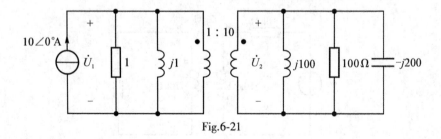

Fig.6-21

Chapter 7

Resonant Circuit Analysis

In the one-port network with inductors and capacitors, when the port voltage and current are in phase, that is, the circuit is purely resistive or purely conductive and the circuit is also called to be resonant. The circuit operating in the resonant state or near the resonant state is called a resonant circuit. Resonance is a special operating state of sinusoidal steady-state circuits. Due to its good frequency selection characteristics, resonant circuit had been widely used in communication and electronic technology. The resonant circuit usually consists of inductors, capacitors and resistors. According to the connection form, resonant circuit can be divided into series resonant circuit, parallel resonant circuit, mutual inductance coupled resonant circuit, etc. This section and the following sections will discuss the resonant conditions, resonant characteristics and frequency characteristics of the series resonant circuit, the parallel resonant circuit, and the mutual inductance coupling resonant circuit, respectively.

7.1 Series Resonant Circuit

7.1.1 *RLC* Series Resonant Circuit

As shown in Fig.7.1.1, it is the *RLC* series circuit, when the port voltage $\dot{U}_S$ and current $\dot{I}$ are in phase, that is, the circuit is purely resistive or purely conductive and the circuit is called to be resonant. The resonance phenomenon occurred in this circuit is also called series resonance. The power supply of the circuit shown in Fig.7.1.1 is a sinusoidal voltage source with angular frequency ω, its voltage phasor is $\dot{U}_S = U_S \angle 0°\text{V}$.

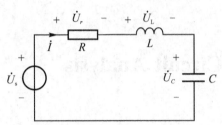

Fig 7.1.1   The *RLC* Series Resonant Circuit

7.1.1.1   Resonant Condition

According to the definition of resonance, while voltage $\dot{U}_s$ and current $\dot{I}$ are in phase, the reactance of the loop impedance must be zero, that is

$$X = \omega_0 L - \frac{1}{\omega_0 C} = 0.$$

Then, resonant angular frequency ω_0 and resonant frequency f_0 are derived as follows

$$\omega_0 = \frac{1}{\sqrt{LC}} \qquad (7.1.1a)$$

$$f_0 = \frac{1}{2\pi\sqrt{LC}} \qquad (7.1.1b)$$

From the above expression, it is seen that the resonant frequency of the circuit depends only on the parameters L, C and is independent of the excitation. So, the resonance reflects the inherent characteristic of the circuit. In addition to making the circuit resonance by changing the excitation frequency, in actual engineering, circuit resonance in a certain frequency is usually achieved by changing the capacitance or inductance parameters in the circuit, this operation is called tuning.

7.1.1.2   Characteristic Impedance

For a resonance circuit, its reactance is zero, but the inductive and capacitive reactance are not equal to zero, their value is $\omega_0 L = \dfrac{1}{\omega_0 C} = \sqrt{\dfrac{L}{C}}$. So, the inductive reactance and the capacitive reactance are independent of resonant frequency and they are important parameters of the resonant circuit. They are called characteristic impedance and denoted as ρ, namely

$$\rho = \omega_0 L = \frac{1}{\omega_0 C} = \sqrt{\frac{L}{C}} \qquad (7.1.2)$$

7.1.1.3 Quality Factor

In electronic technology, the performance of the resonant circuit is usually discussed in terms of the ratio of the characteristic impedance relative to the loss resistance, which is called the quality factor and denoted as Q, namely

$$Q = \frac{\rho}{R} = \frac{\omega_0 L}{R} = \frac{1}{\omega_0 CR} = \frac{1}{R}\sqrt{\frac{L}{C}} \qquad (7.1.3)$$

Quality factor is a dimensionless quantity and can be used to discuss the selectivity of the circuit. In the field of radio technology, Q is generally between 50 ~ 200.

7.1.1.4 Resonant Characteristics

Since the reactance in the resonant circuit is zero, the circuit is pure resistive. Then the resonant impedance is the smallest and is denoted as Z_0, namely

$$Z_0 = R \qquad (7.1.4)$$

Therefore, the current in series resonance circuit is the largest

$$\dot{I}_0 = \frac{\dot{U}}{Z_0} = \frac{\dot{U}}{R} \qquad (7.1.5)$$

And the resistor voltage is equal to the port voltage

$$\dot{U}_r = R\dot{I}_0 = \dot{U} \qquad (7.1.6)$$

Capacitor voltage and inductor voltage are

$$\dot{U}_L = j\omega L \dot{I}_0 = jQ\dot{U}$$
$$\dot{U}_C = \frac{1}{j\omega C}\dot{I}_0 = -jQ\dot{U} \qquad (7.1.7)$$

From above analysis, it can be seen that when the circuit is resonant, LC series branch is equivalent to short circuit, all the source voltage is added on the resistor. As quality factor is generally more than dozens, then the voltage across capacitor and inductor is also dozen times of source voltage, so the series resonance is also known as voltage resonance. In radio technology, due to the signal is weak, series resonance is often applied to obtain a higher voltage. However, in the power system, the high voltage will make the electrical equipment insulation breakdown, so it should be avoided that the circuit is resonant or operates in a frequency near the resonant frequency.

7.1.1.5 Power and Energy

If the circuit is series resonant, the active power absorbed by the circuit is
$$P = UI\cos\varphi = UI = I^2 R$$
The reactive power of the circuit is
$$Q = UI\sin\varphi = 0$$
That is
$$Q = Q_L + Q_C = 0$$

Therefore, when the resonance occurs, the energy is exchanged between the capacitor and the inductor and without energy exchanged with the power supply. The sum of the electric field energy stored in capacitor and the magnetic field energy stored in inductor can be expressed as

$$W = W_L + W_C = \frac{1}{2}LI_m^2 \sin^2\omega_0 t + \frac{1}{2}CU_{Cm}^2 \cos^2\omega_0 t \tag{7.1.8}$$

As
$$U_{cm} = \frac{1}{\omega_0 C}I_m = \sqrt{\frac{L}{C}}I_m$$
$$CU_{cm}^2 = LI_m^2$$

And
$$U_{cm} = QU_m$$

So there is
$$W = \frac{1}{2}CQ^2 U_m^2 \tag{7.1.9}$$

It can be seen that the sum of the electromagnetic energy stored in the inductor and capacitor element is a constant, not varied with time. It is proportional to the square of the quality factor Q of the loop.

Example 7.1.1 In a RLC series circuit, $R = 100\Omega$, $L = 20\text{mH}$, $C = 200\text{PF}$, $U = 10\text{V}$. Try to find its resonance parameters f_0, Q, U_C, U_L.

Solution The resonant frequency, quality factor and capacitor voltage of the series circuit are derived respectively as follows

$$f_0 = \frac{1}{2\pi\sqrt{LC}} = \frac{1}{2\pi\sqrt{2\times10^{-10}\times2\times10^{-2}}} = 79.6\text{KHz}$$

$$Q = \frac{\rho}{r} = \frac{1}{r}\sqrt{\frac{L}{C}} = \frac{1}{100}\sqrt{\frac{2\times10^{-2}}{2\times10^{-10}}} = 100$$

$$U_C = U_L = QU = 100 \times 10 = 1000\text{V}$$

Example 7.1.2 For the circuit shown in Fig.7.1.2, it is known $L_1 = 100$mH, $L_2 = 400$mH, $r = 10\Omega$, $u = 20\sqrt{2} \cos(1000t + 60°)$. If $C = 1.25\mu$F, the current i reaches the maximum value of 2A. Find out the mutual inductance M and quality factor Q.

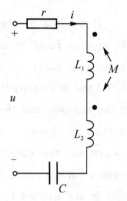

Fig.7.1.2 The Circuit for Example 7.1.2

Solution The circuit contains a sequence series connection of coupling inductor, which can be equivalent to a single inductor. Under the excitation of the power supply, the current i reaches the maximum value, which means that the circuit is in resonance, $\omega_0 = 1000$rad/s. So there is

$$\omega_0(L_1 + L_2 + 2M) - \frac{1}{\omega_0 C} = 0$$

and

$$M = \frac{1}{2}\left(\frac{1}{\omega_0^2 C} - L_1 - L_2\right) = 0.15\text{H}$$

$$Q = \frac{\rho}{r} = \frac{1}{r}\sqrt{\frac{L}{C}} = \frac{1}{10} \times \sqrt{\frac{(100+400+150) \times 10^{-3}}{1.25 \times 10^{-6}}} = 80$$

7.1.2 Frequency Response

The resonant characteristics of the series resonant circuit was discussed earlier. The frequency characteristics of the series resonant circuit are further studied here. The characteristics that circuit response varies with the excitation frequency change, is called frequency response, also known as frequency characteristic. Frequency characteristics includes amplitude and phase frequency characteristics. The amplitude frequency characteristics is the relationship that amplitude varies with frequency change, and the phase frequency characteristics is the relationship of phase varies with frequency change. The frequency characteristics of circuit are usually analyzed with the network function of the sinusoidal steady-state circuit.

For a sinusoidal steady-state circuit, the ratio of the response phasor relative to the excitation phasor is defined as the network function, that is

$$H(j\omega) = \frac{\dot{Y}_m}{\dot{F}_m} = \frac{\dot{Y}}{\dot{F}}$$

Depending on whether the response and the stimulus are on the same port, the network function can be divided into two types: the driving-point function and the transfer function. When the response and excitation in the same port, it is called the driving-point function, otherwise called the transfer function. According to the response and the excitation is the voltage or the current, the driving point function is divided into the driving point impedance and the driving point admittance; the transfer function is divided into the transfer voltage ratio, the transfer current ratio, the transfer impedance and the transfer admittance.

In the following, the frequency characteristics of the current in the series resonant circuit shown in Fig.6.4.1 is discussed. The current in the series resonant circuit can be written as follows

$$\dot{I} = \frac{\dot{U}_s}{R+j\left(\omega L - \frac{1}{\omega C}\right)} = \frac{\frac{1}{r}\dot{U}_s}{1+j\frac{\omega_o L}{R}\left(\frac{\omega}{\omega_o} - \frac{1}{\omega\omega_o LC}\right)}$$

$$= \frac{H_o \dot{U}_s}{1+jQ\left(\frac{\omega}{\omega_o} - \frac{\omega_o}{\omega}\right)} = H_o \frac{\frac{\omega_o}{Q}(j\omega)\dot{U}_s}{(j\omega)^2 + \frac{\omega_o}{Q}(j\omega) + (\omega_o)^2} \quad (7.1.10)$$

where $H_0 = \frac{1}{R}$.

Frequency response of series resonant circuit is

$$H(j\omega) = \frac{\dot{I}}{\dot{U}_s} = H_0 \frac{\frac{\omega_0}{Q}(j\omega)}{(j\omega)^2 + \frac{\omega_0}{Q}(j\omega) + \omega_0^2} \quad (7.1.11)$$

Amplitude frequency response of series resonant circuit

$$|H(j\omega)| = \frac{H_0}{\sqrt{1+Q^2\left(\frac{\omega}{\omega_0} - \frac{\omega_0}{\omega}\right)^2}} = \frac{H_0}{\sqrt{1+Q^2\left(\eta - \frac{1}{\eta}\right)^2}} \quad (7.1.12)$$

where $\eta = \dfrac{\omega}{\omega_0}$ is called relative detuning quantity, which indicates the relative detuning degree of angular frequency ω (source frequency) to ω_0 (resonant frequency).

Normalized amplitude frequency response

$$\frac{|H(j\omega)|}{H_0} = \frac{1}{\sqrt{1+Q^2\left(\eta-\dfrac{1}{\eta}\right)^2}}$$

is called relative inhibition ratio.

Phase frequency characteristics of series resonant circuit is

$$\varphi(\omega) = -\arctan Q\left(\frac{\omega}{\omega_0} - \frac{\omega_0}{\omega}\right) = -\arctan Q\left(\eta - \frac{1}{\eta}\right) \qquad (7.1.13)$$

In electronic technology, the resonant circuit is often used to select the desired signal from many different frequency signals. This property of the resonant circuit is called selectivity. If the source frequency is deviated from resonant frequency, it called detuning. The greater of detuning, the smaller of current.

The normalized amplitude frequency characteristic curve and phase frequency characteristic curve of the series resonant circuit are shown in Fig.7.1.3. It can be seen from the figure, the higher Q is, the more sharp the curve is, the better the circuit selectivity is. In addition, from the expression (7.1.12), it is seen that, as long as Q remains the same, the resonance curve is also the same. Noted that the frequency response curves shown in Fig.7.1.3 are commonly adapted to all RLC

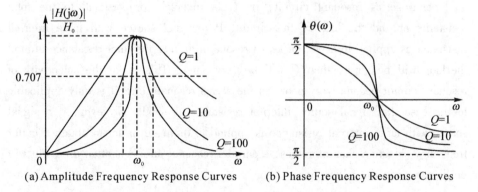

(a) Amplitude Frequency Response Curves (b) Phase Frequency Response Curves

Fig.7.1.3 Frequency Response Curve

series circuits.

7.1.3 Passband

In order to measure the ability of the circuit to transmit a certain bandwidth of the actual signal, it is customary to define the frequency range corresponding to $\frac{|H(j\omega)|}{H_0} = \frac{1}{\sqrt{2}}$ as passband of the circuit, and it is denoted as B, namely

$$B = \omega_2 - \omega_1 (\text{rad/s}) \quad \text{or} \quad B = f_2 - f_1 (\text{Hz}) \qquad (7.1.14)$$

where, ω_2, ω_1 are upper and lower cut-off angular frequency; f_2, f_1 are upper and lower cut-off frequency. They can be derived from the following expression

$$\frac{|H(j\omega)|}{H_0} = \frac{1}{\sqrt{1 + Q^2 \left(\frac{f}{f_0} - \frac{f_0}{f} \right)^2}} = \frac{1}{\sqrt{2}}$$

According to the above expression, an important relationship among the passband, the resonant frequency and the quality factor can be derived as follows

$$B = \frac{\omega_0}{Q} \text{rad/s} \quad \text{or} \quad B = \frac{f_0}{Q} \text{Hz} \qquad (7.1.15)$$

It indicates that the passband B is proportional to ω_0 or f_0 and opposite proportional to Q.

7.2 Parallel Resonant Circuit

For a series resonant circuit, its Q is inversely proportional to the total resistance around the loop of the circuit. If a signal source with large internal resistance is applied to drive the series resonant circuit, the total resistance around the loop will be large, then Q will be very small. This make the selectivity of resonant circuit become very poor. So the series resonant circuit is only applicable to the case that signal source internal resistance is small. However, if a signal source with large internal resistance is applied to drive, in order to obtain a better frequency selection characteristics, a parallel resonant circuit is often used and will be discussed in the following.

7.2.1 GCL Parallel Resonant Circuit

Fig.7.2.1 shows a GCL parallel resonant circuit, which is the dual circuit of the rLC series resonant circuit in Fig.7.1.1. So some of results derived from the rLC series resonant circuit can be applied to parallel resonant circuit by using the duality principle.

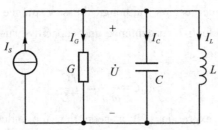

Fig.7.2.1 Parallel Resonant Circuit

The total admittance of the parallel resonant circuit is

$$Y = G + jB = G + j\left(\omega C - \frac{1}{\omega L}\right) \quad (7.2.1)$$

Obviously, when its susceptance $B = 0$, the voltage $\dot{U}$ and current $\dot{I}$ of the parallel circuit are in phase, the circuit will be resonant. And the angular frequency and frequency of the circuit are called the parallel resonant frequency and expressed as ω_0 and f_0. The resonant condition of parallel resonant circuit is that its susceptance $B = 0$

$$\omega C - \frac{1}{\omega L} = 0 \quad (7.2.2)$$

7.2.1.1 Resonant Frequency and Impedance

Resonant frequency can be derived as follows

$$\omega_0 = \frac{1}{\sqrt{LC}}$$
$$f_0 = \frac{1}{2\pi\sqrt{LC}} \quad (7.2.3)$$

It can be seen that, the parallel resonant frequency expression is same as series frequency expression (7.1.1).

When parallel resonance occur, the imaginary part of admittance is zero

$$Y_0 = G = \frac{1}{R} \qquad (7.2.4)$$

It is easy to prove that this resonant admittance is the minimum, the circuit is resistive. Therefore, the resonant impedance will be the maximum

$$Z_0 = \frac{1}{Y_0} = R \qquad (7.2.5)$$

When the resonance occurs, although the susceptance of the circuit is zero, but at this time the inductive susceptance and capacitive susceptance are not equal to zero. They are written as

$$\omega_0 C = \frac{1}{\omega_0 L} = \sqrt{\frac{C}{L}} \qquad (7.2.6)$$

So, from above expression, it is seen that the inductive susceptance and capacitive susceptance are independent of frequency. They are important parameters of the parallel resonant circuit and are called as characteristic susceptance, denoted as ρ, namely

$$\rho = \omega_0 L = \frac{1}{\omega_0 C} = \sqrt{\frac{L}{C}} \qquad (7.2.7)$$

7.2.1.2 Quality Factor

The quality factor of the parallel resonant circuit is

$$Q = \frac{R}{\omega_0 L} = \frac{\omega_0 C}{G} = R\sqrt{\frac{C}{L}} \qquad (7.2.8)$$

7.2.1.3 Resonant Current

The current of each branch is

$$\left.\begin{aligned}\dot{I}_{G0} &= G\dot{U} = G\frac{1}{G}\dot{I}_s = \dot{I}_s \\ \dot{I}_{C0} &= j\omega C\dot{U} = j\frac{\omega_0 C}{G}\dot{I}_s = jQ\dot{I}_s \\ \dot{I}_{L0} &= -j\frac{1}{\omega L}\dot{U} = -j\frac{1}{\omega_0 LG}\dot{I}_s = -jQ\dot{I}_s\end{aligned}\right\} \qquad (7.2.9)$$

It can be seen that in the case of parallel resonance, the amplitude of the capacitor current and inductor current are equal, but the phase is opposite. When Parallel resonance occurs, all port current flows through the resistor element and its value is maximum. There is no current flowing through the parallel connection part of capacitor and an inductor. That part of circuit is equivalent to open circuit. Due to the resonant current of inductance and capacitance may be much greater than the total current, so parallel resonance is called as current resonance.

7.2.1.4 Frequency Response

For the parallel resonant circuit, the frequency response of the output voltage is often studied.

For the circuit shown in Fig.7.2.1, its port voltage can be written as follows

$$\dot{U} = \frac{\dot{I}_s}{Y} = \frac{\dot{I}_s}{G + j\left(\omega c - \frac{1}{\omega L}\right)} = \frac{R\dot{I}_s}{1 + jQ\left(\frac{\omega}{\omega_0} - \frac{\omega_0}{\omega}\right)} = H_0 \frac{\frac{\omega_0}{Q}(j\omega)\dot{I}_s}{(j\omega)^2 + \frac{\omega_0}{Q}(j\omega) + \omega_0^2} \quad (7.2.10)$$

where $H_0 = R = \frac{1}{G}$. The frequency response of the voltage is

$$H(j\omega) = \frac{\dot{U}}{\dot{I}_s} = H_0 \frac{\frac{\omega_0}{Q}(j\omega)}{(j\omega)^2 + \frac{\omega_0}{Q}(j\omega) + \omega_0^2} \quad (7.2.11)$$

The amplitude frequency and phase frequency characteristic curves are similar to that in Fig.7.1.3, and it can be proved that the frequency passband of the parallel resonant circuit is

$$B = \frac{\omega_0}{Q} = \frac{G}{C} = \frac{1}{RC} (\text{rad/s}) \quad (7.2.12)$$

Example 7.2.1 A simplified circuit of the amplifier is shown in Fig.7.2.2. Source voltage $\dot{U}_S = 12\angle 0°\text{V}$, internal resistance $R_i = 200\text{K}\Omega$, $L = 360\mu\text{H}$, $C = 90\text{PF}$, and quality factor $Q = 100$. If it is known the circuit resonate, find the resonant frequency, the voltage across the resistor R and the quality factor of whole the circuit.

Solution When the circuit is resonant, the resonant frequency is

$$\omega_0 = \frac{1}{\sqrt{LC}} = \frac{1}{\sqrt{360\times 10^{-6}\times 90\times 10^{-12}}} = 5.56\times 10^6(\text{rad/s})$$

Resonant impedance is

$$Z_0 = R = Q\sqrt{\frac{L}{C}} = 100\sqrt{\frac{360\times10^{-6}}{90\times10^{-12}}} = 200\times10^3(\Omega)$$

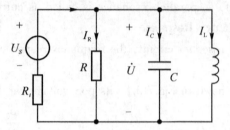

Fig.7.2.2 The Circuit for Example 7.2.1

The voltage of the resistor R is

$$U = U_s \frac{R}{R+R_i} = 6(\text{V})$$

Circuit quality factor is

$$Q_L = R'\sqrt{\frac{C}{L}} = \frac{R_i}{R_i+R} R\sqrt{\frac{C}{L}} = 50$$

It can be seen that, when the source resistance is considered, the quality factor of whole circuit will be decreased.

7.2.2 Practical Parallel Resonant Circuit

In electronic technology, the practical parallel resonant circuit that is often applied is shown in Fig.7.2.3, where R is the internal resistance of inductance coil. Generally, as the loss of internal capacitor is very small, internal capacitor can be ignored. Usually, the circuit operates in the frequency near the resonant frequency, and the Q is very high.

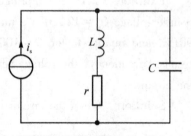

Fig.7.2.3 Practical Parallel Resonant Circuit

Total admittance of the circuit shown in Fig.7.2.3 is

$$Y = j\omega c + \frac{1}{r+j\omega L} = \frac{r}{r^2+(\omega L)^2} + j\left[\omega c - \frac{\omega L}{r^2+(\omega L)^2}\right] \quad (7.2.13)$$

As the Q value of the loop is high, there is $r^2 \ll (\omega L)^2$, then r^2 in the denominator of above expression can be omitted, so the admittance of the circuit can be rewritten as follows

$$Y \approx \frac{r}{(\omega L)^2} + j\left[\omega c - \frac{1}{\omega L}\right] \quad (7.2.14)$$

From this expression, it is seen that if operating in the vicinity of the resonance frequency, the resonant circuit shown in Fig.7.2.4a is equivalent to the circuit shown in Fig.7.2.4b. And resonant impedance will be

$$Z_0 = \frac{1}{Y_0} = \frac{r}{(\omega_0 L)^2} = \frac{L}{rC} = R \quad (7.2.15)$$

The quality factors of the circuits shown in Fig.7.2.4a and Fig.7.2.4b are as follows respectively.

$$Q_a = \frac{\rho_a}{r} = \frac{1}{r}\sqrt{\frac{L}{C}}$$

$$Q_b = \frac{R}{\rho_b} = R\sqrt{\frac{C}{L}} = \frac{L}{rC}\sqrt{\frac{C}{L}} = \frac{1}{r}\sqrt{\frac{L}{C}} = Q_a = Q \quad (7.2.16)$$

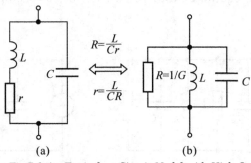

Fig.7.2.4 Equivalent Circuit Model with High Q

It can be seen that, the larger the resistance R of the parallel circuit is, equivalently the smaller the resistance r of the series circuit is, then the higher the Q value is. On the contrary, the smaller the resistance R of the parallel circuit is, the larger resistance r of the series circuit is, the smaller the Q value is.

Example 7.2.2 The circuit shown in Fig. 7.2.5 is a simplified a circuit amplifier, where source voltage $U_S = 12\text{V}$, internal resistance $R_S = 60\text{k}\Omega$; for parallel resonant circuit, $L = 360\text{H}$, $C = 90\text{pF}$, $r = 9\Omega$. The circuit load is capacitive shunt circuit, including $R_L = 60\text{k}\Omega$, $C_L = 10\text{pF}$. If the entire circuit is resonant, try to find the resonance frequency f_0, voltage of the R_L and quality factor Q_L of the entire circuit, passband B.

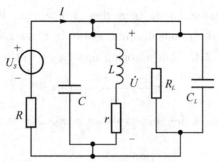

Fig.7.2.5 The Circuit for Example 7.2.2

Solution First, the voltage source in series with a resistor is transformed to a current source in parallel with a resistor. Next, the practical parallel resonant circuit is converted into its equivalent RLC parallel circuit, as shown in Fig.7.2.6a. So there are

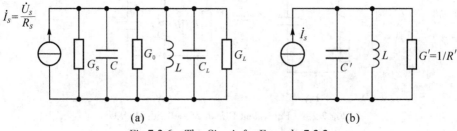

(a)   (b)

Fig.7.2.6 The Circuit for Example 7.2.2

$$\dot{I}_S = \frac{12\angle 0°}{60 \times 10^3} = 200\angle 0°(\mu\text{A})$$

$$C' = C + C_L = 90 + 10 = 100(\text{pF})$$

$$R_0 = \frac{L}{rC'} = \frac{54 \times 10^{-6}}{9 \times 100 \times 10^{-12}} = 60(\text{k}\Omega)$$

Next, the circuit is further simplified to a resonance circuit, as shown in Fig 7.2.6b. There are

$$\frac{1}{R'} = \frac{1}{60 \times 10^3} + \frac{1}{60 \times 10^3} + \frac{1}{60 \times 10^3}$$

$$R' = 20\text{k}\Omega$$

The resonant frequency is

$$f_0 = \frac{1}{2\pi\sqrt{LC'}} = \frac{1}{2\pi\sqrt{360 \times 10^{-6} \times 100 \times 10^{-12}}} = 839 \times 10^3 (\text{Hz})$$

Quality factor of the entire circuit is

$$Q_L = R'\sqrt{\frac{C'}{L}} = 20 \times 10^3 \times \sqrt{\frac{100 \times 10^{-6}}{54 \times 10^{-12}}} = 37$$

Voltage of R_L is

$$U_L = R'I_s = 20 \times 10^3 \times 200 \times 10^{-6} = 4(\text{V})$$

Passband is

$$B = \frac{f_0}{Q_L} = \frac{839000}{37} = 22.68 \times 10^3 (\text{Hz})$$

The series and parallel resonant circuit has been discussed above. As a generalization, for any single-port circuit containing L and C elements, under certain conditions, if the port voltage and current are in phase (the circuit is resistive and reactance is zero), it is called resonant circuit and the corresponding excitation frequency is called the resonant frequency.

7.2.3 Two Inductors, Two Capacitors Parallel Resonant Circuit

In the practical engineering, some complex parallel resonant circuit may be encountered. The most common one is two inductors or two capacitors parallel resonant circuit, as shown in Fig.7.2.7, it is known as the dual inductors or dual capacitors circuit. They can still be analyzed with the admittance.

Assuming that the reactances of two branches are X_1, X_2, we have

$$Y = \frac{1}{R_1 + jX_1} + \frac{1}{R_2 + jX_2} = \left[\frac{R_1}{R_1^2 + X_1^2} + \frac{R_2}{R_2^2 + X_2^2}\right] - j\left[\frac{X_1}{R_1^2 + X_1^2} + \frac{X_2}{R_2^2 + X_2^2}\right] \quad (7.2.17)$$

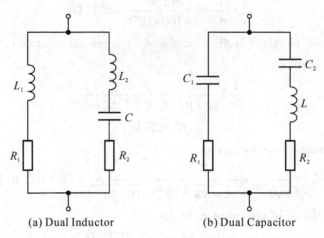

(a) Dual Inductor   (b) Dual Capacitor

Fig.7.2.7 Dual Inductor or Dual Capacitor Parallel Resonant Circuit

IF Q of the circuit is high and the circuit operates in the frequency close to the resonance frequency, then $R_1^2 \ll X_1^2$, $R_2^2 \ll X_2^2$. The items R_1^2 and R_2^2 in the denominator of expression (7.2.17) can be omitted, so it can be derived that

$$Y = \left[\frac{R_1}{X_1^2} + \frac{R_2}{X_2^2}\right] - j\left[\frac{1}{X_1} + \frac{1}{X_2}\right] = G - jB$$

When the parallel resonance occurs, the susceptance is zero, namely

$$B = -\left(\frac{1}{X_1} + \frac{1}{X_2}\right) = -\frac{X_1 + X_2}{X_1 X_2} = 0 \qquad (7.2.18)$$

Therefore

$$X_1 + X_2 = 0 \qquad (7.2.19)$$

In other words, the condition of parallel resonance is: The reactance around the parallel loop is zero (similar to the resonance condition of the series circuit).

According the expression (7.2.19), if resonance occurs in the two inductor circuit shown in Fig.7.2.7a, there is

$$\omega_0(L_1 + L_2) - \frac{1}{\omega_0 C} = 0$$

So, the resonant frequency can be derived as

$$\omega_0 = \frac{1}{\sqrt{(L_1 + L_2)C}} = \frac{1}{\sqrt{LC}} \qquad (7.2.20)$$

$$f_0 = \frac{1}{2\pi\sqrt{LC}} \qquad (7.2.21)$$

where $L = L_1 + L_2$ is the total inductance of the parallel loop in the circuit.

Similarly, if resonance occurs in the dual capacitor circuit shown in Fig.7.2.7b, there is

$$\omega_0 L - \left(\frac{1}{\omega_0 C_1} + \frac{1}{\omega_0 C_2}\right) = 0$$

So, resonant frequency is

$$\omega_0 = \frac{1}{\sqrt{L\dfrac{C_1 C_2}{C_1 + C_2}}} = \frac{1}{\sqrt{LC}} \qquad (7.2.22)$$

where $C = \dfrac{C_1 C_2}{C_1 + C_2}$ is the total capacity along the parallel loop.

From expressions (7.2.20) and (7.2.22), it is seen that if the total inductance or capacitance along of the parallel loop is fixed, regardless the value of L_1, L_2, C_1, C_2, their parallel resonant frequency will be the same.

When susceptance of the circuit is zero, the resonance admittance is

$$Y_0 = G_0 = \frac{R_1}{X_{10}^2} + \frac{R_2}{X_{20}^2} = \frac{R_1 + R_2}{X_{10}^2} = \frac{R}{X_{10}^2}$$

where $R = R_1 + R_2$ is the total resistance of the circuit, X_{10}, X_{20} are the reactance of each branch.

Resonant impedance is

$$Z_0 = \frac{1}{G_0} = \frac{X_{10}^2}{R}$$

So, for the dual inductor circuit, the resonant impedance is

$$Z_0 = \frac{1}{G_0} = \frac{(\omega_0 L_1)^2}{R} = \left(\frac{\omega_0 L_1}{\omega_0 L}\right)^2 \frac{(\omega_0 L)^2}{R} = \left(\frac{L_1}{L}\right)^2 \frac{L}{CR} = p^2 \frac{L}{CR} \qquad (7.2.23)$$

where $p = \dfrac{L_1}{L}$ is the ratio of the inductance of the branch 1 relative to the total inductance in the circuit and it is called inductance distribution coefficient. The resonance impedance can be changed by changing p to achieve the requirement of adjusting the resonance impedance and without changing resonance frequency.

For the two capacitors circuit, the resonant impedance is

$$Z_0 = \left(\frac{1}{\omega_0 C}\right)^2 \frac{1}{R} = \left(\frac{\omega_0 C}{\omega_0 C_1}\right)^2 \frac{1}{(\omega_0 C)^2 R} = \left(\frac{C}{C_1}\right)^2 \frac{L}{CR} = p^2 \frac{L}{CR} \quad (7.2.24)$$

where $p = \dfrac{C}{C_1} = \dfrac{C_2}{C_1 + C_2}$ is called capacitance distribution coefficient. As same as dual inductors circuit, the resonance impedance can be changed by changing p to achieve the requirement of adjusting the resonance impedance and without changing the resonance frequency.

From the above analysis, it is known that the two inductors and dual capacitors circuit have an advantage that the resonance impedance is adjustable and resonant characteristics (such as resonant frequency, quality factor etc.) is invariable. Therefore, they can be more flexibly applied in the circuit to realize the impedance matching.

Example 7.2.3 For the circuit shown in Fig.7.2.8, L is a variable inductor with a movable contact and it forms a parallel resonant circuit with a resistor R and a capacitor C. Given: $L = 100\mu H$, $C = 100pF$, $R = 10\Omega$. If the resonant circuit is connected to the source with effective voltage $U = 100V$ and internal resistance $R_i = 25K\Omega$, in order to obtain the maximum power in the resonant circuit. Try to find the inductance distribution coefficient, the resonance frequency, the branch current and the power absorbed in the loop.

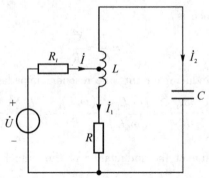

Fig.7.2.8 The Circuit for Example 7.2.3

Solution It can be seen that it is a dual inductors circuit. According to the maximum power matching conditions, there is

$$R_i = Z_0 = p^2 \frac{L}{CR} = 25\text{K}\Omega$$

Then, the inductance distribution coefficient can be obtained

$$p = \sqrt{\frac{R_i CR}{L}} = \sqrt{\frac{100 \times 10^{-12} \times 10 \times 25 \times 10^3}{100 \times 10^{-6}}} = 0.5$$

Resonant frequency is

$$f_0 = \frac{1}{2\pi\sqrt{LC}} = 1.59\text{MHz}$$

Loop quality factor is

$$Q = \frac{1}{R}\sqrt{\frac{L}{C}} = \frac{1}{10}\sqrt{\frac{100 \times 10^{-6}}{100 \times 10^{-12}}} = 100$$

Currents of each branch are

$$\dot{I} = \frac{\dot{U}}{2R_i} = \frac{5\angle 0°}{2 \times 25 \times 10^3} = 0.1(\text{mA})$$

$$\dot{I}_2 = \frac{(R + j\omega_0 L_1)\dot{I}}{R + j\omega_0 L_1 + j\omega_0 L_2 - j\dfrac{1}{\omega_0 C}} = \frac{(R + j\omega_0 pL)\dot{I}}{R}$$

$$= (1 + jQp)\dot{I} = (1 + j0.5 \times 100) \times 10^{-4} = 0.1 + j5(\text{mA})$$

$$\dot{I}_1 = \dot{I} - \dot{I}_2 = -jQp\dot{I} = -j5\text{mA}$$

The power absorbed in the loop is

$$P_{max} = \frac{U^2}{4R_i} = \frac{25}{4 \times 25 \times 10^3} = 0.25(\text{mW})$$

7.3 Examples of Computer Aided Circuit Analysis

In the following, a computer-aided analysis software EWB is applied to analyze resonant circuit. A *RLC* series resonant circuit is shown in Fig.7.3.1, the values of elements are given as follows

$$R = 0.628\Omega, L = 1\text{mH}, C = 25.33\mu\text{F}$$

The resonant frequency of the series resonant circuit can be obtained as follows

Chapter 7 Resonant Circuit Analysis

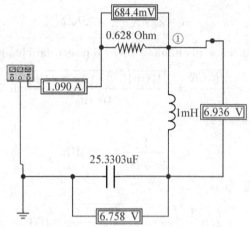

Fig.7.3.1 Series Resonant Circuit

$$f = \frac{1}{2\pi\sqrt{LC}} = \frac{1}{2\pi \times \sqrt{10^{-3} \times 25.33 \times 10^{-6}}} \approx 1000(\text{Hz})$$

And quality factor is

$$Q = \frac{1}{r}\sqrt{\frac{L}{C}} = \frac{1}{0.628} \times \sqrt{\frac{10^{-3}}{25.33 \times 10^{-6}}} = 10$$

An virtual ammeter is connected in series with the circuit to measure its effective current. And three virtual voltmeter are connected in parallel with resistor, capacitor and inductor to measure their effective voltages. The ammeter and voltmeter should set to AC scale. By starting the simulation switch, the current and voltage values can be read from the meters. The reading of Ammeter is 1.5A, the reading of resistor voltmeter is 684mV, the reading of the inductor voltmeter is 6.93V. So inductor voltage is about 10 times the resistor voltage, in line with the actual calculation value.

Next, the series resonant circuit is connected to a AC power supply 1V/1000Hz with the internal resistance $Rs = 628\Omega$, as shown in Fig.7.3.2, Then the resonant frequency of the circuit remains unchanged, is still 1000Hz. However quality factor of the entire circuit is decreased to

$$Q = \frac{1}{R+Rs}\sqrt{\frac{L}{C}} \approx \frac{1}{628} \times \sqrt{\frac{10^{-3}}{25.33 \times 10^{-6}}} = 10^{-2}$$

7.3 Examples of Computer Aided Circuit Analysis — 325

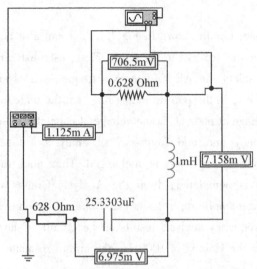

Fig.7.3.2 Series Resonant Circuit with Load

At this time, as shown in Fig.7.3.2, the reading of ammeter is 1.125mA, the reading of voltmeter across resistor is 706mV, the reading of voltmeter across inductor is 7.15mV, so inductor voltage is about 0.01 times the resistor voltage, equal to the actual value. At this point, the waveform can be observed from the oscilloscope. As shown in Fig.7.3.3, it is seen that the voltage across the resistor (that is, the phase of the current) is in phase with the port voltage of the series

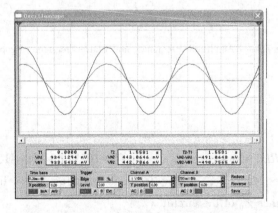

Fig.7.3.3 Voltage and Current Phase

circuit.

For the resonant circuit shown in Fig.7.3.1, it can also be analyzed by using frequency characteristic analysis in the EWB. First, establish circuit diagram in the workspace. Next, select the AC Frequency (frequency analysis) command from Analysis menu. Then, in the pop-up dialog box, set the node for analysis to be the node ①, node voltage at node ① is the voltage of capacitor in series with inductor. The initial frequency and end frequency of analysis are set 1Hz and 1MHz respectively, and other parameters is unchanged. Then click the Simulate button, when the analysis is completed, from the Analysis Graphs window in the AC Analysis column, the amplitude frequency and phase frequency characteristic curve can be derived. Frequency analysis results of the circuit is shown in Fig.7.3.4, it can be seen that in the vicinity of 1000Hz, the circuit resonates, and node voltage at node ① is zero.

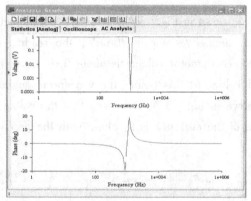

Fig.7.3.4 Amplitude Frequency and Phase Frequency Response

Exercises

7-1 In a RLC series resonant circuit, $R = 10\Omega$, $L = 100\mu H$, $C = 100pF$. Find the resonant frequency f_0, quality factor Q, characteristic impedance ρ and resonant impedance Z_0 of the circuit.

7-2 For a series resonant circuit, if keep the source effective voltage $U_S = 1V$

unchanged, and adjust the source frequency ($f_0 = 100\text{kHz}$) to make circuit resonant, the loop current is measured to be $I_0 = 100\text{mA}$. When the source frequency is changed to $f_1 = 99\text{kHz}$, the loop current is $I_1 = 70.7\text{mA}$. Find:

(1) If the source frequency is $f_1 = 99\text{kHz}$, is the circuit inductive or capacitive?

(2) Find the value of R, L and C.

(3) Find the loop quality factor Q.

7-3 The port voltage of the RLC series circuit is $u = 10\sqrt{2}\cos(2500t + 15°)$ V. If the capacitance $C = 8\mu\text{F}$, the power absorbed in the circuit is the maximum, and $P_{max} = 100\text{W}$.

(1) Find the inductance L and quality factor Q of the circuit;

(2) Draw phasor diagram of the circuit.

7-4 The experimental current resonance curve of series resonant circuit is shown in Fig. 7-1, in which $f_0 = 475\text{kHz}$, $f_1 = 472\text{kHz}$, $f_2 = 478\text{kHz}$ and $L = 500\mu\text{H}$. Find the quality factor Q of the loop and the capacitance C.

7-5 Find the resonant frequency of the circuits shown in Fig.7-2.

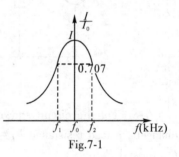

Fig.7-1

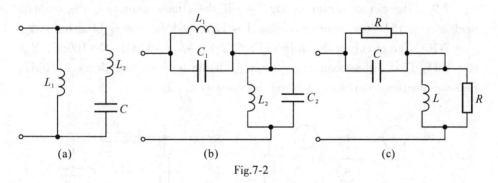

Fig.7-2

7-6 A coil with internal resistance $R = 10\Omega$ and inductance L in series with a capacitor C is connected to a sinusoidal AC power supply with angular frequency $\omega = 1000\text{rad/s}$ and voltage effective $U = 10\text{V}$. The measured current is 1A, the voltage of the capacitor is $U_C = 1000\text{V}$. If the coil and inductor L is reconnected into parallel connection and then they are connected to the same power supply, the measured current is 100μA. Find the value of L, C and the effective values of each branch currents in the parallel circuit.

7-7 The circuit is shown in Fig.7-3, $L=100\mu H$, $C=100pF$, $R=25\Omega$, $I_S=1mA$, $R_i=40k\Omega$, angular frequency $\omega=10^7 rad/s$. Try to find the resonant angular frequency ω_0, quality factor Q, resonant impedance Z_0, current I_0, I_C, port voltage U_0 and bandwidth B of the circuit.

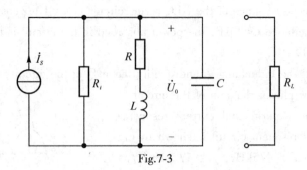

Fig.7-3

7-8 For the circuit shown in the Fig.7-3, if all circuit parameters are not changed, a load resistance $R_L=100k\Omega$ is connect in parallel with capacitor, find Q, U_0 and B.

7-9 The circuit shown in Fig.7-4, if the circuit resonates, the ammeter reading A_1 is 15A, the ammeter reading A is 12A, find the reading of ammeter A_2.

7-10 The circuit is shown in Fig.7-5, $L=L_1+L_2=100\mu H$, $C=100pF$, $R_1+R_2=10\Omega$, Find the resonance frequency f_0. If the resonant impedance is $10k\Omega$, find the distribution coefficient p and the value of L_1, L_2.

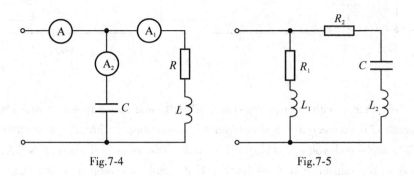

Fig.7-4   Fig.7-5

7-11 The circuit is shown in Fig.7-6, $L = 100\mu H$, $C_1 = C_2 = 200pF$, $I_S = 20mA$, $R_S = 10k\Omega$, the quality factor in the resonant loop itself is $Q = 40$. Try to find the currents of I, I_1 and I_2 in the resonance circuit and the absorbed power of the loop.

7-12 An intermediate-frequency amplifier circuit of a radio is shown in Fig. 7-7. Given: resonant frequency $f_0 = 465kHz$, quality factor of the coil L $Q_L = 100$ (winding in the same magnetic core, it can be regarded as a fully coupled), $C = 200pF$, the turns of each coil is $N = 160$, $N_1 = 40$, $N_2 = 10$, $R_S = 16k\Omega$, $R_L = 1k\Omega$. Try to find inductance L, bandwidth B and Q of the loop with the load.

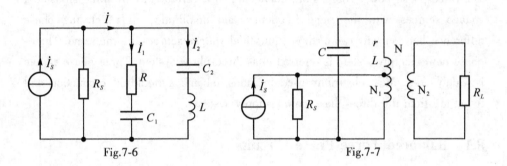

Fig.7-6   Fig.7-7

Chapter 8

Three-Phase Circuits

Three-phase circuit is a kind of circuit in which electric power is supplied by a three-phase sources and delivered to a three-phase load through transmission line. The three-phase power sources are connected in a certain way by three sinusoidal voltage sources with the same frequency and amplitude, in which the phase difference between any two of three sinusoidal voltage sources are the same. Three-phase power supply system is referred to as three-phase system. Three-phase system is widely used. Most electricity used in industrial and agricultural production and living are from the three-phase power supply system.

8.1 Balanced Three-Phase Circuits

8.1.1 Balanced Three-Phase Power Supply

Three-phase circuit power supply is generally generated by the three-phase generator, which can get three electromotive forces with same frequency, same amplitude and 120° phase difference between any two of them, known as balanced three-phase power supply. Fig. 8.1.1 is a schematic diagram of a three-phase synchronous generator. There is a DC current flowing through the excitation coil on the rotor of three-phase generator, so that the rotor become an electromagnet. On the inner side of the generator stator, three identical coils A-X, B-Y, and C-Z are mounted in the groove of stator and separated by 120° in space. When the rotor rotates at an angular velocity ω, the three coils will induce three sinusoidal electromotive forces with the same frequency and same amplitude and 120° phase difference.

Usually, the head-terminals of the three coils in the three-phase generator are denoted by A, B and C, respectively. The tail-terminals are denoted by X, Y, and

Z, and the reference direction of the three-phase voltage is set from the head-terminal to the tail-terminal. As shown in Fig.8.1.2.

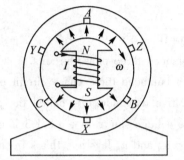

Fig.8.1.1 Three-Phase Synchronous Generator   Fig.8.1.2 Three-Phase Power Sources

The instantaneous expressions of the balanced three-phase voltage are

$$u_A(t) = \sqrt{2}\,U\cos\omega t$$
$$u_B(t) = \sqrt{2}\,U\cos(\omega t - 120°) \tag{8.1.1}$$
$$u_C(t) = \sqrt{2}\,U\cos(\omega t - 240°) = \sqrt{2}\,U\cos(\omega t + 120°)$$

The balanced three-phase voltage phasors are

$$\dot{U}_A = U\angle 0°$$
$$\dot{U}_B = U\angle -120° \tag{8.1.2}$$
$$\dot{U}_C = U\angle -240° = U\angle 120°$$

The waveform of balanced three-phase voltage sources is shown in Fig.8.1.3a and their phasor diagram is shown in Fig.8.1.3b.

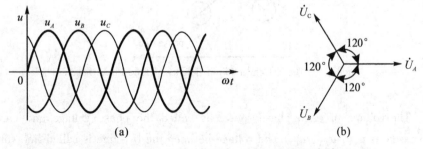

(a)   (b)

Fig.8.1.3 Three-Phase Power Supply Voltage Waveform and Phasor Diagram

It can be proved that the sum of three instantaneous voltages of the balanced three-phase voltage is zero at any time, and the sum of the three voltage phasors is also zero.

$$u_A + u_B + u_C = 0$$
$$\dot{U}_A + \dot{U}_B + \dot{U}_C = 0 \quad (8.1.3)$$

This is an important characteristic of balanced three-phase circuits.

The sequence of each phase voltage in a balanced three-phase circuit passes through a fixed value (such as the first positive maximum) is called the phase sequence. The phase sequence of three-phase voltage shown in Fig.8.1.3 is called positive sequence or ABC sequence. If u_A lags u_B and u_B lags u_C, this sequence is called negative sequence or as CBA sequence. We use positive sequence unless otherwise stated.

8.1.1.1 Y Connection of Three-Phase Sources

If X, Y, Z terminals of the three-phase source coils are connected together, as shown in Fig.8.1.4, this connection of balanced three-phase sources is called Y connection or Y connection. The common point is called neutral point, denoted with N. The wires drawn from the head-terminals of the three-phase sources are called the phase line, commonly known as live line. The wire drawn from the neutral point is called the neutral line.

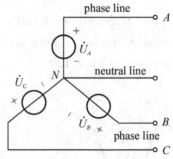

Fig.8.1.4 The Y Connection of Balanced Three-Phase Sources

The voltage of each phase source is called the phase voltage and can be expressed as u_{AN}, u_{BN}, u_{CN}. The voltage between the live line is called line voltage and can be expressed as u_{AB}, u_{BC}, u_{CA}. The relationship between the line voltage and the phase voltage in the balanced three-phase sources are as follows

$$\left.\begin{aligned} u_{AB} &= u_A - u_B \\ u_{BC} &= u_B - u_C \\ u_{CA} &= u_C - u_A \end{aligned}\right\} \quad (8.1.4)$$

If expressed in phasor form, the phase voltages of the balanced three-phase power sources are as follows

$$\left.\begin{aligned} \dot{U}_A &= U \angle 0° \\ \dot{U}_B &= U \angle -120° \\ \dot{U}_C &= U \angle +120° \end{aligned}\right\} \quad (8.1.5)$$

So the line voltage phasors are

$$\left.\begin{aligned} \dot{U}_{AB} &= \dot{U}_A - \dot{U}_B = \sqrt{3}\, \dot{U}_A \angle 30° \\ \dot{U}_{BC} &= \dot{U}_B - \dot{U}_C = \sqrt{3}\, \dot{U}_B \angle 30° \\ \dot{U}_{CA} &= \dot{U}_C - \dot{U}_A = \sqrt{3}\, \dot{U}_C \angle 30° \end{aligned}\right\} \quad (8.1.6)$$

From above expressions, it is seen that, if balanced three-phase sources are connected in the Y connection, the line voltages are also balanced. Effective value of the line voltage (expressed as U_l) is $\sqrt{3}$ times of the phase voltage (expressed as U_p), that is

$$U_l = \sqrt{3}\, U_p$$

It can also be seen that the line voltage leads the corresponding phase voltage by 30°. The relationship between line voltage and phase voltage of Y connection sources is indicated by the phasor diagram shown in Fig.8.1.5.

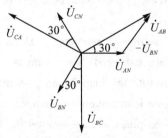

Fig.8.1.5 Line Voltage and Phase Voltage Relation of Y Connection Sources

8.1.1.2 Delta Connection of Three-Phase Sources

If three sources are connected with head terminal to tail terminal, as shown in Fig.8.1.6, this kind of connection of balanced three-phase sources is called Delta connection or Δ connection. In Delta connection, there are only three live lines and without neutral line.

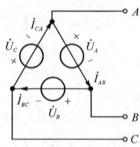

Fig.8.1.6 Delta Connection of Three-Phase Sources

The voltage of each phase is called the phase voltage and can be expressed as u_A, u_B, u_C. The voltage between the live line is called line voltage and can be expressed as u_{AB}, u_{BC}, u_{CA}, as shown in Fig.8.1.6.

Obviously there are

$$\left. \begin{array}{l} u_{AB} = u_A \\ u_{BC} = u_B \\ u_{CA} = u_C \end{array} \right\} \quad \text{or} \quad \left. \begin{array}{l} \dot{U}_{AB} = \dot{U}_A \\ \dot{U}_{BC} = \dot{U}_B \\ \dot{U}_{CA} = \dot{U}_C \end{array} \right\} \quad (8.1.7)$$

That is, phase voltage is equal to line voltage in the Delta connection balanced three-phase sources. This characteristics is different from that of Y connection.

Three-phase balanced sources connected in Delta form a loop for current to flow. Since three voltages are balanced, their sum is equal to zero. According to KVL, the sum of voltage around the loop is zero, so the loop current is also zero. However, if one phase source is mistakenly connected in opposite direction, it will result in that the sum of three-phase voltage around the loop is not zero, then there will be a huge short-circuit current flowing through three sources in the loop and damaging all sources. Therefore, if three-phase balanced sources are connected in Delta connection, special attention should be paid to the mistaken connecting.

8.1.2 Balanced Three-Phase Load

The balanced three-phase load refers to the load which is connected by the three identical impedance loads in a certain way of connection. Similar to the connections of balanced three-phase sources, it is also divided into two type of connections: Y connection and Δ connection, as shown in Fig.8.1.7.

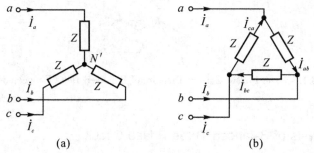

(a)   (b)

Fig.8.1.7 The Star and Delta Connection of Balanced Three-Phase Load

For balanced three-phase load, the voltage of each phase load is called the phase voltage of the load, denoted as $\dot{U}_{AN'}$, $\dot{U}_{BN'}$, $\dot{U}_{CN'}$, and the voltage between the live lines of the load is called the line voltage, denoted as $\dot{U}_{AB}$, $\dot{U}_{BC}$, $\dot{U}_{CA}$. The current flowing through each load is called the phase current, denoted as $\dot{I}_A$, $\dot{I}_B$, $\dot{I}_C$, and the current flowing through each live line is called the line current. Obviously, for a balanced Y-connected three-phase load, its phase current and line current are the same.

For a balanced three-phase load of a Delta connection, as shown in Fig.8.1.7b, it can be proved that the line current is

$$\dot{I}_A = \dot{I}_{ab} - \dot{I}_{ca} = \sqrt{3}\,\dot{I}_{ab} \angle -30°$$
$$\dot{I}_B = \dot{I}_{bc} - \dot{I}_{ab} = \sqrt{3}\,\dot{I}_{bc} \angle -30° \quad\quad (8.1.8)$$
$$\dot{I}_C = \dot{I}_{ca} - \dot{I}_{bc} = \sqrt{3}\,\dot{I}_{ca} \angle -30°$$

So it is seen that, for a balanced three-phase Delta load, the effective value of each line current (expressed as I_l) is $\sqrt{3}$ times of the phase current (expressed as I_p), namely

$$I_l = \sqrt{3}I_p$$

and the line current lags the corresponding phase current by 30°. Their phasor diagram is shown in Fig.8.1.8.

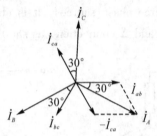

Fig.8.1.8 The Phasor Current Diagram of Balanced Delta Connected Load

8.1.3 Analysis of Balanced Three-Phase Circuit

Three-phase circuit is actually also a kind of sinusoidal AC circuit. Therefore, the sinusoidal AC circuit analysis methods, which is discussed in the chapter 5, can be used to analyze three-phase circuits. For balanced three-phase circuits, based on the symmetry of the circuit, some special law can be evaluated, and they can be applied to simplify the analysis and calculation.

For balanced three-phase circuits shown in Fig.8.1.9, both balanced three-phase sources and balanced three-phase loads are in Y connection. And there is a neutral line connecting between the neutral point of power supply and the neutral

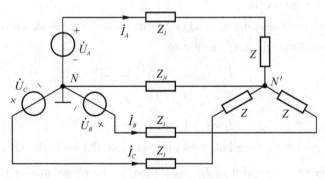

Fig.8.1.9 Three-Phase, Four-Wire System

point of the load, so this power supply method (Y-Y connection) is called the three-phase four-wire system.

Assign N as reference node, by applying Nodal Analysis, node voltage equations are as follows

$$\dot{U}_{N'N}\left(\frac{1}{Z+Z_1}+\frac{1}{Z+Z_1}+\frac{1}{Z+Z_1}+\frac{1}{Z_N}\right)=\frac{\dot{U}_A}{Z+Z_1}+\frac{\dot{U}_B}{Z+Z_1}+\frac{\dot{U}_C}{Z+Z_1}$$

$$=\frac{\dot{U}_A+\dot{U}_B+\dot{U}_C}{Z+Z_1}=0$$

It can be seen that, for a balanced three-phase four-wire system, the voltage between two neutral points N' and N are zero. That is, two neutral points are equipotential and can be shorted with a wire. So that each phase current and voltage can be calculated separately. Because both three-phase sources and three-phase load are balanced, then the three-phase currents are also balanced. Therefore, It is only need to analyze any one phase, voltages and currents of other two phases can be derived directly according to the balanced relationship, this method is known as "one phase calculation method".

In the balanced three-phase circuits of Y-Y connection, as the current on the neutral line is also zero, so the neutral line can be disconnected, and then the circuit is reduced to the three-phase three-wire circuit. The analysis of balanced three-phase three-wire circuit is similar to the analysis of balanced three-phase four-wire circuit. For the balanced three-phase circuits in which power supply or load is Δ-connected, Δ-Y transformation can be used to transform source or load in Delta to Delta first and then analyze.

Example 8.1.1 The circuit is shown in Fig.8.1.10a. The line voltage of balanced three-phase sources is 380V, balanced three-phase load $Z = 30°$ Ω. WFind line current phasors $\dot{I}_A, \dot{I}_B, \dot{I}_C$.

Solution For this Y-Y connection balanced three-phase circuits, a wire can be used to connected between two neutral points, as shown in Fig.8.1.10a, the dashed line is used to connected between two neutral points. Then, the A phase circuit is drawn for analysis, as shown in Fig.8.1.10b.

Assume that $\dot{U}_{AB}=380\angle 30°V$, then $\dot{U}_{AN}=220\angle 0°V$, so there is

$$\dot{I}_A=\frac{\dot{U}_{AN}}{Z}=\frac{220\angle 0°}{100\angle 30°}=2.2\angle -30°(A)$$

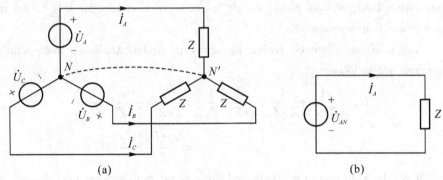

Fig.8.1.10 The Circuit for Example 8.1.1

The other two line currents can be written directly according to the symmetry

$$\dot{I}_B = 2.2\angle-150°\text{A}$$
$$\dot{I}_C = 2.2\angle 90°\text{A}$$

Example 8.1.2 A balanced three-phase circuits is shown in Fig.8.1.11a, the line voltage of power supply is $U_l = 380\text{V}$, $Z_l = 6+j8\Omega$, $Z_2 = -j50\Omega$, and the load impedance is $Z_N = 1+j2\ (\Omega)$. Find each line current phasors and phase current phasors.

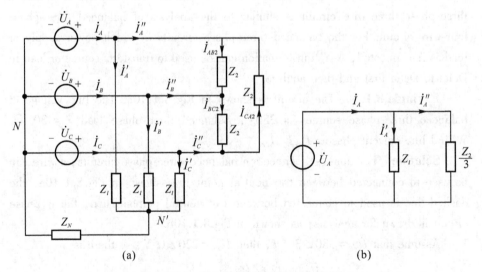

Fig.8.1.11 The Circuit for Example 8.1.2

Solution Assume $\dot{U}_{AN} = 220 \angle 0°\text{V}$, then $\dot{U}_{AB} = 380 \angle 30°$ V. Transforming the Δ-connected load Z_2 to Y-connected, the equivalent Y-connected impedance is $Z_2/3$. According to the conclusion in previous discussion, for a Y-Y-connected balanced three-phase circuits, the voltage between the two neutral points is zero. So, two neutral points can be shorted, then the A phase circuit is derived for analysis, as shown in Fig.8.1.11b. There are

$$\dot{I}'_A = \frac{\dot{U}_{AN}}{Z_1} = \frac{220 \angle 0°}{10 \angle 53.13°} = 22 \angle -53.13° = 13.2 - j17.6(\text{A})$$

$$\dot{I}''_A = \frac{\dot{U}_{AN}}{Z'_2} = \frac{220 \angle 0°}{-j50/3} = j13.2(\text{A})$$

Then

$$\dot{I}_A = \dot{I}'_A + \dot{I}''_A = 13.2 - j4.4 = 13.9 \angle -18.4°(\text{A})$$

According to the symmetry, the line currents of B and C phase are derived as follows

$$\dot{I}_B = 13.9 \angle -138.4°\text{A}$$
$$\dot{I}_C = 13.9 \angle 101.6°\text{A}$$

The phase currents in Y connection load are

$$\dot{I}'_A = 22 \angle -53.1°\text{A}$$
$$\dot{I}'_B = 22 \angle -173.1°\text{A}$$
$$\dot{I}'_C = 22 \angle 66.9°\text{A}$$

The phase currents in Delta load are

$$\dot{I}'_{AB2} = \frac{1}{\sqrt{3}} \dot{I}''_A \angle 30° = 7.63 \angle 120°(\text{A})$$
$$\dot{I}'_{BC2} = 7.63 \angle 0°(\text{A})$$
$$\dot{I}'_{CA2} = 7.63 \angle -120°(\text{A})$$

8.2 Unbalanced Three-Phase Circuits

8.2.1 Unbalanced Three-Phase Circuits

In the three-phase circuits, as long as the power supply or a part of the load is unbalanced, it will be a unbalanced three-phase circuits. Normally, "one phase calculation method" cannot be applied in the analysis of the unbalanced three-phase circuits.

Generally speaking, the power supply is always balanced, and the most unbalanced situation are caused by the unbalanced load.

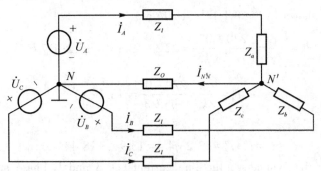

Fig.8.2.1 Three-Phase Load Unbalanced

8.2.1.1 Three-Phase Four-Wire Circuit System

The circuit shown in Fig.8.2.1 is a three-phase four-wire system with a neutral line, and the impedance of neutral line is zero. Due to the existence of neural line, the voltage on each phase load is equal to the voltage of the phase power supply. If power supply is balanced, then the phase voltages of each load are also balanced. However, load impedances may be unbalanced, namely Z_a, Z_b, Z_c may not be equal. So the phase currents may be unbalanced, they can be written as follows

$$\dot{I}_A = \frac{\dot{U}_{AN}}{Z_a}, \ \dot{I}_B = \frac{\dot{U}_{BN}}{Z_b}, \ \dot{I}_C = \frac{\dot{U}_{CN}}{Z_c}$$

The neutral current may not be zero. That is

$$\dot{I}_{N'N} = \dot{I}_A + \dot{I}_B + \dot{I}_C = \frac{\dot{U}_{AN}}{Z_a} + \frac{\dot{U}_{BN}}{Z_b} + \frac{\dot{U}_{CN}}{Z_c} \neq 0$$

If there is impedance Z_o in the neutral line, by applying the node voltage method, node equation is

$$\dot{U}_{N'N}\left(\frac{1}{Z_a} + \frac{1}{Z_b} + \frac{1}{Z_c} + \frac{1}{Z_o}\right) = \frac{\dot{U}_A}{Z_a} + \frac{\dot{U}_B}{Z_b} + \frac{\dot{U}_C}{Z_c}$$

Then, the voltage between two neutral points can be derived as follows

$$\dot{U}_{N'N} = \cfrac{1}{\left(\cfrac{1}{Z_a}+\cfrac{1}{Z_b}+\cfrac{1}{Z_c}+\cfrac{1}{Z_o}\right)}\left(\cfrac{\dot{U}_A}{Z_a}+\cfrac{\dot{U}_B}{Z_b}+\cfrac{\dot{U}_C}{Z_c}\right) \quad (8.2.1)$$

And the neutral line current is

$$\dot{I}_{N'N} = \frac{\dot{U}_{N'N}}{Z_o} \quad (8.2.2)$$

Normally, the voltage between two neutral points is not zero, so if one of Y-connected load impedance varies, the voltage or current of other Y-connected load impedance in Y will be affected. However, if neutral impedance is small enough, this affection will be very small.

8.2.1.2 Three-Phase Three-Wire Circuits System

The circuit shown in Fig. 8.2.2 is a three-phase three-wire system without neutral line. The voltage between two neutral points is

$$\dot{U}_{N'N} = \frac{\dot{U}_{AN}/Z_a + \dot{U}_{BN}/Z_b + \dot{U}_{CN}/Z_c}{1/Z_a + 1/Z_b + 1/Z_c} \neq 0$$

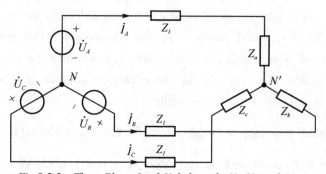

Fig.8.2.2 Three-Phase Load Unbalanced, No Neutral Line

Each phase voltages are

$$\dot{U}_{AN'} = \dot{U}_{AN} - \dot{U}_{N'N}$$
$$\dot{U}_{BN'} = \dot{U}_{BN} - \dot{U}_{N'N}$$
$$\dot{U}_{CN'} = \dot{U}_{CN} - \dot{U}_{N'N}$$

The phasor diagram of the all voltages can be drawn, as shown in Fig.8.2.3. It can be seen that, due to load unbalanced, it results in that the potential at neutral point of Y source is different from the potential of Y load. This phenomenon is called the neutral point displacement.

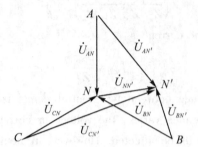

Fig.8.2.3 Neutral Point Displacement

Due to the existence of the neutral point displacement caused by the unbalanced load, it happens that load voltages in some phase may rise, and the load voltages in other phase may drop. If situation is severe, it will cause the load being burned out. In the practical engineering, in order to avoid this phenomenon, the common practice is: Using a high mechanical strength of the wire to connect between the two neutral points, don't install fuse or switch on the neutral wire, so as to force the two neutral points to be the equipotential. This keeps the load voltage balanced even though the load is unbalanced. Since the phase current is unbalanced at this time, the neutral line current is generally not zero. It is an important line and cannot be open-circuited.

8.2.2 General Analysis of Unbalanced Three-Phase Circuits

When a Y-Y connected balanced three-phase circuit is analyzed, if there is a neutral line and the neutral impedance is zero, the analysis method is the same as that of the general balanced three-phase circuit. If there is no central line or there is a an impedance in central line, then the central point voltage is not zero, generally, node analysis can be applied. For non Y-Y connected balanced three-phase circuit, circuit can be transformed by applying the equivalent transformation of the Delta and Y, and then it is analyzed according to analysis method of the balanced three-phase circuit in Y-Y connection.

Example 8.2.1 A Delta connected three-phase load circuit shown in Fig.8.2.4, its port access to balanced three-phase power supply. When the switch S is closed, all ammeters reading are 5A. Find the ammeter reading after opening the switch S.

Solution Since the power supply remains unchanged, the current in the ammeter A2 does not change when the switch S is turned on, which is the same as the current when the switch S is closed. While the current in A1 and A3 is equal to the phase current when the load is balanced. Therefore,

Ammeter A2 reading is 5A

Ammeter A1, A3 readings are $5/\sqrt{3} = 2.89(A)$

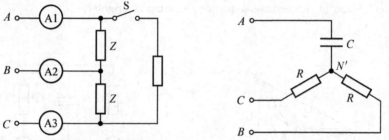

Fig.8.2.4　The Circuit for Example 8.2.1　　Fig.8.2.5　The Circuit for Example 8.2.2

Example 8.2.2 The circuit is shown in Fig.8.2.5, $R = X_C$, the power supply voltage is balanced, and the effective value of the phase voltage is U_p. Find the phase voltages of the loads $\dot{U}_{BN'}$, $\dot{U}_{CN'}$.

Solution Let $\dot{U}_{AN} = U_p \angle 0°$

$$\dot{U}_{BN} = U_p \angle -120°$$

$$\dot{U}_{CN} = U_p \angle 120°$$

Then

$$\dot{U}_{N'N} = \frac{\dfrac{\dot{U}_A}{Z_A} + \dfrac{\dot{U}_A}{Z_B} + \dfrac{\dot{U}_A}{Z_C}}{\dfrac{1}{Z_A} + \dfrac{1}{Z_B} + \dfrac{1}{Z_C}} = \frac{\dfrac{U_p \angle 0°}{Z_A} + \dfrac{U_p \angle -120°}{Z_B} + \dfrac{U_p \angle 120°}{Z_C}}{\dfrac{1}{-jR} + \dfrac{1}{R} + \dfrac{1}{R}}$$

$$= U_p(-0.2 + 0.6) = 0.63 U_p \angle 108.43°$$

so there are

$$\dot{U}_{BN'} = \dot{U}_B - \dot{U}_{N'N} = 1.49 U_p \angle -101.6°$$

$$\dot{U}_{CN'} = \dot{U}_C - \dot{U}_{N'N} = 0.4U_p \angle 138.4°$$

The phasor diagram of the voltages can be drawn as shown in Fig.8.2.6. It is seen that $U_{BN'} > U_{CN'}$. Under the condition of the positive phase sequence, if two resistors R are two lamps, then the lamp in phase B will be brighter than the lamp in phase C.

By applying the above principle, a phase sequence indicator can be made to detect phase sequence. A typical phase sequence indicator is shown in Fig.8.2.7, it is widely used in the shore power box for ship shore electricity. When the shore power relative to the ship's electrical equipment is positive sequence, the B lamp is brighter, when in the reverse sequence, C lamp is brighter.

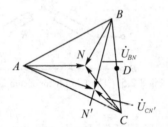
Fig.8.2.6 Phasor Diagram for Example 8.2.2

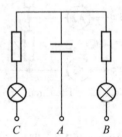
Fig.8.2.7 Phase Sequence Indicator

8.3 Power of Three-Phase Circuits

8.3.1 Power of Three-Phase Circuits

In three-phase circuits, the total active power P and reactive power Q of three-phase load are equal to the summation of all the active power and reactive power absorbed by each phase load.

$$P = P_A + P_B + P_C$$
$$Q = Q_A + Q_B + Q_C$$

If the load is balanced three-phase load, the power of each phase load is the same, the total active power and reactive power Q will be

8.3 Power of Three-Phase Circuits

$$P = 3P_A = 3U_p I_p \cos\varphi$$
$$Q = 3Q_A = 3U_p I_p \sin\varphi \quad (8.3.1)$$

Where, U_p, I_p are the effective value of the phase voltage and phase current, φ is the impedance angle of each phase load.

If the balanced three-phase load is in Y connection, there are

$$U_l = \sqrt{3}\, U_p,\ I_l = I_p \quad (8.3.2)$$

If the balanced three-phase load is in Delta connection, there are

$$U_l = U_p,\ I_l = \sqrt{3}\, I_p \quad (8.3.3)$$

For both connection, there is

$$U_l I_l = \sqrt{3}\, U_p I_p U_p$$

Therefore, for both Y connection or Delta connection, the total active power and reactive power of the three-phase load can also be written as

$$P = \sqrt{3}\, U_l I_l \cos\varphi$$
$$Q = \sqrt{3}\, U_l I_l \sin\varphi \quad (8.3.4)$$

where, U_l, I_l are the effective value of the line voltage and the line current.

Apparent power and power factor of balanced three-phase circuits are expressed as

$$S = \sqrt{P^2 + Q^2}$$
$$\cos\varphi = \frac{P}{S} \quad (8.3.5)$$

The instantaneous power of each phase in the balanced three-phase load are

$$\begin{aligned}
p_A &= u_A i_A = 2U_p I_p \cos\omega t \times \cos(\omega t - \varphi) \\
&= U_p I_p [\cos\varphi - \cos(2\omega t - \varphi)] \\
p_B &= u_B i_B = 2U_p I_p \cos(\omega t - 120°) \times \cos(\omega t - \varphi - 120°) \\
&= U_p I_p [\cos\varphi - \cos(2\omega t - \varphi + 120°)] \\
p_C &= u_C i_C = 2U_p I_p \cos(\omega t + 120°) \times \cos(\omega t - \varphi + 120°) \\
&= U_p I_p [\cos\varphi - \cos(2\omega t - \varphi - 120°)]
\end{aligned} \quad (8.3.6)$$

Then, the total instantaneous power is

$$p = p_A + p_B + p_C = 3U_p I_p \cos\varphi \quad (8.3.7)$$

It can be seen that, in the balanced three-phase circuits, the instantaneous power is equal to the average power, and it is constant at any time. This is an important advantage of the three-phase power supply system, it facilitates the smooth operation of balanced three-phase loads such as three-phase motors.

8.3.2 Power Measurement of Three-Phase Circuits

For a three-phase four-wire system, normally, three single-phase Wattmeters are used to measure the total active power, known as "Three Wattmeters Method". The connection of method is shown in Fig.8.3.1. The reading of each wattmeter is the active power of the phase load. Then the total active power is:

$$P = P_1 + P_2 + P_3$$

Namely, the total active power of three-phase load is the sum of the readings of three wattmeters. If the load is balanced, as the reading of three wattmeter are same, so only one wattmeter is required, the total power of three-phase load is equal to its reading multiplied by 3.

For a three-phase three-wire system, whether the load is balanced or not, and whether the load is Y-connected or Δ-connected, two wattmeters can be used to measure total active power of three-phase load, its specific connection is shown in Fig.8.3.2. The algebra sum of the two wattmeter's reading will be the total active power of three-phase load. This method is customarily called "Two-Wattmeter Method".

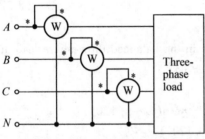
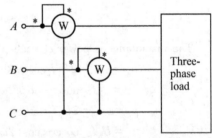

Fig.8.3.1 Three-Wattmeter Method   Fig.8.3.2 Two-Wattmeter Method

The effectiveness of this method is demonstrated below.

Regardless of how the load is connected, it can always be equivalent to a Y-connected load, as shown in Fig.8.3.3.

Then, the instantaneous power of the three-phase load is

$$p = u_{AN} i_A + u_{BN} i_B + u_{CN} i_C$$

$$Qi_A + i_B + i_C = 0 \quad (KCL)$$
$$i_C = -(i_A + i_B)$$
$$\therefore \quad p = (u_{AN} - u_{CN})i_A + (u_{BN} - u_{CN})i_B = u_{AC}i_A + u_{BC}i_B$$
$$\therefore \quad P = U_{AC}I_A\cos\varphi_1 + U_{BC}I_B\cos\varphi_2 = P_1 + P_2$$

where, φ_1 is the phase difference between the voltage u_{AC} and current i_A, φ_2 is the phase difference between the voltage u_{BC} and current i_B.

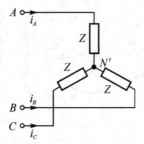

Fig.8.3.3 Y Connection Circuit

Note that only in the condition that $i_A + i_B + i_C = 0$, two wattmeter method can be used, therefore this method cannot be used to the three-phase four-wire system. With the two wattmeters method, the sum of the readings in the two meters is the total active power of three-phases load. According to the correct polarity connection, may show a negative reading, the wattmeter pointer may turn reverse. By reverse connecting the current coil polarity, the pointer will turn the positive, but at this time, the reading should be recorded as negative.

In applying two-wattmeter method, there are three kinds of connection for measuring three-phase power, pay attention to the position of dotted terminal of wattmeters.

Example 8.3.1 For the circuit shown in Fig.8.3.4a, $U_l = 380V$, $Z_1 = 30 + j40 \ \Omega$. The rated power of the motor is $P_D = 1700W$, its power factor is $\cos\varphi = 0.8$ (inductive).

(1) Find the value of line current and the total active power of the three-phase source.

(2) Apply "Two-wattmeters Method" to measure the active power of the motor, draw the wiring diagram and find the readings of the two wattmeters.

Solution The phase voltage of source can be written as $\dot{U}_{AN} = 220\angle 0°\text{V}$.

(1) Equivalent circuit of the motor is shown in Fig.8.3.4b. Equivalent circuit of the phase A is shown in Fig.8.3.4c, so

$$\dot{I}_{A1} = \frac{\dot{U}_{AN}}{Z_1} = \frac{220\angle 0°}{30+j40} = 4.41\angle -53.1°(\text{A})$$

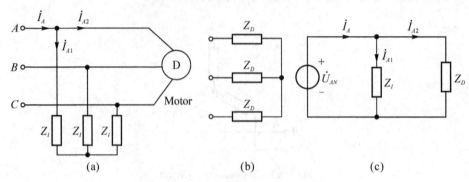

Fig.8.3.4 The Circuit for Example 8.3.1

The active power of the motor is

$$P_D = \sqrt{3}\,U_l I_{A2}\cos\phi = 1700(\text{W})$$

$$I_{A2} = \frac{P_D}{\sqrt{3}\,U_l\cos\phi} = \frac{P_D}{\sqrt{3}\times 380\times 0.8} = 3.23(\text{A})$$

From the power factor of the motor $\cos\varphi = 0.8$ (inductive), it is derived $\varphi = 36.9°$ and $\dot{I}_{A2} = 3.23\angle -36.9°$ A.

Line current $\dot{I}_A$ can be derived as follows

$$\dot{I}_A = \dot{I}_{A1} + \dot{I}_{A2} = 4.41\angle -53.1° + 3.23\angle -36.9° = 7.56\angle -46.2°(\text{A})$$

The total active power P of the three-phase sources can be derived as follows

$$P_{总} = \sqrt{3}\times 380\times 7.56\times\cos 46.2° = 3.44(\text{kW})$$

Another way to find total power: find the power of Z_1 first and then find the total power, that is

$$P_{Z1} = 3\times I_{A1}^2\times R_1 = 3\times 4.41^2\times 30 = 1.74(\text{kW})$$

$$P_{总} = P_{Z1} + P_D = 1.74 + 1.7 = 3.44(\text{kW})$$

(2) The wiring diagram is shown in Fig.8.3.5, the line currents of the motor

are
$$\dot{I}_{A2} = 3.23 \angle -36.9°(A)$$
$$\dot{I}_{B2} = 3.23 \angle -156.9°(A)$$

Line voltages are
$$\dot{U}_{AB} = 380 \angle 30°(V)$$
$$\dot{U}_{AC} = -\dot{U}_{CA} = -380 \angle 150° = 380 \angle -30°(V)$$
$$\dot{U}_{BC} = 380 \angle -90°(V)$$

The readings of the wattmeters are
$$P_1 = U_{AC}I_{A2}\cos\varphi_1 = 380 \times 3.23 \times \cos(-30° + 36.9°)$$
$$= 380 \times 3.23 \cos(6.9°) = 1219(W)$$
$$P_2 = U_{BC}I_{B2}\cos\varphi_2 = 380 \times 3.23 \times \cos(-90° + 156.9°)$$
$$= 380 \times 3.23 \times \cos(66.9°) = 481.6(W)$$

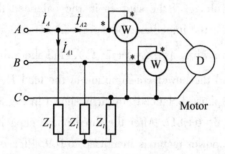

Fig.8.3.5 The Wiring Diagram of Two Wattmeters Method

Exercises

8-1 In the balanced three-phase circuits, the impedance of the Y connection load is $Z = 12 + j16(\Omega)$, the impedances of live wire and neutral line are $0.8 + j0.6(\Omega)$. The line voltage of the balanced three-phase sources is $U_l = 380V$. Try to find the phase current and line voltage of the load impedance, and draw the phasor diagram of the circuit.

8-2 In the balanced three-phase circuits, the impedance of the delta connection load is $Z = 18 + j31.2(\Omega)$, the impedances of live wire are $Z_L = 1.3 +$

$j0.7(\Omega)$. The line voltage of the balanced three-phase sources is $U_l = 380V$. Try to find the line current and phase current of the load impedance, and draw the phasor diagram of the circuit.

8-3 In the balanced three-phase circuits, the line voltage of the sources is $U_l = 380V$.

(1) If the load is a Y connection and the impedances is $Z = 10+j15(\Omega)$, find the value of phase voltage and the absorbed power of the load impedances;

(2) If the load is delta connected and the impedances is $Z = 15+j20(\Omega)$, find the value of line current and the absorbed power of the load impedances.

8-4 In the balanced three-phase circuits, the phase voltage of the sources is 220V. The power of the balanced three-phase load is 12.2kW and the power factor is 0.8(inductive).Try to find the value of line current. If the load is a Y connection, find the load impedance.

8-5 The line voltage of the sources in the balanced three-phase circuits is 380V, $\dot{U}_{AB} = 380\angle 0°$, the impedance of the Y connection load is $Z_L = 12+j9(\Omega)$, the impedances of live wires are $Z = 1+j2(\Omega)$. Find the value of line current $\dot{I}_A$, phase current $\dot{I}_{A'B'}$ and the power consumption of the load P, Q.

8-6 The three-phase balanced circuit is shown in Fig.8-1, the power supply frequency is 50 Hz, $Z = 6+j8\Omega$. After the three-phase capacitor bank is connected to the load side, the power factor is increased to 0.9. Please find the value of the capacitor.

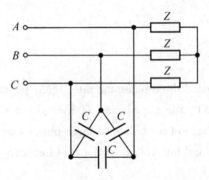

Fig.8-1 The Circuit for Exercise 8-6

8-7 Three-phase balanced inductive load is connected to the three-phase balanced power supply, the power meter is connected between the two line as shown in Fig.8-2. If line voltage is 380V, the power factor of the load is $\cos\varphi = 0.6$, and the Power meter reading is $P = 275.3\text{W}$. Find the value of line current I_A.

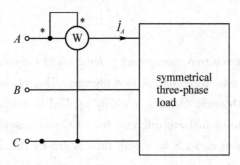

Fig.8-2 The Circuit for Exercise 8-7

Chapter 9
First-Order Circuits

If the circuit structure or component parameters in a dynamic circuit changes, the voltages or currents in the circuit also changes. This phenomenon is known as transition process. Dynamic circuits is widely applied in engineering. There are a lot of important features that are different from DC or sinusoidal AC circuits. The feature that voltages or currents vary with time is greatly different from DC circuit in which the voltages or currents in the circuit are fixed values. And it is also different from sinusoidal AC circuit in which effective voltages or effective currents in the circuit are fixed values.

This chapter mainly discusses the time domain analysis of the first-order dynamic circuit, including the zero-input response, zero-state response, total response, impulse response and step response of the first-order circuit. Among them, the three-factor method of first-order circuit, zero-input response, zero-state response and time constant are very important.

9.1 The Basic Concept and Circuit Switching Rule

9.1.1 The Basic Concept of First-Order Circuit

For the linear resistive circuit discussed in previous chapters, they are described with the a group of linear algebraic equations. However, when the circuit contains the capacitive element and the inductance element, since the relationship between the voltage and the current is described by the derivative or integral equation, the circuit equation established according to KVL, KCL and VCR will be a differential equation.

When the circuit contains only one independent dynamic element (or energy storage element), the circuit equation will be a first order constant coefficient differential equation, the corresponding circuit is called first order circuit, as shown in Fig.9.1.1a below. When the circuit contains two independent dynamic components, the equation of the circuit is a second-order constant coefficient differential equation, the corresponding circuit is called second-order circuit, as shown in Fig.9.1.1b below. When the circuit contains n independent dynamic components, the circuit equation is a n-order constant coefficient differential equation, the corresponding circuit is called the n-order circuit.

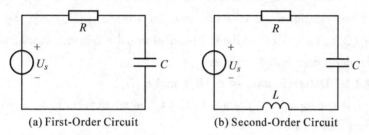

(a) First-Order Circuit   (b) Second-Order Circuit

Fig.9.1.1 RC Dynamic Example

An important feature of dynamic circuits is the existence of a transition process, the so-called transition process is the process from one stable-state to another stable-state. There are two causes for the transition process to occur: (1) there are dynamic components in the circuit, because the dynamic components of the energy storage cannot be changed abruptly, and thus there is a transition process. (2) the circuit structure or component parameters is changed, and then the working state of the circuit is forced to change.

The circuit changes caused by the structure variation or component parameters variation of the circuit described above can be collectively referred to as switching. If it is assumed that switching occurs at $t = 0s$, $t = 0_-$ is the instant just before switching and $t = 0_+$ is the instant immediately after switching.

The common method of analyzing the dynamic circuit transition process is to establish the differential equations of the circuit according to KVL, KCL and the element VCR. The established equation is linear ordinary differential equations, and then the ordinary differential equation is solved to find unknown variables. This method is called the classical method, because this method is carried out in the time domain, so it is also called time-domain analysis.

9.1.2 Determination of Initial Values

To solve the ordinary differential equation by classical method, the integral constant in the solution must be determined according to the initial conditions of the circuit. If the equation describing the dynamic process of the circuit is a n-order differential equation. The initial condition is the variable value of the circuit and its n-1 order derivative value at time $t = 0_+$, also called the initial value. Among them, the initial value of the capacitor voltage $u_C(0_+)$ and the inductor current $i_L(0_+)$, i.e., is called the independent initial condition, and the others are called the dependent initial condition.

9.1.2.1 Determination of $u_C(0_+)$ and $i_L(0_+)$

For a linear capacitor C, at any instant t, the relationship between its charge, voltage and current are

$$q_C(t) = q_C(t_0) + \int_{t_0}^{t} i_C(\xi) d\xi$$

$$u_C(t) = u_C(t_0) + \frac{1}{C} \int_{t_0}^{t} i_C(\xi) d\xi$$

Let $t_0 = 0_-$, $t = 0_+$, then

$$q_C(0_+) = q_C(0_-) + \int_{0_-}^{0_+} i_C(\xi) d\xi \qquad (9.1.1a)$$

$$u_C(0_+) = u_C(0_-) + \frac{1}{C} \int_{0_-}^{0_+} i_C(\xi) d\xi \qquad (9.1.1b)$$

If the current $i_C(t)$ flowing through the capacitor is a limited value in the time interval $(0_- \sim 0_+)$, then integral item in the right hand side of expression (9.1.1a) and (9.1.1b) will be zero. So, the charge and voltage of the capacitor cannot change instantaneously, that is,

$$q_C(0_+) = q_C(0_-) \qquad (9.1.2a)$$

$$u_C(0_+) = u_C(0_-) \qquad (9.1.2b)$$

For a linear inductor, at any instant t, the relationship between its flux, current and voltage are

$$\psi_L(t) = \psi_L(t_0) + \int_{t_0}^{t} u_L(\xi) d\xi$$

9.1 The Basic Concept and Circuit Switching Rule

$$i_L(t) = i_L(t_0) + \frac{1}{L}\int_{t_0}^{t} u_L(\xi)d\xi$$

Let $t_0 = 0_-$, $t = 0_+$, then

$$\psi_L(0_+) = \psi_L(0_-) + \int_{0_-}^{0_+} u_L(\xi)d\xi \tag{9.1.3a}$$

$$i_L(0_+) = i_L(0_-) + \frac{1}{L}\int_{0_-}^{0_+} u_L(\xi)d\xi \tag{9.1.3b}$$

If the voltage $u_L(t)$ across inductor in the time interval $(0_- \sim 0_+)$ is a limited value, then integral item on the right hand side of expression (9.1.3a) and (9.1.3b) will be zero. So, the flux and current of the capacitor cannot change instantaneously, that is

$$\psi_L(0_+) = \psi_L(0_-) \tag{9.1.4a}$$

$$i_L(0_+) = i_L(0_-) \tag{9.1.4b}$$

The expressions of (9.1.2a), (9.1.2b), (9.1.4a), (9.1.4b) are called continuity.

9.1.2.2 Determination of Initial Value of Other Variables in the Circuit

Except u_C and i_L, the initial value of other variables in the circuit can be determined according to following steps:

(1) according to the equivalent circuit at $t = 0_-$, determine $u_C(0_-)$ and $i_L(0_-)$. For the DC excitation circuit, if the circuit is in steady state at $t = 0_-$, the inductor can be regarded as short circuit, the capacitor can be regarded as open circuit, and the equivalent circuit at $t = 0_-$ can be derived. Then, $u_C(0_-)$ and $i_L(0_-)$ can be derived with any analysis methods of the DC circuit learned before.

(2) $u_C(0_+)$ and $i_L(0_+)$ can be derived by applying circuit switching rule.

(3) drawing the 0_+ equivalent circuit. In the 0_+ equivalent circuit, the capacitor is replaced by a voltage source $u_C(0_+)$, the inductor is replaced by the current source $i_L(0_+)$, the independent source take its value $t = 0_+$.

(4) Find the initial value of the other variables based on the 0_+ equivalent circuit.

9.1.2.3 Determination of $\left.\dfrac{du_C}{dt}\right|_{0_+}$ and $\left.\dfrac{di_L}{dt}\right|_{0_+}$

If the voltage and current of capacitor and inductor are assumed in the associated reference directions, with $i_C = C\dfrac{du_C}{dt}$, $u_L = L\dfrac{di_L}{dt}$, $\dfrac{du_C}{dt}\bigg|_{0_+} = \dfrac{1}{C}i_C(0_+)$ and $\dfrac{di_L}{dt}\bigg|_{0_+} = \dfrac{1}{L}u_L(0_+)$ can be derived. Initial value of the other variables can be found based on the 0_+ equivalent circuit.

Example 9.1.1 For the circuit shown in Fig.9.1.2a, it is known that the circuit had been reached steady state before the switch action. It is assumed the switch S turns on at $t = 0$. Find: $u_C(0_+)$, $i_L(0_+)$, $i_C(0_+)$, $u_L(0_+)$, $i_R(0_+)$, $\dfrac{du_C}{dt}\bigg|_{0_+}$ and $\dfrac{di_L}{dt}\bigg|_{0_+}$.

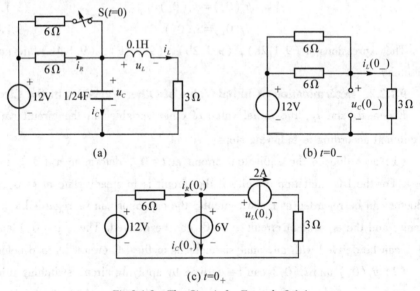

Fig.9.1.2 The Circuit for Example 9.1.1

Solution Due to the circuit had been reached steady state before the switch action, the 0_- equivalent circuit can be drawn as shown in Fig.9.1.2b. Then, there is

$$i_L(0_-) = \dfrac{12}{6//6+3} = 2(\text{A}), u_C(0_-) = 3i_L(0_-) = 6(\text{V})$$

According to circuit switching rule, there are

$$u_C(0_+) = u_C(0_-) = 6(V)$$
$$i_L(0_+) = i_L(0_-) = 2(A)$$

Then, 0_+ equivalent circuit can be drawn as shown in Fig.9.1.2c, applying KVL, there is

$$6i_R(0_+) + 6 - 12 = 0$$

Thus

$$i_R(0_+) = 1(A), i_C(0_+) = i_R(0_+) - 2 = -1(A), u_L(0_+) = 6 - 3 \times 2 = 0$$

$$\left.\frac{du_C}{dt}\right|_{0_+} = \frac{1}{C}i_C(0_+) = -24 V/S, \left.\frac{di_L}{dt}\right|_{0_+} = \frac{1}{L}u_L(0_+) = 0$$

9.2 Zero-Input Response of First-Order Circuit

The zero input response is the response generated only by the initial energy storage of the energy storage unit (dynamic element), and there is no excitation in the circuit after circuit switching.

9.2.1 Zero Input Response in RC Circuit

In the RC circuit shown in Fig.9.2.1a, in the beginning, the switch is at position 1, the capacitor have been charged, its voltage $u_C(0_-) = U_0$, its current $i(0_-) = 0$. At instant $t = 0$, the switch is switched from 1 to 2. Since the capacitor voltage cannot jump, so $u_C(0_+) = u_C(0_-) = U_0$. However, in this instant, current of the circuit jumps to maximum, $i(0_+) = U_0/R$, that is, at the moment of switching, the circuit in the current jumps. After the circuit switching, the capacitor discharges through the resistor R, so u_C decreases. If time $t \to \infty$, then $u_C(t) \to 0$, $i(t) \to 0$. In this process, the energy stored in the capacitor is gradually consumed by the resistor and is converted into heat energy. The above is a qualitative analysis of the physical concept. In the following, the changing law of the circuit current and voltage will be analyzed mathematically.

When $t \geq 0$, the circuit is shown in Fig.9.2.1b. Applying KVL, gives

$$u_C - u_R = 0,$$

And

$$u_R = Ri, i = -C\frac{du_C}{dt}$$

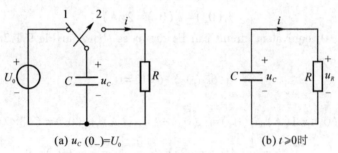

(a) $u_C(0_-)=U_0$ (b) $t \geqslant 0$时

Fig.9.2.1　Zero Input Response in RC Circuit

Substituting then into KVL equation, yields
$$RC\frac{du_C}{dt}+u_C=0$$

This is a first-order homogeneous differential equation, and its initial condition is
$$u_C(0_+)=u_C(0_-)=U_0$$

The corresponding characteristic equation is
$$RCp+1=0$$

The characteristic root is
$$p=-\frac{1}{RC}$$

The general solution of homogeneous differential equation
$$u_C(t)=Ae^{pt}=Ae^{-\frac{1}{RC}t}$$

Substituting the initial condition into equation, gives
$$A=u_C(0_+)=U_0$$

So, the solution of differential equation is
$$u_C(t)=u_C(0_+)e^{-\frac{1}{RC}t}=U_0e^{-\frac{1}{RC}t}$$

This is the expression of the capacitor voltage u_C during discharge process.

The current of the circuit is
$$i(t)=-C\frac{du_C}{dt}=\frac{U_0}{R}e^{-\frac{1}{RC}t}$$

The voltage across the resistor is

$$u_C(t) = u_R(t) = U_0 e^{-\frac{1}{RC}t}$$

The waveforms of $u_C(t)$ and $i(t)$ are shown in Fig.9.2.2a, b.

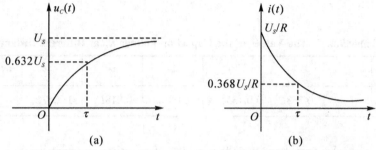

(a)   (b)

Fig.9.2.2 Zero Input Responses of u_C and i and Their Waveforms

From the above waveform, it can be seen that, in the moment of circuit switching, $i(0_-) = 0$, $i(0_+) = U_0/R$, the current has jumped and the capacitor voltage did not jump. As can be seen from their expressions, the voltage $u_C(t)$, $u_R(t)$ and the current $i(t)$ vary according to the same exponential law, and the speed of their attenuation depends on the value of $1/RC$ in the index.

To study the speed of their attenuation, a time constant is introduced. The time constant is defined as the reciprocal value of the characteristic root p of the first order circuit homogeneous equation, it is denoted by τ.

$$\tau = -1/p$$

For RC circuit, its time constant is

$$\tau = -1/p = RC$$

The unit of time constant τ is

$$\Omega \cdot F = \frac{V}{A} \cdot \frac{C}{V} = \frac{V}{A} \cdot \frac{A \cdot s}{V} = s$$

If the circuit structure and the component parameters is fixed, τ will be a constant. And because it's unit is same as unit of time, so τ is called the time constant. After introducing the time constant, the above $u_C(t)$ and $i(t)$ can be expressed as

$$u_C(t) = U_0 e^{-t/\tau}, i(t) = \frac{U_0}{R} e^{-t/\tau}$$

The time constant τ reflects the speed of the first-order transition process, and it is an important quantity which reflects the characteristics of the transition process. Table 9.2.1 lists the values of the capacitor voltage u_C at time instant $t=0$, τ, 2τ, 3τ, $\cdots$

Table 9.2.1 The Values of the Capacitor Voltage u_C at Different Instant

t	0	τ	2τ	3τ	4τ	5τ	$\cdots$	∞
$u_C(t)$	U_0	$0.368U_0$	$0.135U_0$	$0.05U_0$	$0.018U_0$	$0.0067U_0$	$\cdots$	0

As it can be seen from the above table, after a time constant τ, the capacitor voltage $u_C(t)$ attenuates to 36.8% of the initial value or attenuation of 63.2%. Theoretically, it will decay to zero by going through infinite time. But, it is generally considered that, after 3τ to 5τ time range, the transition process ends.

The time constant can be calculated from the circuit parameters or the eigenvalue of the circuit characteristic equation, it can also be determined from the response curve.

(1) with the Circuit Parameters

① Find τ with circuit parameters.

There is a formula to find time constant, as follows

$$\tau = R_{eq} C$$

where R_{eq} is which is derived by seen from the two terminals of capacitor.

For example, For the RC circuit shown in Fig.9.2.3, by seen from the two terminals of capacitor, the equivalent resistance $R_{eq} = R_2 \mathbin{/\mkern-5mu/} R_3 + R_1$, so, time constant of the circuit is

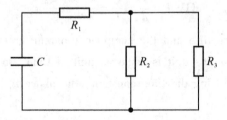

Fig.9.2.3 A RC Circuit

$$\tau = R_{eq}C = \left(\frac{R_2 R_3}{R_2 + R_3} + R_1\right)C$$

② Find τ with the eigenvalue

The relationship between τ and the eigenvalue is

$$\tau = -1/p$$

③ Find τ from the response curve

For a capacitor voltage shown in Fig.9.2.4, select a point A on the capacitor voltage curve, draw a tangent line AC over point A, as shown in Fig.9.2.4, then the sub-tangent in figure can be derived as follows

$$BC = \frac{AB}{\tan\alpha} = \frac{u_C(t_0)}{-\left.\frac{du_C}{dt}\right|_{t=t_0}} = \frac{U_0 e^{-t/\tau}}{\frac{1}{\tau}U_0 e^{-t/\tau}} = \tau$$

Namely, the length of the sub-tangent on time axis is equal to time constant τ.

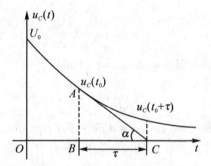

Fig.9.2.4 Find τ from the Response Curve

9.2.2 Zero Input Response of RL Circuit

In the RL circuit shown in Fig.9.2.5a, the voltage and current are stabilized before the switch S is operated, $i_L(0_-) = U_0/R_0 = I_0$. When switch from 1 to 2, due to the inductor current cannot jump, $i_L(0_+) = i_L(0_-) = I_0$. This current will gradually decrease to zero in the RL loop. In this process, the inductor energy stored in the magnetic field at the initial moment is gradually consumed resistor, and is converted into heat energy. In the following, the changing law of the circuit current and voltage will be analyzed mathematically.

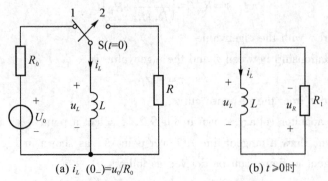

(a) $i_L(0_-) = U_0/R_0$ (b) $t > 0$时

Fig.9.2.5 Zero Input Response of RL Circuit

For the circuit shown in Fig.9.2.5b, it is obtained from KVL
$$u_L + u_R = 0$$
And
$$u_R = Ri_L, \quad u_L = L\frac{di_L}{dt}$$
Substituting it into KVL equation, we obtain
$$L\frac{di_L}{dt} + Ri_L = 0$$
This is a first order homogeneous differential equation, its initial condition is
$$i_L(0_+) = i_L(0_-) = I_0$$
The corresponding characteristic equation is
$$Lp + R = 0$$
The characteristic root is
$$p = -R/L$$
The General Solution of Homogeneous Differential Equation
$$i_L(t) = Ae^{pt} = Ae^{-\frac{R}{L}t}$$
Substituting the initial condition into equation, gives
$$A = i_L(0_+) = I_0$$
So, the solution of differential equation is
$$i_L(t) = i_L(0_+)e^{-\frac{R}{L}t} = I_0 e^{-\frac{R}{L}t}$$
This is the expression of the capacitor current i_L during transition process.

The time constant of RL circuit is
$$\tau = -1/p = L/R$$
The voltage across the resistor is
$$u_R(t) = Ri_L = RI_0 e^{-t/\tau}$$
The voltage across the inductor is
$$u_L(t) = L\frac{di_L}{dt} = -RI_0 e^{-t/\tau}$$
The current of the circuit is
$$i_L(t) = I_0 e^{-\frac{R}{L}t} = I_0 e^{-t/\tau}$$
The waveforms of $i_L(t)$, $u_L(t)$ and $u_R(t)$ are shown in Fig.9.2.6a, b.

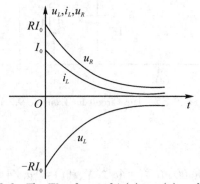

Fig.9.2.6 The Waveforms of $i_L(t)$, $u_L(t)$ and $u_R(t)$

From the above analysis, it can be seen that: both zero input response of RC circuit or RL circuit vary from the initial value according to the same exponential law. If the initial value increases by K times, the zero input response also increases by a factor of K, this characteristic is called the proportionality of the zero input response. Therefore, the general form of zero-input response can be written as:
$$f(t) = f(0_+) e^{-t/\tau} \quad t > 0$$
where, $f(t)$ is zero input response of the circuit, $f(0_+)$ is its initial value, τ is time constant.(For RC circuit, $\tau = RC$; for RL circuit, $\tau = L/R$).

Example 9.2.1 For the circuit shown in Fig.9.2.7a, when $t < 0$, switch S is on position 1 and the circuit is stable. At $t = 0$, switch from position 1 to position 2. Find $u_C(t)$ and $i(t)$ for $t > 0$.

Solution Due to the circuit is table before circuit switching, the initial capacitor voltage is

$$u_C(0_+) = u_C(0_-) = \frac{10}{2+4+4} \times 4 = 4(\text{V})$$

After circuit switching, the circuit is shown in Fig.9.2.7b. Capacitor discharges through resistor R_1 and R_2, so, the response is zero input response. Time constant can be derived as follows

$$R_{eq} = 4//4 = 2, \tau = R_{eq}C = 2 \times 1 = 2(\Omega)$$

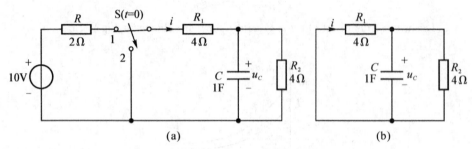

Fig.9.2.7 The Circuit for Example 9.2.1

Thus

$$u_C(t) = u_C(0_+)e^{-t/\tau} = 4e^{-0.5t}\text{V}, i(t) = -u_C/4 = -e^{-0.5t}\text{A}$$

$i(t)$ can also be derived from the formula $i = i(0_+)e^{-t/\tau}$.

Example 9.2.2 For the circuit shown in Fig.9.2.8a, given: $i_L(0_+) = 150\text{mA}$, find voltage $u(t)$ when $t>0$.

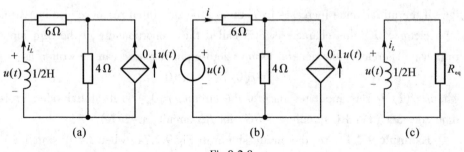

Fig.9.2.8

Solution Let's find equivalent resistance R_{eq} first. By removing the inductor from the circuit and connecting a voltage source to the port, a circuit for finding R_{eq} is derived, as shown in Fig.9.2.8b. Applying KVL, there is
$$u = 6i + 4(i + 0.1u)$$
So
$$R_{eq} = u/i = 50/3 \, (\Omega)$$
The equivalent circuit is shown in Fig.9.2.8c, then
$$u(0_+) = R_{eq} i_L(0_+) = \frac{50}{3} \times 0.15 = 2.5 \, (V)$$
Thus
$$u(t) = u(0_+) e^{-t/\tau} = 2.5 e^{-100t/3} \, (V) \quad t>0$$

9.3 Zero-State Response of First-Order Circuit

The zero-state response is the response generated only by the excitations of the circuit with zero initial state (the initial energy storage of the dynamic element is zero).

9.3.1 Zero State Response of the *RC* Circuit

For the circuit shown in Fig.9.3.1, before the switch is closed, the circuit is in steady state and initial state is zero. At instant $t = 0$, switch S is closed, the capacitor is been charged. At switch closed moment, the capacitor voltage cannot jump, the capacitor is equivalent to short circuit, it can be seen that $u_R(0_+) = U_S$.

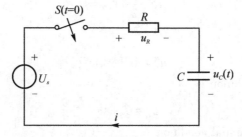

Fig.9.3.1 Zero State Response of *RC* Circuits

And the charging current $i(0_+) = U_S/R$ will be the maximum. After this moment, with the charging of capacitor by power source, u_C increases, and the current gradually reduced, When $u_C = U_S$, $i = 0$, $u_R = 0$, the charging process ends and the circuit enters a new steady state.

In the following, the changing law of the circuit current and voltage will be analyzed mathematically.

From KVL,
$$u_R + u_C = U_S$$

Substituting
$$u_R = Ri, i = C\frac{du_C}{dt}$$

into KVL equation, gives
$$RC\frac{du_C}{dt} + u_C = U_S$$

This equation is a first order linear non-homogeneous differential equation, the initial condition is $u_C(0_+) = u_C(0_-) = 0$. The solution of the equation consists of two components, i.e. the special solution u'_C of the non-homogeneous equation and the general solution u''_C of the homogeneous equation. That is
$$u_C = u'_C + u''_C$$

It is easy to derive the special solution
$$u'_C = U_S$$

And the general solution can be derived from its corresponding homogeneous equation
$$RC\frac{du_C}{dt} + u_C = 0$$

That is
$$u''_C = Ae^{-\frac{t}{RC}} = Ae^{-\frac{t}{\tau}}$$

So complete solution is
$$u_C = U_S + Ae^{-\frac{t}{\tau}}$$

Substitute the initial condition
$$u_C(0_+) = u_C(0_-) = 0$$

we obtain

$$A = -U_S$$

Therefore, the voltage of capacitor is

$$u_C(t) = U_S - U_S e^{-t/\tau} = U_S(1 - e^{-t/\tau})$$

The current of the circuit is

$$i(t) = C\frac{du_C}{dt} = \frac{U_S}{R} e^{-t/\tau}$$

The waveforms of zero-state responses $u_C(t)$ and $i(t)$ are shown in Fig.9.3.2.

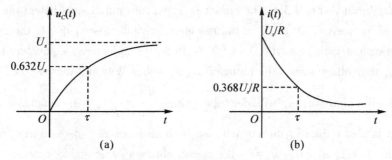

Fig.9.3.2 The Waveforms of Zero-State Responses $u_C(t)$ and $i(t)$

Here are a few concepts. The special solution of the differential equation is called the mandatory component, which is related to the change law of the excitation. When the mandatory component is a constant or periodic function, this component is also called the steady-state component. The general solution of the differential equation depends on the structure and component parameters of the circuit, which is independent of the external excitation and decays to zero with the increase of time. Therefore, it is called the free component or the transient component.

The process by connecting a RC circuit to the DC power source is also a process that the capacitor is charged by the power source through the resistor. The energy consumed by the resistor during charging is:

$$W_R = \int_0^\infty i^2 R dt = \int_0^\infty \left(\frac{U_S}{R} e^{-t/\tau}\right)^2 R dt = \frac{U_S^2}{R}\left(-\frac{RC}{2}\right) e^{-\frac{2}{RC}t} \bigg|_0^\infty = \frac{1}{2}CU_S^2$$

The energy stored in capacitor is

$$W_C = \frac{1}{2}CU_C^2(\infty) = \frac{1}{2}CU_S^2$$

It can be seen that only half of the energy supplied by the power source during the charging process is converted into electric field energy stored in the capacitor, while the other half is consumed by the resistor. Therefore, the charging efficiency is only 50%.

9.3.2 Zero State Response of RL Circuit

As shown in Fig.9.3.3, the circuit is in the zero initial state before the switch is closed, namely $i_L(0_-) = 0$. In the moment of switch closed, due to the inductor current cannot jump, so $i_L(0_+) = i_L(0_-) = 0$, So the inductor is equivalent to open circuit, the voltage across the inductor $u_L(0_+) = U_S$. With the increase of current, u_R will also increase, u_L will decrease. Since $\dfrac{di_L}{dt} = \dfrac{1}{L}u_L$, the changing rate of current is also reduced, the current rise become more and more slowly. Finally, when $i_L = U_S/R$, $u_R = U_S$, $u_L = 0$, the circuit enters another stable state.

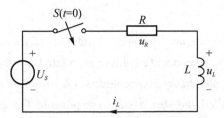

Fig.9.3.3 Zero State Response of RL Circuit

The differential equation of the circuit can be derived as follows

$$L\frac{di_L}{dt} + Ri_L = U_S$$

This equation is a first order linear non-homogeneous differential equation, and initial condition is

$$i_L(0_+) = i_L(0_-) = 0$$

The solution of current i_L is

$$i_L = i_L' + i_L'' = \frac{U_S}{R} + Ae^{-\frac{R}{L}t} = \frac{U_S}{R} + Ae^{-\frac{t}{\tau}}$$

By substituting initial condition, gives
$$A = -U_S/R$$
Thus
$$i_L(t) = \frac{U_S}{R} - U_S e^{-\frac{t}{\tau}} = \frac{U_S}{R}(1 - e^{-\frac{t}{\tau}})$$

The voltage across the inductor is
$$u_L(t) = L\frac{di_L}{dt} = U_S e^{-\frac{t}{\tau}}$$

The waveforms of zero-response $i_L(t)$ and $u_L(t)$ are shown in Fig.9.3.4.

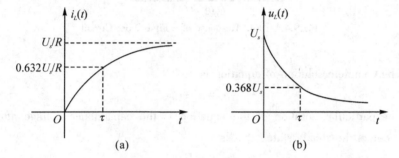

Fig.9.3.4 The Waveform of Aero-Response of $i_L(t)$ and $u_L(t)$

From the above expression of zero-state response, it can be seen that the zero-state response is proportional to the excitation, when the excitation increases K times, the zero-state response also increased K times. This linear relationship is called the proportionality of zero-state responses.

9.4 Short-Cut Method for Complete Response of First-Order Circuit

9.4.1 Complete Response

For a first-order circuit with a nonzero initial state, its response generated by external excitation is called full response.

For the circuit shown in Fig. 9.4.1, the initial voltage of the capacitor is assumed to be U_0 and switch S is closed at instant $t = 0$. Then, according to KVL, there is

$$RC\frac{du_C}{dt}+u_C=U_S$$

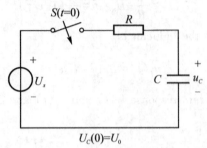

$U_C(0)=U_0$

Fig.9.4.1 Full Response of a First-Order Circuit

The complete solution of equation is

$$u_C=u'_C+u''_C$$

The particular solution of the equation is the capacitance voltage after the circuit enters the steady state, that is

$$u'_C=U_S$$

The general solution corresponding to the homogeneous equation is

$$u''_C=Ae^{-t/\tau}$$

So

$$u_C=U_S+Ae^{-t/\tau}$$

Substitute the initial condition: $u_C(0_+)=u_C(0_-)=0$, gives

$$A=U_0-U_S$$

Thus the capacitor voltage is

$$u_C(t)=U_S+(U_0-U_S)e^{-t/\tau},t>0 \quad\quad\quad (9.4.1)$$

This is the expression of full response of capacitor voltage.

As can be seen from equation (9.4.1), the first term on the right hand side is the steady-state component, which is equal to the applied DC voltage, and the second term is the transient component, which will decrease to zero as time increases. So the full response can be expressed as

Complete response = steady state component + transient component

Complete response = forced component + free component

The formula (9.4.1) is rewritten as
$$u_C(t) = U_S(1-e^{-t/\tau}) + U_0 e^{-t/\tau}$$

The first term on the right hand side of the equation is the zero-state response of the circuit, because it is the response when $u_C(0_-) = 0$. The second term is the zero-input response of the circuit, because the circuit's response when $U_S = 0$ is exactly equal to $U_0 e^{-t/\tau}$. This shows that in the first-order circuit, the complete response is superposition of zero input response and zero state response, it is the embodiment of linear circuit superposition theorem in the dynamic circuit.

The above two analysis methods of full response are only different in view of points. The former focus on reflecting that, after circuit switching, it has to go through a period of time, the linear dynamic circuit will enter the steady state. While the latter is focused on the causal relationship between the circuit. Not all linear circuits are capable of separating both transient and steady states, but as long as circuit is linear, the total response can be decomposed into zero-input and zero-state responses.

9.4.2 Shortcut Method

From the above analysis, it is seen that the response of the circuit can be determined when the initial value $f(0_+)$, the special solution $f_s(t)$ and the time constant τ (called the three elements of the first order circuit) are determined, whether it is the zero input response, the zero state response or the full response. So, it can be proved that the response of the circuit can be calculated by the following formula

$$f(t) = f_s(t) + [f(0_+) - f_s(0_+)] e^{-t/\tau} \qquad (9.4.2)$$

When the three elements of the circuit is determined, according to formula (9.4.2), the response of the circuit can be directly written, this method is called shortcut method. For the DC excitation circuit, the special solution $f_s(t)$ is constant, and $f_s(t) = f_s(0_+) = f(\infty)$, So formula (9.4.2) can also be written as

$$f(t) = f(\infty) + [f(0_+) - f(\infty)] e^{-t/\tau}$$

For the sinusoidal excitation, the special solution $f_s(t)$ is a sine function, $f_s(0_+)$ take the value of $f_s(t)$ at the time instant, $t = 0_+$. In the formula, the meaning of $f(0_+)$ and τ is the same as described above. It should be noted that the shortcut method is only applicable to the first-order circuit, however the circuit can be excited in the DC, sine function, step function.

Example 9.4.1 As shown in Fig.9.4.2a, the circuit has reached steady state before the switch is turned on and the switch S is turned on when $t=0$. Time of time. Find $u_C(t)$ and $i_C(t)$ when $t>0$.

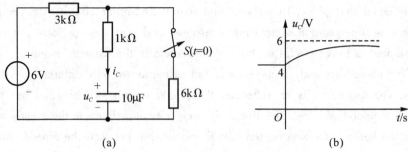

(a)   (b)

Fig.9.4.2   The Circuit for Example 9.4.1

Solution The initial value of capacitor voltage is

$$u_C(0_+)=u_C(0_-)=\frac{6}{6+3}\times 6=4(\text{V})$$

Its particular solution is

$$u'_C=u_C(\infty)=6(\text{V})$$

Time constant is

$$\tau=R_{eq}C=(1+3)\times 10^3\times 10\times 10^{-6}=0.04(\text{s})$$

It is derived from formula (9.3.2), that

$$u_C(t)=6+(4-6)e^{-t/0.04}=6-2e^{-25t}\text{V} \quad t>0$$

$$i_C(t)=C\frac{du_C}{dt}=0.5e^{-25t}\text{mA} \quad t>0$$

The waveform of u_C is shown in Fig.9.4.2b.

Example 9.4.2 For the circuit shown in Fig.9.4.3a, given: $i_L(0_-)=2\text{A}$, find: $i_L(t)$, $i_1(t)$ when $t\geqslant 0$.

Solution First, Thevenin's equivalent circuit for the part in the left side of inductor can be derived, as shown in Fig.9.4.3b, where $u_{OC}=24\text{V}$, $R_{eq}=6\Omega$.

$$i_L(0_+)=i_L(0_-)=2(\text{A})$$

$$i_{LS} = i_L(\infty) = u_{OC}/R_{eq} = 4(\text{A})$$

$$\tau = \frac{L}{R_{eq}} = 3/6 = 0.5(\text{s})$$

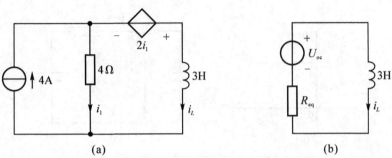

(a)   (b)

Fig.9.4.3 The Circuit for Example 9.4.2

Thus

$$i_L(t) = 4 + (2-4)e^{-2t}(\text{A}) = 4 - 2e^{-2t}\,\text{A}$$

$$i_1(t) = 4 - i_L = 2e^{-2t}(\text{A})$$

9.5 Step Response and Impulse Response of First Order Circuit

9.5.1 Step Function and Impulse Function

9.5.1.1 Unit Step Function

The unit step function is a singular function, as shown in Fig.9.5.1a, which is defined as

$$\varepsilon(t) = \begin{cases} 0 & t \leq 0_- \\ 1 & t \geq 0_+ \end{cases}$$

There is a unit step jumping in the interval $(0_-, 0_+)$. This function can be used to describe the switching action from position 1 to position 2, as shown in Fig.9.5.1b. It indicates that the circuit is connected to the unit DC voltage at instant $t = 0$. The step function can be used as a mathematical model of the switch, so it is sometimes called a switching function.

If the switching action does not occur at $t = 0$, but at the time $t = t_0$, it can be defined by the unit step function

$$\varepsilon(t-t_0) = \begin{cases} 0 & t \leq t_{0-} \\ 1 & t \geq t_{0+} \end{cases}$$

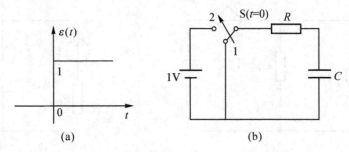

(a)   (b)

Fig.9.5.1   Unit Step Function and a RC Circuit

It is called the delayed unit step function, which can be seen as the result of $\varepsilon(t)$ by moving t_0 on the time axis, as shown in Fig.9.5.2.

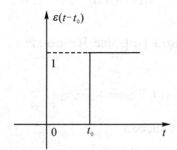

Fig.9.5.2   Delayed Unit Step Function

If the circuit is connected to a 3 A DC current source at time $t=t_0$, then the current of this current source can be written as $3\varepsilon(t-t_0)$ A.

The unit step function can be used to "start" any function. If $f(t)$ is an arbitrary function defined for all t, as shown in Fig.9.4.3a, then there is

$$f(t)\varepsilon(t-t_0) = \begin{cases} 0 & t \leq t_{0-} \\ f(t) & t \geq t_{0+} \end{cases}$$

Its waveform is shown in Fig.9.5.3b.

9.5 Step Response and Impulse Response of First Order Circuit

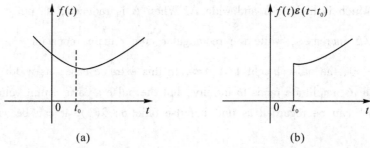

Fig.9.5.3 The Unit Step Function Can Be Used to "Start" Any Function

The unit step function can be used to describe the rectangular pulse. For the pulse signal shown in Fig.9.5.4a, it can be decomposed into the sum of the two step functions, as shown in Fig.9.5.4b. That is

$$f(t) = \varepsilon(t) - \varepsilon(t-t_0)$$

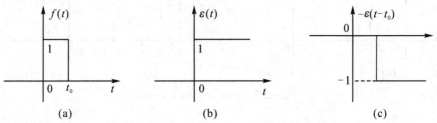

Fig.9.5.4 Decomposition of the Pulse Signal

9.5.1.2 Unit Impulse Function

The unit impulse function is also a singular function, as shown in Fig.9.5.5, which can be defined as

$$\begin{cases} \delta(t) = \begin{cases} 0, & t \neq 0 \\ \infty, & t = 0 \end{cases} \\ \int_{-\infty}^{+\infty} \delta(t) dt = 1 \end{cases}$$

The unit impulse function is also called a delta function. It is zero at time $t \neq 0$, but it is singular at $t=0$.

The unit impulse function can be regarded as the limit of the unit step function. Fig.9.4.5a shows the waveform of a unit rectangular pulse function $p_\Delta(t)$, which is high $1/\Delta$ and wide Δ. When Δ is reduced, its pulse function height $1/\Delta$ increases, while the rectangular area remains constant $\frac{1}{\Delta} \cdot \Delta = 1$. When $\Delta \to 0$, the pulse height $1/\Delta \to \infty$. In this extreme case, its width tends to zero, and its amplitude tends to infinity, but the pulse area is a unit value. Then this $p_\Delta(t)$ can be regarded as unit impulse function $\delta(t)$. It can be written as follows

$$\lim_{\Delta \to 0} p_\Delta(t) = \delta(t)$$

The waveform of the unit impulse function is shown in Fig.9.5.5b, sometimes marked "1" next to the arrow. The impulse function of intensity K is denoted by Fig.9.5.5c and marked "K" next to the arrow.

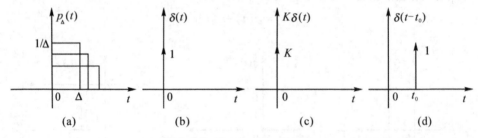

Fig.9.5.5 Unit Impulse Function

Delayed unit impulse function can be defined as

$$\delta(t - t_0) = 0, \ t \neq 0; \int_{-\infty}^{+\infty} \delta(t - t_0) dt = 1$$

Its waveform is shown in Fig.9.5.5d.

If the impulse function occurs at the moment $t = t_0$ and the impulse intensity is K, it is expressed as $K\delta(t-t_0)$.

The impulse function has two main properties:

(1) The unit impulse function is the derivative of the unit step function, that is,

$$\frac{d\varepsilon(t)}{dt} = \delta(t)$$

On the other hand, the unit step function is the integral of the unit impulse function, namely

$$\int_{-\infty}^{t} \delta(t) dt = \varepsilon(t)$$

(2) The "sieving" nature of the unit impulse function. Due to $\delta(t) = 0$ at the time $t \neq 0$, so, for any function $f(t)$ that is continuous at $t=0$, there is

$$f(t)\delta(t) = f(0)\delta(t)$$

Then

$$\int_{-\infty}^{+\infty} f(t)\delta(t) dt = \int_{-\infty}^{+\infty} f(0)\delta(t) dt = f(0) \int_{-\infty}^{+\infty} \delta(t) dt = f(0)$$

Similarly, it can be proved that

$$\int_{-\infty}^{+\infty} f(t)\delta(t - t_0) dt = f(t_0)$$

This means that the impulse function can filter the function value at the moment of impulse operating, so it is called "sieving" property, also known as sampling property.

9.5.2 Step Response

The zero-state response of the circuit generated by the input of the unit step function is called the unit step response, it is denoted by $s(t)$. Analysis of the step response is the same as the zero state response under DC excitation. If the input of the circuit is a step function with amplitude A, then according to the proportionality of the zero-state response, the zero-state response of the circuit is $As(t)$. Since the circuit parameters of the time-invariant circuit do not change with time, the response under the action of the delayed unit step signal is $s(t-t_0)$. This property is called time-invariant.

Example 9.5.1 The u_S waveforms in the circuit shown in Fig. 9.5.6 are shown in Fig. 9.5.6b. $R = 1\Omega$, $L = 1H$. Find the zero state response of $i(t)$ is when $t \geqslant 0$, and draw its waveform is drawn.

Solution The example will be solved with two ways.

(1) Segmentation calculation.

When $t < 0$, $i(t) = 0$

When $0 \leqslant t \leqslant 2s$, $u_S = 10V$, the response of circuit is zero-state response. Applying three-element method.

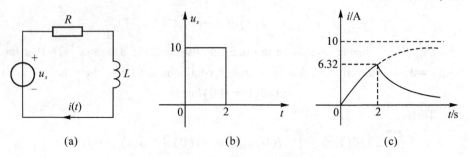

Fig.9.5.6　Figure for Example 9.5.1

Due to
$$i_L(0_+) = i_L(0_-) = 0$$
$$i(\infty) = u_S/R = 10$$
$$\tau = L/R = 2$$

So
$$i(t) = 10(1 - e^{-t/2}) \text{ A}$$

When $t \geq 2s$, $u_S = 0$, the response of circuit is zero-input response

Due to $i(2_+) = i(2_-) = 10(1 - e^{-1}) = 6.32\text{A}$

So
$$i(t) = 6.32 e^{-(t-2)/2} \text{ A}$$

(2) Calculation with the step function.

Source voltage u_S can be represented by step function as follows
$$u_S(t) = 10\varepsilon(t) - 10\varepsilon(t-2)$$

The step response of circuit can be derived as
$$s(t) = (1 - e^{-t/2}) \varepsilon(t)$$

Based on proportional and time-invariant property of zero-state response, it can be derived that
$$i(t) = 10(1 - e^{-t/2})\varepsilon(t) - 10(1 - e^{-(t-2)/2})\varepsilon(t-2) \text{ A}$$

The waveform of $i(t)$ is shown in Fig.9.5.6c.

9.5.3　Impulse Response

The zero-state response of the circuit under the excitation of the impulse function is called the unit impulse response and is expressed by $h(t)$.

If a impulse function is acted on the zero-state circuit, the capacitor voltage or the inductor current will jump during the interval $(0_-,0_+)$. After the moment $t \geqslant 0_+$, due to the impulse function excitation is zero, the impulse response of the circuit is equivalent to the zero input response caused by the initial state. Therefore, a method to find the impulse response is that: first calculated $u_C(0_+)$ or $i_L(0_+)$ caused by the action of $\delta(t)$, and then solve for the zero input response caused by the initial state, which is the impulse response for $t>0$.

Now, the key is how to determine the capacitor voltage and inductor current when $t = 0_+$. As the storage capacity of the capacitor and inductor is limited, so the impulse voltage should not appear across two terminals of the capacitor, the impulse current cannot flow through the inductor. In other words, in the moment of the impulse source operating on circuit, the capacitor should be regarded as short circuit, the inductor should be regarded as open circuit. Based on this analysis, the equivalent circuit in the moment of the impulse source operating on circuit can be derived. Then, distribution of the impulse current and impulse can be determined. If the impulse current flows through the capacitor, the capacitor voltage will jump; if the impulse voltage occurs at both terminals of the inductor, the inductor current will jump. By applying expression (9.1.1b) and (9.1.3b), $u_C(0_+)$ and $i_L(0_+)$ can be obtained.

Example 9.5.2 Find the impulse response of the capacitor voltage u_C in the circuit shown in Fig.9.5.7.

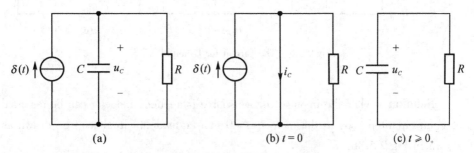

Fig.9.5.7 The Circuit for Example 9.5.2

Solution When the impulse current source is applied, capacitor can be regarded as short-circuited, so, at the moment $t=0$, an equivalent circuit can be drawn as shown in Fig.9.4.7b. The impulse current of current source flows through the capacitor only and there is not current flowing through the resistor. This impulse current will make the capacitor voltage jumping, that is,

$$u_C(0_+) = u_C(0_-) + \frac{1}{C}\int_{0_-}^{0_+} i_C dt = \frac{1}{C}\int_{0_-}^{0_+} \delta(t)dt = \frac{1}{C}$$

When $t \geq 0_+$, $\delta(t)=0$, so there is not source in the circuit, as shown in Fig.9.4.7c, the impulse response of capacitor voltage can be derived as follows

$$h(t) = \frac{1}{C}e^{-t/\tau}$$

where, $\tau = RC$.

Therefore, combining above analysis, the impulse response expression of capacitor voltage can be rewritten as:

$$h(t) = \frac{1}{C}e^{-t/\tau}\varepsilon(t) \text{ V}$$

Example 9.5.3 For the circuit shown in Fig.9.5.8a, $i_L(0_-)=0$, $R_1=6\Omega$, $R_2=4\Omega$, $L=100$mH. Find the impulse response of $u_L(t)$ and $i_L(t)$ when $t>0$.

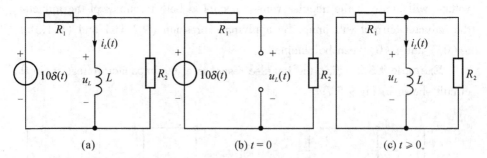

Fig.9.5.8 The Circuit for Example 9.5.3

Solution When the impulse voltage source is applied, inductor can be regarded as open-circuited, so, at the moment $t=0$, an equivalent circuit can be drawn as shown in Fig.9.5.8b.

The voltage across the inductor can be derived as follows

$$u_L = \frac{R_2}{R_1+R_2} \times 10\delta(t) = \frac{4}{6+4} \times 10\delta(t) = 4\delta(t)$$

This impulse voltage will make inductor current jumping, so, there is

$$i_L(0_+) = i_L(0_-) + \frac{1}{L}\int_{0_-}^{0_+} u_L dt = \frac{1}{100 \times 10^{-3}}\int_{0_-}^{0_+} 4\delta(t)dt = 40(\text{A})$$

When $t \geq 0_+$, the equivalent circuit can be drawn as shown in Fig.9.5.8c, Then

$$\tau = \frac{L}{R_1 // R_2} = \frac{100 \times 10^{-3}}{2.4} = \frac{1}{24}(\text{s})$$

The inductor current can be derived as follows

$$i_L(t) = i_L(0_+) e^{-\frac{t}{\tau}} = 40 e^{-24t} \varepsilon(t) (\text{A})$$

The inductor voltage will be

$$u_L(t) = L\frac{di_L}{dt} = 100 \times 10^{-3} \times 40 [-24 e^{-24t} \varepsilon(t) + e^{-24t}\delta(t)]$$
$$= 4\delta(t) - 96 e^{-24t}\varepsilon(t) (\text{V})$$

The waveform of $i_L(t)$ and $u_L(t)$ is shown in Fig.9.5.9. Pay attention to the impulse and jump in $i_L(t)$ or $u_L(t)$.

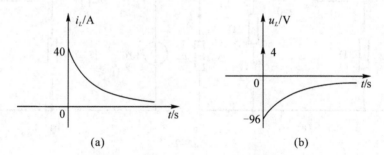

Fig.9.5.9 The Waveform of $i_L(t)$ and $u_L(t)$

Exercise

9-1 For the circuit shown in Fig.9-1, the switch K is closed at $t = 0$. Before switch is closed, the circuit has reached steady state. Find the voltage and current of each circuit at the moment $t = 0_+$.

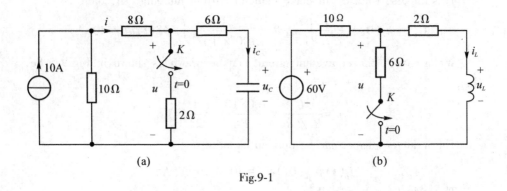

Fig.9-1

9-2 For the circuit shown in Fig.9-2, the switch is closed at $t=0$. Before switch is closed, the circuit has reached steady state. Find the voltage and current labeled in each circuit at the moment $t=0_+$.

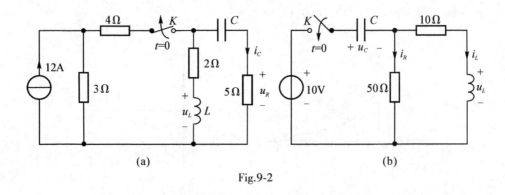

Fig.9-2

9-3 For the circuit shown in Fig.9-3, the switch is closed at $t=0$. Before switch is closed, the circuit has reached steady state. Find the voltage $u_C(t)$ and current when $t \geqslant 0$.

9-4 For the circuit shown in Fig.9-4, it is known that, when $t<0$, S is on position "1" and the circuit has reached steady state. At the moment $t=0$, S is turn to position "2".

(1) Find response $u_C(t)$ when $t \geqslant 0$ by applying three-element method;

(2) Find the instant t_0 when response $u_C(t)$ passes zero;

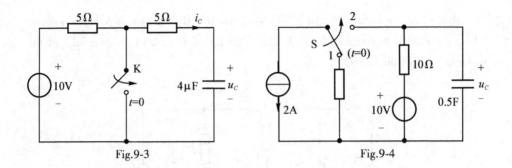

Fig.9-3   Fig.9-4

9-5   For the circuit shown in Fig. 9-5, it is known that initial voltage of capacitor is zero and all sources start acting at instant $t=0$, find $i(t)$.

9-6   For the circuit shown in Fig.9-6, before switch K is closed, the circuit has reached steady state. Find voltage u_C after the switch is closed.

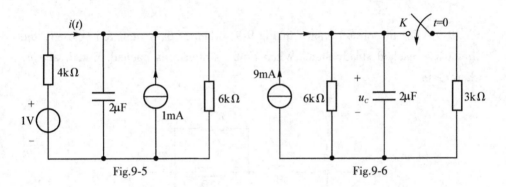

Fig.9-5   Fig.9-6

9-7   For the circuit shown in Fig.9-7, $u_C(0_-) = 0$. Find u_C when $t \geq 0$.

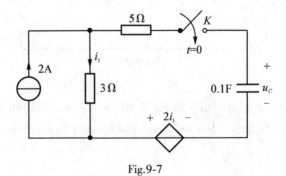

Fig.9-7

9-8 For the circuit shown in Fig.9-8, when $t<0$, the switch K is on position "1", the circuit has reached steady state. Switch K is turn to position "2" at the moment $t=0$, find i_L and u.

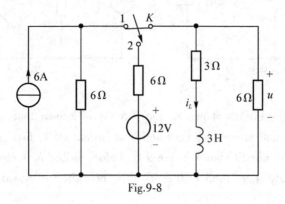

Fig.9-8

9-9 For the circuit shown in Fig.9-9, when $t<0$, switch K is closed, the circuit has reached steady state. When $t=0$, switch K is opened. find i_L and u_L when $t \geqslant 0$.

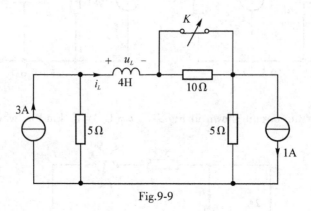

Fig.9-9

9-10 For the circuit shown in Fig.9-10, when $t=0$, switch is closed. Before switch is closed, the circuit has reached steady state and there is $u_C(0_-)=0$, find u_C when $t \geqslant 0$.

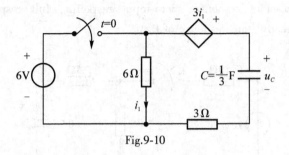

Fig.9-10

9-11 For the circuit shown in Fig.9-11, switch K is opened at $t = 0$. Find zero-state response of u_C and u_0.

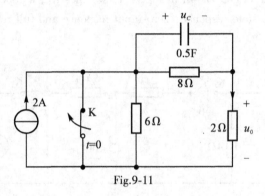

Fig.9-11

9-12 For the circuit shown in Fig.9-12, switch K is closed at $t = 0$. Find zero-state response of u_L and i_L.

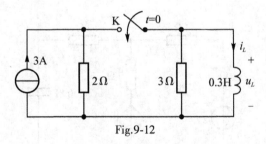

Fig.9-12

9-13 For the circuit shown in Fig.9-13, $u_C(0) = 3\text{V}$, switch K is closed at

$t=0$. Find zero-state response, zero-input response, full response, transient response and steady state response of u_C.

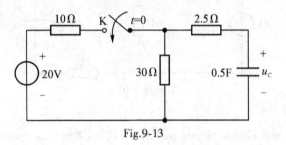

Fig.9-13

9-14 For the circuit shown in Fig.9-14, switches K_1, K_2 operate simultaneously at $t=0$. Find zero-state response, zero-input response and full response of i_L. when $t \geqslant 0$.

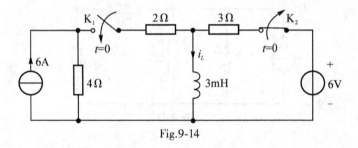

Fig.9-14

9-15 For the circuit shown in Fig.9-15, initial storage energy of capacitor is zero, switch K is closed at $t=0$. Find i_1 when $t>0$.

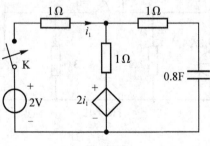

Fig.9-15

9-16 For the circuit shown in Fig.9-16, when $t<0$, switch K is on position "1" and circuit is on steady state. At the moment $t=0$, switch K is turned to position "2". Find i_L and u when $t \geq 0$.

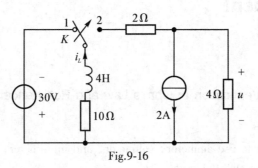

Fig.9-16

9-17 For the circuit shown in Fig.9-17, find the impulse response of the capacitor voltage and current.

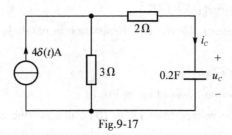

Fig.9-17

9-18 For the circuit shown in Fig.9-18, find the impulse response of the inductor current and voltage.

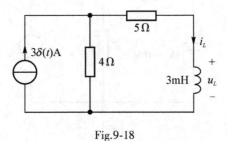

Fig.9-18

Appendix A

Experiment

Experiment 1 Verification of Ohm's Law and Resistance Measurement

1. Objectives

To learn how to use ammeter, voltmeter, and multimeter;

To understand Ohm's law through experiment;

To learn how to use Multimeter to measure resistance;

2. Principles

Ohm's law: $V = IR$

Resistance measured: $R = V/I$

Resistance in series: $R_t = R_1 + R_2$; Resistance in parallel: $R_t = R_1 R_2 / (R_1 + R_2)$

3. Steps

(1) Study Ohm's law:

a. Connect the circuit according to Fig.1;

b. Change source voltage from 1V to 10V, observe the changing in current;

c. Record currents and voltages in the circuit into table 1;

d. Plot the VCR curve and find the resistance to verify Ohm's law;

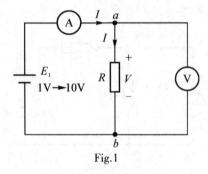

Fig.1

Table 1

Voltage					
Current					
Resistance					

(2) Resistance measure: use Ohmmeters with its proper scale to measure some resistances.

(3) Resistances in series: use Ohmmeters to measure total resistance of two resistances in series.

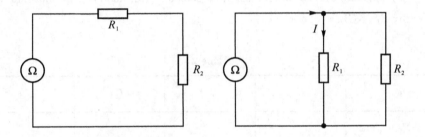

(4) Resistances in parallel: use Ohmmeters to measure total resistance of two resistances in parallel.

Experiment 2   Verification of Kirchhoff's Law

1. Objectives

To better understand and verify Kirchhoff's Law.

2. Principles

(1) KCL: The algebraic sum of branch currents entering a node of a circuit is zero.

(2) KVL: The algebraic sum of branch voltages drop along any loop of a circuit is zero.

3. Steps

(1) Connect the circuit according to Fig.2.

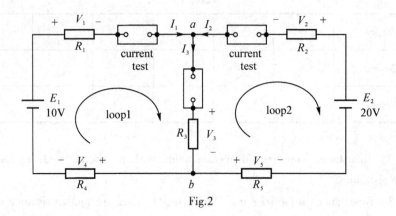

Fig.2

(2) Measure every branch currents associated with node a. Fill data into table 2. Verify the KCL.

Table 2

Items	I_1	I_2	I_3	ΣI
Node a				
Node b				

(3) Measure every branch voltage drops associated with loop 1 and loop 2. Fill data into table 3. Verify the KCL.

Table 3

Items	V_1	V_2	V_3	V_4	V_5	ΣV
Loop 1						
Loop 2						

Experiment 3 Superposition Theorem

1. Objectives
To verify Superposition Theorem.

2. Principles
The current in any circuit element or voltage across any element of a linear, bilateral network is the algebraic sum of the currents or voltages separately produced by each source of energy.

3. Steps
(1) Connect circuit according to Fig.3;

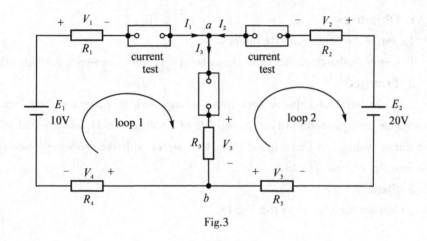

Fig.3

(2) Consider single source E_1 in operation, the source E_2 is removed (you can do this by replacing it with a wire or moving the terminal A to B.), measure the branch currents and voltages. Fill data measured into table 1.

(3) Consider single source E_2 in operation, the source E_1 is removed (you can do this by replacing it with a wire or moving the terminal C to D.), measure the branch currents and voltages. Fill data into table 1.

(4) Consider both sources E_1, E_2 in operation, no source is removed, measure the branch currents and voltages. Fill data into table 4.

(5) Verify superposition Theorem.

Table 4

Data measured Source actived	I_1	I_2	I_3	V_1	V_2	V_3	V_4	V_5
Kill Source E_1								
Kill Source E_2								
Source E_1, E_2 both								

Experiment 4 Thevenin's Theorem

1. Objectives

To verify the Thevenin's Theorem

To better understand the VCR characteristic of linear two-terminal network

2. Principles

Any two terminal network containing voltage and/or current sources can be replaced by an equivalent circuit, consisting of a voltage source which equal to the open circuit voltage of the original circuit in series with the resistance measured back into the original circuit.

3. Steps

a. Connect the circuit as the Fig.4a.

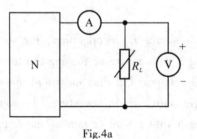

Fig.4a

b. Change the value of R, measure the voltage across R and current flowing through R, fill data into following table (at least 9 group data). Plot the curve $V=f(I)$.

V									
I									

c. Measure the open circuit voltage V_{oc}

d. Measure the short circuit current I_{sc}, and then, compute the equivalent resistance: $R_o = V_{oc}/I_{sc}$

e. Reconnect the circuit according to the Thevenin's equivalent circuit as Fig.4b, measure voltage across R and current flowing through R when R is assigned to different value. Plot the VCR curve $V = f(I)$.

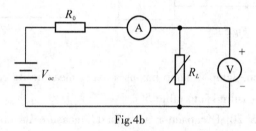

Fig.4b

f. By comparing two curves got from above to verify Thevenin's Theorem.

Experiment 5 Impedance Measurement with Three-Meter Method

1. Objectives

To learn how to use wattmeter;

To learn the method of impedance measurement by using ammeter, voltmeter and wattmeter.

2. Principles

Impedance can be determined by voltage phasor and current phasor:

$$Z = \frac{\dot{V}}{\dot{I}} = \frac{V}{I} \angle (\phi_V - \phi_i) = |Z| \angle \theta$$

The magnitude of impedance:

$$|Z| = \frac{V}{I}.$$

To determine the angle of impedance, we need to measure power P more.

Then we have

$$\theta = \cos^{-1}\frac{P}{VI}$$

3. Steps

(1) Connect circuit according to Fig.5a;

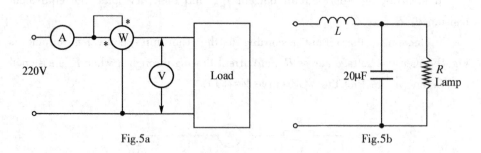

Fig.5a　　　　　　　　　　Fig.5b

(2) Choose one lamp in lamp box as a load, measure its current, voltage and power. Fill data measured into table 5.

(3) Choose a 20μF capacitor as a load, measure its current, voltage and power.

(4) Choose an inductor (a coil containing a ferric core) as a load, measure its current, voltage and power.

(5) Choose the circuit shown in Fig.5b as a load, measure its current, voltage and power.

(6) Compute the impedance in each case above.

Table 5

Data Item	Current	Voltage	Power	magnitude $|Z|$	angle θ	Impedance Z
Lamp: R						
Capacitor: C						
Inductor: L						
RLC circuit						

Experiment 6 Power Factor Measurement and Correction

1. Objectives

To learn how to measure and correct power factor;

To learn the operation principle of a fluorescent lamp.

2. Principles

Most industrial and many residential electrical loads are inductive, that is, they operate at a lagging power factor or a lower power factor. The consequence of a lower power factor is that: more currents needed to transmission same power, and more energy will loss in transmission line.

Power factor can be measured by using a power factor meter.

Power factor of an inductive circuit can be corrected by a parallel capacitor.

3. Steps

(1) Connect the circuit of a fluorescent lamp according to Fig.6.

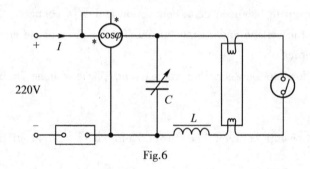

Fig.6

(2) Set capacitance to zero, turn on power supply to make the fluorescent lamp bright. Measure current, power, and voltages across ballast and lamp tube. Fill data measured into table 6.

(3) Increase the capacitance, observe the variation of power factor. When power factor reaches unity, measure the current and capacitor. Suppose this capacitance is C_o.

(4) Increase the capacitance to make it greater than, measure the current and capacitor.

(5) Decrease the capacitance to make it less than C_o, measure the current

and capacitor.

(6) Plot the relationship figure between I and C: $I=f(C)$

Table 6

Item \ Data	1	2	3	4	5	6	7	8	9
Current									
power factor					1				
capacitor					C_0				

Experiment 7 Three-Phase Circuit

1. Objectives

To verify the relationship between line voltage and phase voltage, line current and phase current in balanced delta connection and Wye connection.

To study the voltage and current in unbalanced three phase circuit.

2. Principles

The relationship between line voltage and phase voltage in balanced delta connection is

$$V_l = V_p$$

The relationship between line current and phase current in balanced delta connection is

$$I_l = \sqrt{3} I_p$$

The relationship between line voltage and phase voltage in balanced Wye connection is

$$V_l = \sqrt{3} V_p$$

The relationship between line current and phase current in balanced Wye connection is

$$I_l = I_p$$

3. Steps

(1) Balanced Wye connection:

Connect the circuit according to Fig.7a, turn on two lamps in each phase, measure each line voltage and phase voltage. Verify that: $V_l = \sqrt{3} V_p$.

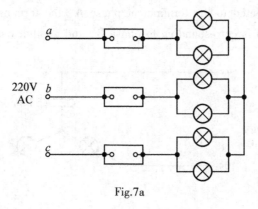

Fig.7a

(2) Unbalanced Wye connection:

In the Fig.7b, turn on two lamps in phase b and c,

(a) Switch on one lamp in phase a, measure each line voltage(current) and phase voltage (current). Fill the data measured into table 7.

(b) Short circuit of phase a, measure each line voltage(current) and phase voltage (current). Fill the data measured into table 7.

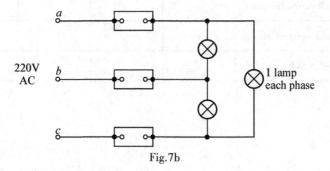

Fig.7b

(3) Balanced delta connection:

Connect the circuit according to Fig.7b, measure each line voltage(current) and phase voltage (current). Verify that: $I_l = \sqrt{3} I_p$.

(4) Phase sequence indicator:

Connect the circuit according to Fig. 7c. Because the three-phase load is unbalanced, so the voltages across each phase load are difference. When the capacitor is connected to the terminal of phase A, the terminal which a brighter lamp is connected is corresponding to phase B, and another one is phase C.

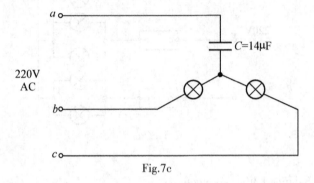

Fig.7c

Table 7

Data Item	line voltage	phase voltage	line current	phase current
Balanced Wye connection				
Unbalanced Wye connection				
Balanced delta connection				
Phase sequence indicator				

Appendix B

Reference Answers for Partial Exercises

Chapter 1

1-1 (1) -50W; (2) 8mW; (3) -1A; (4) 10V

1-2 $p(t)=\begin{cases} 10t & 0\leqslant t<1 \\ 10(t-2) & 1\leqslant t<2 \\ 0 & \text{other} \end{cases}$

1-3 $I_3=0.31\mu\text{A}$, $I_4=9.3\mu\text{A}$, $I_6=9.6\mu\text{A}$

1-4 $u_1=-2\text{V}$, $u_{ab}=9\text{V}$

1-5 $P_1=-20\text{W}$, $P_2=10\text{W}$, $P_3=15\text{W}$, $P_4=-5\text{W}$

1-6 $i=0.5\text{A}$

1-7 $R=4\Omega$

1-8 $u=8\text{V}$, $i_S=1\text{A}$

1-9 $i=\begin{cases} 2\times 10^{-10}\text{A} & 1\leqslant t\leqslant 2 \\ 0 & \text{other} \end{cases}$

1-10 $u=\begin{cases} 0.2\text{A} & 0\leqslant t<1 \\ 0 & 1\leqslant t<2 \\ -0.2\text{A} & 2\leqslant t<3 \end{cases}$

1-11 $u=\begin{cases} 0 & t<0 \\ 10t\text{V} & 0\leqslant t<1 \\ 10\text{V} & 1\leqslant t<3 \\ 10(t-2)\text{V} & 3\leqslant t<4 \\ 20\text{V} & t\geqslant 4 \end{cases}$

1-12 $u_R=2e^{-t}\text{V}$, $u_L=e^{-t}\text{V}$, $u_C=10(1-e^{-t})\text{V}$

1-13 $u=50\text{V}$; no effect

1-14 (1) $i=-1\text{A}$, (2) $u=16\text{V}$, (3) $i=3\text{A}$

1-15 $u_1=-5\text{V}$, 50W, -100W, 100W, -100W, 50W

1-16 (1) $V_a = 6V$, $V_b = 2V$, $V_C = 0V$;
(2) $V_a = 4V$, $V_b = 0V$, $V_C = -2V$;
(3) $V_a = 115V$, $V_b = 70V$, $V_C = 0V$

1-17 (1) $V_A = 1V$; (2) $u = 2V$

1-18 (1) $i_1 = \dfrac{20}{9}A$, $u_{ab} = \dfrac{8}{9}V$;
(2) $u_{ab} = -3V$, $u_{cb} = -13V$;
(3) $u = 10V$, $i_1 = 2A$, $i_2 = 2.5A$

1-19 $i_1 = 1A$, $u = 3V$

1-20 $u_{ab} = 4V$

Chapter 2

2-1 (a) $R_{ab} = 2\Omega$; (b) $R_{ab} = 3\Omega$; (c) $R_{ab} = 10\Omega$

2-2 $R_2 = 54\Omega$

2-3 $R_{ab} = 24\Omega$

2-4 (a) $R_{ab} = 40\Omega$; (b) $R_{ab} = 26.6\Omega$

2-5 (a) 5V, 2.5Ω; (b) 4V, 4Ω; (c) 66V, 10Ω

2-6 (a) 10V voltage source; (b) 4V voltage source in series with 1Ω

2-7 $\dfrac{15}{11}V$, $\dfrac{30}{11}\Omega$

2-8 (a) $i = -0.075A$; (b) $i = -0.5A$

2-9 (a) $R_{ab} = \dfrac{6}{5-r}\Omega$; (b) $R_{ab} = \dfrac{2}{3-\alpha}\Omega$; (c) $R_{ab} = \dfrac{2}{3}\Omega$

2-10 $U_{OC} = -\dfrac{8}{15}V$, $R_0 = -\dfrac{4}{15}\Omega$

Chapter 3

3-1 5, 5

3-2 5, 6, 6

3-3 (a) $i_1 = \dfrac{15}{7}A$, $i_2 = \dfrac{6}{7}A$, $i_3 = -3A$;
(b) $i_1 = -\dfrac{1}{2}A$, $i_2 = 1A$, $i_3 = -\dfrac{1}{2}A$

3-4 (a) $i_1 = 2A$; (b) $i_1 = -2A$, $P = 20W$

3-5 $i_1 = \dfrac{9}{11}A$, $i_2 = -\dfrac{8}{11}A$, $i_3 = -\dfrac{1}{11}A$

3-6 $i_1 = \dfrac{3}{35}A$, $i_2 = -\dfrac{6}{7}A$, $i_3 = \dfrac{9}{70}A$

3-7 $i = 3A$

3-8 $I_A = 0.02A$, $0.24W$

3-9 $64W$

3-10 $u = \dfrac{22}{3}V$

3-12 $R_1 = 2\Omega$, $R_2 = 1\Omega$, $R_3 = 3\Omega$, $k = 0.5$, $u_{S1} = 8V$, $u_{S2} = 12V$

3-13 $i_1 = 15A$, $i_2 = 11A$, $i_3 = 17A$

3-14 $117W$

3-15 $u = 7V$, $i = 3A$

3-16 $u_1 = 8V$, $i = 1A$

3-17 $I_{AB} = -2mA$

3-18 $u = -\dfrac{120}{7}V$, $122W$

3-21 $i = 2A$

3-22 $u = 20V$

Chapter 4

4-1 (1) $u = 6V$; (2) $i_X = \dfrac{15}{11}A$

4-2 $I_1 = 2A$, $I_2 = -1A$, $I_3 = 9A$

4-3 $u_{ab} = 0.1V$

4-4 $52W$, $78W$

4-5 (1) $2V$, $4.2V$, $6.82V$;
  (2) $1A$, $1.1A$, $1.651A$;
  (3) $u = 10.122V$; (3) $i_7 = 9.88A$

4-6 $u_X = -4V$

4-7 $i_X = 3A$

4-8 $i_L = 6A$

4-9 (a) $u_{OC}=6\text{V}$, $R_0=2\Omega$, $i_{SC}=3\text{A}$;
    (b) $u_{OC}=5\text{V}$, $R_0=2\Omega$, $i_{SC}=2.5\text{A}$

4-10 (a) $u_{OC}=4\text{V}$, $R_0=1\Omega$;
    (b) $u_{OC}=\dfrac{400}{17}\text{V}$, $R_0=\dfrac{110}{17}\Omega$

4-11 1.8A, 1A

4-12 $i=8/13\text{mA}$

4-13 $u_{OC}=10\text{V}$, $R_0=5\text{k}\Omega$

4-14 $R_L=7\Omega$, $P_{L\max}=\dfrac{36}{7}\text{W}$

4-15 (1) $I=1\text{A}$, $P_R=5\text{W}$; (2) $R=5\Omega$, $P_{L\max}=2.45\text{W}$

4-16 $R_L=6\Omega$, $P_{L\max}=6\text{W}$

4-17 $R_L=6\Omega$, $P_{L\max}=1.5\text{W}$

4-18 (1) $R=\dfrac{12}{7}\Omega$; (2) $\dfrac{1200}{49}\text{W}$, $\dfrac{48}{7}\text{W}$, $\dfrac{144}{49}\text{W}$ $\eta=20\%$;
    (3) $\dfrac{48}{7}\text{W}$, $\eta=20\%$

4-19 $u_2=4\text{V}$

4-20 $i_2=0.2\text{A}$

4-21 $u_1=4\text{V}$

4-22 $i=-\dfrac{3}{4}\text{A}$

Chapter 5

5-1 (1) $U_m=30\text{V}$, $f=50\text{Hz}$, $\varphi=60°$;
    (2) $I_m=10\text{A}$, $f=500\text{Hz}$, $\varphi=-120°$;
       $U_m=15\text{V}$, $f=100\text{Hz}$, $\varphi=90°$

5-2 $i(t)=8\cos(10^3+45°)\text{mA}$, $I=4\sqrt{2}\text{A}$

5-3 (a) $U_m/\sqrt{3}$, (b) 7.75mA

5-4 (1) $\dot{U}=150\angle-45°\text{V}$; (2) $\dot{I}=10\angle 60°\text{A}$;
    (3) $\dot{I}=5\sqrt{5}\angle-26.6°\text{A}$;
 (4) $\dot{U}=100\sqrt{10}\angle 26.6°\text{V}$;

5-6 $u_S = 1.58\cos(10^6 t + 26.6°)$ V

5-7 $i_S = 1.58\cos(10^3 t + 33.4°)$ V

5-8 $R = 4\Omega$, $L = 1.5$H

5-9 (1) 67.08V, 30V, 25V;
 (2) (a) $V_1 = 12$V, $V_2 = 0$V;
 (b) $V_1 = 12$V, $V_2 = 0$V; $V_1 = V_2 = 0$V, $V_3 = 12$V

5-10 5A, $R = \dfrac{100}{3}\Omega$, $X_C = 25\Omega$

5-11 $\dot{I}_R = 0.2\angle 0°$A; $\dot{I}_L = 0.4\angle -90°$A;
 $\dot{I}_C = 0.5\angle 90°$A; $\dot{I}_R = 0.22\angle 26.6°$A

5-12 (1) capacitor, $C = 0.02$F; (2) resistor, $R = 10\Omega$;
 (3) inductor, $L = 0.5$H

5-13 (a) $Z_{ab} = \dfrac{\sqrt{2}}{2}\angle 45°\Omega$; (b) $Z_{ab} = 2\Omega$

5-14 $U = 40.28$V

5-15 $\dot{U}_S = 2\sqrt{2}\angle 45°$V

5-16 $R_L = 13.75\Omega$, $L = 0.102$H

5-17 $I = 5\sqrt{2}$A, $R = 10\sqrt{2}\Omega$, $X_L = 5\sqrt{2}\Omega$, $X_C = 10\sqrt{2}\Omega$

5-18 $r = 750\Omega$, $X_L = 375\Omega$

5-19 4.8V, $C = 0.025$F

5-22 (a) $\dot{U}_{OC} = \sqrt{2}\angle -45°$V, $Z_0 = \dfrac{\sqrt{2}}{2}\angle 45°\Omega$;
 (b) $\dot{U}_{OC} = 3\angle 0°$V, $Z_0 = 3\angle 0°\Omega$

5-23 $P = 12$W, $Q = -16$var, $S = 20$VA, $\lambda = 0.6$

5-24 $P = 38$W, $Q = -8$var, $S = 38.83$VA, $\lambda = 0.98$

5-25 $R_L = 40\Omega$, $L = 0.03$H

5-26 $I = 2.24$A, $U_{ab} = 20$V, $\tilde{S} = 40 + j20$VA

5-27 3.70μF or 6.57μF

5-28 (1) 22.36A, 2000W, $\lambda = 0.89$; (2) 12.08Ω, $\lambda = 0.94$;
 (3) 3.3μF or 179.9μF

5-29 (1) $Z_L = (3 + j4)$kΩ; (2) 6.75mW; (3) 5.06mW

5-30 $Z_L = 500 + j500\Omega$, $P_{L\max} = 625$W

5-31 $Z_L = 3+j3\Omega$, $P_{Lmax} = 1.5W$

Chapter 6

6-1 (a) $\begin{cases} u_1 = L_1 \dfrac{di_1}{dt} - M \dfrac{di_2}{dt} \\ u_2 = M \dfrac{di_1}{dt} - L_2 \dfrac{di_2}{dt} \end{cases}$; (b) $\begin{cases} \dot{U}_1 = j\omega L_1 \dot{I}_1 + j\omega M \dot{I}_2 \\ \dot{U}_2 = -j\omega M \dot{I}_1 - j\omega L_2 \dot{I}_2 \end{cases}$

6-2 (a) 2H; (b) 6H; (c) 4H

6-3 $u_{ab} = -8e^{-4t}$ V; $u_{bc} = -16e^{-4t}$ V; $u_{ca} = 24e^{-4t}$ V

6-4 $M = 10$mH

6-5 $u_1 = 40\sqrt{10}\cos(10^4 t - 10.3°)$ V; $u_2 = 160\cos(10^4 t + 8.13°)$ V

6-6 $M = 35.5$mH

6-7 (a) $2+j1\Omega$; (b) $3.5+j1.5\Omega$

6-9 $\dot{U} = 2.83\angle -135°$V; $\dot{U} = 0.591\angle -164°$V

6-10 $i_1 = 20\cos(100t - 45°)$ A; $i_2 = 5\sqrt{2}\cos(100t - 180°)$ A

6-12 $\dot{U}_2 = -\dfrac{50}{37}(1+j6)$ V

6-13 (a) $1.5+j10.5\Omega$; (b) $400+j600\Omega$

6-15 open: $R_{ab} = \dfrac{12}{7}\Omega$; closed: $R_{ab} = \dfrac{4}{3}\Omega$

6-16 $\dot{I} = \sqrt{2}\angle 45°$A

6-17 2000W, 3200W

6-18 $Z_X = 0.2+j10.2\Omega$

6-19 (1) $n = 100$; (2) $P_{max} = 0.25$W

6-20 $\dot{U}_{OC} = 17.68\angle -45°$V, $R_0 = 50\sqrt{2}\angle -45°$V

6-21 $\dot{U}_1 = 3.2+j2.4$V, $\dot{U}_2 = 32+j24$V

Chapter 7

7-1 $f_0 = 1591.6$kHz, $Q = 100$, $\rho = 10^3\Omega$, $Z_0 = 10\Omega$

7-2 (1) capacitive; (2) $R = 10\Omega$, $L = 796\mu$H, $C = 3180$pF; (3) $Q = 50$

7-3 $L = 0.02$H; $Q = 50$

7-4 $Q=79.2$, $C=225\text{pF}$

7-5 (a) $\dfrac{1}{2\pi\sqrt{L_2C}}$, $\dfrac{1}{2\pi\sqrt{(L_1+L_2)C}}$;

(b) $\dfrac{1}{2\pi\sqrt{L_1C_1}}$, $\dfrac{1}{2\pi\sqrt{L_2C_2}}$, $\dfrac{\sqrt{L_1+L_2}}{2\pi\sqrt{L_1L_2(C_1+C_2)}}$; (c) $\dfrac{1}{2\pi\sqrt{LC}}$

7-6 $L=1\text{H}$, $C=1\mu\text{F}$, 10mA, 10mA

7-7 $\omega_0=10^7\text{rad/s}$, $Q=20$, $Z_0=20\text{k}\Omega$, $I_0=0.5\text{mA}$, $I_C=20\text{mA}$, $U_0=20\text{V}$, $B=79.62\text{kHz}$

7-8 $Q=16.67$, $U_0=16.67\text{V}$, $B=95.52\text{kHz}$

7-9 9A

7-10 $p=0.316$, $L_1=31.6\mu\text{H}$, $L_2=68.4\mu\text{H}$

7-11 $I=10\text{mA}$, $I_1=0.2\text{A}$, $I_2=0.2\text{A}$, $P=1\text{W}$

7-12 $L=586\mu\text{H}$, $Q=42.8$, $B=10.86\text{kHz}$

Chapter 8

8-1 10.5A, 363.73V

8-2 16.56A, 9.56A, 344.35V

8-3 (1) 220V, 4.45kW; (2) 26.3A, 10.4kW

8-4 $I_l=40\text{A}$, $Z=3.18\angle 36.9°\Omega$

8-5 $\dot{I}_A=22\sqrt{2}\angle-75°\text{A}$, $\dot{I}_{A'B'}=17.96\angle-45°\text{A}$, $P=11616\text{W}$, $Q=8712\text{var}$

8-7 $I_A=1.207\text{A}$

Chapter 9

9-1 (a) $i(0_+)=3.85\text{A}$, $i_C(0_+)=-11.54\text{A}$, $u(0_+)=30.78\text{V}$, $u_C(0_+)=100\text{V}$;

(b) $i(0_+)=5\text{mA}$, $u_L(0_+)=-6.25\text{V}$, $u(0_+)=3.75\text{V}$

9-2 (a) $i_C(0_+)=-i_L(0_+)=-4\text{A}$; $u_R(0_+)=-20\text{V}$; $u_L(0_+)=-20\text{V}$

(b) $u_C(0_+)=0\text{V}$, $i_L(0_+)=0\text{A}$, $i_R(0_+)=0.2\text{A}$, $u_L(0_+)=10\text{V}$

9-3 $u_C(t)=10e^{-5\times10^4 t}\text{V}$, $i_C(t)=-2e^{-5\times10^4 t}\text{A}$

9-4 $u_C(t)=-10+20e^{-0.2t}\text{V}$

9-5 $i(t)=-0.5+0.75e^{-\frac{5}{24}\times10^3 t}\text{mA}$

9-6 $u_C = 18 + 36e^{-250t}$ V

9-7 $u_C = 10(1-e^{-t})$ V

9-8 $i_L = 1 + 2e^{-2t}$ A, $u = 3 - 6e^{-2t}$ V

9-9 $i_L = 1 + e^{-5t}$ A, $u = -20e^{-5t}$ V

9-10 $u_C = 9 - 9e^{-t}$ V

9-11 $u_C = 6(1-e^{-0.5t})$ V, $u_0 = 1.5(1-e^{-0.5t})$ V

9-12 $u_L = 3.6e^{-4t}$ V, $i_L = 3 - 3e^{-4t}$ A

9-13 $u_{Cf} = 15(1-e^{-0.2t})$ V, $u_{Cx} = 15(1-e^{-0.2t})$ V, $u_C = 15 - 12e^{-0.2t}$ V,
$u_{C,\text{ steady}} = 15$ V, $u_{C,\text{ transient}} = -12e^{-0.2t}$ V

9-14 $i_{Lf} = 2e^{-2\times 10^3 t}$ A, $i_{Lx} = 4 - 4e^{-2\times 10^3 t}$ A, $i_L = 4 - 2e^{-2\times 10^3 t}$ A

9-15 $i_1 = 0.5 + 0.3e^{-t}$ A

9-16 $i_L = 0.5 + 2.5e^{-4t}$ A, $u = -6 + 10e^{-4t}$ V

9-17 $u_C(t) = 12e^{-t}\varepsilon(t)$ V, $i_C(t) = 2.4[\delta(t) - e^{-t}\varepsilon(t)]$ A

9-18 $u_L(t) = 12\delta(t) - 3.6\times 10^4 e^{-3\times 10^3 t}\varepsilon(t)$ V,
$i_L(t) = 4\times 10^3 e^{-3\times 10^3 t}\varepsilon(t)$ A

References

[1] 单潮龙,王向军,嵇斗,等.电路第二版[M].北京:国防工业出版社,2015.

[2] James W. Nilsson, et al.. Electric Circuits (10th Edition)[M]. Prentice Hall, 2007.

[3] James A. Svoboda, et al.. Introduction to Electric Circuits (9th Edition)[M]. WILEY, 2014.

[4] 邱关源.电路(第五版)[M].北京:高等教育出版社,2006.

[5] 吴大正.电路基础[M].西安:西安电子科技大学出版社,2000.

[6] 李瀚荪.电路分析基础(上、中、下册)[M].北京:高等教育出版社,2000.

[7] 韩力,等.EWB应用教程[M].北京:电子工业出版社,2003.

[8] 侯勇严,孙瑜,郭文强.MATLAB在复杂电路分析中的应用研究[J].微计算机信息(测控自动化),2004,20(10).

[9] John O. Attia. Electronics and Circuit Analysis Using Matlab.[M] CRC Press, 2000.